macROBERTS

SCOTTISH LIQUIDATION
HANDBOOK

(Third Edition)

AUSTRALIA
LBC Information Services—Sydney

CANADA and USA
Carswell—Toronto

NEW ZEALAND
Brooker's—Auckland

SINGAPORE and MALAYSIA
Sweet & Maxwell
Singapore and Kuala Lumpur

macROBERTS

SCOTTISH LIQUIDATION HANDBOOK

Third Edition

Third Edition

David Flint
LL.B., LL.M., Dip. ICEI, NP, FABRP, MIPA, MICM
Solicitor in Scotland

THOMSON
™
W. GREEN

Published in 2004 by
W. Green & Son Ltd
21 Alva Street
Edinburgh
EH2 4PS

First edition © 1987 Jordan & Sons Limited
Second edition © 1990 Jordan & Sons Limited

Typeset by J&L Composition, Filey, North Yorkshire

Printed in Great Britain by
Creative Print & Design
(Wales), Ebbw Vale

No natural forests were destroyed to make this product;
only farmed timber was used and replanted

A CIP catalogue record for this book is available from
the
British Library

ISBN 0 414 015 754

© W. Green & Son Ltd 2004

CONTENTS

PREFACE

This Handbook has been prepared for use by insolvency practitioners, accountants, solicitors and other professional advisers called upon to advise on corporate liquidation and to assist those concerned with the provision of credit in understanding the manner in which liquidations are conducted, and the rights and remedies of creditors, and shareholders therein.

This is the Third Edition of a Handbook designed to assist with the procedures brought into effect by the Insolvency Act 1986, the Insolvency (Scotland) Rules 1986 as amended by the Insolvency (Scotland) Amendment Rules 1987 and various other pieces of subordinate legislation. The Handbook follows the scheme of the Insolvency (Scotland) Rules 1986 (Winding-up by the Court, Creditors' Voluntary Winding-up, and Members' Voluntary Winding-up) considering in each case the procedural steps which require to be taken in the order in which each step will occur. Thereafter, general provisions regarding the convening and conduct of insolvency meetings; claims in liquidation and proxies are considered. Finally, a brief consideration of diligence and lien, adjustment of prior transactions, the conduct of directors and prohibited names is made. With the Scotland Act 1998 and the enactment of the EC Regulation on Insolvency Proceedings, there is need enough to update the previous edition, now some 15 years ago.

In September 2003, the new insolvency procedures of the Enterprise Act 2002 came into force, bringing with them the most revolutionary changes in corporate insolvency practice for over 15 years. There are now over 20 pieces of primary and 30 pieces of secondary legislation with which a practitioner would have to acquaint himself. A far cry from the pre-1986 position which relied on the Companies Act 1985, the Bankruptcy (Scotland) Act 1913 and two statutes from the seventeenth century (the Act of 1621 and the Act of 1696).

Following many requests by users, this Third Edition includes sections on employment law, pensions, data protection and on taxation.

These are included as appendices, a Form of Proxy for use by creditors, styles of court applications, minutes, resolutions and advertisements which comply with the various Rules. As with all styles, these are a starting point for drafting and many require substantial additional information to be added if the requisite court orders are to be obtained.

I am grateful to my colleagues at MacRoberts and, in particular, Gillian Craig, Jamie Grant, Isobel d'Inverno, David Mallon, Stephen Miller, Alan McAdams, Sara Du Terroil and Peter Trotter, and to the Recovery and Reorganisation Department of Grant Thornton for their assistance in preparing this Third Edition.

Finally, this Third Edition is dedicated to my wife Marie and my daughters Jennifer and Aimée.

David Flint
February 2004

PLEASE NOTE

References to sections are to sections of the Insolvency Act 1986, and references to Rules are to the Insolvency (Scotland) Rules 1986, unless the context indicates otherwise. EC Regulation means Council Regulation (EC) No 1346/2000.

TABLE OF CASES

TABLE OF STATUTES

Acts of the Scottish Parliament

Table of Statutory Instruments

CHAPTER 1

INTRODUCTION

1.1 Applicability of the Insolvency Act 1986

(1) The Insolvency Act 1986, and its associated Rules, applies to all companies.[1] It also applies to unregistered companies[2] (including open-ended investment companies[3]), building societies,[4] industrial and provident societies[5] and friendly societies.[6]

(2) The winding-up of insurance companies (and certain other financial services bodies) is subject to a special regime.[7]

(3) Companies, formed under private Acts of Parliament or Royal Charter, are included by virtue of Part XXII, Chapter II of the Companies Act 1985.

(4) The Act does not apply to a Scottish partnership[8] or a limited partnership,[9] but it does apply to Limited Liability Partnerships.[10]

(5) The Act, and the Company Directors Disqualification Act 1986, apply to European Economic Interest Groupings.[11]

1.2 Accountant in Bankruptcy

Following the Scotland Act 1998, certain of the Insolvency Act functions of the Registrar of Companies were transferred to the Accountant in Bankruptcy[12] either exclusively or concurrently.

1.3 Excluded Areas

Special rules apply in relation to the winding-up of banks, financial institutions and insurance companies and these are largely excluded from this Handbook. Limited coverage is contained in Chapter 20.

---

[1] As defined in s.735 of the Companies Act 1985.

[2] Section 220 of the Companies Act 1985.

[3] Regulation 31, Open Ended Investment Companies Regulations 2001 (SI 2001/1228).

[4] Section 90 of and Sch.15 to the Building Societies Act 1986.

[5] Section 55(a) of the Industrial and Provident Societies Act 1965, as amended.

[6] Pt V of the Insolvency Act 1986 dealing with unregistered companies.

[7] Insurers (Reorganisation and Winding-up) Regulations 2003 (SI 2003/1102)

[8] Other than as provided for in s.367(2) Financial Services and Markets Act 2000.

[9] *Smith, Petitioner*, 1999 S.L.T. 5.

[10] Limited Liability Partnerships (Scotland) Regulations 2001 (SI 2001/128), regs 4 and 6, and Sch.2.

[11] Council Regulation (EEC) No. 2137/85 of 25th July 1985 on the European Economic Interest Grouping (EEIG); See Chapter 22.10.

[12] By virtue of the Scotland Act 1998 (Consequential Modifications) (No. 2) Order 1999 (SI 1999/1820), art.4, Sch.2, Pt II, para.141(1).

CHAPTER 2

WINDING-UP BY THE COURT

2.1 Jurisdiction (Sections 120, 220 and 225)

(1) The Court of Session has jurisdiction to wind up any company registered in Scotland.[1]

(2) Where the amount of a company's share capital paid, or credited as paid up, does not exceed £120,000, the sheriff court of the Sheriffdom in which the company's registered office, or in the case of an unregistered company or an overseas company, where its principal place of business, is situated, has concurrent jurisdiction with the Court of Session to wind up the company. Where the company is a company limited by guarantee (without a share capital) or an unlimited company, it has been suggested that only the Court of Session will have jurisdiction to wind-it up. There is a decision of the Sheriff Court supporting this view,[2] but it must be wondered whether (particularly in light of the EC Regulation) this is a correct interpretation.

(3) "Registered Office" means the place which has longest been the company's registered office during the six months immediately preceding the presentation of the petition for winding-up. However, "registered office" can also mean the place which is the registered office as at the date of the winding-up.[3]

(4) It is also possible (in addition to the general principle contained in section 6(2) of the Bankruptcy (Scotland) Act 1985) for a Scottish Partnership to be wound-up as an unregistered company by virtue of the powers contained in section 367(2) of the Financial Services and Markets Act 2000.

(5) A company may not be wound-up by the court where it is an EEA insurer or a branch of an EEA insurer.

2.2 Grounds for Winding-up (Sections 122 and 221)

(1) A company registered under the Companies Acts may be wound-up by the court if:

---

[1] Although there has been some discussion amongst practitioners, it is considered that a proper reading of s.120(1) (and the corresponding provisions for England in s.117(1)) is that an English company cannot be wound-up in Scotland, and a Scottish company cannot be wound-up in England. This assumes that the phrase "exclusive (subject to the provisions of the EC Regulation)" is read into the applicable section before "jurisdiction".

[2] See *Pearce and Cannon – Re: Visual Communications Instant Muscle Ltd*, [1991] S.C.L.R. 861.

[3] See *Ross v Invergordon Distillers Ltd* [1961] S.L.T. 258.

(a) the company has by special resolution resolved that the company be wound-up by the court;

(b) it is a public company that has not been issued with a certificate under section 117 of the Companies Act 1985;

(c) it is an old public company;

(d) it does not commence business within a year of incorporation, or suspends its business for a year;

(e) except in the case of a private company limited by shares or by guarantee, the number of members is reduced below two;

(f) the company is unable to pay its debts[4];

(g) at the time at which a moratorium for the company under section 1A (of the Insolvency Act 1986) comes to an end, no voluntary arrangement approved under Part I (of the Insolvency Act 1986) has effect in relation to the company (only one or more creditors may present a petition on this ground);

(h) the court is the option that it is just and equitable that the company be wound-up[5]; or

(i) the court is satisfied that the security of a creditor entitled to the benefit of a floating charge is in jeopardy (*i.e.* that events have occurred or about to occur which render it unreasonable in the creditor's interest that the company should retain power to dispose of the property which is subject to the floating charge).

(2) An unregistered company (which includes an overseas company) may be wound-up by the court if:

(a) the company is dissolved, or has ceased to carry on business, or is carrying on business only for the purpose of winding-up its affairs;

(b) the company is unable to pay its debts (see in *Re A Company (No. 00359 of 1987)* [1987] 3 W.L.R. 139, where it was held that for the court to make a winding-up order against a foreign company, it was not necessary to show that the company had assets within the jurisdiction, but a significantly close connection with the jurisdiction had to be established)[6];

(c) the court is of the opinion that it is just and equitable that the company should be wound-up[7]; or

(d) the court is satisfied that the security of a creditor entitled to the benefit of a floating charge over property comprised in the company's property and undertaking is in jeopardy.

---

[4] See also s.367 of the Financial Services and Markets Act 2000 and *Re DPR Futures Ltd,* [1999] 1 W.L.R. 778.

[5] See *Teague Petitioner* [1985] S.L.T. 469; *Ebrahami v Westbourne Galleries Ltd* [1983] A.C. 360; see *Levy v Napier*; also s.72 of the Financial Services Act 1986; and *DPR Futures Ltd* above.

[6] *Re Drax Holdings Limited; Re InPower Limited,* [2003] EWHC 2743 (Ch).

[7] See *Rocks v Brae Hotel (Shetland) Ltd* [1997] S.L.T. 474; *Secretary of State for Trade and Industry v Hasta International Ltd* [1998] S.L.T. 73; *Hyndman v RC Hyndman Ltd* [1989] S.C.L.R. 294

(For an analysis of the conditions under which a foreign company may be wound-up see in *Re Compania Merabello San Nicholas SA*, 1973 Ch. 75, at 91–92. Even if no assets exist within the court's jurisdiction it may be possible for the court to have jurisdiction to wind up the company — although the case in question was slightly unusual see in *Re Eloc Electro-Optieck and Communicate BV* [1982] Ch. 43. See also *International Westminster Bank plc v Okeanos Maritime Corporation* [1987] B.C.L.C. 450.) See also the EC Regulation.

   (3) An unregistered company may be wound-up voluntarily, but only in accordance with the EC Regulation.
   (4) A European Economic Interest Grouping may be wound-up, additionally, for infringement of Articles 3, 12 or 31(3) of the Regulation,[8] (on petition by the Secretary of State) or if it is "just and proper"[9] (on the application of a member).

2.3 Inability to Pay Debts (Sections 123, 222, 223 and 224)

   (1) A company registered under the Companies Acts is deemed unable to pay its debts if:

   (a) A creditor (by assignation or otherwise) to whom the company is indebted in a sum exceeding £750 then due has served on the company, be leaving at the company's registered office, a written demand (using Form 4.1 (Scotland)) requiring the company to pay the sums so due, and the company has for three weeks thereafter neglected to pay the sum or to secure of compound for it to the reasonable satisfaction of the creditor. In *Iona Hotels v Craig* [1988] S.C.L.R. 130, it was held that the written demand could not be sent by post, but required to be "left" at the company's registered office. The practice since that date has been to serve such demands by Sheriff Officer, but the author questions whether the judgment is in fact a correct interpretation of the Act. Nonetheless, it is clear that the demand must be served by a person authorised by the creditor to do so and this fact must be narrated in the petition.[10] The English courts have permitted service by post[11] and service by fax may be permitted. However, in *Re a Company* [1985] B.C.L.C. 37, it was held that a statutory demand could not be made by telex.

   If there is a genuine dispute to the debt a winding-up process is not the appropriate forum for its resolution (see *Re a Company* [1984] B.C.L.C. 322), but a dispute which his not genuine will not be a ban to the presentation of a winding-up petition.

---

   [8] Council Regulation (EEC) No. 2137/85 of 25th July 1985 on the European Economic Interest Grouping (EEIG), Art.32.
   [9] Article 32(2).
   [10] *Lord Advocate v Blairwest Investments Ltd.* [1989] S.L.T. (Sh. Ct) 97. Approved *in Lord Advocate, Petitioner* [1993] S.L.T. 1324.
   [11] *Re a Company No. 008790 of 1990* [1992] B.C.C. 11.

In *Blue Star Security Services (Scotland) Ltd, Petitioners,*[12] the Sheriff Principal held that a demand for payment of an undisputed sum, then overdue, within 48 hours, was, when unsatisfied, evidence of inability to pay debts.

(b) In England and Wales, execution or other process issued on a judgment, decree or order of any court in favour of a creditor of the company is returned unsatisfied in whole or in part.

(c) In Scotland, the *induciae* of a charge for payment on an extract decree, or an extract registered bond or an extract registered protest, have expired without payment being made.

(d) In Northern Ireland, a certificate of unenforceability has been granted in respect of a judgement against the company.

(e) It is proved to the satisfaction of the court that the company is unable to pay its debts as they fall due; the mere fact that the debtor company is a well known and substantial public company does not prevent a petition being presented for its winding-up even it is solvent if it ignores a Statutory Demand.[13]

(f) It is proved to the satisfaction of the court that the value of the company's assets is less than the amount of its liabilities, taking into account its contingent and prospective liabilities.[14] However, the mere fact that a company can only pay its debts with borrowed money does not show that it is unable to pay its debts within the meaning of the Act.[15]

(2) An unregistered company (including an overseas company) is deemed unable to pay its debts if:

(a) a creditor by assignment or otherwise who is owed £750 or more has served on the company, by leaving at its principal place of business, or delivering to the secretary or some director, manager or principal office of the company, or by otherwise serving in such manner as the court may approve or direct, a written demand in the prescribed form requiring the company to pay the sum due and the company has three weeks after the service of the demand neglected to pay the sum or to secure or compound for it to the creditor's satisfaction;

(b) an action or other proceedings has been instituted against any member for any debt or demand due, or claimed to be due, from the company, or from him in his character of member and notice in writing of the institution of the action or proceeding has been served on the company by leaving it at the company's principal place of business (or by delivering it to the secretary, or some director, manager or principal

---

[12] [1992] S.L.T. (Sh. Ct) 80.
[13] *Cornhill Insurance plc v Improvement Services Ltd* [1986] B.C.L.C. 26.
[14] See *Walter L Jacob & Co Ltd v FIMBRA* [1988] S.C.L.R. 184.
[15] *Re A Company* [1986] B.C.L.C. 261.

officer of the company, or by otherwise serving it in such manner as the court may approve or direct) and the company has not within three weeks after service of the notice paid, secured or compounded for the debt or demand, or procured the action or proceeding to be stayed or sisted, or indemnified the defendant or defender to his reasonable satisfaction against the action or proceedings, and against all costs, damages and expenses to be incurred by him because of it;

(c) in England and Wales, execution or other process issued on a judgment, decree or order obtained in any court in favour of a creditor against the company, or any member of it as such, or any person authorised to be sued as nominal defendant on behalf of the company, is returned unsatisfied;

(d) in Scotland, the induciae of a charge for payment on an extract decree, or an extract registered bond, or an extract registered protect, have expired without payment being made;

(e) if in Northern Ireland, a certificate of unenforceability has been granted in respect of any judgment, decree or order obtained as mentioned in paragraph (a);

(f) if it is otherwise proved to the satisfaction of the court that the company is unable to pay its debts as they fall due[16]; and even where no statutory demand has been served[17]; or

(g) it is proved to the satisfaction of the court that the value of the company's assets is less than the amount of its liabilities, taking into account its contingent and prospective liabilities.[18]

2.4   Competent Petitioners (Sections 124 – 124A)

(1) A petition may be represented by:

(a) the company;

(b) the directors (all directors require to present the petition — a majority is not sufficient)[19];

(c) any creditor or creditors — a person whose debt is disputed on substantial grounds will not be regarded as a creditor[20] — including any contingent or prospective creditor or creditors; for the position of contingent creditors, see *Walter L Jacob & Co Ltd v FIMBRA* [1988] S.C.L.R. 184; in *Re William Hockley Ltd* [1962] 2 All E.R. 111, it was stated that "the expression 'contingent creditor' is not defined in the Companies Act 1948, but must, I think, denote a person to whom under the existing obligations the company may or

---

[16] See *Cornhill Insurance plc v Improvement Services Ltd* [1986] 1 W.L.R. 114.

[17] See *Taylor's Industrial Flooring Ltd* [1990] B.C.C. 44; *Blue Star Security Services (Scotland) Ltd, Petitioners* [1992] S.L.T. (Sh. Ct) 80.

[18] See *In Re a Company (No. 00359 of 1987)* [1987] 3 W.L.R. 339.

[19] See *Re Instrumentation Electrical Services Ltd* [1988] B.C.L.C. 550.

[20] See *Mann v Goldstein* [1968] 2 All E.R. 769.

will become subject to a present liability on the happening of some future event or at some future date". In *Stonegate Securities Ltd v Gregory*,[21] Buckley LJ stated (at 243):

> "In that context, in my opinion, the expression 'contingent creditor' means a creditor in respect of a debt which will only become due in an event which may or may not occur; and a prospective creditor is a creditor in respect of a debt which will certainly become due in the future, either on some date which has been already determined or on some date determinable by reference to future events."

For a consideration of what constitutes a "prospective creditor", see *Re A Company* [1983] B.C.L.C. 492; and *Re: Healing Research Trustee Co Ltd* [1991] B.C.L.C. 716. An unascertained debt which has never been demanded and for which no opportunity to repay has been given cannot form the basis of a liquidation petition;

(d) any contributory or contributories, but only where the number of members is reduced below two,[22] or some of the shares in respect of which a person is a contributory have been held by him and registered in his name for at least six months, however, in relation to just and equitable petitions[23]; it would appear that a contributory is not a competent petitioner in the case of a petition based on the insolvency of the company[24];

(e) a liquidator (within the meaning of Article 2(b) of the EC Regulation) appointed in proceedings by virtue of Article 3(1) of the EC Regulation;

(f) a temporary administrator (within the meaning of Article 38 of the EC Regulation);

(g) a justices' chief executive in the exercise of the power conferred by section 87A of the Magistrates Court Act 1980 (enforcement of fines imposed on companies);

(h) all or any of the parties in paragraphss (a)–(g) above, together or separately;

(i) a receiver of the company (section 55 and paragraph 21 of Schedule 2);

(j) an administrator of the company (section 14 and paragraph 21 of Schedule 1), but see *Re Brooke Marine Ltd/Re Brooke Yachts Ltd* [1988] B.C.L.C. 546;

---

[21] [1980] 1 All E.R. 241.
[22] Presumably, this would not be the case for a single member company.
[23] See *Re Instrumentation Electrical Ser vices Ltd* [1988] B.C.L.C. 550.
[24] *Re Chesterfield Catering Co Ltd* [1977] Ch. 373, [1976] 3 All E.R. 294; *Re Ottery Construction Ltd* [1966] 1 All E.R. 145.

(k) the Secretary of State (sections 124 or 124A)[25];

(l) the Financial Services Authority under section 367 of the Financial Services and Markets Act 2000[26];

(m)the supervisor of a voluntary arrangement;

(n) the depositary of an open-ended investment company[27]; or

(o) the Secretary of State in terms of reg.7(1) and 7(2) of the EEIG Regulations.[28]

It is suggested that it is not competent to attempt to wind up more than one company with the same petition.[29]

(2) Where a petitioner is subsequently found not entitled to present a petition, fails to intimate, serve or advertise the petition, moves or consents to withdraw the petition or fails to move for an order in terms of the petition, the court may, on such terms as it thinks fit, sist as petitioner any creditor or contributory who in the opinion of the court is entitled to present the petition.[30] The court may allow the cause to be continued for a specified period to allow a note to be presented to achieve same.

2.5 Provisional Liquidators (Section 135)

(1) A provisional liquidator may be appointed at any time before the appointment of a liquidator.[31] He shall carry out such functions as the court may confer on him, and his powers may be limited by the order appointing him (*Levy v Napier*, above).

(2) Application for the appointment of a provisional liquidator may be made by:

(a) the petitioner in the winding-up;

(b) any creditor of the company;

(c) a contributory[32];

(d) the company itself;

(e) any other person entitled to present a petition for winding-up the company (rule 4.1); or

(f) the Secretary of State (Sheriff Court Company Insolvency Rules 1986, rule 23(1)(b) (Rules of the Court of Session 1994, rule 74.25(5)).

---

[25] See *Re Walter L Jacob & Co Ltd, The Times*, December 29, 1988; For jurisdiction to be exercised under a public interest petition there is no requirement that the company be insolvent, nor is insolvency as such sufficient in itself to justify winding-up the company on public interest grounds. *Re Marann Brooks CSV Limited* [2003] B.P.I.R. 1159.

[26] The Financial Services Authority may not present a petition to the court under s.367 for the winding-up of an EEA firm which qualifies for authorisation under Sch.3, FSMA or a Treaty firm which qualifies for authorisation under Sch.4, FSMA unless it has been asked to do so by the home state regulator of the firm concerned.

[27] Regulation 31, Open Ended Investment Companies Regulations 2001 (SI 2001/1228).

[28] The European Economic Interest Grouping Regulations 1989 (SI 1989/638).

[29] *Re a Company* [1984] B.C.L.C. 307.

[30] Act of Sederunt (Rules of the Court of Session 1994) 1994, Sch.2, Pt V, r.74.24; Act of Sederunt (Sheriff Court Company Insolvency Rules) 1986, r.21.

[31] See *Levy v Napier* [1962] S.L.T. 264 and cases therein cited.

[32] See *Teague, Petitioner* [1985] S.L.T. 469.

(3) Forthwith after his appointment the provisional liquidator shall give notice of his appointment to:

(a) the Accountant in Bankruptcy[33] (using Form 4.9 (Scotland));
(b) the Registrar of Companies;
(c) the company; and
(d) any receiver of the whole or any part of the company's assets.

The provisional liquidator shall advertise his appointment in accordance with any directions of the court (rule 4.2) once in the *Edinburgh Gazette* and once in one or more newspapers as the court shall direct for ensuring that it comes to the notice of the creditors of the company (Sheriff Court Corporate Insolvency Rules, rule 23(5)) (Rules of the Court of Session, rule 74.25(b)).

(4) The remuneration[34] of the provisional liquidator shall be fixed by the court from time to time, on the basis of section 53(4) of the Bankruptcy (Scotland) Act 1985. The provisional liquidator's remuneration[35] shall be paid to him:

(a) if a winding-up order is not made, out of the property of the company; or
(b) if the winding-up order is made, as an expense of the liquidation: rule 4.5.

(5) The appointment of the provisional liquidator may be terminated by the court on his application, or on that of any of the persons entitled to make application for his appointment under paragraph 2.4 above. On termination of his appointment, in consequence of the dismissal of the winding-up petition or otherwise, the court may give such directions as it thinks fit with respect to:

(a) the accounts of his administration;
(b) the expenses properly incurred by the provisional liquidator; and
(c) any other matters which it thinks appropriate: rule 4.6.

Even if the petition is dismissed, the company will generally still be liable for the costs and expenses of the appointment.[36]

(6) The author does not consider it necessary to seek the discharge of a provisional liquidator where a winding-up order is made, as it follows that the provisional appointment falls automatically. The Rules of the Sheriff Court and of the Court of Session contain provisions for the seeking of the discharge of a provisional liquidator[37]

---

[33] By virtue of the Scotland Act 1998 (Consequential Modifications) (No. 2) Order 1999 (SI 1999/1820), art.4, Sch.2, Pt II, para.141(1).

[34] Regard should also be had to the Statement of Insolvency Practice No. 9, issued by the Insolvency Practitioners Association, and published on the R3 website: *http://www.r3.org.uk*

[35] *ibid.*

[36] *Re Walter L Jacob & Co Ltd* [1987] 3 B.C.L.C. 532; *Re a Company (No. 001951 of 1987)* [1988] B.C.L.C. 182

[37] Act of Sederunt (Sheriff Court Company Insolvency Rules) 1986, r.23(6); Act of Sederunt (Rules of the Court of Session 1994) 1994, Sch.2, Pt V, r.74.25(5).

(7) The remuneration[38] of a provisional liquidator is fixed by the Court[39]

2.6   Matters Relative to the Petition (Sections 125–127)

(1) On hearing a petition for winding-up, the court may dismiss it,[40] or adjourn the hearing conditionally or unconditionally, or make an interim order or any other order it thinks fit.

(2) At any time after the presentation of a winding-up petition and before a winding-up order has been made, the company or any contributory or creditor may apply to the court having jurisdiction to wind up the company to restrain further proceedings in any pending action or proceeding.

(3) Any disposition of the company's property and any transfer of shares, or alteration in the status of the company's members, made after the commencement of the winding-up, unless the court otherwise orders, is void.[41]

This provision has no effect in respect of anything done by an administrator of a company while a winding-up petition is suspended under paragraph 40 of Schedule B1 to the Insolvency Act.

(4) In *Rose v AIB Group (UK) PLC,*[42] the court restated the general principles on which it will validate a transaction:

(a) first, the discretion is at large;
(b) the basic principle is one of pari passu distribution;
(c) the court should ensure that the interests of the unsecured creditors are not prejudiced;
(d) the court should not, except in exceptional circumstances where it was in the interests of creditors generally, validate a transaction which would result in one or more pre-liquidation creditors being preferred; and
(e) a disposition carried out by the parties in good faith when they were unaware that a petition had been presented would normally be validated unless there were grounds for thinking that the transaction was an attempt to prefer.

(5) Where the position of a bank changed to its detriment after presentation of a petition where it would be inequitable in all the cir-

---

[38] Regard should also be had to the Statement of Insolvency Practice No. 9, issued by the Insolvency Practitioners Association, and published on the R3 website: *http://www.r3.org.uk*
[39] Insolvency (Scotland) Rules 1986, r.4.5; Act of Sederunt (Sheriff Court Company Insolvency Rules) 1986, r.29; Act of Sederunt (Rules of the Court of Session 1994) 1994, Sch.2, Pt V, r.73.30.
[40] See *Craig v Iona Hotels Ltd* [1988] S.C.L.R. 130.
[41] *Re Webb Electrical Ltd* [1988] B.C.L.C. 382; *Re McGuinness Bros (UK) Ltd* (1987) 3 B.C.C. 571; *Gray's Inn Construction Co Ltd* [1987] 1 W.L.R. 711; *Re Tramway Building and Construction Co Ltd* [1987] B.C.L.C. 632.
[42] Ch. D, June 9, 2003.
[43] *Lipkin Gorman v Carpnale Limited* [1991] 2 A.C. 548.

cumstances to require it to make restitution.[43] As this seems to rely on the English doctrine of Equity, it may not be good law in Scotland.

(4) Any attachment, sequestration, distress or execution put in force against the estate or effects of the company situated in England and Wales after the commencement of the winding-up is void.

(5) In addition, by virtue of the provisions of sections 227 and 229, in the case of an unregistered company, the provisions of the Act with respect to staying, sisting or restraining actions and proceedings against a company at any time after the presentation of a petition to wind up, but before the making of a winding-up order, also extend to actions and proceedings against any contributors of the company.

(6) Where a petititioner is subsequently found not entitled to present a petition, fails to intimate, serve or advertise the petition, moves or consents to withdraw the petition or fails to move for an order in terms of the petition, the court may, on such terms as it thinks fit, sist as petitioner any creditor or contributory who in the opinion of the court is entitled to present the petition.[44] The court may allow the cause to be continued for a specified period to allow a note to be presented to achieve same.

2.7 Commencement of the Winding-up (Section 129)

(1) Save where the winding-up by the court follows a voluntary winding-up (see paragraph 2.26 below — in which case the winding-up is deemed to have commenced at the time of the passing of the resolution) the winding-up of a company by the court is deemed to commence at the time of presentation of the petition for winding-up. Note that it is the time and not the date of the petition which is important.

(2) Where the court makes a winding-up order by virtue of paragraph 13(1)(e) of Schedule B1, the winding-up is deemed to commence on the making of the order.

(3) Note however that in relation to an Open-Ended Investment Company, the commencement of the winding-up is calculated differently.[45]

2.8 Making of a Winding-up Order (Sections 130 and 138)

(1) On the making of a winding-up order, a copy of the order must forthwith be forwarded by the company (or otherwise as may be prescribed) to the Accountant in Bankruptcy,[46] using Form 4.2 (Scotland).

(2) Where a winding-up order is made by the court, a liquidator shall

---

[44] Act of Sederunt (Rules of the Court of Session 1994) 1994, Sch.2, Pt. V, r.74.24; Act of Sederunt (Sheriff Court Company Insolvency Rules) 1986, r.21

[45] Open-Ended Investment Companies Regulations 2001 (SI 2001/1228), See Ch.20.6.2, *infra*.

[46] By virtue of the Scotland Act 1998, s.125, Sch.8, para.23.

be appointed by the court, referred to as "the interim liquidator", who continues in office until another person becomes liquidator in his place.

(3) Where a winding-up order has been made, or a provisional liquidator appointed, no action or proceeding shall be proceeded with or commenced against the company or its property, except by leave of the court and subject to terms as the court may impose.[47] For an action of specific performance, see *Re Coregrange Ltd.*[48] In *Canon (Scotland) Business Machines Ltd, Noter,*[49] Lord Caplan held that in considering an application for leave to commence proceedings, the court had wide discretion and should seek to do what was right and fair according to the circumstances of each case.

(4) An interim liquidator has all the powers of a liquidator in terms of section 167. There has been some discussion of this point in academic circles, but the author considers the proposition that an interim liquidator has no powers except those necessary to fulfil his duties under section 138 to be wholly without foundation.

2.9   Duties of the Interim Liquidator (Section 138)

(1) To give notice to the Accountant in Bankruptcy,[50] using Form 4.9 (Scotland), of his appointment within seven days thereof: rule 4.18(4).

(2) To give notice of his appointment within 28 days thereof to the creditors and contributories, or if the court so permits, to advertise his appointment in accordance with the directions of the court: rule 4.18(4).

(3) As soon as practicable in the period of 28 days, beginning with the day on which the winding-up order was made, to summon separate meetings of the company's creditors and of the company's contributories for the purpose of choosing a person (who may be the interim liquidator) to be liquidator of the company in place of the interim liquidator (unless, that is, the company is being wound-up on the grounds that include inability to pay its debts: in which case, a meeting of contributories need not be summoned). Any such meeting shall be summoned for a date not later than 42 days after the date of the winding-up order or such longer period as the court may allow.

(4) If at one or more meetings held in pursuance of this section no person is appointed or nominated, to make a report to the court, which shall appoint either the interim liquidator or some other person.

---

[47] See *Anderson's Trustees v Donaldson & Co Ltd* [1908] S.C. 385
[48] [1984] B.C.L.C. 453.
[49] [1992] B.C.C. 621.
[50] By virtue of the Scotland Act 1998, s.125, Sch.8, para.23,

2.10 First Statutory Meeting (Section 138 and Rule 4.12)

(1) The purpose is to choose a person to be liquidator of the company in place of the interim liquidator.

(2) Only the following resolutions may be taken:

(a) a resolution to appoint one or more insolvency practitioners to be liquidator and, in the case of joint liquidators, as to whether they can act individually;

(b) a resolution to appoint a liquidation committee under section 142;

(c) unless a liquidation committee is to be appointed, a resolution to specify the terms on which the liquidator is to be remunerated, or to defer consideration of that matter;

(d) a resolution to adjourn the meeting for not more than three weeks; or

(e) any other resolution which the chairman considers it right to allow for special reason.

(3) A contributories' meeting cannot pass any resolution to the effect of (c) above. The creditors do not need to fix a date for proving claims — this requires to be done by the court; nor do they need to sanction the appointment by the liquidator of solicitors — he merely requires to advise the Liquidation Committee (if any) that he has done so.

2.11 Appointment of the Liquidator (Section 139; Rules 4.18 and 4.19)

(1) The creditors and contributories at their respective meetings (if there be a meeting of both) may nominate a person to be liquidator.

(2) The liquidator shall be the person nominated by the creditors or, where no person has been so nominated, the person nominated by the contributories.

(3) Where the two meetings nominate different persons, an aggrieved party may apply to the court for any order that the contributories nominee or some other person be appointed. (Rule 4.18 will apply, and its terms should be noted carefully.)

(4) The interim liquidator, as chairman of the meting or, where he is to be nominated as liquidator, some other person as chairman of the meeting, shall certify the appointment of a person as liquidator by the meeting, but not unless and until the person to be appointed has provided a written statement that he is a duly qualified insolvency practitioner, and that he consents so to act (Form 4.8 (Scotland)). It is suggested that, since in almost all cases, the interim liquidator will be offering himself for appointment as liquidator, it is probably good practice for someone other than the interim liquidator to deal with any election of the liquidator to avoid any question being raised as to the way in which proxies in favour of "the chairman" are exercised.

(5) The appointment is effective from the date of the certificate.

(6) Where no person is nominated by either meeting, the court appoints the liquidator: section 138(5); rule 4.18.

2.12   Duties of the Liquidator (Rule 4.19(4))

(1) To give notice of his appointment to the court and to the Accountant in Bankruptcy[51] within seven days, using Form 4.9 (Scotland).
(2) Within 28 days of his appointment, to give notice of it in a newspaper circulating in the pace where the company has its principal place of business, or in another appropriate newspaper, to ensure that it comes to the notice of the company's creditors and contributories.
(3) The provisions of rule 4.18(5) apply to such an advertisement.

2.13   Transitional Matters (Rule 4.21)

Where there is a change in responsible insolvency practitioner, the one being replaced must hand over all assets to his successor and give him all information etc. which the former has.

2.14   The Liquidation Committee (Section 142)[52]

2.14.1   *Until creditors are paid in full*

(1) At the first statutory meeting, those meeting may establish a liquidation committee. If such a committee is not then established, the liquidator may call meetings (and is required so to do if requested by one-tenth in value of the company's creditors) to establish a committee.
(2) Where there is no liquidation committee, its functions are exercised by the court.
(3) The committee consists of at least three and not more than five creditors. Those eligible must have lodged a claim of debt in the liquidation; and that claim must not have been wholly rejected for voting purposes or for the purposes of dividend: rule 4.41.
(4) The liquidation committee comes into existence when the liquidator issues a certificate of due constitution, using Form 4.20 (Scotland). The certificate is issued when three members agree to act, and when up to two more agree to be members, an amended certificate or amended certificates is/are issued, using Form 4.20 (Scotland). Unless a proxy contains a statement to the contrary, agreement may be given by the proxy holder on behalf of the member.

---

[51] By virtue of the Scotland Act 1998 (Consequential Modifications) (No. 2) Order 1999 (SI 1999/1820), art.4, Sch.2, Pt II, para.141(1).
[52] For information on Liquidation Committees, see the Guidance published by the Association of Business Recovery Professionals at *http://www.r3.org.uk*

(5) The certificate (and any amended certificate) is to be sent to the Accountant in Bankruptcy,[53] using Form 4.22 (Scotland).

(6) There is the possibility (rule 4.43) of the liquidation committee having contributory members.

(7) The liquidator is under an obligation to report to the committee such matters as appear to him, or the committee has indicated to be of interest. In the latter case, the liquidator need not comply if:

    (a) the request is frivolous or unreasonable;

    (b) the cost of compliance is out of proportion to the importance of the information; or

    (c) there are insufficient assets: rule 4.44.

(8) The liquidation committee meets as and when the liquidator decides, subject to the following conditions:

    (a) the first meeting must be held within three months of the committee's establishment or the liquidator's appointment, whichever is the later; and

    (b) thereafter, meetings shall be called if requested by a creditor member (the meeting to be held within twenty-one days of the request being received), or on a specified date if the committee has previously so resolved.

Meetings are held on seven days' notice — which can be waived: rule 4.45.

(9) The liquidator, or his qualified representative, chair the liquidation committee, and its quorum is two creditor members: rules 4.46 and 4.47.

(10) Members of the liquidation committee may appoint representatives to attend on their behalf: rule 4.48.

(11) The liquidator shall report to the liquidation committee in writing as directed by it (but not more often then once in any period of two months), setting out the position as regards the progress of the winding-up and matters arising out of it: rule 4.56.

(12) Members of the liquidation committee are entitled to reasonable travelling expenses as an expense of the liquidation, unless the previous meeting was held less than three months before: rule 4.57.

(13) There is a basic prohibition on dealings by members of the liquidation committee, and the terms of rule 4.58 should be referred to in all cases.

(14) The author would strongly recommend the appointment of a liquidation committee in all cases; the technical difficulties of applications to the court in its absence are very serious and time consuming.

---

[53] By virtue of the Scotland Act 1998 (Consequential Modifications) (No. 2) Order 1999 (SI 1999/1820), art.4, Sch.2, Pt II, para.141.

2.14.2   *When Creditors have been Paid in Full (Rule 4.59)*

(1) Once the liquidator issues a certificate that the creditors have been paid in full with interest in accordance with section 189 (Form 4.23 (Scotland)), a copy of that certificate is sent to the Accountant in Bankruptcy[54] using Form 4.24 (Scotland).

(2) Thereupon the creditor members of the liquidation committee cease to be members of the committee.

(3) The committee continues in being unless and until abolished by decision of a meeting of contributories, and (subject to the next paragraph) so long as it consists of at least two contributory members.

(4) The committee does not cease to exist on account of the number of contributory members falling below two, unless and until 28 days have lapsed since the issue of the liquidator's certificate under paragraph (1), but at any time when the committee consists of less than two contributory members, it is suspended and cannot act.

(5) Contributories may be co-opted by the liquidator, or appointed by a contributories' meetings to be members of the committee; but the maximum number of members is five.

2.15   Distribution of Assets (Rules 4.66 and 4.67)

The order of priority in the distribution of the company's assets is as follows:

(1) The expenses of the liquidation, according to the following order of priority:

    (a)   (i) any outlays of the provisional liquidator and liquidator (except those outlays specifically mentioned below);

        (ii) where the winding-up by the court follows immediately on a voluntary winding-up, such outlays and remuneration[55] of the voluntary liquidator as the court may allow;

    (b) the cost of any caution for the provisional liquidator, liquidator or special manager;

    (c) the remuneration[56] of the provisional liquidator (if any)[57];

    (d) the expenses of the petitioner and any intervener whose expenses are allowed by the court;

    (e) the remuneration of any special manager;

---

[54] By virtue of the Scotland Act 1998 (Consequential Modifications) (No. 2) Order 1999 (SI 1999/1820), art.4, Sch.2, Pt II, para.141.

[55] Regard should also be had to the Statement of Insolvency Practice No. 9, issued by the Insolvency Practitioners Association, and published on the R3 website: *http://www.r3.org.uk*

[56] *ibid.*

[57] For possible guidance on dealing with remuneration of provisional liquidators in a major case with a lengthy period of provisional liquidation see *Re Independent Insurance Company Limited* [2003] EWHC 51.

    (f) any allowance made by the liquidator under rule 4.9(1) (expenses of statement of affairs);

    (g) the remuneration of any person employed by the liquidator, but legal expenses still require to be taxed[58] unless there is a liquidation committee[59];

    (h) the remuneration[60] of the liquidator determined in accordance with rule 4.32;

    (i) any corporation tax on chargeable gains accruing on the realisation of any asset (without regard to whether the realisation is effected by the liquidator, a secured creditor or otherwise).

(2) Preferential debts within the meaning of section 386.

(3) Ordinary debts (*i.e.* neither secured nor preferential).

(4) Interest at the official rate (presently 15 per cent[61]) on (2) and (3) above for the period between the commencement of the winding-up and the date of payment of the debt. Interest ranks equally on all debts of the company, irrespective of their respective rankings.

(5) Postponed debts.

(6) Any remaining surplus is returned to the members of the company, according to their respective rights and interests.

2.16 Information (Sections 131, 133, 157 and 192; Rules 4.7–4.11, 4.14 and 4.74)

(1) The provisional liquidator, using Form 4.3 (Scotland), may require present and past officers and employees of the company to make out and submit a statement as to the affairs of the company: rule 4.7.

(2) Such a statement of affairs must be submitted to the liquidator (or provisional liquidator) within 21 days of the request, using Form 4.4 (Scotland), and must be sworn by the deponent.

(3) The liquidator (or provisional liquidator) may, at the request of the deponent, authorise an allowance for the preparation of the statement of affairs.

(4) The liquidator shall report to the creditors and, except where he considers it inappropriate, the contributories, with respect to the proceedings in the winding-up within six weeks after the end of each accounting period; or he may submit such a report to a meeting of creditors or of contributories held within the same period. (*N.B.*: the accounting period is 26 weeks).

(5) Where a statement of affairs has been submitted to the liquidator, he may send it out to creditors and contributories with the next convenient report to be made in terms of rule 4.10(1).

---

[58] See *Scotatlas Limited, http://wwwlscotcourts.gov.uklopinionsvlp276_02.html*

[59] See s.53(2A) of the Bankruptcy (Scotland) Act 1985.

[60] Regard should also be had to the Statement of Insolvency Practice No. 9, issued by the Insolvency Practitioners Association, and published on the R3 website: *http://www.r3.org.uk*

[61] Rule 4.66(2)(b). Given present interest rates, the failure to change this rate since 1986 looks like an oversight. Curiously, the rate of interest in an English winding-up is 8 per cent by virtue of section 189(4) and SI 1993/564. Compare the rate of 12 per cent under the Late Payment of Commercial Debts (Interest) Act 1998. The interface between the late payment legislation and the insolvency legislation is unclear.

(6) Within 30 days after the expiry of one year from the commencement of the liquidation and of each accounting period (26 weeks) thereafter, the liquidator is required to send to the Accountant in Bankruptcy a statement, using Forms 4.5 (Scotland) and 4.6 (Scotland).

(7) The liquidator may require the attendance of an one or more of the company's personnel at any meeting of creditors or contributories: section 157.

(8) At any time during the liquidation, the liquidator may — and if one-half in value of the company's creditors request it, unless the court otherwise orders shall — apply to the court for the public examination of any present or past office of the company, or of any person otherwise engaged in its affairs: section 133. The examination may be made by:

(a) the liquidator;
(b) any special manager of the company's property or business;
(c) any creditor of the company who has submitted a claim in the winding-up;
(d) any contributory of the company.

(9) At least 14 days' notice of the examination diet must be given to the persons mentioned in (8)(b)–(d) above, unless the court otherwise orders, and the liquidator may advertise the diet in one or more newspapers, provided that at least seven days have elapsed since the person to be examined was served with the order: rule 4.74.

(10) If any person without reasonable excuse fails to attend his examination, he is guilty of contempt of court and a warrant may be issued for his arrest and imprisonment: section 134(1).[62]

(11) A person subject to examination under section 133 is not entitled to refuse to answer questions on the ground that he may incriminate himself.[63]

(12) If the winding-up is not concluded within a year after its commencement, if the liquidator is required to send to the Accountant in Bankruptcy a statement in the prescribed form: Form 4.5 (Scotland).

2.17 Getting in the Company's Property (Sections 234–237)

(1) Where any person has under his possession or control any property, books, papers or such records to which the company appears to be entitled, the court may require that person to pay, deliver, convey, surrender or transfer the property, books, papers or records to the liquidator.

(2) Officers of the company, employees, past employees, any former administrator, administrative receiver or liquidator of the com-

---

[62] See *Re Avatar Communications Ltd* (1988) 4 B.C.C. 473.
[63] See *Bishopsgate Investment Management Ltd (in provisional liquidation) v Maxwell* [1993] Ch 1.

pany are each obliged to give to the liquidator such information concerning the company and its promotion, formation, business dealings, affairs or property as the liquidator may reasonably require and shall attend on the liquidator at such times as he may reasonably require: section 235.

(3) The relevant period for investigations (other than in the case of an officer of the company is one year before administration, administrative receivership, appointment of a provisional liquidator or the date on which the company went into liquidation.

(4) The court may summon to appear before it[64]:

    (a) any officer of the company;

    (b) any person known or suspected to have in his possession any property of the company or supposed to be indebted to the company; or

    (c) any person whom the court thinks capable of giving information concerning the promotion, formation, business affairs or property of the company: section 236.

(5) There is no requirement that the examination be preceded by a written statement of questions.

(6) The use of information obtained in a section 236 examination in later criminal proceedings has been held to contrary to the European Convention on Human Rights.[65] For this reason it is considered that an objection to the proceedings on the grounds on possible self-incrimination is unlikely to be upheld.

(7) According to an English case[66] an application under section 236 could be made even if the liquidator's sole purpose was to get information for the purpose of commencing disqualification proceedings against the director under the Company Directors Disqualification Act 1986.[67] Whilst this decision was overturned on appeal,[68] in a subsequent case[69] Millett LJ stated that the powers conferred by section 236 were more properly conferred for the better discharge of the liquidator's wider statutory functions which included the provision of information to the Secretary of State for the purpose of disqualification proceedings.

(8) The scope of section 236 is not limited to persons within the jurisdiction of the court or to persons who had been served personally with the petition within the jurisdiction.[70]

(9) A distinction between sections 235 and 236 (which have to be read together) is that persons covered by section 235 (insiders) are under a greater duty and compulsion than outsiders to assist the

---

[64] See *Re Highgrade Traders Ltd* [1983] B.C.L.C. 137; *Re Norton Warburg Holdings Ltd and Norton Warburg Investment Management Ltd* [1983] B.C.L.C. 235.

[65] *Saunders v United Kingdom* [1997] B.C.C. 872.

[66] *Re Pantmaenog Timber Co Ltd* [2003] B.C.C. 659; [2003] UKHL 49.

[67] See *R. v Secretary of State for Trade and Industry, Ex parte. McCormick* [1998] B.C.C. 379.

[68] *Re Pantmaenog Timber Co Ltd* [2003] B.C.C. 659; [2003] UKHL 49.

[69] *Official Receiver v Wadge Rapps & Hunt* [2003] UKHL 49.

[70] *McIsaac and Wilson, Petitioners* [1995] S.L.T. 498.

liquidator. As a result the ability of an insider to resist an order under section 236 has to be reduced.[71]

2.18   Annual Meetings (Rule 4.13)

The liquidator is required to summon a meeting of the creditors each year during which the liquidation is in force.

2.19   Removal of the Liquidator and his Vacation of Office (Section 172)

(1) A provisional liquidator may be removed from office only by an order of the court.

(2) A liquidator may be removed from office only by an order of the court or by a general meeting of creditors summoned especially for that purpose.

(3) A liquidator or provisional liquidator shall vacate office if he ceases to be qualified to act as an insolvency practitioner in relation to the company.

(4) Where an order is made for early dissolution under section 204, the liquidator vacates office when the dissolution of the company takes effect in accordance with that section.

(5) Where a final meeting has been held under section 146 to receive the liquidator's report on completion of the winding-up, the liquidator whose report was considered at the meeting shall vacate office as soon as he has given notice to the court and the Accountant in Bankruptcy that the meeting has been held and of the decisions (if any) of the meeting.

(6) A meeting for removal of a liquidator must be convened by the liquidator if requested so to do by not less than one-quarter in value of the creditors.

(7) The notice convening such a meeting shall draw attention to the provisions of section 174(4) with respect to the liquidator's release.

(8) If, at the meeting, it is resolved that the liquidator be removed, the chairman of the meeting shall (rule 4.24):

    (a) if another liquidator was not appointed, send a copy of the certificate of the liquidator's removal to the court, and to the Accountant in Bankruptcy, using Forms 4.10 (Scotland) and 4.11 (Scotland);

    (b) otherwise, deliver the certificate to the new liquidator, who shall send a copy of such certificate to the court and to the Accountant in Bankruptcy, using the same Forms: rule 4.24.

(9) Where a new liquidator is appointed, he shall advertise his appointment according to rules 4.19–4.21 (see paragraph 2.12, above), but the notice under rule 4.19(4), using Form 4.9 (Scotland), shall also state that his predecessor as liquidator has been removed, and whether the latter has been released.

---

[71] *Re RBG Resources Limited* [2002] EWCA Civ 1624.

2.20 Resignation of the Liquidator (Section 172(6))

(1) A meeting of creditors must be called to receive his resignation. Notice thereof must draw attention to section 174(4)(*c*) and rule 4.29(4) with respect to the liquidator's release, and shall be accompanied by a statement of his intromissions: rule 4.28. It must also contain a statement as to the amount paid to unsecured creditors by virtue of the application of section 176A (prescribed part).

(2) The only grounds for resignation are:

(a) ill health;
(b) the intention to cease practising as an insolvency practitioner;
(c) a conflict of interest or change in personal circumstances which precludes or makes impracticable the further discharge by him of the duties of liquidator: rule 4.28(3). This would, however, not include the realisation that the assets are insufficient to meet the liquidator's proposed fees.

(3) If the resignation is accepted it is effective from such date as the meeting of creditors may determine: rule 4.29(2).

(4) The liquidator gives notice of his accepted resignation to the court and to the Accountant in Bankruptcy, using Forms 4.15 (Scotland) and 4.16 (Scotland): rule 4.29(3).

(5) If the liquidator's resignation is not accepted, the court may, on the liquidator's application, make an order giving him leave to resign, using Form 4.16 (Scotland).

(6) If there is no quorum at the meeting of creditors convened, the resolution is deemed to have been passed.

2.21 Final Meeting of Creditors (Section 146)

(1) If it appears to the liquidator that the winding-up is for practical purposes complete, he shall summon a final meeting of creditors which shall:

(a) receive the liquidator's report of the winding-up; and
(b) determine whether the liquidator should have his release under section 174.

(2) Notice of the final meeting may be given at the same time as notice of a final distribution is given.

(3) At lease 28 days' notice of the final meeting of creditors shall be given, and shall be sent to all creditors whose claims in the liquidation have been accepted.

2.22 Release of the Liquidator (Section 174)

(1) After removal of a liquidator by a meeting of creditors:

(a) if there is no resolution against his release, it is from the time stated on the notice which is given to the court and the

Accountant in Bankruptcy,[72] using Forms 4.10 (Scotland) and 4.11 (Scotland), that that person has ceased to hold office;

(b) if there is a resolution against release, the liquidator must apply to the Accountant of Court for his discharge: Form 4.12 (Scotland). When the Accountant of Court releases the former liquidator, he shall issue a certificate of release to the new liquidator, who shall send a copy of it to the court and the Accountant in Bankruptcy, using Forms 4.13 (Scotland) and 4.14 (Scotland): rule 4.25.

(2) On the resignation of the liquidator:

(a) if there is no resolution against release, it shall be from such date as the meeting convened to consider the resignation may determine;

(b) if there is a resolution against release, the liquidator must apply to the Accountant of Court for his discharge: Form 4.12 (Scotland). When the Account of Court releases the former liquidator, he shall issue a certificate of release to the new liquidator, who shall send a copy of it to the court and to the Accountant in Bankruptcy,[73] using Forms 4.13 (Scotland) and 4.14 (Scotland): rule 4.25;

(c) if there was no quorum present at the meeting convened, the liquidator has his release from the date for which the meeting was summoned: rule 4.29(7)(b).

(3) On the death of the liquidator, notice must be given to the court and to the Accountant in Bankruptcy,[74] using Form 4.18 (Scotland): rule 4.36. Release is from the time at which notice is given to the court that that person has ceased to hold office.

(4) On an early dissolution of the company under section 204, release shall be from such time as the Accountant of Court, on the application of the liquidator, may determine: section 174(4)(b).

(5) On completion of the winding-up:

(a) if, at the final meeting of creditors under section 146, there is no resolution against release, release shall be from the time the liquidator vacates office and gives notice to the court, to the Registrar of Companies and to the Accountant in Bankruptcy,[75] using Form 4.17 (Scotland);

(b) if, at the final meeting of creditors, there is a resolution against release, the liquidator must apply to the Accountant of Court for his discharge: Form 4.12 (Scotland). When the Accountant of Court releases the former liquidator, he shall issue a certificate of release to the new liquidator, who shall

---

[72] By virtue of the Scotland Act 1998 (Consequential Modifications) (No. 2) Order 1999 (SI 1999/1820), art.4, Sch.2, Pt II, para.141.

[73] *ibid.*

[74] *ibid.*

[75] *ibid.*

send a copy of it to the court and to the Accountant in Bankruptcy,[76] using Forms 4.13 (Scotland): rule 4.25;

(c) if there is no quorum present at the final meeting the liquidator reports this fact to the court, and the meeting is deemed to have been held and no resolution against release to have been passed: rule 4.31.

2.23 Outlays and Remuneration (Rules 4.32–4.35)

(1) In questions of remuneration regard should always be had by the liquidator to Statement of Insolvency Practice 9 (Scotland), published on the website of the Association of Business Recovery Professionals.[77]

(2) Claims by the liquidator for the outlays reasonably incurred by him, and for his remuneration[78], shall be made in accordance with section 53 of the Bankruptcy (Scotland) Act 1985: rule 4.32(1).

(3) The liquidator may, at any time before the end of an accounting period (26 weeks), submit to the liquidation committee (if any) an interim claim in respect of that period for the outlays reasonably incurred by him and for his remuneration; and the liquidation committee may make an interim determination in relation to the amount of the outlays and remuneration[79] payable to the liquidator. Where there is not a liquidation committee, its functions are exercised by the court. However, it is suggested that if there is to be no liquidation committee, the liquidator should seek a resolution of creditors at the first statutory meeting in terms of rule 4.12 on the basis upon which he is to be remunerated.

(4) If the liquidator considers the remuneration fixed by the liquidation committee to be insufficient, he may request that it be increased by the resolution of the creditors: rule 4.33.

(5) Thereafter, if the liquidator is still dissatisfied, he may apply to the court for an order increasing the amount or rate. The liquidation committee may be heard on such application, or if there is no such committee, the court may order that notice of the application be sent to one or more creditors, who may nominate one or more of their number to appear to be represented: rule 4.34.

(6) Any remuneration fixed by the liquidation committee or by resolution of creditors may be challenged on application by creditors representing 25 per cent or more in value of the creditors, on the basis that the liquidator's remuneration is excessive. The court may, if it finds the application well founded, order the remuneration to be fixed at a reduced rate: rule 4.35.

---

[76] By virtue of the Scotland Act 1998 (Consequential Modifications) (No. 2) Order 1999 (SI 1999/1820), art.4, Sch.2, Pt II, para.141.

[77] *http://www.r3.org.uk*

[78] Regard should also be had to the Statement of Insolvency Practice No. 9, issued by the Insolvency Practitioners Association, and published on the R3 website: *http://www.r3.org.uk*

[79] *ibid.*

(7) Section 53 of the Bankruptcy (Scotland) Act 1985 provides that the basis of remuneration may be a commission calculated by reference to the value of the company's estate, but in any event there shall be taken into account:

(a) the work which, having regard to that value, was reasonably undertaken by the liquidator; and
(b) the extent of his responsibilities in administering the company's assets.

(8) Accounts for legal services shall be submitted for taxation before payment, but the court may authorise the liquidator to pay any such account without taxation.

(9) Within six weeks after the end of an accounting period (26 weeks):

(a) the liquidation committee or the court shall audit the accounts and issue a determination fixing the amount of the outlays and the remuneration[80] payable to the liquidator;
(b) the liquidator shall make the audited accounts scheme and the said determination available for inspection by the company and the creditors.

(10) Not later than eight weeks after the end of an accounting, the liquidator, the company and any creditor may appeal to the court against a determination.

(11) For the remuneration[81] of a provisional liquidator, see paragraph 2.5(4) above.

2.24 Powers of the Liquidator (Section 167)

(1) The liquidator may exercise any of the powers contained in Parts I and II of Schedule 4 to the Act with the sanction of the court or the liquidation committee, and may exercise those contained in Part III of the said Schedule with or without such sanction.

(2) If the liquidator, in pursuant of his powers, disposes of any assets to any person associated with the company, or employs a solicitor to assist him in the carrying out of his functions, notice thereof must be given to the liquidation committee (if any).

2.25 General Powers of Court (Sections 147–159)

2.25.1 *Power to Stay or Sist Winding-up (Section 147)*

(1) The court may at any time after an order for winding-up, on the application of the liquidator or any creditor or contributory and on proof to the satisfaction to the court that the winding-up ought to be stayed or sisted, make an order staying or sisting the

---

[80] Regard should also be had to the Statement of Insolvency Practice No. 9, issued by the Insolvency Practitioners Association, and published on the R3 website: http://www.r3.org.uk
[81] *ibid.*

proceedings, either altogether or for a limited time, on such terms and conditions as the court thinks fit.

(2) In such an event the company requires to send a copy of the order to the Accountant in Bankruptcy[82] using From 4.27 (Scotland).

2.25.2 Settlement of List of Contributories (Section 148)

If it appears to the court that there are unlikely to be sufficient funds to meet the claims of creditors in full, the court may dispense with the settlement of a list of contributories. Contrary to popular belief, this power may not be exercised either by the creditors or by the liquidation committee.

2.25.3 Debt by Contributory (Section 149)

The court may make an order ordering any contributory to pay any moneys due from him to the company exclusive of any money payable by him by virtue of any calls in pursuant of the Companies Act or the Insolvency Act.

2.25.4 Power to Make Calls (Section 150)

The court may, at any time after making the winding-up order and either before or after it has ascertained the sufficiency of the company's assets, make calls on all or any of the contributories for the time being settled on the list of contributories to the extent of their liability for payment of the money which the court considers necessary to satisfy the company's debts and liabilities and the expenses of winding-up. In making such a call, the court may take into consideration the probability that some of the contributories may partly or wholly fail to pay it.

2.25.5 Fixing of Date for Claims (Section 153)

The court may fix a time or times within which creditors are to prove their debts or claims or to be excluded from the benefit of any distribution made before those debts are proved. Here again, there have been instances in which either a liquidation committee or meeting of the creditors has attempted to fix such a date, but in a winding-up of the court it is only the court which has the power so to do.

2.25.6 Any Inspection of Books by Creditors, etc. (Section 155)

The court may make such order for inspection of the company's books and papers by creditors and contributories as the court thinks just; and any books and papers in the company's possession may be inspected by creditors and contributories accordingly, but not further or otherwise.

---

[82] By virtue of the Scotland Act 1998 (Consequential Modifications) (No. 2) Order 1999 (SI 1999/1820), art.4, Sch.2, Pt II, para.141.

2.26   Dissolution of the Company (Sections 204 and 205)

2.26.1   Early Dissolution (Section 204)

(1) If after the first statutory meeting (and there appears to be no maximum period which can elapse) it appears to the liquidator that the realisable assets of the company are insufficient to cover the expenses of the winding-up, he may apply to the court for an order that the company be dissolved. There does not appear to be any requirement for the liquidator to bring to the attention of the company's creditors and contributories the fact that such an application to the court is being made. Presumably this will be self apparent from the reports given at the first statutory (or any subsequent) meeting.

(2) If the court makes such an order, a copy of it is to be forwarded to the Accountant in Bankruptcy[83] within 14 days.

(3) The court may, on application by any person who appears to the court to have an interest, order that the date at which the dissolution of the company is to take effect be deferred for such period as the court thinks fit.

(4) If such deferment is granted, the court order shall be sent to the Registrar of Companies within seven days, using Form 4.28 (Scotland).

(5) Unless a deferred date for dissolution is fixed, the company will be dissolved at the end of the period of three months after registration of the order.

2.26.2   Dissolution at the Conclusion of the Winding-up

(1) Where the Registrar of Companies has received a notice served for the purposes of section 172(8) on Form 4.17 (Scotland) (final meeting of creditors and the vacation of office by the liquidator), the company is dissolved after a period of three months following registration of the notice.

(2) The court may, on application of any person who appears to have an interest, defer the dissolution of the company for such period as the court thinks fit.

(3) If a deferment is granted, the court order in question must be sent to the Accountant in Bankruptcy[84] within seven days, using Form 4.28 (Scotland).

2.27   Winding-up by the Court and Voluntary Winding-up

(1) It is clear that the fact that a company has passed a resolution for voluntary winding-up is not a bar to the granting of a winding-up order by the court. In *Re J D Swain*,[85] Diplock L.J. stated (at 914):

---

[83] By virtue of the Scotland Act 1998 (Consequential Modifications) (No. 2) Order 1999 (SI 1999/1820), art.4, Sch.2, Pt II, para.141.

[84] *ibid.*

[85] [1965] 1 W.L.R. 909.

There are four cases to which I think it is desirable to refer. The first is *Re James Millward & Co Ltd,*[86] which was the first case coming before the court after section 137(2) of the Companies (Consolidation) Act 1908 had been replaced by section 255 of the Companies Act 1929. The decision of the Court of Appeal in that case, it seems to me, comes to no more than that in a contest between a creditor and the company where no other creditors are concerned, *prima facie* the fact that the company has entered into voluntary liquidation is not a ground which weighs either way in the determination by the judge as to the way in which his discretion should be exercised.

(2) This view was also supported by Harman J. in *Re Surplus Properties (Huddersfield) Ltd.*[87] In that case, a declaration of solvency had been given by the directors and Harman J. considered that, in such circumstances, the contributories' view is relevant.

(3) In *Re Lowestoft Traffic Services Ltd,*[88] Hoffman J. stated that in determining the wishes of creditors as to whether or not a winding-up order should be granted, it is proper to discount the opposition from those opposing creditors who are clearly associated with the management of the company, particularly when, as in this case, it is said that the main reason why there should be an order for compulsory winding-up is the necessity for an independent investigation into their management.[89]

(4) Even if the creditors in favour of a continuation of the voluntary liquidation are a minority in value, the court may refuse a compulsory order if there appears to be no advantage to creditors in making one (see *Re Medisco Equipment Ltd,*[90] in which the voluntary winding-up had been almost completed and a compulsory order would only have been added to the expense and see also *William Thorpe and Son Ltd).*[91]

(5) It would therefore appear that if a creditor wishes to challenge the appointment of a liquidator which was made at a creditors' meeting due, in whole or in part, to votes exercised by the directors and those associated with them, the time to make application to the court for a compulsory winding-up order is as soon as possible after the creditors' meeting.

---

[86] [1940] 1 All E.R. 347.
[87] [1984] B.C.L.C. 89.
[88] [1986] B.C.L.C. 881.
[89] (See also *Re Palmer Marine Surveys Ltd* [1986] B.C.L.C. 106; *Re Falcon Developments Ltd* [1987] B.C.L.C. 437; *Re MCH Services Ltd* [1987] B.C.L.C. 535).
[90] [1983] B.C.L.C. 305.
[91] [1989] 5 B.C.C. 156.

CHAPTER 3

CREDITORS' VOLUNTARY WINDING-UP
(PART IV OF THE ACT AS APPLIED BY SCHEDULE 1 TO THE RULES)

3.1 Commencement of the Winding-up (Sections 84–86)

(1) A company may be wound-up voluntarily if it resolves by extraordinary resolution to the effect that it cannot, by reason of its liabilities, continue its business, and that it is advisable to wind up.

(2) Before a company passes a resolution for voluntary winding-up it must give written notice of the resolution to the holder of any qualifying floating charge to which section 72A[1] applies. Thereafter, the resolution may not be passed until a period of five days has elapsed or the holder of the qualifying floating charge has consented in writing to the passing of the resolution.

(3) A copy of that resolution must be sent to the Registrar of Companies and to the Accountant in Bankruptcy[2] within 15 days.[3]

(4) Within 14 days of passing the resolution, the company must give notice of the resolution by advertisement in the *Edinburgh Gazette*.

(5) A voluntary winding-up is deemed to commence at the time of the passing of the resolution for voluntary winding-up. This is an important point. Where a liquidation is being timed to cut down an illegal preference or transaction at an undervalue, it may be more advantageous to pass a resolution for voluntary winding-up rather than petition the court in view of the provisions of section 185. Note that it is the time, not the date, which is important.

(6) However, regard should be had to the requirement introduced by section 84(2A) to give notice to the holder of any qualifying floating charge.

(7) Failure to publish the resolution in the *Edinburgh Gazette* may lead to a fine on the company, its directors and the liquidator.

3.2 Creditors' Meeting (Section 98 and 99)

(1) The company shall cause:

(a) a meeting of its creditors to be summoned for not later than the 14th day after the company meeting at which the

---

[1] A qualifying floating charge is basically a charge created after September 15, 2003.

[2] By virtue of the Scotland Act 1998 (Consequential Modifications) (No. 2) Order 1999 (SI 1999/1820), art.4, Sch.2, Pt II, para.141.

[3] Section 380 of the Companies Act 1985.

resolution for voluntary winding-up is to be considered; it is probably good practice for the directors to resolve to summon the creditors' meeting before the members appoint a liquidator (if this is to be done at the initial stage), as some doubt has been expressed as to whether it is competent to call it after a liquidator has been appointed by the members. In such a situation, the author considers that the liquidator could call the meeting although there could then be problems in having a director chair the creditors' meeting;

(b) notices of the creditors' meeting to be sent by post to the creditors not less than seven days before the date of the meeting;

(c) notice of the meeting to be advertised once in the *Edinburgh Gazette* and once at least in two newspapers circulating in the locality in which the company's principal place of business in Great Britain is situated; such an advertisement must be at least seven days before the date of the creditors' meeting.

(2) The notice of the meeting shall state:

(a) either the name and address of a person qualified to act as an insolvency practitioner in relation to the company who, during the period before the day on which the meeting is to be held, will furnish creditors free of charge with such information concerning the company's affairs as they may reasonably require; or

(b) a place in the locality of the company's principal place of business where, on the two business days falling next before the date on which the meeting is to be held, a list of the names and addresses of the company's creditors will be available for inspection free of charge.

To date, in Scotland, it has been almost invariable practice to select option (b); perhaps the open-ended nature of paragraph (a) has been a disincentive to insolvency practitioners, whose choice this will be.

(3) In terms of rule 7.26, a creditor who has the right to inspect documents can also require a list of the company's creditors and the amounts of their respective debts to be furnished to him. A copy of the list may be taken on payment of the appropriate fee (presently, 15p per A4 or A5 page, and 30p per A3 page). Only creditors and their duly authorised representatives are entitled to inspect and take copies of the list of creditors. It is not possible for a person to require that he be permitted to inspect the list to ascertain whether any of his "clients" are on the list. Such activity comes very close to the solicitation which is prohibited by rule 4.39 and in any event, in the author's opinion, constitutes very poor practice.

(4) The directors of the company shall:

(a) make out a statement, using Form 4.4 (Scotland), as to the affairs of the company;

> (b) cause that statement to be laid before the meeting of creditors; and
>
> (c) appoint one of their number to preside at that meeting. The failure of the director to attend the meeting, and the necessity of the creditors there present to appoint a chairman to preside will not vitiate the conduct of the meeting.[4]

(5) Such a statement must be verified by affidavit of the directors.

(6) Where the members appoint a liquidator before the creditors' meeting, the directors must send him a copy of the statement of affairs forthwith.

(7) Where the statement of affairs laid before the meeting of creditors is not as at the date of that meeting, the directors shall cause a report to be made to the meeting (possibly by the director who was chosen to preside at the meeting) on any material transactions between the date of the statement and that of the meeting.

3.3 Appointment of the Liquidator (Sections 100, 101 and 109)

(1) The creditors and the company at their respective meetings may nominate a person to be liquidator of the company and distribute its assets.

(2) The liquidator shall be the person nominated by the creditors or, where no person has been so nominated, the person, if any, nominated by the company.

(3) If neither the creditors nor the members make a nomination, the appointment is made by the court having jurisdiction to wind up the company.

(4) If different persons are nominated by the creditors and the company, application may be made to the court by any director, member or creditor of the company may apply to the court for an order either directing that the person nominated by the company shall be liquidator instead of or jointly with the person nominated by the creditors, or appointing some other person to be liquidator instead of the person nominated by the creditors.

(5) The court is required to grant an application pursuant to (4) where it is made by the holder of a qualifying floating charge in respect of the company's property unless the court thinks it right to refuse the application because of the particular circumstances of the case.

(6) The chairman of the meeting shall certify the appointment, using Form 4.8 (Scotland), after the person to be appointed has provided him with a written statement to the effect that he is an insolvency practitioner, duly qualified, and that he consents to act.

(7) The appointment takes effect from the passing of the resolution for his appointment.

---

[4] *Re Salcombe Hotel Development Co Ltd* (1989) 5 B.C.C. 807.

(8) The liquidator shall, within 14 days of his appointment, publish in the *Gazette* and deliver to the Accountant in Bankruptcy[5] a notice of his appointment, using Forms 600 and 600a; and publish notice thereof, within twenty-eight days of his appointment, in one newspaper circulating in the area in which the company carried on business: rule 4.19(4)(b).

(9) On the appointment of a liquidator, all the powers of the directors cease, except so far as the liquidation committee (or, if there is no liquidation committee, the court) sanctions their continuance. The directors, however, remain in office.

3.4 Initial Expenses (Rules 4.9 and 4.14A, Schedule 1)

(1) Payment may be made, as an expense of the liquidation:

    (a) of any reasonable and necessary expenses incurred in preparing the statement of affairs under section 99 — provided such expenditure has been authorised in advance by the liquidator; and

    (b) of any reasonable and necessary expenses incurred in connection with the summoning, advertisement and holding of a creditors' meeting under section 98.

(2) Where such payments are made before the commencement of the winding-up, the director presiding at the creditors' meeting shall inform the meeting of their amount and of the identity of the person to whom they were made.

(3) The liquidator may make such a payment but, if there is a liquidation committee, he must give it seven days' notice of his intention to make the payment.

(4) Such a payment may not be made by the liquidator to himself, or to any associate of his, without the consent of the liquidation committee, the creditors or the court.

3.5 Information (Rules 4.10 and 4.11, Section 192)

(1) Within 28 days of the creditors' meeting, the liquidator shall send creditors a copy of summary of the statement of affairs and a report of the proceedings at the meeting.

(2) Within 30 days after the first year of the winding-up, and six monthly thereafter, the liquidator shall send to the Accountant in Bankruptcy a statement of receipts and payments, using Forms 4.5 (Scotland) and 4.6 (Scotland).

3.6 Annual Meetings (Section 105 and Rule 4.13)

The liquidator is required to call a meeting of creditors at the end of the first year of the winding-up, and annually thereafter. This meeting is to be

---

[5] By virtue of the Scotland Act 1998 (Consequential Modifications) (No. 2) Order 1999 (SI 1999/1820), art.4, Sch.2, Pt II, para.141.

no later than three months after the year end. There shall be laid before each meeting an account of the liquidator's acts and dealings, and of the conduct of the winding-up during the preceding year.

3.7 The Liquidation Committee (Section 101 and Rules 4.40–4.59A)

3.7.1   Until Creditors are Paid in Full

(1) At the first creditors' meeting, or at any subsequent meeting, the creditors may appoint a liquidation committee.

(2) The committee consists of at least three and not more than five creditors. Those eligible must have lodged a claim of debt in the liquidation; and that claim must not have been wholly rejected for voting purposes or for the purposes of dividend: rule 4.41.

(3) The liquidation committee comes into existence when the liquidator issues a certificate of due constitution, using Form 4.20 (Scotland). The certificate is issued when three members agree to act, and when up to two more agree to be members, an amended certificate or amended certificates (Form 4.20 (Scotland)) is/are issued.

(4) The certificate (and any amended certificate) is to be sent to the Accountant in Bankruptcy,[6] using Form 4.22 (Scotland).

(5) The liquidator is under an obligation to report to the committee such matters as appear to him, or they have indicated, are of interest to them. In the latter case, the liquidator need not comply if:

(a) the request is frivolous or unreasonable;
(b) the cost of compliance is out of proportion to the importance of the information; or
(c) there are insufficient assets: rule 4.44.

(6) The liquidation committee meets as and when the liquidator decides, subject to the following conditions:

(a) the first meeting must be held within three months of the committee's establishment or the liquidator's appointment, whichever is the later;
(b) thereafter, meetings shall be called if requested by a creditor member (the meeting to be held within twenty-one days of the request being received), or for a specified date if the committee has previously so resolved.

Meetings are held on seven days' notice — which can be waived: rule 4.45.

(7) The liquidator or his representative chairs the liquidation committee, and its quorum is two members: rules 4.46 and 4.47.

(8) Members of the liquidation committee may appoint representatives to attend on their behalf: rule 4.48.

(9) The liquidator shall report to the liquidation committee in writ-

---

[6] By virtue of the Scotland Act 1998 (Consequential Modifications) (No. 2) Order 1999 (SI 1999/1820), art.4, Sch.2, Pt II, para.141.

ing as directed by it (but not more often than once in any period of two months), setting out the position as regards the progress of the winding-up and matters arising out of it: rule 4.56.

(10) Members of the liquidation committee are entitled to reasonable travelling expenses as an expense of the liquidation unless the previous meeting was held less than three months before: rule 4.57.

(11) There is a basic prohibition on dealing by members of the liquidation committee, and the terms of rule 4.58 should be referred to in all cases.

3.7.2 When Creditors have been Paid in Full (Rule 4.59)

(1) Once the liquidation issues a certificate that the creditors have been paid in full with interest in accordance with section 189 (Form 4.23 (Scotland)) a copy of that certificate is sent to the Accountant in Bankruptcy using Form 4.24 (Scotland).

(2) Thereupon, the creditor members of the liquidation committee cease to be members of the committee.

(3) The committee continues in being unless and until abolished by decision of a meeting of contributories, and (subject to the next paragraph) so long as it consists of at least two contributory members.

(4) The committee does not cease to exist on account of the number of contributory members falling below two, unless and until twenty-eight days have elapsed since the issue of the liquidator's certificate under paragraph (1), but at any time when the committee consists of less than two contributory members, it is suspended and cannot act.

(5) Contributories may be co-opted by the liquidator, or appointed by a contributories' meeting to be members of the committee; but the maximum number of members is five.

3.8 Getting in the Company's Property (Sections 234–237)

(1) Where any person has under his possession or control any property, books, papers or such records to which the company appears to be entitled, the court may require that person to pay, deliver, convey, surrender or transfer the property, books, papers or records to the liquidator.

(2) Officers of the company, employees, past employees, any former administrator, administrative receiver or liquidator of the company is obliged to give to the liquidator such information concerning the company and its promotion, formation, business dealings, affairs or property as the liquidator may reasonably require and shall attend on the liquidator at such times as he may reasonably require: section 235.

(3) The relevant period for investigations (other than in the case of an officer of the company is one year before administration, administrative receivership, appointment of a provisional liquidator or the date on which the company went into liquidation.

(4) The court may summon to appear before it:

(a) any officer of the company;

(b) any person known or suspected to have in his possession any property of the company or supposed to be indebted to the company; or

(c) any person whom the court thinks capable of giving information concerning the promotion, formation, business affairs or property of the company: section 236.[7]

(5) There is no requirement that the examination be preceded by a written statement of questions.

(6) The use of information obtained in a section 236 examination in later criminal proceedings has been held to contrary to the European Convention on Human Rights.[8] For this reason it is considered that an objection to the proceedings on the grounds on possible self-incrimination is unlikely to be upheld.

(7) According to one English case[9] an application under section 236 can be made even if the liquidator's sole purpose was to get information for the purpose of commencing disqualification proceedings against the director under the Company Directors Disqualification Act 1986.

(8) The scope of section 236 is not limited to persons within the jurisdiction of the court or to persons who had been served personally with the petition within the jurisdiction.[10]

3.9 Distribution of Assets (Rules 4.66 and 4.67)

The order of priority in the distribution of the company's assets is as follows:

(1) The expenses of the liquidation according to the following order of priority:

(a) any outlays of a provisional liquidator and liquidator (except those outlays specifically mentioned below);

(b) the cost of any caution for the provisional liquidator, liquidator or special manager;

(c) the remuneration[11] of the provision liquidator (if any);

(d) the expenses of the petitioner and any intervener whose expenses are allowed by the court;

(e) the remuneration of any special manager;

(f) any allowance made by the liquidator under rule 4.9(1) (expenses of statement of affairs);

(g) the remuneration of any person employed by the liquidator, but legal expenses may still require to be taxed[12] unless there

---

[7] See *Re Highgrade Traders Ltd* [1983] B.C.L.C. 137; *Re Norton Warburg Holdings Ltd and Norton Warburg Investment Management Ltd* [1983] B.C.C. 235.

[8] *Saunders v United Kingdom* [1997] B.C.C. 872.

[9] *Re Pantmaenog Timber Co Ltd.* [2003] B.C.C. 659; [2003] UKHL 49.

[10] *McIsaac and Wilson, Petitioners*, 1995 S.L.T. 498.

[11] Regard should also be had to the Statement of Insolvency Practice No. 9, issued by the Insolvency Practitioners Association, and published on the R3 website: *http://www.r3.org.uk*

[12] See *Scotatlas Limited, http://wwwlscotcourts.gov.uklopinionsvlp276_02.html*

is a liquidation committee[13]; The meaning of the section is unclear as the liquidation is not "pending" before any court;

    (h) the remuneration of the liquidator determined in accordance with rule 4.32;

    (i) any capital gains tax on realisation of any asset.

(2) Preferential debts within the meaning of section 386.

(3) Ordinary debts (*i.e.* neither secured nor preferential).

(4) Interest at the official rate (presently 15 per cent) on (2) and (3) above for the period between the commencement of the winding-up and the date of payment of the debt.

(5) Postponed debts.

(6) Any remaining surplus to the members of the company, according to their respective rights and interests.

3.10 Early Dissolution of the Company (Section 204)

(1) Although section 204 does not appear to be immediately applicable in cases of creditors' voluntary winding-up, it has been so held by virtue of the application of section 112 of the Act.[14]

    If after the first statutory meeting (and there appears to be no maximum period which can elapse) it appears to the liquidator that the realisable assets of the company are insufficient to cover the expenses of the winding-up, he may apply to the court for an order that the company be dissolved. There does not appear to be any requirement for the liquidator to bring to the attention of the company's creditors and contributories the fact that such an application to the court is being made. Presumably this will be self apparent from the reports given at the first statutory (or any subsequent) meeting.

(2) If the court makes such an order, a copy of it is to be forwarded to the Accountant in Bankruptcy[15] within 14 days.

(3) The court may, on application by any person who appears to the court to have an interest, order that the date at which the dissolution of the company is to take effect be deferred for such period as the court thinks fit.

(4) If such deferment is granted, the court order shall be sent to the Registrar of Companies within seven days, using Form 4.28 (Scotland).

(5) Unless a deferred date for dissolution is fixed, the company will be dissolved at the end of the period of three months after registration of the order.

---

[13] See s.53(2A) of the Bankruptcy (Scotland) Act 1985.

[14] *Summary Application of Maureen E Leslie as Liquidator of EX1 Limited*, Edinburgh Sheriff Court, July 16, 2003.

[15] By virtue of the Scotland Act 1998 (Consequential Modifications) (No. 2) Order 1999 (SI 1999/1820), art.4, Sch.2, Pt II, para.141.

3.11 Removal of the Liquidator and his Vacation of Office (Sections 108 and 171)

(1) A liquidator may be removed from office only by an order of the court or by resolution of a general meeting of creditors summoned specifically for that purpose. See *Re Keypak Homecare Ltd*,[16] where it was held that the phrase "on cause shown" did not require evidence of personal misconduct or unfitness — however, some unfitness in a wide sense of the terms was required.

(2) A liquidator shall vacate office if he ceases to be qualified to act as an insolvency practitioner in relation to the company.

(3) Where a final meeting has been held under section 106 (liquidator's report on completion of winding-up), the liquidator whose report was considered at the meeting shall vacate office as soon as he has given notice to the Accountant in Bankruptcy[17] that the meeting has been held, and of the decisions (if any) of the meeting.

(4) A meeting for removal of the liquidator must be convened by the liquidator if requested so to do by not less than one-quarter in value of the creditors.

(5) The notice convening such a meeting shall draw attention to the provisions of section 173(2)(a) or (b) with respect to the liquidator's release.

(6) If at the meeting it is resolved that the liquidator be removed, the chairman of the meeting shall:

    (a) if another liquidator was not appointed, send a certificate of the liquidator's removal to the Accountant in Bankruptcy,[18] using Forms 4.10 (Scotland) and 4.11 (Scotland);

    (b) otherwise, deliver the certificate to the new liquidator, who shall send it to the Accountant in Bankruptcy,[19] using Forms 4.10 (Scotland) and 4.11 (Scotland).

(7) Where a new liquidator is appointed, he shall advertise his appointment according to rules 4.19 and 4.21 (see 3.3 above), but the notice under rule 4.19(4), using Form 4.9 (Scotland), shall also state this his predecessor as liquidator has been removed, and whether the latter has been released: rule 4.27.

3.12 Resignation of the Liquidator (Section 171(5))

(1) A meeting of creditors must be called to receive his resignation. Notice thereof must draw attention to section 172(2)(c) and rule 4.29(4) with respect to the liquidator's release, and shall be accompanied by a statement of his intromissions: rule 4.28.

---

[16] [1987] B.C.L.C. 409.
[17] By virtue of the Scotland Act 1998 (Consequential Modifications) (No. 2) Order 1999 (SI 1999/1820), art.4, Sch.2, Pt II, para.141.
[18] *ibid.*
[19] *ibid.*

(2) The only grounds for resignation are:

   (a) ill health;
   (b) the intention to cease to be in practice as an insolvency practitioner;
   (c) a conflict of interest or change of personal circumstances which precludes or makes impracticable the further discharge by him of the duties of liquidator: rule 4.28(3). This would, however, not include the realisation that the assets of the company would be insufficient to meet the liquidator's proposed fees.

(3) If the resignation is accepted it is effective from such date as the meeting of creditors may determine: rule 4.29(2).

(4) The liquidator is to give notice of his accepted resignation to the Accountant in Bankruptcy,[20] using Form 4.16 (Scotland).

(5) If the liquidator's resignation is not accepted, the court may, on the liquidator's application, make an order giving him the leave to resign using Form 4.16 (Scotland). Also Form 4.15 (Scotland) which require to be sent to the Accountant in Bankruptcy

3.13   Final Meeting of Creditors (Section 106)

(1) As soon as the company's affairs are fully wound-up, the liquidator shall make an account of the winding-up, showing how it has been conducted and how the company's property has been disposed of. Thereupon, he shall call a general meeting of the company and of the creditors, for the purpose of laying the account before the meetings and giving an explanation of it.

(2) At least 28 days' notice of the final meeting of creditors shall be given, and the notice shall be sent to all creditors whose claims in the liquidation have been accepted.

(3) Within seven days of the meeting, notice shall be given to the Registrar of Companies and to the Accountant in Bankruptcy[21], using Form 4.17 (Scotland), that the final meeting has been held. The notice shall state whether or not the liquidator has been released.

(4) If not quorum is present at the final meeting, the liquidator shall make a return that the meeting was duly summoned and that no quorum was present. Upon such return being made, the provisions of the subsection as to the making of the return are, in respect of that meeting, deemed to be complied with.

(5) The liquidator shall vacate office as soon as he has sent notice of the decisions of the final meeting to the Registrar of Companies: rule 4.31.

---

[20] By virtue of the Scotland Act 1998 (Consequential Modifications) (No. 2) Order 1999 (SI 1999/1820), art.4, Sch.2, Pt II, para.141.
[21] *ibid.*

3.14   Release of the Liquidator (Section 173)

(1) After removal of the liquidator by a meeting of creditors:

(a) if there is no resolution against his release, it is from the time stated on the notice which is given to the Accountant in Bankruptcy[22] that that person has ceased to hold office, using Forms 4.10 (Scotland) and 4.11 (Scotland);

(b) if there is a resolution against release, the liquidator must apply to the Accountant of Court for his discharge: Form 4.12 (Scotland); when the Accountant of Court releases the former liquidator, he shall issue a certificate of release to the new liquidator, who shall send a copy of it to the Accountant in Bankruptcy[23] using Forms 4.13 (Scotland) and 4.14 (Scotland): rule 4.25.

(2) On the resignation of the liquidator:

(a) if there is no resolution against his release, it shall be from such date as the meeting convened to consider the resignation may determine;

(b) if there is a resolution against release, the liquidator must apply to the Accountant of Court for his discharge: Form 4.12 (Scotland); when the Accountant of Court releases the former liquidator, he shall issue a certificate of release to the new liquidator, who shall send a copy of it to the Accountant in Bankruptcy[24] using Forms 4.13 (Scotland) and 4.14 (Scotland): rule 4.25.

(3) On the death of the liquidator, notice must be given to the liquidation committee or any member thereof, and to the Accountant in Bankruptcy, using Form 4.18 (Scotland): rule 4.36. Release is from the time at which notice is given to the Accountant in Bankruptcy[25] that that person has ceased to hold office.

(4) On completion of the winding-up (rule 4.13):

(a) if, at the final meeting of creditors under section 106, there is no resolution against release, it shall be from the time the liquidator vacates the office and gives notice to the Registrar of Companies, and to the Accountant in Bankruptcy[26], using Forms 4.17 (Scotland) and 4.26 (Scotland);

(b) if there is a resolution against release the liquidator must apply to the Accountant of Court for his discharge: Form 4.12 (Scotland); when the Accountant of Court releases the

---

[22] By virtue of the Scotland Act 1998 (Consequential Modifications) (No. 2) Order 1999 (SI 1999/1820), art.4, Sch.2, Pt II, para.141.

[23] *ibid.*

[24] *ibid.*

[25] *ibid.*

[26] *ibid.*

former liquidator, he shall issue a certificate of release to the new liquidator, who shall send a copy of it to the Accountant in Bankruptcy[27] using Forms 4.13 (Scotland) and 4.14 (Scotland): rule 4.25.

3.15 Outlays and Remuneration (Rules 4.32–4.35)

(1) In questions of remuneration regard should always be had by the liquidator to Statement of Insolvency Practice 9 (Scotland), published on the website of the Association of Business Recovery Professionals.[28]

(2) Claims by the liquidator for the outlays reasonably incurred by him and for his remuneration shall be made in accordance with section 53 of the Bankruptcy (Scotland) Act 1985: rule 4.32(1);

(3) The liquidator may at any time before the end of an accounting period (26 weeks) submit to the liquidation committee (if any) an interim claim in respect of that period for the outlays reasonably incurred by him, and for his remuneration; and the liquidation committee may make an interim determination in relation to the amount of outlays and remuneration to the liquidator. Where they do so, the committee shall take into account that interim determination when making their final determination: rule 4.32(2).

(4) If the liquidator considers the remuneration fixed by the liquidation committee to be insufficient, he may request that it be increased by resolution of the creditors: rule 4.33.

(5) Thereafter, if the liquidator is still dissatisfied, he may apply to the court for an order increasing the amount or rate. The liquidation committee may be hears on such application or, if there is no such committee, the court may order that notice of the application be sent to one or more creditors, who may nominate one or more of their number to appear or be represented: rule 4.34.

(6) Any remuneration fixed by the liquidation committee or by resolution of creditors may be challenged on application by creditors representing 25 per cent or more in value of the creditors, on the basis that the liquidator's remuneration is excessive. The court may, if it finds the application well founded, order the remuneration to be fixed at a reduced rate: rule 4.35.

(7) Section 53 of the Bankruptcy (Scotland) Act 1985 provides that the basis of remuneration[29] may be a commission calculated by reference to the value of the company's estate, but in any event there shall be taken into account:

(a) the work which, having regard to that value, was reasonably undertaken by the liquidator; and

---

[27] By virtue of the Scotland Act 1998 (Consequential Modifications) (No. 2) Order 1999 (SI 1999/1820), art.4, Sch.2, Pt II, para.141.

[28] *http://www.r3.org.uk*

[29] Regard should also be had to the Statement of Insolvency Practice No. 9, issued by the Insolvency Practitioners Association, and published on the R3 website: *http://www.r3.org.uk*

(b) the extent of his responsibilities in administering the company's assets.

(8) The Rules state that accounts for legal services shall be submitted or taxation before payment, but the court may authorise the liquidator to pay any such account without taxation. However, given that the legal accounts are to be taxed by the auditor of "the court before which the liquidation is pending" and in a voluntary liquidation there is no court before which the liquidation is pending, the author considers there to be at least a reasonable argument that in voluntary windings-up a legal account can be paid without taxation.

(9) Within six weeks after the end of an accounting period (26 weeks):

(a) the liquidation committee or the court shall audit the accounts and issue a determination fixing the amount of the outlays and the remuneration payable to the liquidator;

(b) the liquidator shall make the audited accounts scheme of division and the said determination available for inspection by the company and the creditors.

(10) Not later than eight weeks after the end of an accounting period, the liquidator, the company or any creditor may appeal against a determination to the court.

(11) Where there is no liquidation committee, its functions are exercised by the creditors in general meeting. However, if no committee is appointed at the first or any subsequent meeting of creditors, it is suggested that the liquidator seek authority fro the creditors at that meeting as to the method of his remuneration.[30] Although there is no equivalent in creditors' voluntary liquidation to rule 4.12(3)(c) in winding-up by the court, the author considers there to be no reason that this matter not be dealt with specifically if appropriate.

3.16   Powers of the Liquidator (Sections 112, 165 and 166)

(1) The liquidator may exercise any of the powers contained in Part 1 of Schedule 4 to the Act with the sanction of the court or the liquidation committee (or there is no liquidation committee), any provision making reference thereto shall be construed as reference to a meeting of creditors), and may exercise those contained in Parts II and III of the said Schedule with or without such sanction.

(2) If the liquidator, in pursuance of his powers, disposes of any assets to any person associated with the company, notice thereof must be given to the liquidation committee (if any).

---

[30] Regard should also be had to the Statement of Insolvency Practice No. 9, issued by the Insolvency Practitioners Association, and published on the R3 website: *http://www.r3.org.uk*

(3) Except with the sanction of the court, no powers other than those to protect the assets may be exercised by the liquidator (*i.e.* the members' nominee) before the holding of the creditors' meeting in terms of section 98.

(4) By virtue of section 112(1), a liquidator in a creditors' voluntary winding-up may apply to the court to exercise all or any of the powers which the court might exercise if the company were being wound-up by the court. The court need not accede to the request. Any such order requires to be filed with both the Accountant in Bankruptcy and the Registrar of Companies

(5) Significantly, the liquidator may use the power in section 112 to avail himself of the rights of investigation set out in section 133.[31]

(6) At any time during the liquidation, the liquidator may — and if one-half in value of the company's creditors request it, unless the court otherwise orders — shall apply to the court for the public examination of any present or past office of the company, or of any person otherwise engaged in its affairs: section 133. The examination may be made by:

　(a) the liquidator;
　(b) any special manager of the company's property or business;
　(c) any creditor of the company who has submitted a claim in the winding-up;
　(d) any contributory of the company.

(7) At least 14 days' notice of the examination diet must be given to the persons mentioned in (8)(b)–(d) above, unless the court otherwise orders, and the liquidator may advertise the diet in one or more newspapers, provided that at least seven days have elapsed since the person to be examined was served with the order: rule 4.74.

(8) If any person without reasonable excuse fails to attend his examination, he is guilty of contempt of court and a warrant may be issued for his arrest and imprisonment: section 134(1).[32]

(9) A person subject to examination under section 133 is not entitled to refuse to answer questions on the ground that he may incriminate himself.[33]

(10) For a consideration of the situation of a company incorporated in a jurisdiction in which disclosure of information may be a criminal offence in relation to section 133 applications see *Re Casterbridge Properties Limited.*[34]

---

[31] See *Bishopsgate Investment Management Ltd (in provisional liquidation) v Maxwell* [1993] Ch 1.

[32] See *Re Avatar Communications Ltd* (1988) 4 B.C.C. 473.

[33] See *Bishopsgate Investment Management Ltd (in provisional liquidation) v Maxwell* [1993] Ch 1.

[34] [2003] EWHC 1731 (Ch).

3.17   Dissolution of the Company (Sections 201 and 205(6))

At the conclusion of the winding-up:

(1) Where the Accountant in Bankruptcy[35] receives a notice, on Forms 4.17 (Scotland) (also sent to the Registrar of Companies) and 4.26 (Scotland), served for the purposes of section 106 (final meeting and vacation of office by the liquidator), the company shall be dissolved after a period of three months following registration of the notice.

(2) The court may, on application of any person who appears to have an interest, defer the dissolution of the company for such period as the court thinks fit.

(3) If a deferment is granted, the court order in question must be sent to the Accountant in Bankruptcy[36] within seven days, using Form 4.28 (Scotland).

---

[35] By virtue of the Scotland Act 1998 (Consequential Modifications) (No. 2) Order 1999 (SI 1999/1820), art.4, Sch.2, Pt II, para.141.

[36] *ibid.*

CHAPTER 4

MEMBERS' VOLUNTARY WINDING-UP (PART IV AS APPLIED BY SCHEDULE 2 TO THE RULES)

4.1 Commencement of the Winding-up (Sections 84–86 and 89)

(1) A company may be wound-up voluntarily by an extraordinary resolution to that effect.

(2) A copy of this resolution must be sent to the Registrar of Companies and to the Accountant in Bankruptcy[1] within 15 days.

(3) Within 14 days of passing the resolution, the company must give notice of the resolution by advertisement in the *Edinburgh Gazette*.

(4) A voluntary winding-up is deemed to commence at the time of the passing of the resolution for voluntary winding-up. This is an important point. Where a liquidation is being timed to cut down an illegal preference or transaction at an undervalue, it may be more advantageous to pass a resolution for voluntary winding-up rather than petition the court in view of the provisions of section 185. However, regard should be had to the requirement introduced by section 84(2A) to give notice to the holder of any qualifying floating charge.

(5) The directors of the company (or a majority of them) must make a statutory declaration to the effect that, after a full enquiry into the company's affairs, they have formed the opinion that the company will be able to pay its debts in full, together with interest at the official rate (as defined in section 251), (presently 15 per cent[2]) within such period (not exceeding 12 months from the commencement of the winding-up) as may be specified in the declaration. It is unusual to see a period of less than 12 months provided in such a declaration.

(6) Such declaration of solvency must be made within five weeks immediately preceding the date on which the resolution to wind up the company is passed, or on that date, but before the passing of the resolution.

(7) The declaration, using Form 4.25 (Scotland), must be forwarded to the Registrar of Companies and to the Accountant in

---

[1] By virtue of the Scotland Act 1998 (Consequential Modifications) (No. 2) Order 1999 (SI 1999/1820), art.4, Sch.2, Pt II, para.141.

[2] R.4.66(2)(b). Given present interest rates, the failure to change this rate since 1986 looks like an oversight. Curiously, the rate of interest in an English winding-up is 8 per cent by virtue of s.189(4) and SI 1993/564. Compare the rate of 12 per cent under the Late Payments of Commercial Debts (Interest) Act 1998. The interface between the late payment legislation and the insolvency legislation is unclear.

Bankruptcy[3] within 15 days immediately following the date on which the resolution for winding-up is passed.

(8) A director making a declaration without having reasonable grounds for the opinion stated is liable to a fine or imprisonment or both. In terms of section 89(5) the burden of proof is on the director to establish that he had reasonable grounds for making the declaration.

4.2 Appointment of the Liquidator (Sections 91 and 109)

(1) The members of the company at their meeting shall appoint a person (or persons) to be liquidator of the company for the purpose of winding-up the company's affairs and distributing its assets.

(2) The chairman of the meeting shall certify the appointment of the liquidator, using Form 4.8 (Scotland), after the person to be appointed has provided him with a written statement to the effect that he is an insolvency practitioner, duly qualified, and that he consents to act: rule 4.19(5), as amended. This certificate is placed in the Sederunt Book for the liquidation.

(3) The liquidator's appointment takes effect from the passing of the resolution for his appointment: rule 4.19(5), as amended.

(4) The liquidator shall, within fourteen days of his appointment, publish in the *Gazette* and deliver to the Accountant in Bankruptcy[4] a notice of his appointment, using Forms 600a and 600 respectively; and shall, within 28 days of his appointment, publish notice thereof in one newspaper circulating in the area in which the company carried on business: rule 4.19(4)(b).

(5) On the appointment of a liquidator, all the powers of the directors cease, except in so far as the company in general meeting or the liquidator sanctions their continuance.

4.3 Information

Within 30 days after the first year of the winding-up, and in respect of every period of 26 weeks thereafter, the liquidator shall send to the Registrar of Companies and the Accountant in Bankruptcy[5] a statement of receipts and payments, using Form 4.5 (Scotland): rule 4.11.

4.4 Annual Meetings (Section 93)

The liquidator is required to call a meeting of the company at the end of the first year of the winding-up, and annually thereafter. This meeting is to be no later than three months after the year end. There shall be laid before each meeting to an account of the liquidator's acts and dealings, and of the conduct of the winding-up during the preceding year.

---

[3] By virtue of the Scotland Act 1998 (Consequential Modifications) (No. 2) Order 1999 (SI 1999/1820), art.4, Sch.2, Pt II, para.141.

[4] *ibid.*

[5] *ibid.*

4.5 Removal of the Liquidator and his Vacation of Office (Sections 106 and 171)

(1) A liquidator may be removed from office only by an order of the court or by a general meeting of the company summoned especially for that purpose.

(2) A liquidator shall vacate office if he ceases to be qualified to act as an insolvency practitioner in relation to the company.

(3) Where a final meeting has been held under section 94 to consider the liquidator's report on completion of the winding-up, the liquidator shall vacate office as soon as he has given notice to the Registrar of Companies and to the Accountant in Bankruptcy,[6] using Form 4.26 (Scotland), that the meeting has been held and of the decisions (if any) of the meeting.

(4) Where a new liquidator is appointed, he shall advertise his appointment according to rules 4.19–4.21 (see paragraph 4.2(4) above), but the notice under rule 4.19(4) shall also stated that his predecessor as liquidator has been removed, and whether the latter has been released: rule 4.27.

4.6 Resignation of the Liquidator (Section 171(5))

(1) A meeting of the company must be called to receive his resignation. Notice thereof must draw attention to section 173(2)(c) and rule 4.28A with respect to the liquidator's release, and shall be accompanied by a statement of his intromissions: rule 4.28, as amended.

(2) The only grounds for resignation are:

   (a) ill health;
   (b) the intention to cease to be in practice as an insolvency practitioner;
   (c) a conflict of interest or change in personal circumstances which precludes or makes impracticable the further discharge by him of the duties of the liquidator: rule 4.28(3). This would, however, not include the realisation that the company's assets would be insufficient to meet the liquidator's proposed fees.

(3) If the resignation is accepted, it is effective from the date on which notice is given to the Accountant in Bankruptcy,[7] and the Registrar of Companies using Form 4.16 (Scotland).

4.7 Final Meeting of the Company (Section 94)

(1) As soon as the company's affairs are fully wound-up, the liquidator makes an account of the winding-up, showing how it has been

---

[6] By virtue of the Scotland Act 1998 (Consequential Modifications) (No. 2) Order 1999 (SI 1999/1820), art.4, Sch.2, Pt II, para.141.

[7] *ibid.*

conducted and how the company's property has been disposed of. Thereupon, he shall call a general meeting of the company, for the purpose of laying the account before the meeting and giving an explanation of it.

(2) At least one month's notice of the final meeting of the company is to be given.

(3) Within one week after the meeting, notice is to be given to the Registrar of Companies and to the Accountant in Bankruptcy,[8] using Form 4.26 (Scotland), that the final meeting has been held.

(4) If no quorum is present at the final meeting, the liquidator makes a return that the meeting was duly summoned and that no quorum was present: Form 4.26 (Scotland). Upon such return being made, the provisions of the subsection as to the making of the return are, in respect of that meeting, deemed complied with.

(5) The liquidator shall vacate office as soon as he has sent notice of the decisions of final meeting to the Registrar of Companies and to the Accountant in Bankruptcy, using Form 4.26 (Scotland).

4.8   Release of the Liquidator (Section 173)

(1) After the removal of the liquidator by a general meeting of the company, his release is from the time at which notice is given to the Accountant in Bankruptcy, using Form 4.11 (Scotland), that he has ceased to hold office.

(2) On the resignation of the liquidator, his release is from the date on which he gives notice to the Accountant in Bankruptcy, using Form 4.16 (Scotland): rule 4.28A.

(3) On the death of the liquidator, notice must be given to the directors of the company or any one of them, and to the Accountant in Bankruptcy, using Form 4.18 (Scotland): rule 4.36, as amended. Release is from the time at which notice is given to the Accountant in Bankruptcy[9] that that person has ceased to hold office.

(4) On completion of the winding-up, release of the liquidator is from the time he gives notice to the Registrar of Companies and to the Accountant in Bankruptcy[10] that he has vacated office, using Forms 4.17 (Scotland) and 4.26 (Scotland).

4.9   Outlays and Remuneration

(1) There are no particular Rules prescribed for the recovery of outlays and remuneration in a members' voluntary winding-up. The declaration of solvency provides that the company is able to meet all its liabilities, and this would include the expenses of winding-up.

---

[8] By virtue of the Scotland Act 1998 (Consequential Modifications) (No. 2) Order 1999 (SI 1999/1820), art.4, Sch.2, Pt II, para.141.
[9] *ibid.*
[10] *ibid.*

(2) In questions of remuneration regard should always be had by the liquidator to Statement of Insolvency Practice 9 (Scotland), published on the website of the Association of Business Recovery Professionals.[11]

4.10 Liquidation Committee

There is no liquidation committee in a members' voluntary winding-up.

4.11 Powers of the Liquidator (Sections 112 and 165)

(1) The liquidator may exercise any of the powers contained in Part I of Schedule 4 to the Act with the sanction of an extraordinary resolution of the company, and those contained in Parts II and III of the Schedule with or without such sanction.

(2) By virtue of section 112(1), a liquidator in members' voluntary winding-up may apply to the court to exercise all or any of the powers which the court might exercise if the company were being wound-up by the court.

4.12 Getting in the Company's Property (Sections 234–237)

(1) Where any person has under his possession or control any property, books, papers or such records to which the company appears to be entitled, the court may require that person to pay, deliver, convey, surrender or transfer the property, books, papers or records to the liquidator.

(2) Officers of the company, employees, past employees, any former administrator, administrative receiver or liquidator of the company is obliged to give to the liquidator such information concerning the company and its promotion, formation, business dealings, affairs or property as the liquidator may reasonably require and shall attend on the liquidator at such times as he may reasonably require: section 235.

(3) The relevant period for investigations (other than in the case of an officer of the company) is one year before administration, administrative receivership, appointment of a provisional liquidator or the date on which the company went into liquidation.

(4) The court may summon to appear before it[12]:

    (a) any officer of the company;

    (b) any person known or suspected to have in his possession any property of the company or supposed to be indebted to the company; or

    (c) any person whom the court thinks capable of giving information concerning the promotion, formation, business affairs or property of the company: section 236.

---

[11] *http://www.r3.org.uk*
[12] See *Re Highgrade Traders Ltd* [1983] B.C.L.C. 137; *Re Norton Warburg Holdings Ltd and Norton Warburg Investment Management Ltd* [1983] B.C.L.C. 235.

(5) There is no requirement that the examination be preceded by a written statement of questions.

(6) The use of information obtained in a section 236 examination in later criminal proceedings has been held to contrary to the European Convention on Human Rights.[13] For this reason it is considered that an objection to the proceedings on the grounds on possible self-incrimination is unlikely to be upheld.

(7) According to one English case[14] an application under section 236 can be made even if the liquidator's sole purpose was to get information for the purpose of commencing disqualification proceedings against the director under the Company Directors Disqualification Act 1986.

(8) The scope of section 236 is not limited to persons within the jurisdiction of the court or to persons who had been served personally with the petition within the jurisdiction.[15]

4.13 Distribution of Assets

(1) There are no specific Rules regarding distribution of assets in a Members' Voluntary Winding-up, presumably on the basis that, in order to comply with the provisions of the Act, all creditors must be paid within such period as was stated by the directors in their Declaration of Solvency (being a period of no greater than 12 months).

4.14 Effect of Insolvency (Sections 95 and 96)

(1) Where the liquidator in a Members' Voluntary Winding-up reaches the opinion that the company will not be able to pay its debts within the period stated in the declaration of solvency, he shall:

(a) summon a meeting of creditors for a date not later than 28 days after he reaches his opinion;

(b) send notices to creditors at least seven days before the meeting;

(c) cause notice of the creditors' meeting to be advertised once in the *Edinburgh Gazette* and once in at least two newspapers circulating in the locality in which the company's principal place of business was situated — such advertisement must be at least seven days before the date of the creditors' meeting;

(d) during the period before the day on which the creditors' meeting is to be held, furnish creditors free of charge with such information concerning the affairs of the company as they may reasonably require; and include a statement of this duty in the notice of the creditors' meeting.

---

[13] *Saunders v United Kingdom* [1997] B.C.C. 872.

[14] *Re Pantmaenog Timber Co Ltd.* [2003] B.C.C. 659; [2003] UKHL 49.

[15] *McIsaac and Wilson, Petitioners* [1995] S.L.T. 498.

(2) The liquidator shall also make out a statement of affairs, using Form 4.4 (Scotland), and lay that statement before the creditors' meeting, which he must attend and at which he presides.

(3) As from the date on which the creditors' meeting is held, the liquidation is treated as a creditors' voluntary winding-up and the rules in Chapter IV of the Act (other than sections 98 and 99) will apply. The meeting of creditors held under section 95 is treated as the meeting of creditors under section 98.

4.15 Dissolution of the Company (Section 201)

At the conclusion of the winding-up:

(1) Where the Registrar of Companies and Accountant in Bankruptcy[16] each receives a notice, on Form 4.26 (Scotland) served for the purposes of section 94 (final meeting of the company and vacation of office by liquidator), the company shall be dissolved after a period of three months following registration of the notice.

(2) The court may, on application of any person who appears to have an interest, defer the dissolution of the company for such period as the court thinks fit.

(3) If a deferment is granted, the court order in question must be sent to the Registrar of Companies within seven days, using Form 4.28 (Scotland).

4.16 Early Dissolution of the Company (Section 204)

(1) Although section 204 does not appear to be immediately applicable in cases of members' voluntary winding-up, it is theoretically possible by virtue of the application of section 112 of the Act.[17]

(2) However, it is difficult to envisage such a situation as it would require all creditors to be paid in full and this would include creditors which were the expenses of the liquidation. In such a case (*i.e.* no pre-liquidation creditors) it is more likely that application would be made under section 652 of the Companies Act 1985 to have the company struck off.

---

[16] By virtue of the Scotland Act 1998 (Consequential Modifications) (No. 2) Order 1999 (SI 1999/1820), art.4, Sch.2, Pt II, para.141.

[17] *Summary Application of Maureen E Leslie as Liquidator of EX1 Limited*, Edinburgh Sheriff Court, July 16, 2003.

CHAPTER 5

LIQUIDATION AND ADMINISTRATION

5.1 Appointment (Section 140)

(1) Where a winding-up order is made immediately upon the appointment of an administrator ceasing to have effect, the court may appoint as liquidator of the company, the person whose appointment as administrator has ceased to have effect.

(2) Although the wording is not perfect, it appears that the liquidator appointed under section 140 would, in fact, be an interim liquidator with obligations to convene a meeting of creditors as provided in the Act.

5.2 Commencement of the Winding-up — Unsuccessful Administration Application

(1) Where the winding-up follows the presentation of a petition for an administration order which is not granted (but where the court makes a winding-up order),[1] the winding-up is deemed to commence on the date of the order and not the date when the petition was presented.

5.3 Winding-up during Administration

(1) The general rule is that on making of an administration order, any pending petition for winding-up will be dismissed and (unless it is a petition presented under section 124A of the Insolvency Act or section 367 of the Financial Services and Markets Act 2000) shall be suspended where the administrator was appointed by the holder of a floating charge.[2]

(2) No resolution may be passed or order made for winding-up the company during administration.

(3) Where a winding-up order is made under section 124A or section 367 of the Financial Services and Markets Act 2000 (or a provisional liquidator was appointed following the presentation of a petition for winding-up under those sections), the court has discretion as to whether to allow the administration to continue or cease.[3] In such circumstances the court may specify which of the powers in Schedule B1 may be exercised by the administrator.

---

[1] Paragraph 13(1)(e) of Sch.B1 to the Act.
[2] Paragraph 40(1) of Sch.B1 to the Act.
[3] Paragraph 82 of Sch.B1 to the Act.

5.4 Winding-up on Conclusion of Administration (Paragraph 83(2) of Schedule B1 to the Insolvency Act)

(1) Where the administrator of a company thinks:

   (a) that each secured creditor of the company will receive payment in respect of his debt, and
   (b) that a distribution will be made to unsecured creditors (if there are any).

(2) The administrator may send to the Registrar of Companies a notice that this paragraph applies.
(3) On receipt of a notice under sub-paragraph (2) the registrar shall register it.
(4) If an administrator sends a notice under sub-paragraph (2) he shall as soon as is reasonably practicable:

   (a) file a copy of the notice with the court, and
   (b) send a copy of the notice to each creditor of whose claim and address he is aware.

(5) On the registration of a notice under sub-paragraph (2):

   (a) the appointment of an administrator in respect of the company shall cease to have effect; and
   (b) the company shall be wound-up as if a resolution for voluntary winding-up under section 84 were passed on the day on which the notice is registered.

(6) The liquidator for the purposes of the winding-up shall be:

   (a) a person nominated by the creditors of the company in the prescribed manner and within the prescribed period, or
   (b) if no person is nominated under paragraph (a), the administrator.

(7) In the application of Part IV to a winding-up by virtue of this paragraph:

   (a) section 85 shall not apply;
   (b) section 86 shall apply as if the reference to the time of the passing of the resolution for voluntary winding-up were a reference to the beginning of the date of registration of the notice under sub-paragraph (3);
   (c) section 89 does not apply;
   (d) sections 98, 99 and 100 shall not apply;
   (e) section 129 shall apply as if the reference to the time of the passing of the resolution for voluntary winding-up were a reference to the beginning of the date of registration of the notice under sub-paragraph (3); and
   (f) any creditors' committee which is in existence immediately before the company ceases to be in administration shall continue in existence after that time as if appointed as a liquidation committee under s.101.

5.5   Effect of a Paragraph 83 Winding-up

(1) Although paragraph 83(7) of Schedule B1 states that the liquidator will be a person "nominated by the creditors in the prescribed manner and within the prescribed period", it is very unclear as to what that would be (if at all) given that in terms of paragraph 83(8), sections 98–100 which deal with creditors' meetings to select a liquidator are expressly excluded.

(2) This would appear to suggest that the only way in which creditors would have a say in the process would be to convene a meeting for removal of the (former) Administrator] liquidator.

(3) However, rule 2.47(3) provides that for the purposes of paragraph 83(7) a person shall be nominated by the creditors either:

(a) by approval by the creditors of the Administrator's statement of proposals under paragraph 49(1) (or revised proposals under paragraph 54(2) in which he is proposed to be nominated as liquidator[4];

(b) where the creditors wish to appoint someone else, at the meeting held to consider the statement of proposals or revised proposals in which the move from administration to creditors' voluntary liquidation is proposed.

(4) The import of this would appear to be that if the creditors do not turn up at the administration meeting, they cannot expect to be surprised if their options thereafter are limited.

(5) If the liquidator is intending to apply to the court for his appointment as liquidator, he requires to give notice of this fact to the creditors.[5]

5.6   Commencement of the Winding-up — following Administration Period

(1) Where the winding-up is a creditors voluntary winding-up pursuant to paragraph 83 of Schedule B1, the winding-up would be deemed to commence on the date of registration of the Notice to the Registrar of Companies pursuant to paragraph 83(3) of Schedule B1.[6]

(2) Where the winding-up is a winding-up by the court, the winding-up would be deemed to commence on the date of presentation of the petition for winding-up.

5.7   Liquidation Committee

The Liquidation Committee in a creditors' voluntary liquidation following administration will automatically be the creditors' committee from the Administration if there were one.[7]

---

[4] See Form 2.25B.
[5] R.2.46(4); Form 2.24B.
[6] Form 2.25B.
[7] Paragraph 83(8(f) of Sch.B1.

5.8 Conversion of Secondary Insolvency Proceedings from Administration to Liquidation

(1) A liquidator in main proceedings under the EC Regulation may request[8] that an Administration previously opened in Scotland as secondary proceedings be converted into winding-up proceedings if this proves to be in the interests of the creditors in the main proceedings.[9]

(2) The effect of an order for winding-up made by the court pursuant to an application made under rule 2.57 may provide that the company be wound-up as if a resolution for winding-up under section 84 (creditors' voluntary winding-up) were passed on the day on which the order is made.[10]

(3) However, the court has total discretion about what order to make.[11]

---

[8] Article 37 of the EC Regulation.
[9] R.2.57.3
[10] R.2.59(3).
[11] R.2.59(1).

CHAPTER 6

MEETINGS
(RULES 7.1–7.13)

The following provisions apply to all meetings held in liquidation proceedings (court appointment and both types of voluntary) other than meetings of a liquidation committee.

6.1 Convening of Meetings (Rules 7.2 and 7.3)

(1) In fixing the date, time and place for a meeting, the person summoning the meeting ("the convenor") shall have regard to the convenience of the persons who are to attend: rule 7.2(1).

(2) Meetings in all cases shall be summoned to commence between 10am and 4pm on a business day (*i.e.* not a Saturday, Sunday, Christmas Day, Good Friday, or a day which is a bank holiday in any part of Great Britain (note that there are different bank holidays in Scotland, England and Wales and Northern Ireland)), unless the court otherwise directs: rule 7.2.

(3) The convenor shall give at least 21 days' notice (14 days' notice in the case of a meeting called under sections 138(3) or (4) of the Act and seven days in the case of a meeting called under sections 95 or 98, which meeting is to be advertised in accordance with those sections) of the meeting to every person known to him as being entitled to attend the meeting: rule 7.3(1).

(4) The convenor may also publish notice of the date, time and place of the meeting in a newspaper circulating in the area of the principal place of business of the company, or in such other newspaper as he thinks most appropriate for ensuring that it comes to the attention of the persons who are entitled to attend the meeting: rule 7.3(2). Such an advertisement, if made is to be published before the date of the meeting on the same period of notice as the notice is required to be given as set out in (3) above.

(5) Any notice shall state:

(a) the purpose of the meeting;

(b) the persons who are entitled to attend and vote at the meeting;

(c) the effects of rules 7.9 or 7.10 (entitlement to vote) and of the relevant provisions of rule 7.12 (resolutions); it is not sufficient merely to refer to the particular Rules, a statement as to their effect must be given;

(d) that proxies may be lodged at or before the meeting, and the place where they may be lodged; and

(e) in the case of a meeting of creditors, that claims (which must be on the prescribed Form 4.7 (Scotland)) may be lodged by those who have not already done so at or before the meeting, and the place where they may be lodged: rule 7.3(4).

(6) Where a meeting of creditors is summoned specially for the purpose of removing the liquidator, or of receiving his resignation, the notice convening it shall also include the information required by rule 4.23(2) or rule 4.28(2) (liquidator's release): rule 7.3(4).

(7) With the notice given, the convenor shall also send out a proxy form: rule 7.3(5). The proxy sent out must be in the form of Form 4.29, although, at the meeting itself, any proxy to like effect may be used.

(8) In the case of any meeting of creditors or contributories, the court may order that notice of the meeting be given by public advertisement in such form as may be specified in the order, and not by individual notice to the persons concerned: rule 7.3(6).

6.2 Chairman of the Meeting (Rule 7.5)

(1) The chairman of the meeting of creditors or contributories shall be either the responsible insolvency practitioner (except in the case of a meeting of creditors summoned under section 98) or (except in the case of a meeting convened by the liquidator under section 95), a person nominated by him in writing: rule 7.5(1).

(2) The person nominated must be a person who is qualified to act as an insolvency practitioner in relation to the company, or an employee of his or of his firm: rule 7.5(2). Although it has sometimes been the erroneous practice, it is not permissible for the nominee to ask his solicitor to chair the meeting (particularly in relation to the dealing with resolutions to appoint the liquidator) unless the solicitor in question is himself an authorised insolvency practitioner.

(3) At the first meeting of creditors or contributories in a winding-up by the court, the interim liquidator shall be the chairman, except that where a resolution is proposed to appoint the interim liquidator to be the liquidator, another person may be elected to act as chairman for the purpose of choosing the liquidator: rule 7.5(4). The author would suggest that it is good practice for the interim liquidator to insist that someone else is elected to avoid any problems arising in relation to proxies in favour of "the chairman". Although rule 7.5(1) talks of a person "nominated" to chair the meeting (see (2) above) and rule 7.5(4) of someone "elected" so to do, it is felt better practice to have a director chair the meeting rather than someone selected by the liquidator (albeit elected by the creditors).

(4) Any meeting to remove the liquidator must observe the provisions of rule 4.23(3) (which deals with the circumstances in which the liquidator may adjourn the meeting): rule 7.5(5).

(5) Note, however, that in a creditors' voluntary winding-up, it is a director of the company who is to preside at the first meeting of creditors: section 99(1)(c).

6.3 Requisitioned Meetings (Rule 7.6)

(1) Any request to a liquidator for a meeting of creditors under section 142(3), section 171(3) or section 172(3) shall be accompanied by:

> (a) a list of creditors concurring with the request, showing the amount of their claims;
> (b) from each creditor concurring, written confirmation of his concurrence; and
> (c) a statement of the purpose of the proposed meeting: rule 7.6(2).

(2) The expenses of summoning and holding a meeting under this Rule shall be paid by the creditor or creditors making the request, who shall deposit with the liquidator caution for their payment. The sum to be deposited shall be as the liquidator may determine, and he shall not act without the deposit having been made: rules 7.6(4) and (5).

(3) The meeting may resolve that the expenses of summoning and holding it are to be payable out of the assets of the company as an expense of the liquidation: rule 7.6(6).

(4) To the extent that any caution deposited under this Rule is not required for the payment of expenses of summoning and holding the meeting, it shall be repaid to the person or persons who paid it: rule 7.6(7).

6.4 Quorum (Rule 7.7)

(1) A quorum is:

> (a) in the case of a creditors' meeting, at least one creditor entitled to vote;
> (b) in the case of a meeting of contributories, at least two contributories entitled to vote.[1]

(2) In calculating the constitution of a quorum, there is to be included those represented by proxy by any person (including the chairman).

(3) However, if the quorum were to be satisfied by the chairman or the chairman and one other person, and the chairman is aware that one or more additional persons would, if attending, be entitled to vote, the meeting shall not commence until the expiry of fifteen minutes after the time appointed for its commencement: rule 7.7(3).

6.5 Adjournment (Rule 7.8)

(1) If, within 30 minutes from the time appointed for the commencement of a meeting, a quorum is not present, then — unless the chairman otherwise decides — the meeting shall be adjourned to

---

[1] Presumably unless there is only one contributory.

the same time and place in the following week (or the next business day thereafter): rule 7.8(2).

(2) In the course of a meeting, the chairman may and shall, if the meeting so resolves, adjourn it to such a date, time and place (within 21 days) as seems to him to be appropriate in the circumstances but this is subject to rule 4.23(3) (removal of liquidator): rule 7.8(3).

(3) The chairman of the meeting may give notice of the adjourned meeting: rule 7.8(5). Although the text of this Rule is opaque, it is assumed that the "notice" to which reference is made is notice to those entitled to attend other than those who attended the meeting which was adjourned. It is not clear what will happen if the reason for the adjournment is that a quorum was absent from the meeting; perhaps in such a circumstance notice should be given.

(4) Proxies given for a meeting may be used at any adjourned meeting: rule 7.8(6).

6.6 Entitlement to Vote (Rules 7.9 and 7.10)

(1) A creditor is entitled to vote at any meeting if he has submitted his claim to the responsible insolvency practitioner and if his claim has been accepted in whole or in part: rule 7.9(2). A distinction requires to be made here between acceptance for the purpose of voting, and acceptance for the purpose of ranking for a dividend; it is submitted that in relation to rules 7.9 and 7.10, where the voting is at a preliminary stage in the liquidation up — including the first meeting of creditors — the acceptance for the purpose of determining entitlement to vote should be on a *prima facie* basis as set out in the creditor's claim. Unless the company (or the nominee) has actual knowledge that the creditor's claim is false (or that set off or a counterclaim exists) the claim should not be rejected. The acceptance of the claim is (at this stage) a procedural question of whether the Rules have been satisfied.

(2) Chapter 5 of Part 4 of the Rules (see Chapter 7 below), (claims in liquidation) shall apply for the purpose of determining a creditor's entitlement to vote at a meeting of creditor in a liquidation: rule 7.9(3).

(3) Members of a company or contributories at their meetings shall vote according to the rights attaching to their shares respectively in accordance with the Articles of Association: rule 7.10(1).

6.7 Resolutions (Rules 7.12 and 7.13)

(1) At a meeting of creditors, contributories or members of a company, a resolution is passed when a majority in value of those voting, in person or by proxy, has voted in favour of it (unless there is a contrary provision in the Act or the Rules): rule 7.12(1).

(2) Where the chairman at a meeting holds a proxy which requires him to vote for a particular resolution, and no other person proposes that resolution:

(a) he shall propose it himself, unless he considers that there is good reason for not doing so; and

(b) if he does not propose it, he shall forthwith, after the meeting, notify the person who granted him the proxy of the reason why he did not do so: rule 7.11(1).

(3) In the case of a resolution for the appointment of a liquidator:

(a) if, on any vote, there are two nominees for appointment, the person for whom a majority in value has voted shall be appointed;

(b) if there are three or more nominees, and one of them has a clear majority over both or all of the others together, that one is appointed; and

(c) in any other case, the chairman of the meeting shall continue to take votes (disregarding at each vote any nominee who has withdrawn and, if no nominee has withdrawn, the nominee who obtained the least support last time) until a clear majority is obtained for any one nominee: rule 7.12(3).

(4) The chairman may, at any time, put to the meeting a resolution for the joint appointment of any two or more nominees: rule 7.12(3).

(5) Where a resolution is proposed which affects a person in respect of his remuneration or conduct as a responsible insolvency practitioner the vote of that person, or of his firm or of any partner or employee of his, shall not be reckoned in the majority required for passing the resolution. This applies with respect to a vote given by a person (whether personally or on his behalf by a proxy-holder) either as creditor or contributory or member, or as a proxy-holder for a creditor or contributory or member: rule 7.12(4).

(6) The chairman at any meeting shall cause a report to be made of the proceedings at the meeting which shall be signed by him: rule 7.13(1). The report of the meeting shall include:

(a) a list of all creditors or, as the case may be, contributories who attended the meeting either in person or by proxy;

(b) a copy of every resolution passed; and

(c) if the meeting established a liquidation committee, a list of the names and addresses of those elected to be members of the committee: rule 7.13(2).

(7) The chairman (who may not, in all cases, be the liquidator) shall keep a copy of the report of the meeting as part of the sederunt book in the liquidation.

CHAPTER 7

CLAIMS IN LIQUIDATION
(RULES 4.15–4.17 AND BANKRUPTCY (SCOTLAND) ACT 1985, SECTIONS 48–49)

7.1 Making the Claim

In general the Rules applicable to claims in a liquidation follow precisely, *mutatis mutandis*, the Rules contained in the Bankruptcy (Scotland) Act 1985 in relation to personal insolvency.

(1) A creditor, in order to obtain an adjudication as to his entitlement:

   (a) to vote at any meeting of the creditors in the liquidation; or
   (b) to a dividend (so far as funds are available) out of the assets of the company in respect of any accounting period,

   shall submit his claim to the liquidator:

   (i) at or before the meeting; or, as the case may be
   (ii) not later than eight weeks before the end of the accounting period: rule 4.15(1).

(2) A creditor shall submit his claim by producing to the liquidator:

   (a) a statement of claim, using Form 4.7 (Scotland); and
   (b) an account or voucher (according to the nature of the debt claimed) which constitutes *prima facie* evidence of the debt;

   but the liquidator may dispense with any requirement of this paragraph in respect of any debt or class of debt: rule 4.15(2).

(3) A claim submitted by a creditor which has been accepted in whole or in part by the liquidator for the purpose of voting at a meeting, or of drawing a dividend in respect of any accounting period, shall be deemed to be resubmitted for the purpose of obtaining an adjudication as to his entitlement both to vote at any subsequent meeting and (so far as funds are available) to a dividend in respect of an accounting period, or as the case may be, any subsequent accounting period: rule 4.15(3). This rule seems to make it clear than adjudication for voting is a separate process from adjudication for dividend, albeit that the claim does not require to be resubmitted.

(4) Votes are calculated according to the amount of:

   (a) a creditor's debt as at the date of commencement of the winding-up, deducting any amounts paid in respect of that debt after that date; or

(b) in relation to a Member State liquidator, the debt claimed to be due to creditors in proceedings in relation to which he holds office: rule 4.15(5).

(5) No vote may be cast by virtue of a debt more than once on any resolution put to a meeting: rule 4.15(5A).

(6) Where a creditor:

(a) is entitled to vote under the Rules;
(b) has lodged his claim in one or more sets of other proceedings; and
(c) votes (either in person or by proxy) on a resolution put to the meeting,

only the creditor's vote shall be counted.

(7) Where:

(a) a creditor has lodged his claim in more than one set of other proceedings; and
(b) more than one Member State liquidator seeks to vote by virtue of that claim,

the entitlement to vote by virtue of that claim is exercisable by the Member State liquidator in the main proceedings, whether or not the creditor has lodged his claim in the main proceedings. It is not clear how such a liquidator will become aware of a claim which has not been lodged with him.

(8) The liquidator, for the purpose of satisfying himself as to the validity or amount of a claim submitted by a creditor, may require:

(a) the creditor to produce further evidence; or
(b) any other person whom he believes can produce relevant evidence, to produce such evidence: Bankruptcy (Scotland) Act 1985, section 48(5).

If the creditor or other person refuses or delays to do so, the liquidator may apply to the sheriff for an order requiring the creditor or other person to attend for his private examination before the sheriff. It is not clear why the liquidator would do this, as he has the alternative remedy of adjudicating against the claim in question and waiting for the creditor to challenge that.

(9) At the commencement of every meeting of creditors, the liquidator shall, for the purpose of entitlement to vote, accept or reject the claim of each creditor: Bankruptcy (Scotland) Act 1985, section 49(1). The practice does not appear to be to require a formal acceptance or rejection of such claims at each meeting, although tacit acceptance is not ruled out. It is also the fact that at few meetings is a formal resolution put to a vote.

(10) Where funds are available for payment of a dividend in respect of an accounting period, the liquidator for the purpose of determining who is entitled to such a dividend shall, not later than four weeks before the end of the period, accept or reject every claim submitted: Bankruptcy (Scotland) Act 1985, section 49(2).

(11) Where a claim is rejected, the liquidator shall forthwith notify the

creditor, giving reason for the rejection: Bankruptcy (Scotland) Act 1985, section 49(4). Any decision on acceptance or rejection of a claim requires to be inserted in the sederunt book.

(12) The company or any creditor may, if dissatisfied with the acceptance or rejection of any claim, appeal to the court within two weeks of that acceptance or rejection (where it relates to entitlement to vote at a meeting) or not later than two weeks before the end of the accounting period (where it relates to entitlement to a dividend: Bankruptcy (Scotland) Act 1985, section 49(6).

(13) The provisions of Schedule 1 to the Bankruptcy (Scotland) Act 1985 (determination of amount of creditor's claim) are to be applied: rule 4.16(1)(f).

(14) Foreign currency claims are to be converted into Sterling at the exchange rate prevailing at the close of business on the date of commencement of the winding-up: rule 4.17(2) and Bankruptcy (Scotland) Act 1985, section 49(3).[1] In a court winding-up, this may be a different date for calculation than would have been the case under the English Insolvency Rules, as the relevant date in England is the date on which the court makes the winding-up order (section 247(1)) whereas in Scotland it is the date of presentation of the petition (section 129(2)).

(15) Although rule 4.16(1)(d) incorporates section 50 of the Bankruptcy (Scotland) Act 1985, the Insolvency (Scotland) Regulations 2003[2] make the same change in the Insolvency (Scotland) Rules 1986, at rules 4.15(5) and (5A).

---

[1] *Re Lines Bros Ltd (No.1)* [1983] Ch 1.
[2] SI 2003/2109.

CHAPTER 8

PREFERENTIAL CLAIMS IN LIQUIDATION

8.1 Section 386 and Schedule 6

One of the changes brought about by the Enterprise Act 2002 was a reduction in the number of preferential creditors in a liquidation. These are now limited to the following:

(a) Contributions to occupational pension schemes and state scheme premiums — if Schedule 4 to the Pension Schemes Act 1993 applies.[1]

(b) Employee remuneration:

   (i) for the four month period prior to the winding-up; and
   (ii) not exceeding the prescribed maximum (£270 per week[2]).

(c) Accrued Holiday pay.

(d) Wages advances which would have fallen under (b) and (c).

(e) Sums ordered to be paid under the Reserve Forces (Safeguard of Employment) Act 1985.

(f) Levies on coal and steel production.

---

[1] Basically employee deductions in relation to the 4 months prior to liquidation (or sums due in respect of that period).

[2] SI 2003/3038 (Employment Rights (Increase of Limits) Order 2003). The Order took effect on February 1, 2004. A similar Order is made each year.

CHAPTER 9

THE PRESCRIBED PART

9.1 Share of Assets for Unsecured Creditors (Section 176A)

(1) As part of the reforms brought about by the Enterprise Act 2002, the government decided to restrict the extent of preferential creditors under the insolvency legislation and, as a *quid pro quo*, determined that part of the assets of the insolvent company should be set aside for ordinary creditors — the fear being that, absent such a provision, the amount sacrificed by the preferential creditors would merely go to improve the position of the floating charge holders. Needless to say, the rules are complex and their impact — at least initially — limited.

(2) The provisions only apply:

    (a) where a floating charge[1] relates to the property of a company:

        (i) which has gone into liquidation; or
        (ii) of which there is a provisional liquidator.

(3) In such circumstances the liquidator is required to make available for unsecured creditors a prescribed part of the company's net property.[2] Section 176A(2)(a). He may not distribute any of such prescribed part to a floating charge creditor unless the unsecured debts have previously been satisfied.

(4) The prescribed part Rules do not apply if the company's net property is less than the prescribed minimum[3] AND the liquidator thinks that the costs of making a distribution to unsecured creditors would be disproportionate to the benefits.

(5) These Rules do not apply also where the liquidator applies to the court for an order on the ground that the costs of making a distribution to unsecured creditors would be disproportionate to the benefits and the court orders than the prescribed part Rules do not apply. Section 176A(5).

(6) The prescribed part is calculated[4] as follows:

    (a) where the net property does not exceed £10,000 in value, 50 per cent of that property;
    (b) where the net property exceeds £10,000 in value:

---

[1] Being a floating charge created after September 15, 2003.

[2] Net property is the amount which would otherwise have been available for floating charge creditors.

[3] £10,000 as at September 15, 2003 by virtue of the Insolvency Act 1986 (Prescribed Part) Order 2003 (SI 2003/2097) art.2.

[4] Insolvency Act 1986 (Prescribed Part) Order 2003 (SI 2003/2097), art.3 .

(i) 50 per cent of the first £10,000 in value; and

(ii) 20 per cent of the excess over £10,000 in value,

Provided that the value of the prescribed part shall not exceed £600,000.

(7) Thus for the maximum value to be made available to ordinary creditors for this purpose there will require to be available assets of £2,985,000.

9.2   Application under Section 176A(5)

(1) The liquidator may apply to the court for an order on the ground that the costs of making a distribution to unsecured creditors would be disproportionate to the benefits.

(2) Such an application is made pursuant to the provisions of section 176A(5) and of rules 7.13A and 7.13B.

(3) The application must include averments as to:

(a) the type of insolvency proceeding in which the application arises;

(b) the financial position of the company;

(c) the basis of the applicant's view that the cost of making a distribution to the unsecured creditors would be disproportionate to the benefits;

(d) whether any other insolvency practitioner is acting in relation to the company and, if so, his address.

(4) The application is by way of petition where there is no existing process in relation to the liquidation and by way of note in that process where there is.[5]

(5) After lodging the petition or note a hearing is fixed to hear same and this is intimated to the liquidator.

(6) The liquidator is not required to give notice of the hearing to any person unless the insolvency judge/sheriff rules otherwise.

(7) Where the court makes an order under section 176A(5) the liquidator must, as soon as reasonably practicable:

(a) send a court-certified copy of the order to the company;

(b) send the Accountant in Bankruptcy a copy of the order together with Form 4.31;

(c) give notice of the order to each known creditor.

(8) The liquidator may, if the court so directs, give the notice required by the publication of a notice in a newspaper designed to cope to the attention of the creditors: rule 7.13B(2).

---

[5] See Act of Sederunt (Rules of the Court of Session 1994) 1994 (SI 1994/1443), as amended by Act of Sederunt (Rules of the Court of Session Amendment No. 5) (Insolvency Proceedings) 2003, (SSI 2003/385), r.74.30A. See also Act of Sederunt (Sheriff Court Company Insolvency Rules) 1986 (SI 1986/2297) as amended by Act of Sederunt (Sheriff Court Company Insolvency Rules 1986) Amendment 2003 (SSI 2003/388), r.31A.

9.3 Information (Rule 4.10(1))

(1) Within six weeks after the end of each accounting period the liquidator shall provide a report to the creditors which shall include:

(a) to the best of the liquidator's knowledge and belief:

(i) an estimate of the value of the prescribed part (whether or not he proposes to make an application to the court under section 176A(5) or 176A(3), and

(ii) an estimate of the value of the company's net property,

provided that the report need not include information whose disclosure could seriously prejudice the commercial interests of the company. In such case estimates must include a statement to that effect.

(b) whether, and, if so, why, the liquidator proposes to make an application to the court under section 176A(5).

CHAPTER 10

PROXIES AND COMPANY REPRESENTATION
(RULES 7.14–7.20)

10.1 General

(1) A person may authorise another person to attend, speak and vote as his representative at meetings of creditors or contributories of the company in insolvency proceedings, and any such authority is referred to as a proxy.

(2) A proxy may be given either generally for all meetings in insolvency proceedings, or specifically for any meetings or class of meeting.

(3) Only one proxy may be given by the principal for any one meeting; alternatives may be nominated. A proxy may be given to whoever is to be the chairman of the meeting.

(4) A proxy may require the holder to vote on behalf of the principal on matters arising for determination at any meeting, or to abstain, either as directed or in accordance with the holder's own discretion; and it may authorise or require the holder to propose, in the principal's name, a resolution to be voted on by the meeting.

10.2 Procedure

(1) A form of proxy in the form of Form 4.29 (Scotland) shall be sent out with every notice summoning a meeting of creditors or contributories of the company in insolvency proceedings. However, the Form 4.29 (Scotland) proxy need not be used, as any form of proxy to substantially the same effect may be used.

(2) A form of proxy shall not be sent with the name or description of any person (*i.e.* the "Chairman of the Meeting") inserted in it.

(3) A form of proxy shall be filled out and signed by the principal, or by someone acting on his authority.

(4) A proxy given for a particular meeting may be used at any adjournment thereof. It may be lodged at or before the meeting at which it is to be used.

(5) Proxies used for voting shall be retained by the chairman of the meeting, and delivered by him to the responsible insolvency practitioner.

(6) Proxies may be lodged at or before any meeting of creditors at which it is proposed the proxy be used. Proxies for meetings of contributories require to be lodged in accordance with the provisions of the Companies Acts and the company's Articles of Association. This may not be what rule 7.16 states in relation to meetings of contributories but, it is submitted, must be right.

(7) In an English case[1] it was held that a proxy form could be lodged by fax. Given the close similarity of words in rule 8.2 of the English Insolvency Rules[2] and rule 7.15 in Scotland, it is likely that faxed proxies should also be accepted in Scotland.

10.3 At the Meeting

(1) A proxy holder may not vote in favour of any resolution which would directly or indirectly place him or any associate of his in a position to receive any remuneration out of the insolvent estate, unless the proxy specifically directs him to vote in that way.
(2) The proxies lodged at a meeting are open to inspection by creditors at all reasonable times. For the purposes of this provision, a Member State liquidator in main proceedings is deemed to be a creditor[3]: rule 7.20A.

10.4 Corporate Representation

(1) Where a person is authorised under section 375 of the Companies Act 1985 to represent a corporation at a meeting of creditors or contributories, he shall produce to the chairman of the meeting a copy of the resolution from which he derives his authority.
(2) The copy resolution must be executed in accordance with section 36(3) of the Companies Act 1985, or certified by the secretary or a director of the corporation to be a true copy.

---

[1] *Inland Revenue Commissioners v Conbeer* [1996] B.C.C. 189. In his judgment, Laddie J. said that it was common ground between the parties that signing could not be restricted to the narrow concept of marking a substrate manually by direct use of a pen or similar writing instrument. It was conceded that a form could be signed by use of a stamp or if it had a signature impressed on it by a printing machine in the way that share dividend cheques frequently do. Once this was accepted, it was difficult to see why some forms of non-human agency for impressing the mark on the paper should be acceptable while others were not. With these considerations in mind, he came to the conclusion that a proxy form was signed for the purposes of r.8.2(3) if it bore upon it some distinctive or personal marking which had been placed there by or with the authority of the creditor. When a creditor faxed a proxy form to the chairman of a creditors meeting he transmitted two things at the same time: the contents of the form and the signature applied to it. The receiving fax machine was, in effect, instructed by the transmitting creditor to reproduce his signature on the proxy form which was created at the receiving station. It followed that the received fax was a proxy form signed by the principal or by some person authorised by him.

[2] Insolvency Rules 1986 (SI 1986/1925).

[3] Insolvency (Scotland) Regulations 2003 (SSI 2003/2109).

CHAPTER 11

DILIGENCE AND LIEN

11.1 Diligence (Section 185 of the Insolvency Act 1986 and Sections 37 and 39 of the Bankruptcy (Scotland) Act 1985)

(1) A winding-up order shall have effect, as from the date of commencement of the winding-up (defined for the purposes of this section in a winding-up by the court as being the date upon which the winding-up order is made — compare that with section 129, which provides (for other purposes) that a winding-up (other than one following a refused Administration Petition[1]) is deemed to commence on the date of presentation of a petition for winding-up), of:

(a) a decree of adjudication of the company's heritable estate for payment of its debts which has been duly recorded in the register of inhibitions and adjudications on that date; and

(b) an arrestment in execution and decree of forthcoming, an arrestment in execution and warrant of sale, and a completed poinding;

in favour of the creditors according to their respective entitlements.

11.2 Inhibitions

No inhibition within 60 days of the winding-up (defined (for the purposes of this section) in a winding-up by the court as being the date upon which the winding-up order is made), shall be effectual to create a preference in favour of the inhibitor, provided that the liquidator shall be entitled neither to receive any payment made to the inhibitor before the date of liquidation, nor to affect the validity of anything done before that date in consideration of such payment. The right of challenge of any deed voluntarily granted by the company (if vested in the inhibitor as a result of the inhibition) shall vest in the liquidator as shall the right of the inhibitor to receive payment for discharge of the inhibition.

11.3 Arrestments and Attachments

No arrestment or attachment[2] executed within 60 days before the commencement of the winding-up, defined as aforesaid, and whether or not subsisting at the date, or on or after the date of commencement of the

---

[1] Paragraph 13(1)(e) of Sch.B1 to the Act.

[2] Formerly poinding – see Debt Arrangement and Attachment (Scotland) Act 2002, s.61, Sch. 3, Pt 1, para.15(1), (4).

winding-up, shall be effectual to create a preference for the arrester or attacher[3]; and the assets so arrested or attached,[4] or the proceeds of the sale thereof, shall be handed over to the liquidator.[5]

11.4 Poinding of the Ground

No poinding of the ground in respect of the company's assets executed within 60 days before the date of commencement of the winding-up is effectual in a question with the liquidator except for the interest on the debt of a secured creditor, being interest for the current half-yearly terms and arrears of interest for one year immediately before the commencement of that term.

11.5 Actions of Maills and Duties

However, an action of maills and duties is available to a secured creditor whose security includes an assignation of rents during a winding-up. While this might seem contrary to the restriction on poinding of the ground, such a poinding is directed at moveables on the property, whereas an action of maills and duties is directed at the heritable property itself.

11.6 Adjudications

Since a winding-up order is equivalent to a decree of adjudication of the company, any adjudications within a year and a day of the date of commencement of the winding-up will be equalised: Diligence Act 1661; Adjudications Act 1672.

11.7 Effectual Diligence

Despite the fact that arrestments within 60 days of winding-up are ineffectual to create a preference, this has been interpreted by the courts as not applying in a case where the arrestment had been superseded by payment and was no longer subsisting at the date of commencement of the winding-up in *Johnston v Cluny Estates Trustees*.[6]

11.8 Expenses

An arrester or attacher[7] of an ineffectual diligence is entitled to the expenses of the diligence.

---

[3] Formerly poinder — see Debt Arrangement and Attachment (Scotland) Act 2002, s.61, Sch. 3, Pt 1, para.15(1), (4).

[4] Formerly poinded — see Debt Arrangement and Attachment (Scotland) Act 2002, s.61, Sch. 3, Pt 1, para.15(1), (4).

[5] See *Commercial Aluminium Windows Ltd v Cumbernauld Development Corporation* [1978] S.L.T. (Sh. Ct) 91.

[6] [1957] S.L.T. 293.

[7] Formerly poinder — see Debt Arrangement and Attachment (Scotland) Act 2002, s.61, Sch. 3, Pt 1, para.15(1), (4).

11.9   Miscellaneous

(1) The provisions of sections 38(3), (4), (7) and (8) of the Bankruptcy (Scotland) Act 1985 apply in liquidation.

(2) It is important to note that section 39(8) declares it to be incompetent for the liquidator or any associate of his, or for any member of the liquidation committee, to purchase any of the company's assets.

(3) A very important provision relating to diligence, which is frequently overlooked, is section 64 of the Taxes Management Act 1970 which provides:

> "(1) If at any time at which any moveable goods and effects belonging to any person (in this section referred to as "the person in default") are liable to be taken by virtue of any poinding,[8] sequestration for rent, or diligence whatever, or by any assignation, the person in default is in arrears in respect of any such sums as are referred to in subsection (1A) below, the goods and effects may not be so taken unless on demand made by the collector the person proceeding to take the goods and effects pays such sums as have fallen due at or before the date of poinding[9] or, as the case may be, other diligence or assignation.
>
> (1A) The sums referred to in subsection (1) above are:
>
>> (a) sums due from the person in default on account of deductions of income tax from emoluments paid during the period of twelve months next before the date of poinding, being deductions which the person in default was liable to make under section 203 of the principal Act (pay as you earn) less the amount of the repayments of income tax which he was liable to make during that period; and
>>
>> (b) sums due from the person in default in respect of deductions required to be made by him for that period under section 559 of the [Income and Corporation Taxes Act 1988] (sub-contractors in the construction industry)."

The amount for which a person can be made liable in terms of this section is not limited to the benefit he receives by way of the sequestration for rent, but is for all arrears. It is very much a double-edged sword.

11.10   Lien (Section 246 and Rule 4.22)

(1) The liquidator shall:

> (a) as soon as may be after his appointment take possession of the whole assets of the company and any property, books,

---

[8] Presumably this should read "attachment".
[9] *ibid.*

papers or records in the possession or control of the company or to which the company appears to be entitled; and

(b) make up and maintain an inventory and valuation of the assets which he shall retain in the sederunt book.

(2) The liquidator shall be entitled to have access to all documents or records relating to the assets of the property or the business or financial affairs of the company sent by or on behalf of the company to a third party and in that third party's hands and to make copies of any such documents or records.

(3) If any person obstructs a liquidator who is exercising, or attempting to exercise, a power conferred by subsection (2) above, the court, on application of the liquidator, may order that person to cease so to obstruct the liquidator.

(4) The liquidator may require delivery to him of any title deed or other documents or record of the company, notwithstanding that a right of lien is claimed over the title deed or document or record, but this paragraph is without prejudice to any preference of the holder of the lien.

(5) Sections 39(4) and (7) of the Bankruptcy (Scotland) Act 1985 shall apply in relation to a liquidation of a company as it applies in relation to a sequestration of a debtor's estate, subject to the modifications specified in rule 4.16(2) and to any other necessary modifications.

(6) In terms of section 246(2) a lien or other right to retain possession of any of the books, papers or other records of the company is unenforceable to the extent that its enforcement would deny possession thereof to the liquidator. This does not apply to a lien on documents which give a title to property and are held as such.

CHAPTER 12

ADJUSTMENT OF PRIOR TRANSACTIONS

12.1 Gratuitous Alienations (Section 242)

(1) Where any part of the company's property is transferred, or any claim or right of the company is discharged or renounced, and the alienation took place on a relevant day, the alienation is challengeable by any creditor or by the liquidator. This would include an alienation which became completely effectual after the relevant date.[1]

(2) "Relevant day" means, if the alienation has the effect:

(a) of favouring an associate (as defined in the Bankruptcy (Scotland) Act 1985), a day not earlier than five years before the date on which the winding-up of the company commences;

(b) of favouring any other person, a day not earlier than two years before that date.

(3) "Associate" includes directors and employees of the company, and includes associated companies.

(4) Decree of reduction, or for restoration of property to the company's assets, shall not be granted if the person seeking to uphold the alienation establishes:

(a) that immediately, or at any other time, after the alienation the company's assets were greater than its liabilities; or

(b) that the alienation was made for adequate consideration[2]; or

(c) that the alienation:

(i) was a birthday, Christmas or other conventional gift; or

(ii) was a gift, made for a charitable purpose to a person who is not an associate of the company;

which, having regard to all circumstances, it was reasonable for the company to make;

Provided that this paragraph is without prejudice to any right or interest acquired in good faith and for value from or through the transferee in the alienation.

(5) The "consideration" for the alienation need not be in cash. A guarantee to an associated company in order to obtain a tax exemption certificate may constitute adequate consideration[3]; on

---

[1] See *Jackson v Royal Bank of Scotland plc* [2002] S.L.T. 1123

[2] Including consideration received (or to be received) at some future time: *Nova Glaze Replacement Windows Limited v Clark Thomson & Co* [2001] S.C. 815.

[3] *John E Rae (Electrical Services) Linlithgow Ltd v Lord Advocate* [1994] S.L.T. 788.

the other hand the granting of a (financial) guarantee for the obligations of an already insolvent party will not.[4]

(6) In addition to the statutory framework of section 242 of the Act, it is also possible for a gratuitous alienation to be challenged by a creditor at common law[5] (hence avoiding the time limits in section 242)[6].

(7) Under section 242(1) a challenge may be made by the liquidator or any creditor of the company. In the latter case such proceedings are not taken on behalf of or in the name of the company.

(8) No sanction is required under section 167 for the liquidator to commence proceedings under section 242.[7]

12.2 Unfair Preferences (Section 243)

(1) Any transaction entered into by a company which has the effect of creating a preference in favour of a creditor to the prejudice of the general body of creditors, being a preference created not earlier than six months before the commencement of the winding-up, is challengeable by any creditor or by the liquidator.

(2) A transaction is not challengeable if it is:

(a) a transaction in the ordinary course of trade or business;

(b) a payment in cash for a debt due and payable,[8] unless the transaction was collusive with the purpose of prejudicing the general body of creditors;

(c) a transaction whereby the parties to it undertake reciprocal obligations, unless the transaction was collusive as aforesaid[9];

(d) the granting of a mandate by a company authorising an arrestee to pay over the arrested funds to the arrester where:

(i) there has been a decree for payment or warrant for summary diligence[10]; and

(ii) the decree or warrant has been preceded by an arrestment on the dependence of the action, or followed by an arrestment in execution.

(3) On a successful challenge, the court shall grant decree or reduction, or for such restoration of property to the company's assets or other redress as may be appropriate.[11] Provided that this

---

[4] *Jackson v Royal Bank of Scotland plc* [2002] S.L.T. 1123.

[5] See *Bank of Scotland v Pacific Shelf* [1988] 4 B.C.C. 457 and *R W Forsyth Ltd* [1988] S.C.L.R. 487; [1988] S.C. 245.

[6] See *Stuart Eves Limited (In Liquidation) v Smiths Gore* [1993] S.L.T. 1274.

[7] See *Dyer v Hislop* [1994] S.C.L.R. 171.

[8] This does not mean that payment required to be made immediately after the debt became payable in order to fall within the scope of s.243(2(b) of the Act. *Secretary of State for Trade and Industry v Burn* [1998] S.L.T. 1009.

[9] But see *Nicoll v Steel Press (Supplies) Limited* [1991] S.C. 119.

[10] A payment is exchange for the lifting of arrestments on the dependence of an action may be an unfair preference; *R Gaffney & Son Ltd (In Liquidation) v Davidson* [1996] S.L.T. (Sh. Ct) 36.

[11] On the meaning of this see *Baillie Marshall Ltd (In Liquidation) v Avian Communications Ltd* [2002] S.L.T. 189.

paragraph is without prejudice to any right or interest acquired in good faith and for value from or through the creditor in whose favour the preference was created.[12]

(4) Unlike the English law position, section 243 does not require any intention to prefer.

(5) Notwithstanding the statutory provisions, the common law still survives.[13]

12.3   Extortionate Credit Transactions (Section 244)

(1) Where, in a period of three years prior to the date on which the company went into liquidation, the company has entered into a transaction for the provision of credit the court may, on the application of the liquidator make an order in respect of the transaction if the transaction is or was extortionate.

(2) For the purposes of this section, a transaction is deemed to be extortionate if, having regard to the risk accepted by the person providing the credit, the terms of it are or were such as to require grossly exorbitant payments to be made (whether unconditionally or in certain contingencies) in respect of the provision of the credit or it otherwise grossly contravened ordinary principles of fair dealing. In terms of the section there is a presumption, unless the contrary is proved (presumably by the provider of the credit), a transaction with respect to which an application is made by the liquidator is or was extortionate.

(3) An order by the court under this section in respect of any transaction may set aside the whole or part of any obligation created by the transaction, vary the terms of the transaction or the terms on which any security for the purposes of the transaction is held, require any person who is or was a party to the transaction to pay to the liquidator any sums paid to him by virtue of the transaction by the company, and require any person to surrender to the liquidator any property held by him as security for the purposes of that transaction or direct amounts to be taken between any persons.

(4) The section does not give any indication whatsoever as to what is likely to be the bench-mark used in determining whether or not a credit transaction is "extortionate". In the situation of a company which is verging on insolvency, it is not unexpected that the company will be paying a higher rate of interest on its normal borrowings than would a company which is highly successful. In addition, because of difficulties of raising funds for its business, it is likely that the company in difficulty will have had to resort to lenders whose credit terms are generally less favourable than those which are afforded by mainstream lenders.

(5) It is therefore difficult to see exactly what role this section will play although it would attack transactions with moneylenders

---

[12] See *Walkraft Paint Co Ltd v Kinsey Ltd* [1964] S.L.T. 104; *Bob Gray (Access) Ltd v TM Standard Scaffolding Ltd* [1987] S.C.L.R. 720.

[13] *Bank of Scotland v Pacific Shelf* [1988] 4 B.C.C. 457.

and other similar persons. It could also be used to attach transactions which were, in the past, common where associates of the
directors of the company provided funds to the company on
terms which were grossly exorbitant.

(6) In this final regard, note should be had that the powers contained
in section 244 are expressly stated to be concurrent of any powers
exercised in relation to the transaction as a transaction at an
undervalue or as a gratuitous alienation.

12.4 Avoidance of Floating Charges (Section 245)

(1) Where a company grants a floating charge within a period of two
years prior to liquidation in the case of a charge to a person connected with the company, or within a period of one year to any
other person (but only in the latter case if at the time the charge
is created the company is unable to pay its debts in consequence
of the transaction under which the charge is created) the charge is
invalid except to the extent of the aggregate of:

(a) the value of so much of the consideration for the creation of
the charge as consists of moneys paid or goods or services
supplied to the company at the same time as or after the
creation of the charge;

(b) the value of so much of that consideration as consists of the
discharge or reduction at the same time as or after the
creation of the charge or any debt of the company; and

(c) the amount of such interest (if any) as is payable on the
amount following within paragraph (a) or (b) in pursuance of
any agreement under which the money was so paid, the
goods or services were so supplied, or the debt was so
discharged or reduced.

(2) For the purposes of the section, the value of any goods or services supplied by way of consideration for a floating charge is the
amount in money which at the time they were supplied could reasonably have been expected to be obtained for supplying the
goods or services in the ordinary course of business under the
same terms (apart from the consideration) as those on which they
were supplied to the company.

12.5 Tainted Gifts (Section 427 of the Proceeds of Crime Act 2002)

(1) The Proceeds of Crime Act 2002 ("PCA") effectively excludes
from the ambit of the assets under the liquidator's control assets
which are the proceeds of crime. This is dealt with further in
Chapter 18.

(2) Under section 427 of the PCA, a decree cannot be granted under
sections 242 or 243 in respect of the making of the gift at any time
when:

(a) any property of the recipient of the tainted gift is subject to
a restraint order under sections 41, 120 or 190 of the PCA; or

    (b) there is in force in respect of such property an order under sections 50, 52, 128(3), 198 or of the 2002 PCA.

(3) Any order under sections 242 or 243 after the discharge of an order mentioned in (2)(a) or (b) above must take into account any realisation under the Proceeds of Crime Act of property held by the recipient of the tainted gift.

(4) The purpose of the provision is to ensure that where restraint or receivership action has been taken against property in the hands of the gift recipient, then the power to void the gift under the insolvency legislation cannot be exercised for as long as that action is underway.

(5) A "tainted gift" is one which was made by a criminal (see Chapter 18).

(6) If action is taken under the Proceeds of Crime Act before a winding-up order is made, confiscation takes precedence over insolvency. Section 426 of the PCA.

CHAPTER 13

PUBLIC AND PRIVATE EXAMINATIONS
(SECTIONS 133, 198, 235 AND 236)

13.1 Public Examination of Officers

(1) The liquidator may at any time prior to dissolution, apply to the court for the public examination of any person who has been an officer of the company, its liquidator, receiver, administrator or manager or is a person who has been concerned in the promotion, formation or management of the company.

(2) Except where the court otherwise orders, application must be made for examination where the liquidator is requested to do so by one half in value of the creditors of the company or three quarters in value of the contributories of the company.

(3) The examination may be made by:

(a) the liquidator;
(b) any special manager of the company's property or business;
(c) any creditor of the company who has submitted a claim in the winding-up;
(d) any contributory of the company.

(4) At least 14 days' notice of the examination diet must be given to the persons mentioned in (3)(b)–(d) above, unless the court otherwise orders, and the liquidator may advertise the diet in one or more newspapers, provided that at least seven days have elapsed since the person to be examined was served with the order: rule 4.74.

(5) If any person without reasonable excuse fails to attend his examination, he is guilty of contempt of court and a warrant may be issued for his arrest and imprisonment: section 134(1).[1]

(6) A person subject to examination under section 133 is not entitled to refuse to answer questions on the ground that he may incriminate himself.[2]

(7) For a consideration of the situation of a company incorporated in a jurisdiction in which disclosure of information may be a criminal offence in relation to section 133 applications see *Re Casterbridge Properties Limited*[3].

---

[1] See *Re Avatar Communications Ltd* (1988) 4 B.C.C. 473
[2] See *Bishopsgate Investment Management Ltd (in provisional liquidation) v Maxwell* [1993] Ch 1.
[3] [2003] EWHC 1731 (Ch).

13.2   Private Examination (Section 198)

(1) The court may direct the examination in Scotland of any person
for the time being in Scotland (whether a contributory of the
company or not), in regard to the trade, dealings affairs or property of any company in course of being wound-up, or of any person being a contributory of the company, so far as the company
may be interested by reason of his being a contributory.

(2) The order or commission to take the examination shall be
directed to the sheriff principal of the Sheriffdom in which the
person to be examined is residing or happens to be for the time;
and the sheriff principal shall summon the person to appear
before him at a time and place specified in the summons for examination on oath as a witness or as a haver, and to produce any
books or papers called for which are in his possession or power.

(3) The sheriff principal may take the examination either orally or on
written interrogatories, and shall report the same in writing in the
usual form to the court, and shall transmit with the report the
books and papers produced, if the originals are required and
specified by the order or commission, or otherwise copies or
extracts authenticated by the sheriff.

(4) If a person so summoned fails to appear at the time and place
specified, or refuses to be examined or to make the production
required, the sheriff principal shall proceed against him as a witness or haver duly cited; and failing to appear or refusing to give
evidence or make production may be proceeded against by the
law of Scotland.

Basically, a warrant can be issued for his arrest.

13.3   Duty to Co-operate (Section 235)

(1) Officers of the company, employees, past employees, any former
administrator, administrative receiver or liquidator of the company is obliged to give to the liquidator such information concerning the company and its promotion, formation, business
dealings, affairs or property as the liquidator may reasonably
require and shall attend on the liquidator at such times as he may
reasonably require: section 235.

(2) The relevant period for investigations (other than in the case of
an officer of the company) is one year before administration,
administrative receivership, appointment of a provisional liquidator or the date on which the company went into liquidation.

(3) Unlike section 236, no court order is needed under section 235.

(4) If any person fails without reasonable cause to comply with an
obligation under section 235 he is liable to a fine.[4]

---

[4] See *Re Wallace Smith Trust Co Ltd* [1992] B.C.C. 707 – failure to submit a Statement of
Affairs.

13.4   Public Examination (Section 236)

(1) The court may summon to appear before it[5]:

    (a) any officer of the company;

    (b) any person known or suspected to have in his possession any property of the company or supposed to be indebted to the company; or

    (c) any person whom the court thinks capable of giving information concerning the promotion, formation, business affairs or property of the company.

(2) There is no requirement that the examination be preceded by a written statement of questions.

(3) The court may require any such person as to submit an affidavit to the court containing an account of his dealings with the company or to produce any books, papers or other records in his possession or under his control relating to the company or the matters mentioned.

(4) If a person fails to appear for examination under this section or there are reasonable grounds for believing that he has absconded or is about to abscond with a view to avoiding his appearance before the court, a warrant can be issued for his arrest and for the seizure of any books, papers, records, money or goods in that person's possession.

(5) Once arrested a person can be kept in custody until he is brought before the court.

(6) If it appears to the court, on consideration of any evidence obtained under sections 236 or 237, that any person has in his possession any property of the company, the court may, on the application of the liquidator, order that person to deliver the whole or any part of the property to the liquidator at such time, in such manner and on such terms as the court thinks fit.

(7) If it appears to the court, on consideration of any evidence so obtained, that any person is indebted to the company, the court may, on the application of the liquidator, order that person to pay to the liquidator, at such time and in such manner as the court may direct, the whole or any part of the amount due, whether in full discharge of the debt or otherwise, as the court thinks fit.

(8) The court may, if it thinks fit, order that any person who if within the jurisdiction of the court would be liable to be summoned to appear before it under sections 236 or 237 shall be examined in any part of the United Kingdom where he may for the time being be, or in a place outside the United Kingdom.

(9) Any person who appears or is brought before the court under sections 236 or 237 may be examined on oath, either orally or (except in Scotland) by interrogatories, concerning the company or the matters mentioned in section 236(2)(c).

---

[5] See *Re Highgrade Traders Ltd* [1983] B.C.L.C. 137; *Re Norton Warburg Holdings Ltd and Norton Warburg Investment Management Ltd* [1983] B.C.L.C. 235.

(10) The use of information obtained in a section 236 examination in later criminal proceedings has been held to contrary to the European Convention on Human Rights.[6] For this reason it is considered that an objection to the proceedings on the grounds on possible self-incrimination is unlikely to be upheld.

(11) According to one English case[7] an application under section 236 can be made even if the liquidator's sole purpose was to get information for the purpose of commencing disqualification proceedings against the director under the Company Directors Disqualification Act 1986.[8]

(12) The scope of section 236 is not limited to persons within the jurisdiction of the court or to persons who had been served personally with the petition within the jurisdiction.[9]

---

[6] *Saunders v United Kingdom* [1997] B.C.C. 872.
[7] *Re Pantmaenog Timber Co Ltd.* [2003] B.C.C. 659; [2003] UKHL 49.
[8] See *R v Secretary of State for Trade and Industry, ex parte McCormick* [1998] B.C.C. 379.
[9] *McIsaac and Wilson, Petitioners* [1995] S.L.T. 498.

CHAPTER 14

REPORTS ON DIRECTORS, ETC.

14.1   Company Directors Disqualification Act 1986 (as amended)

(1) In terms of section 7(3) of the Company Directors Disqualification Act 1986 and rule 3 of the Insolvent Companies (Reports on Conduct of Directors) (Scotland) Rules 1996,[1] the liquidator is required to submit a report (Form D1) where it appears to him that:

  (a) a person is or has been a director of a company which has at any time become insolvent (whether while he was a director or subsequently); and

  (b) that person's conduct as a director of that company (either taken alone or taken together with his conduct as a director of any other company or companies), makes him unfit to be concerned in the management of a company.

(2) Unless the report mentioned in section 7(3) is made, the liquidator is required by rule 4 of the 1996 Rules to make a return (Form D2) in respect of every person who was, at the date the company went into liquidation, a director or shadow director of the company, or had been a director or shadow director of the company at any time in the three years immediately preceding that date.

(3) The said reports and returns contain details of the company, its affairs and the directors and their conduct, all as per the specified forms.

(4) In addition, the liquidator should have regard to the provisions of sections 218 and 219 of the Insolvency Act 1986 which require the liquidator, either on the direction of the court or *ex proprio motu*, to report to the Lord Advocate any matter which it appears that any past or present officer or any member of the company has been guilty of any offence for which he is criminally liable. Whether or not such a report is required by the Act, in appropriate cases it should be made by the liquidator, it is for the courts — and not the liquidator — to determine whether a person is or is not guilty of a criminal offence.

---

[1] SI 1996/1910 (S.154).

CHAPTER 15

DISQUALIFICATION

15.1 General

Limited liability is a privilege, not a right; and as a corollary of that privilege the Companies Act 1985 imposes obligations on directors requiring them to disclose detailed information about themselves, the company and the financial affairs of the business on an annual or more frequent basis to enable creditors and others dealing or proposing to deal with the company to determine whether they should do so and, if so, on what credit terms.

15.2 Company Directors Disqualification Act 1986

(1) If these obligations are not complied with, the Company Directors Disqualification Act 1986 ("CDDA") empowers the court to make a disqualification order against a director (or shadow director) to the effect that, for a specified period, he (or she) shall not be, *inter alia*, a director of a company or in any way, whether directly or indirectly, be concerned or take part in the promotion, formation or management of a company. In addition to preventing a person from being a director, this could also prevent him from being employed in a managerial or executive position and indeed, arguably, could also prevent him from being a majority or even a major shareholder in a company where such shareholding enable him to exercise an influence over the activities of a company.[1]

(2) An individual who is the subject of a disqualification order cannot obtain the leave of the court to act as an Insolvency Practitioner.[2]

(3) Leaving aside disqualification following conviction of an indictable offence in relation to a company (which can be imposed by the court *ex proprio motu* for a period of between five and fifteen years), disqualification falls into three main categories; disqualification for persistent breaches of companies' legislation[3]; disqualification for cartel offences under the Enterprise Act 2002[4]; and disqualification of unfit directors of insolvent companies.[5] It is also possible for disqualification orders to be

---

[1] For a consideration of what is meant by "be concerned or take part in", see *R v Campbell* [1984] B.C.L.C. 83. The *Campbell* case was an appeal by a management consultant against a two year conditional discharge. The appeal was unsuccessful and in its judgement the Court of Appeal stated that the said wording should not be construed narrowly.

[2] Section 1(1)(b), CDDA; Section 1A(1)(b), CDDA.

[3] Section 3, CDDA.

[4] Section 9A, CDDA.

[5] Section 6, CDDA.

made by the court following the making of a declaration under sections 213 or 214 of the Insolvency Act 1986[6]; or for fraud in the course of the winding-up of a company[7]; or on summary conviction for contravention of, or failure to comply with any filing requirements of the Companies Acts.[8]

(4) A disqualification is something like the passing of a sentence in a criminal case and ought to be dealt with comparatively briefly and without elaborate reasoning. The degree of blame and seriousness of the actions of the persons involved would vary with each case, and accordingly there is no point in rehearsing in great detail the defaults in question.[9]

15.3 Disqualification for Persistent Breaches of Companies' Legislation

Application[10] for the order may be made by, *inter alia*, the liquidator or any past or present creditor or members of the company. The order may be for up to five years.[11] There is, however, no requirement for there to be an actual conviction for default.[12]

15.4 Disqualification for Cartel Offences under the Enterprise Act 2002

(1) In terms of section 9A of the CDDA,[13] the court must make a disqualification order against a person if a company of which he was a director commits a breach of competition law and the court considers that his conduct as a director makes him unfit to be concerned in the management of a company.

(2) The scope of the Competition Disqualification Order falls outwith the ambit of this Handbook.

15.5 Disqualification following upon Insolvency

(1) Application[14] for an order on the basis of unfitness may be made by the Secretary of State and may be for a period of not less than two or more than 15 years; application for an order on the basis of breach of his duties as a director may be made by, *inter alia*, the liquidator or any past or present creditor or member of the company and may be for up to 15 years.

---

[6] Section 10, CDDA.

[7] Section 4, CDDA.

[8] Section 5, CDDA.

[9] *Re Civica Investment Ltd* [1983] B.C.L.C. 456 (at 457i).

[10] Act of Sederunt (Rules of the Court of Session) 1994, Sch 2, Pt V, r.74.33; Act of Sederunt (Company Directors Disqualification) 1986 (SI 1986/2296) (S.168).

[11] See *Civica Investments Ltd* [1983] B.C.L.C. 456, where there were, in relation to 13 companies, a total of 298 separate defaults since 1976, of which 59 had been the subject of criminal convictions. A disqualification period of one year was imposed (although it was stated that this was unusually lenient) in view of the director's attempts to regularise the position.

[12] See *Re Arctic Engineering and Others (No. 2)* [1986] B.C.L.C. 253.

[13] Inserted by s.204(1), (2) of the Enterprise Act 2002.

[14] Act of Sederunt (Rules of the Court of Session 1994) 1994, Sch 2, Pt V, r.74.33; Act of Sederunt (Company Directors Disqualification) 1986 (SI 1986/2296) (S.168).

(2) The Act provides an illustrative but not exhaustive list of matters to be taken into account in determining whether or not an order should be made. A director, and those advising him, should be aware, therefore, of those matters to which reference is made (which are, of course, matters to which directors should always have regard)[15]:

(a) to keep accounting records sufficient to show and explain the company's transaction and disclose with reasonable accuracy, at any time the financial position of the company at that time; and to retain such records for at least three years;

(b) to maintain up to date the register of directors and the particulars therein;

(c) to maintain up to date the register of members of the company;

(d) to make an annual return at least once in every year containing the particulars required by the Act and file this timeously;

(e) to register with the Registrar of Companies the charges the company creates;

(f) to prepare annual accounts and file these timeously with the Registrar of Companies, *i.e.* within ten months from the end of each year in the case of a private limited company[16];

(g) in cases of insolvency, the extent of the director's responsibilities (i) for the causes of the company becoming insolvent, (ii) for the failure by the company to supply any goods or services which have been paid for (in whole or in part), and (iii) for any failure to comply with various obligations of the Insolvency Act 1986.

(3) It has been suggested that failure to account to the Inland Revenue or Customs & Excise for PAYE and VAT is a particular point which should be taken into account in determining whether or not to make a disqualification order. It is thought by the Official Receiver in England (and presumably by the Secretary of State in Scotland) that the use of crown moneys to finance trading is a particularly serious breach of a director's duty — either as a breach of his duty to inform himself as to the company's current trading position or as acting improperly in continuing to trade by using these moneys.[17] Other matters in that case, where a two year disqualification was made included carrying on the business with inadequate capital with the result that they were carried on at risk to the creditors, and failure to file annual returns and accounts in accordance with the provisions of the Companies Act.

---

[15] See *Secretary of State for Trade and Industry v Goldberg* [2003] EWHC 2843 (Ch). – re: *Crystal Palace FC (1986) Limited* – an undertaking was accepted from Mr Goldberg early in the case which then proceeded against Mr McAvoy alone.

[16] *Re Churchill Hotel (Plymouth) Ltd and Others* [1988] B.C.L.C. 341; *Re J & B Lynch (Builders) Ltd* [1988] B.C.L.C. 376.

[17] See *Re Stanford Services Ltd* [1987] B.C.L.Cz. 607.

(4) In *Re Wedgecroft*,[18] Harman J classified crown debts as "quasi-trust moneys", but in *Dawson Print Group Ltd*,[19] Hoffman J commented:

> "I can see that in some cases that view can be taken, but the fact is that, no doubt for good reasons, the Exchequer and the Commissioners of Customs & Excise have chosen to appoint traders to be tax collectors on their behalf with the attendance risk. That risk is, to some extent, compensated by the preference which they have on insolvency. There is, as yet, no obligation on traders to keep moneys in a separate account, as there might be if they were really trust moneys; they are simply a debt owned by the company to the Revenue or the Commissioners of Customs & Excise. I cannot accept that the failure to pay these debts is regarded in the commercial world generally as such a breach of commercial morality that it requires, in itself, a conclusion that the directors concerned are unfit to be involved in the management of the company."

(5) However, in *Stanford Services Ltd*, Vinelott J stated:

> "The position of the Crown in relation to PAYE, national insurance contributions and VAT is very different. The Crown is an involuntary creditor. The fact is, of course, recognised by and is one of the reasons for the preference afforded to Crown debts. More importantly, the trade is under a statutory obligation to keep full and up-to-date records of the sum due by way of PAYE, national insurance contributions and VAT and to account for these sums at regular intervals, monthly in the case of PAYE and national insurance contributions and quarterly in the case of VAT. The directors of a company ought to conduct is affairs in such a way that it can meet these liabilities when they fall due, not only because they are not moneys by its trading activities, which the company is entitled to treat as part of its cash flow (entitled that is in that the persons with whom it deals expects the company to do so) but, more importantly, because the directors ought not to use moneys which the company is currently liable to pay over to the Crown to finance its current trading activities. If they do so and if, in consequence, PAYE, national insurance contributions and VAT become overdue and, in a winding-up, irrevocable, the court may draw the inference that the directors were continuing to trade, at a time when they ought to have known that the company was unable to meet its current and accruing liabilities, and was unjustifiably putting at risk moneys which ought to have been paid over to the Crown as part of

---

[18] March 17, 1986, unreported.
[19] [1987] B.C.L.C. 601.

the public revenues to finance trading activities which might or might not produce a profit. It is, I think, misleading (or at least unhelpful) to ask whether a failure to pay debts of this character would be generally regarded as a breach of commercial morality. A director who allows such a situation to arise is either in breach of his duty to keep himself properly informed, with reasonable accuracy, as to the company's current financial position (as to which see section 221 of the 1985 Act) or is acting improperly in continuing to trade at the expense and jeopardy of moneys which he ought not to use to finance the company's current trade.'"

(6) Whatever the status of failure to pay Crown debts, in *Churchill Hotel (Plymouth) Ltd*,[20] Peter Gibson J. made it clear that gross incompetence without any breach of commercial morality would plainly entitle the court to disqualify a director; use of crown debts to finance trading was improper. In *Re Lo-Line Electric Motors Ltd*,[21] Brown-Wilkinson V.C. stated (at 705) that the use of moneys which should have been paid to the Crown to finance continuation of an insolvency company's business was more culpable than the failure to pay commercial debts.

(7) Any misconduct of a director, qua director, could be relevant even if it did not fall within a specific section of the Insolvency Act 1986.[22] The court only requires to be satisfied that the director has been guilty of a serious failure or failures, whether deliberate or through incompetence, to perform those duties of directors which are attendant on the privilege of trading through companies with limited liability.

(8) However cynical exploitation of the privilege of limited liability or gross incompetence constitute grounds for the making of a disqualification order.[23] In the cited case, the director and his wife had exposed themselves to the risks of business failure and, as a result, had lost a considerable sum of money in connection with two companies, also the director had relied on advice which he had every reason to believe was competent; accordingly, the court did not make a disqualification order.

15.6　Disqualification Undertakings (Insolvency Act 2000)

(1) One of the perceived shortcomings of the CDDA 1986 system was the necessity in each case for court proceedings to be taken against the director etc. concerned with the resultant costs for both prosecution and director.

(2) As a result, the Insolvency Act 2000 formalised a system which had existed on an informal basis hitherto. In some cases a director could avoid a formal disqualification if he gave an undertak-

---

[20] [1988] B.C.L.C. 3341.
[21] [1988] B.C.L.C. 698.
[22] *Re Bath Glass Ltd* [1988] B.C.L.C. 329.
[23] *Douglas Construction Services Ltd* [1988] B.C.L.C. 397.

ing that he would behave as if such an order had been made against him. However, this undertaking was not legally enforceable — save by fresh proceedings — and it was considered that a legally enforceable form of undertaking was needed.[24]

(3) Under the 2000 Act (which introduced new sections 1A, 7(2A) and 8(2A) to the CDDA 1986), the Secretary of State may accept an undertaking by any person to the same effect as a disqualification order. The undertaking would be for a period of between 2 and 15 years.

(4) Application for variation of the disqualification undertaking (or its cessation) may be made by the subject thereof after grant.[25]

(5) In determining whether or not to accept a disqualification undertaking, regard is to be had by the Secretary of State to the same matters as would be relevant in a petition for disqualification.

(6) The disqualification undertakings are entered in the register of disqualification orders in the same way as a court order.[26]

(7) As a result of the changes effected by the Insolvency Act 2000, there are now very few disqualification orders and almost all cases are dealt with by undertakings.

(8) However, the Secretary of State has unfettered discretion as to whether or not to accept an undertaking which has been offered.[27]

15.7 Disqualification of Officers of Other Bodies

The provisions of the CDDA apply (with modifications) to Building Societies[28] and Friendly Societies[29]; to European Economic Interest Groupings[30]; and to Limited Liability Partnerships.[31]

15.8 Waivers of Disqualification

A person who is the subject of a disqualification order or undertaking may seek the leave of the court[32] to allow him to be a director of a company, act as receiver of a company's property (but not act as an Insolvency Practitioner[33]), or be concerned in the promotion, formation or management of a company.[34]

---

[24] See *Secretary of State for Trade and Industry v Goldberg* [2003] EWHC 2843 (Ch). – re: *Crystal Palace FC (1986) Limited*, in which an undertaking was accepted from Mr Goldberg early in the case which then proceeded against Mr McAvoy alone.

[25] Section 8A, CDDA.

[26] Section 18(2A), CDDA.

[27] *Re Blackspur Group Plc (No. 3)* [2001] EWCA Civ 1595.

[28] Section 22A, CDDA.

[29] Section 22B, CDDA.

[30] European Economic Interest Grouping Regulations 1989, (SI 1989/638), reg.20.

[31] Limited Liability Partnerships Regulations 2001, (SI 2001/1090)

[32] Act of Sederunt (Rules of the Court of Session 1994) 1994, Sch 2, Pt V, r.74.33; Act of Sederunt (Company Directors Disqualification) 1986 (SI 1986/2296) (S.168).

[33] Section 1(1)(b), CDDA; s.1A(1)(b), CDDA.

[34] Section 1(1)(a), CDDA; s.1A(1)(a), CDDA.

CHAPTER 16

OFFENCES BY DIRECTORS ETC
(SECTIONS 206, 207, 208, 212, 213 AND 214)

16.1 Fraud in Anticipation of Winding-up (Section 206)

When a company is ordered to be wound up by the court, or passes a resolution for voluntary winding up, any person, being a past or present officer of the company, is deemed to have committed an offence if, within the 12 months immediately preceding the commencement of the winding up, he has:

(1) concealed any part of the company's property to the value of £120 or more, or concealed any debt due to or from the company, or

(2) fraudulently removed any part of the company's property to the value of £120 or more, or

(3) concealed, destroyed, mutilated or falsified any book or paper affecting or relating to the company's property or affairs, or

(4) made any false entry in any book or paper affecting or relating to the company's property or affairs, or

(5) fraudulently parted with, altered or made any omission in any document affecting or relating to the company's property or affairs, or

(6) pawned, pledged or disposed of any property of the company which has been obtained on credit and has not been paid for (unless the pawning, pledging or disposal was in the ordinary way of the company's business).

16.2 Transactions in Fraud of Creditors (Section 207)

(1) When a company is ordered to be wound-up by the court or passes a resolution for voluntary winding-up, a person is deemed to have committed an offence if he, being at the time an officer of the company:

(a) has made or caused to be made any gift or transfer of, or change on, or has caused or connived at the levying of any execution against, the company's property, or

(b) has concealed or removed any part of the company's property since, or within 2 months before, the date of any unsatisfied judgment or order for the payment of money obtained against the company.

(2) A person is not guilty of an offence under this section:

(a) by reason of conduct constituting an offence under subsection (1)(a) which occurred more than 5 years before the commencement of the winding-up, or

(b) if he proves that, at the time of the conduct constituting the offence, he had no intent to defraud the company's creditors.

(3) A person guilty of an offence under this section is liable to imprisonment or a fine, or both.

16.3 Misconduct in the Course of Winding-up (Section 208)

(1) When a company is being wound up, whether by the court voluntarily, any person, being a past or present officer of the company, commits an offence if he:

(a) does not to the best of his knowledge and belief fully and truly discover to the liquidator all the company's property, and how and to whom and for what consideration and when the company disposed of any part of that property (except such part as has been disposed of in the ordinary way of the company's business), or

(b) does not deliver up to the liquidator (or as he directs) all such part of the company's property as is in his custody or under his control, and which he is required by law to deliver up, or

(c) does not deliver up to the liquidator (or as he directs) all books and papers in his custody or under his control belonging to the company and which he is required by law to deliver up, or

(d) knowing or believing that a false debt has been proved by any person in the winding up, fails to inform the liquidator as soon as practicable, or

(e) after the commencement of the winding up, prevents the production of any book or paper affecting or relating to the company's property or affairs.

(2) Such a person commits an offence if after the commencement of the winding up he attempts to account for any part of the company's property by fictitious losses or expenses; and he is deemed to have committed that offence if he has so attempted at any meeting of the company's creditors within the 12 months immediately preceding the commencement of the winding up.

16.4 Falsification of Company's Books (Section 209)

When a company is being wound up, an officer or contributory of the company commits an offence if he destroys, mutilates, alters or falsifies any books, papers or securities, or makes or is privy to the making of any false or fraudulent entry in any register, book of account or document belonging to the company with intent to defraud or deceive any person.

16.5 Material Omissions from Statement of Affairs/False Representations to Creditors (Sections 210–211)

(1) When a company is being wound up, whether by the court or voluntarily, any person, being a past or present officer of the company, commits an offence if he makes any material omission in any statement relating to the company's affairs.

(2) When a company has been ordered to be wound up by the court, or has passed a resolution for voluntary winding up, any such person is deemed to have committed that offence if, prior to the winding up, he has made any material omission in any such statement.

(3) When a company is being wound up, whether by the court or voluntarily, any person, being a past or present officer of the company:

  (a) commits an offence if he makes any false representations or commits any other fraud for the purpose of obtaining the consent of the company's creditors or any of them to an agreement with reference to the company's affairs or to the winding up, and

  (b) is deemed to have committed that offence if, prior to the winding up, he has made any false representation, or committed any other fraud, for that purpose.

16.6 Misfeasance (Section 212)

(1) If it appears during the course of the winding up that a person who has been an officer of the company or has been concerned or has taken part in the promotion, formation or management of the company, has misapplied or retained or become accountable for any money or other property of the company or been guilty of any misfeasance or breach of any fiduciary or other duty in relation to the company,[1] the court may on application of the liquidator or any creditor or contributory examine into that person's conduct and compel him:

  (a) to repay, restore or account for the money or property or any part of it within interest at such rate as the court thinks just; or

  (b) to contribute such sum to the company's assets by way of compensation in respect of the misfeasance or breach of fiduciary or other duty as the court thinks just.

---

[1] In *Colin Gwyer & Associates Limited v London Wharf (Limehouse) Limited* [2002] EWHC 2748, (approving *West Mercia Safetywear v Dodds* [1988] B.C.L.C. 250 and *Russell Kinsella Property Limited* [1986] 4 N.S.W.L.R. 722) the court stated that "where a company is insolvent *or on the verge of insolvency* (emphasis added) the directors must consider the interests of the creditors as paramount and take them into account in reaching decisions."

(2) In *Gray v Davidson*,[2] it was held that section 212 was not a method of obtaining information but rather a means of ordering payment on the basis of information which the liquidator already had. Whether this is a correct interpretation of the wording of the section must be a moot point.

(3) For a consideration of what is meant by 'be concerned or take part in' (see *R v Campbell* [1984] B.C.L.C. 83).

(4) Misfeasance itself is not a concept which falls easily within the law of Scotland and the section itself does not contain any new offences, but is merely a shorthand method of obtaining for the company and its creditors the remedies which are open to the liquidator or the company itself under other section of the Insolvency and Companies Legislation.[3]

(5) In *West Mercia Safetywear Ltd (In Liquidation) v Dodd* [1988] B.C.L.C. 250, it was held that the fact that a director authorised payment, by way of fraudulent preference, was misfeasance on the part of the managing director of West Mercia, who as a director owed a fiduciary duty to that company. However, as he had used the assets merely to pay in part a debt owed by the West Mercia company to the other company, the judge at the first instance decided that there had not been a breach of any duty of care, fiduciary or otherwise, to the company or in relation to that company. On appeal, however, Dillon L.J. quoted with approval the statement of Street C.J. in *Kinsela v Russell Kinsela pty Ltd (In Liquidation)* [1986] 4 N.S.W.L.R. 722 at 730 where he said:

> "In a solvent company the proprietary interests of the shareholders entitle them as a general body to be regarded as a company when questions of the duty of director arise. If, as a general body, they authorise or ratify a particular action of the directors there can be no challenge to the validity of what the directors have done. But where the company is insolvent the interests of the creditors intrude. They become respectively entitled, through the mechanism of liquidation to displace the power of the shareholders and directors to deal with the company's assets. It is in a practical sense their assets and not the shareholders' assets that, through the medium of the company, or under the management of the directors pending either liquidation, return to solvency, or the imposition of some alternative administration."

(6) In these circumstances, it was held that the director had been guilty of breach of duty when, for his own purposes, he caused sums to be transferred in disregard of the interest of the general creditors of the insolvent company. In that case the director was ordered to repay the full sum which had been paid by fraudulent preference with interest.

---

[2] [1991] S.L.T. (Sh. Ct) 61.
[3] See *Blin v Johnstone* [1988] S.L.T. 335.

(7) The misfeasance rules in section 212 apply also to liquidators and receivers of the company. Administrators, however, are not mentioned.

16.7   Fraudulent Trading (Section 213)

(1) If in the course of a winding up, it appears that any business of the company has been carried on with intent to defraud creditors of the company, or creditors of any other person, or for any fraudulent person, the court on the application of the liquidator (and unlike the previous legislation, creditors and contributories can no longer make this application) may declare that any persons who are knowingly parties to the carrying on of the business in the said manner are to be liable to make such contributions (if any) to the company's assets as the court thinks proper.

(2) The problem, however, with section 213 (and with its predecessors section 322 of the 1948 Companies Act and sections 458 and 630 of the 1985 Act) was, as the court stated in *Rossleigh Ltd v Carlaw*,[4] that that section contains penal provisions and this the words "with intent to defraud" therein contained related to fraud in the criminal sense and that actual dishonesty would require to be proved. In addition, it requires to be established that the person was knowingly party to the action in question. The mere fact that the person was a director does not mean he was knowingly party to all the transactions carried out by the company; it required to be averred and proved that he was party to the particular transaction founded upon. In the circumstances in that case the application was refused.

(3) What requires to be approved is criminal intent and "actual dishonesty" involving, according to current notions of fair trading among commercial men, real moral blame.[5] The onus of proof is on the liquidator to establish that the business had been carried on with intent to defraud.[6] One transaction itself may be enough to establish liability where the acceptance of a deposit of the purchase price of goods in advance knowing that goods cannot be supplied or the deposit repaid[7] — but the mere giving or receipt of a preference over other creditors will not necessarily constitute fraudulent trading.[8] The company must have been party to a fraud in which an individual being prosecuted played an active part.[9] It is not sufficient that the director merely failed to present the transaction or failed to advise against it.[10]

(4) Unlike the test which will be considered in relation to wrongful trading, the offence is committed if credit is obtained at a time

---

[4] [1986] S.L.T. 204.

[5] See *R v Hodges* [1983] B.C.L.C. 169.

[6] See *Re Patrick and Lyon* [1933] Ch. 786 at 790.

[7] See *Re Gerald Cooper Chemicals Ltd* [1978] Ch. 262.

[8] *Re Sarflax* [1979] Ch. 592; *R v Grantham* [1984] Q.B. 675; *Rossleigh v Carlaw* [1986] S.L.T. 204).

[9] See *Re Augustus Barnett* [1986] B.C.L.C. 170.

[10] See *Re Maidstone Builders* [1971] 1 W.L.R. 1085.

when a person knows that there is no good reason for thinking that funds will become available to pay the debt when it becomes due or shortly thereafter. It is unnecessary to establish knowledge that funds will never become available, although as long as the director honestly believes that funds will become available this is probably sufficient to avoid the penalties of section 213.[11] The *Grantham* case was already moving the test of fraudulent trading very much closer to the test of wrongful trading which is now included in the legislation.

(5) It should be noted in addition to the civil penalties of fraudulent trading under section 213 of the Insolvency Act that the person who has been engaged in fraudulent trading is also liable criminally under section 458 of the Companies Act 1985.

(6) It is only a liquidator who can apply to the court for a finding of fraudulent trading; creditors cannot make an application.

(7) Any sums recovered by the liquidator from a defender go into the general pool of assets in the liquidation available for creditors.

(8) In addition to any financial penalty, a person liable to pay compensation may also face the possibility of a disqualification order under the Company Directors Disqualification Act 1986, sections 4 and 10.

16.8 Wrongful Trading (Section 214)

(1) The 1986 Act introduced the concept of wrongful trading to insolvency legislation. This applies where the company has gone into insolvent liquidation and at some time before the commencement of the winding up of the company the person knew or ought to have concluded that there was no reasonable prospect that the company would avoid going into solvent liquidation, the court on the application of the liquidator may declare that the person is to be liable to make such contribution if any to the company's assets as the court thinks proper.

(2) However, the court will not make a declaration under this section if it is satisfied that after the person knew or ought to have concluded that the company would not avoid liquidation that the director took every step with a view to minimising the potential loss to the company's creditors as (assuming him to have know that there was no reasonable prospect that the company would avoid going into insolvent liquidation) he ought to have taken. Unfortunately, there is no objective list of what steps should be taken and the test — all steps — is a particularly onerous one. In addition the test is one which is applied with the benefit of the hindsight which the director clearly could not have had.

(3) In ascertaining what facts a director should have known, the conclusion which he ought to have reached and the steps which he ought to have taken, the standards are those which would be known or ascertained or reached or taken by a reasonably diligent

---

[11] See *Re William C Leitch Brothers Ltd* (No.1) [1932] Ch 71; *R v Grantham* [1984] Q.B. 675.

person having both the general knowledge, skill and experience that may reasonably be expected of a person carrying out the same functions as are carried out by that director in relation to the company and the general knowledge, skill and experience that director has.[12]

(4) There is thus a general test and a higher test and the fact that a director does not possess the intellectual capability to satisfy the tower test does not excuse him from it, although if he is of greater ability he will be bound by the higher test as well.

(5) In *Halls v David (Re Produce Marketing Consortium Ltd* (March 22, 1989)), Knox J. gave a very full consideration of the provisions and effect of sections 213 and 214 before ordering payment of £75,000 plus interest at 15 per cent from the date of commencement of the liquidation. In that case it was held:

> "In my judgement the jurisdiction under section 214 is primarily compensatory rather than penal. *Prima Facie* the appropriate amount that a direct is declared to be liable to contribute is the amount by which the company's assets can be discerned to have been depleted by the director's conduct which caused the discretion under subsection (1) to arise.

> But Parliament has indeed chosen very wide words of discretion and it would be undesirable to seek to spell out limits on that discretion, more especially since this is, so far as Counsel were aware, the first case to come to judgement under this section. The fact that there was no fraudulent intent is not of itself a reason for fixing the amount at a nominal or low figure, for that would amount to frustrating what I discern as Parliament's intention in adding sections 214 to 213 in the Insolvency Act 1986, but I am not persuaded that it is right to ignore that fact totally."

(6) The difference between fraudulent and wrongful trading (albeit that there have been few major cases to date) would appear to be, first, in fraudulent trading the onus is on the liquidator to establish intent to defraud, whereas in wrongful trading it is for the director to establish that he took all steps which he should have taken once the company's position is known or should have been known to be beyond doubt. Secondly, in the case of fraudulent trading, some act is positively required, whereas in wrongful trading omissions can also found the basis of a case. Thirdly, for fraudulent trading it is necessary that the director in question actually knew that the transaction was being carried on with intent to defraud creditors and required to know that the company was insolvent, whereas in wrongful trading it is merely sufficient that the situation was such that he ought to have known

---

[12] See *Walker Pennifold & Walker v Secretary of State*, Chancery Division, February 12, 2003.

that the company could not avoid going into liquidation. It is therefore clear that the concept of wrongful trading moves the burden of proof very substantially on to the director of the insolvent company and should hopefully be an improvement in the protection of creditors of companies generally.

(7) Where more than one director is pursued, their liability is not joint and several and payment by one does not discharge the others.[13]

(8) Action under section 214 is available against both present and former directors and against shadow directors. A bank may be liable under this section if it makes recommendations to the directors of a company in trouble as to the future conduct of its business.[14]

(9) As with section 213, it is only a liquidator who has standing to bring proceedings under this section.

(10) Again, any proceeds recovered go into the general assets for the benefit of all creditors. It will NOT be caught by a charge over the assets of the company.

(11) Where a person is found liable under this section 214, a disqualification order may be made under the Company Directors Disqualification Act 1986.

(12) However, unlike the wider provisions of section 213, which apply to anyone who has been party to the fraudulent trading, section 214 only applies to persons who are or have been directors of the company.

(13) In an application against a director under section 214, the director is not entitled to relief under section 727(1) of the Companies Act 1985 (which provides relief to directors where he acted honestly and reasonably and ought fairly to be excused).[15]

---

[13] *Re Continental Assurance Co. of London plc* [2001] B.P.I.R. 733, at 846–848.
[14] *Re a company No. 005009 of 1987* (1988) 4 B.C.C. 424.
[15] *Dyer v Hislop* [1994] S.C.L.R. 171.

CHAPTER 17

PROHIBITED NAME (SECTION 216)

17.1 Restriction on Re-use of Company Names

(1) Prior to enactment of the 1986 Insolvency Act, there was great concern among creditors that directors, having had one company go into insolvent liquidation, would then immediately set up a new business with a name which was almost identical to that of the business which had failed.

(2) Accordingly, section 216 of the 1986 Act provides that a person who was a director or shadow director of a company at any time in the period of 12 months prior to the company going into liquidation is prohibited from being a director of any company, or being directly or indirectly concerned or taking part in the promotion, formation or management of any company, or in any way being concerned or taking part in the carrying on of a business carried on (otherwise than by a company), under a name by which the liquidating company was known at any time in that period of 12 months or a name which is so similar to a name by which the liquidating company was known as to suggest an association with that company.

(3) In determining an application under section 216, it should be noted that all that is required is that the new name suggests an association with the previous company. Where such an association occurs, the court has no option but to find the director concerned to have personal liability, even in the absence of proof that there has been any express misrepresentation or that anyone has actually been deceived or confused into thinking that there was an association.[1]

(4) Chapter 13 of the Insolvency (Scotland) Rules 1986 provides the rules for establishing how an application for leave required under section 216 for a person to act as mentioned in that section in relation to a company with a prohibited name is to be dealt with.

(5) In considering that application the court may call on the liquidator or any former liquidator of the liquidating company for a report of the circumstances in which that company became insolvent and the extent (if any) of the applicant's apparent responsibility for its doing so: rule 4.79.

(6) There are, however, a number of exceptions to the general prohibition of section 216 which may be used by a party wishing to obtain leave to become a director of a company with an otherwise prohibited name which are necessary to make effective the bene-

---

[1] *Ricketts v Ad Valorem Factors Ltd* [2003] EWCA Civ 1706.

fits which may be derived from the insolvency process or to provide a system which is fair to parties generally.

(7) The first case is where a company acquires the whole or substantially the whole of the business of an insolvent company under arrangements made by an insolvency practitioner. Under these circumstances, the successor company may, for the purposes of section 216, give notice to the insolvent company's creditors within 21 days from the completion of the arrangements specifying:

(a) the name and registered number of the insolvent company and the circumstances in which its business has been acquired by the successor company;

(b) the name which the successor company has assumed or proposes to assume for the purpose of carrying on the business if that name is or will be a prohibited name under section 216; and

(c) any change of name which it has made or proposes to make for that purpose under section 28 of the Companies Act 1985.

(8) The notice given by the successor company may name a person to whom section 216 may apply as having been a director or shadow director of the insolvent company and given particulars as to the nature and duration of that directorship with a view to his being a director of the successor company or being otherwise associated with its management.

(9) If the successor company has effectively given notice under the Rules to the insolvent company's creditors, a person who is named in the notice may act in relation to the successor company in any of the ways mentioned in section 216(3) notwithstanding that he has not the leave of the court under that section: rule 4.80.

(10) The second expected case is to cover the position where, but for the exception, a director who is already a director of a company with a very similar name, would automatically be prohibited from acting in connection with that company until the court's leave was obtained. Rule 4.81 provides that where a person to whom section 216 applies, applies for leave of the court under that section not later than seven days from the date on which the company went into liquidation he may, during the period of whichever is the shorter of six weeks and the period until the court disposes of the application for leave, act in any of the ways mentioned in section 216(3), notwithstanding that he has not the leave under that section: rule 4.81.

(11) This would emphasise the importance of seeking the leave of the court as quickly as possible, as a six week period is not particularly long when it comes to court procedures and there is no provision in the Rules for extension of that period, although it is always possible for the court to consider an application on cause shown and to extend the period.

(12) The third excepted case is where a company is already in existence with the name which, by the application of section 216, becomes a prohibited name.

(13) This third excepted case provides that leave of the court under section 216(3) is not required where the company there referred to, although known by a prohibited name within the meaning of the section:

(a) has been known by that name for the whole of the period of twelve months ending with the day before the liquidating company went into liquidation; and

(b) has not at any time in those twelve months been dormant within the meaning of section 252(5) of the Companies Act 1985.

(14) While this third exception would provide an important safeguard where there was a group situation, it is probably unwise to rely too heavily upon it and in particular it would be unwise for the director of the company which is not in liquidation to set itself up in a business identical to that which had been carried on by the now liquidating company as this would give rise to questions as to the director's conduct in relation to the two companies.

(15) The prohibition in section 216 does not only apply in relation to the formation of a new company; if an existing company were to change its name, to one which was a prohibited name, in the period of five years, leave would require to be sought.

17.2   Personal Liability for Breach of Section 216 (Section 217)

(1) Where a person acts in contravention of section 216 (or acts, or is willing to act, on the instructions of someone whom he knows to be in contravention of section 216 in relation to the company), that person is personally responsible for all the debts of the company incurred at a time when such contravention existed.

(2) Once a third party acts at any time on the instructions of a person whom he knows to be in contravention of section 216, he is deemed to have been willing to act on that person's instructions at any time thereafter.

CHAPTER 18

PROCEEDS OF CRIME LEGISLATION
(PROCEEDS OF CRIME ACT 2002)

18.1 Scope of Coverage

It is outwith the scope of this book to deal in detail with the Proceeds of Crime legislation and it is included only insofar as it is necessary for a liquidator to be aware of its scope — particularly in limiting his ability to reduce prior transactions.

18.2 Tainted Gifts

Section 144 of the Proceeds of Crime Act 2002 ("PCA") sets out, in relation to Scotland, the definition of a "tainted gift":

"144 Tainted gifts and their recipients
(1) Subsections (2) and (3) apply if—

>(a) no court has made a decision as to whether the accused has a criminal lifestyle, or
>(b) a court has decided that the accused has a criminal lifestyle.

(2) A gift is tainted if it was made by the accused at any time after the relevant day.
(3) A gift is also tainted if it was made by the accused at any time and was of property—

>(a) which was obtained by the accused as a result of or in connection with his general criminal conduct, or
>(b) which (in whole or part and whether directly or indirectly) represented in the accused's hands property obtained by him as a result of or in connection with his general criminal conduct.

(4) Subsection (5) applies if a court has decided that an accused does not have a criminal lifestyle.
(5) A gift is tainted if it was made by the accused at any time after—

>(a) the date on which the offence concerned was committed, or
>(b) if his particular criminal conduct consists of two or more offences and they were committed on different dates, the earliest of those dates.

(6) For the purposes of subsection (5) an offence which is a continuing offence is committed on the first occasion when it is committed.

(7) A gift may be a tainted gift whether it was made before or after the passing of this Act.

(8) The relevant day is the first day of the period of six years ending with—

   (a) the day when proceedings for the offence concerned were instituted against the accused, or

   (b) if there are two or more offences and proceedings for them were instituted on different days, the earliest of those days.

(9) If the accused transfers property to another person (whether directly or indirectly) for a consideration whose value is significantly less than the value of the property at the time of the transfer, he is to be treated as making a gift.

(10) If subsection (9) applies the property given is to be treated as such share in the property transferred as is represented by the fraction—

   (a) whose numerator is the difference between the two values mentioned in subsection (9), and

   (b) whose denominator is the value of the property at the time of the transfer.

(11) References to a recipient of a tainted gift are to a person to whom the accused has (whether directly or indirectly) made the gift."

18.3   Excluded Assets

Property which is the subject of a restraint order or a confiscation order falls outwith the assets of the company over which the liquidator can exercise his powers. Section 426 of the PCA.

18.4   Priority of Powers

In all cases the powers of receivers and administrators under the Proceeds of Crime Act are to have priority and preference over the powers of liquidators under the Insolvency Act. Section 426 of the PCA. It is unfortunate that the statute uses the same terms to describe appointees under the two Acts but that is the position.

18.5   General

In cases where it is thought that the Proceeds of Crime legislation might apply, specialist advice must be taken as the interplay between the Acts is complex and tortuous.

CHAPTER 19

THE EC REGULATION

19.1 Application of the EC Regulation

(1) The EC Regulation on Insolvency Proceedings[1] came into force on May 31, 2002 and applies in every EU Member State, except Denmark.

(2) The Regulation applies to corporate collective insolvency proceedings which are court based and give rise to the partial or total divestment by a debtor of its assets and the appointment of a liquidator. It does not apply to financial services industry insolvencies including that of insurance companies.

It only applies where the centre of main interests of the company is situated in the EU.

19.2 Main and Secondary Proceedings

(1) The Regulation differentiates between main (Article 3.1) and secondary (Article 3.2) proceedings;

    (a) Main proceedings are those in the country in which the company conducts most of its business (generally presumed to be where the registered office is situated); the test is one of economic activity not assets. They may be winding up or reorganisation proceedings.

    (b) Secondary proceedings are all proceedings which are not the main proceedings. The criteria is a place of operations where the company carries out a non-transitory economic activity with personnel or goods. Only winding-up proceedings may be secondary proceedings.

(2) The purpose of secondary proceedings is to protect local creditors — particularly where there is a difference in substantive law between two or more jurisdictions. The Regulation does not seek to harmonise insolvency law, but merely deal with procedural matters including recognition. Secondary proceedings are confined to the assets of the company situated within the territory of the secondary Member State.

(3) Secondary proceedings may be initiated by the liquidator in the main proceedings or anyone with standing in the second Member State.

---

[1] Council Regulation (EC) No. 1346/2000.

(4) Generally, main proceedings will be commenced before second-ary proceedings.
(5) The applicable national law of each set of proceedings will apply (Article 4) except for:

(a) rights *in rem* (Article 5);
(b) set off (Article 6);
(c) retention of title (Article 7);
(d) contracts relating to immoveable property (Article 8);
(e) rights related to financial and settlement systems (Article 9);
(f) contracts of employment (Article 10);
(g) rights relating to registered property (Article 11);
(h) Community patents and trade marks (Article 12).

(8) Any judgment handed down by a court in the main proceedings will be recognised in all the other Member States.
(9) Such judgments may be enforced in accordance with the Brussels Convention on Jurisdiction and Enforcement of Judgments in Civil and Commercial Matters as amended.
(10) There exist provisions to ensure that creditors who receive a div-idend in one set of proceedings have this taken into account in all other proceedings to ensure that all creditors are treated equally.
(11) Should there be a surplus in the main or secondary proceedings, it must be remitted to the liquidator in the remaining proceedings.

19.3   Exclusions

(1) A Member State may refuse to recognise insolvency proceedings or judgments of another Member State where doing so would be contrary to public policy.
(2) Public interest petitions do not fall within the scope of the EC Regulation.[2]

---

[2]   *Re Marann Brooks CSV Limited* [2003] B.P.I.R. 1159.

CHAPTER 20

LIQUIDATION AND THE FINANCIAL SERVICES MARKETS

20.1 General

(1) Special rules apply in relation to the winding up of financial institutions and insurance companies and these are largely excluded from this Handbook. The comments that follow are not a substitute for a detailed examination of the primary secondary legislation and the Financial Services Authority Handbook, which contains the rules made by the Financial Services Authority ("FSA") under section 138 of the Financial Services and Markets Act 2000 ("FSMA").

(2) Where a Scottish partnership is an authorised person/appointed representative/is carrying on (or has carried on) a regulated activity in contravention of a general prohibition under the FSMA, the FSA may present a petition either on the grounds of inability to pay its debts or if it is just and equitable that a winding-up order be made.[1] In those cases, the Scottish partnership is treated as an unregistered company as defined in section 220 of the Insolvency Act 1986.

(3) The special rules applying to liquidation in the financial services industry is contained in sections 365–371 of the FSMA, and relative Statutory Instruments.

(4) A liquidator is exempt from the prohibition[2] in section 19 of the FSMA which makes it an offence for any person other than an authorised person or an exempt person to carry on a regulated activity in the United Kingdom.[3] The exemptions are specified by reference to the types of activity enumerated in the Order:

Article 14 — Dealing in investments as principal;
Article 21 — Dealing in investments as agent;
Article 25 — Arranging deals in investments;
Article 37 — Managing investments;
Article 40 — Safeguarding and administering investments;
Article 45 — Sending dematerialised instructions;
Article 51 — Establishing, operating or winding up a collective investment scheme, acting as trustee of an authorised unit trust scheme, or acting as depository or sole director of an open-ended investment company;

[1] Section 367(2) of the FSMA.
[2] By virtue of The Financial Services and Markets Act 2000 (Exemption) Order 2001 (SI 2001/1201).
[3] By virtue of art.5 and Pt III of the Schedule to the Order.

Article 52 — Establishing, operating or winding up a stake-holder pension scheme;
Article 53 — Advising on investments.

It is only the liquidator who is exempt, the company still requires to be authorised in terms of the FSMA — even if it is in liquidation.

20.2 Creditors' Voluntary Winding-up

(1) Where the company being wound up is an authorised person not being an insurer effecting or carrying out contracts of long term insurance, the FSA is entitled to make applications to the court under section 112 (reference of questions) of the FSMA in respect of the company; is entitled to be heard at any court hearing; must receive copies of all documents sent to creditors; may attend any meeting of creditors or a liquidation committee and make representations.[4]

(2) Where the company does effect or carry out contracts of long term insurance it cannot be wound up voluntarily without the consent of the FSA.[5]

20.3 Winding up by the Court

(1) The FSA may present a petition to the court to wind up a body which is an authorised person/appointed representative/is carrying on (or has carried on) a regulated activity in contravention of a general prohibition under the FSMA.[6]

(2) A petition by any person for winding up or appointment of a provisional liquidator other than the by FSA must be served on the FSA.

(3) The FSA is given wide rights to be informed, attend meetings, and make representations at all stages of the winding up.

20.4 Obligations in respect of Contravening Party

Where a company is being wound up voluntarily or on a petition by any person other than the FSA and it appears to the liquidator that it has been carrying on a regulated activity in contravention of the general prohibition of the FSMA, this must be reported to the FSA without delay.

20.5 Ongoing Business

Where the company in liquidation effects or carries out contracts of long term insurance the liquidator must, unless the court otherwise orders, carry on the insurer's business insofar as it consists of carrying on the insurer's contracts of long term insurance with a view to those being transferred as a going concern to a person who may lawfully carry out those contracts.

---

[4] Section 365 of the FSMA.
[5] Section 366 of the FSMA.
[6] Section 367 of the FSMA.

20.6 Amendment to Insolvency Act provisions

20.6.1 *The Insurers (Reorganisation and Winding Up) Regulations 2003*

(1) The Insurers (Reorganisation and Winding Up) Regulations 2003[7] came into force on April 20, 2003. The Regulations implement the EU Insurers' Reorganisation and Winding Up Directive.[8]

(2) A Scottish court cannot make a winding-up order, or appoint a provisional liquidator to an EEA insurer (an undertaking (other than a UK insurer) pursuing insurance business under authorisation granted in an EEA State).

(3) The court requires to advise the FSA of any winding-up order made or provisional liquidator appointed; Where a liquidator is appointed in a creditors' voluntary winding up or a members' voluntary winding up, he has to advise the FSA forthwith.

(4) Following upon the making of a winding-up order, appointment of a provisional liquidator or appointment of a liquidator in a voluntary winding up, the liquidator is required to publish this in the Official Journal of the European Communities.[9]

(5) The liquidator is also required, as soon as reasonably practicable, to notify all creditors of the insurer of the order or appointment and its relevant date and the effect which it will have on their contract of insurance and of any resulting variation in the risks covered or sums recoverable under the contract.[10]

(6) The liquidator must report to all the creditors in writing at least annually.[11]

(7) The Regulations make some amendments to the priority of debts in an insolvency — basically inserting "insurance debts" after preferential debts, but before all other debts.[12]

20.6.2 *Open-Ended Investment Companies Regulations 2001*

(1) The Open-Ended Investment Companies Regulations 2001[13] came into force on December 1, 2001.

(2) They allow an Open-Ended Investment Company to be wound up as an unregistered company under section 220 of the Insolvency Act 1986.

(3) Where a petition for winding up is presented (other than by the FSA) it must be served on the FSA who are entitled to be heard on the petition.

(4) However, the commencement of the winding up is not pursuant to section 129(2) of the 1986 Act, but at the time the FSA gave its

---

7 SI 2003/1102.
8 2001/178/EC.
9 Regulation 11.
10 Regulation 12.
11 Regulation 14.
12 Pt IV of the Regulations.
13 SI 2001/1228.

approval to a proposal mentioned in regulation 21(1)(d) or in a case falling within regulation 21(3)(b), following the end of the one month period mentioned in that paragraph.

20.6.3 *The Financial Collateral Arrangements (No.2) Regulations 2003*

(1) The Financial Collateral Arrangements (No.2) Regulations 2003[14] came into force on December 26, 2003 to give effect to the European Financial Collateral Directive.[15]

(2) The Regulations only apply to security over cash (which is defined to include claims for repayment of money) or financial instruments. Thus, they do not cover security over property, plant, machinery, stock or book debts.

(3) The Regulations also disapply certain provisions of insolvency law[16]:

> (a) In relation to winding-up proceedings of a collateral-taker or collateral-provider, section 127 of the Insolvency Act 1986 (avoidance of property dispositions, etc) shall not apply (if it would otherwise do so)—
>
> > (i) to any property or security interest subject to a disposition or created or otherwise arising under a financial collateral arrangement; or
> > (ii) to prevent a close-out netting provision taking effect in accordance with its terms.
>
> (b) Section 88 of the Insolvency Act 1986 (avoidance of share transfers, etc after winding-up resolution) shall not apply (if it would otherwise do so) to any transfer of shares under a financial collateral arrangement.
>
> (c) Section 176A of the Insolvency Act 1986 (share of assets for unsecured creditors) shall not apply (if it would otherwise do so) to any charge created or otherwise arising under a financial collateral arrangement.
>
> (d) Section 178 of the Insolvency Act 1986 (power to disclaim onerous property) or, in Scotland, any rule of law having the same effect as that section, shall not apply where the collateral-provider or collateral-taker under the arrangement is being wound up, to any financial collateral arrangement.
>
> (e) Section 245 of the Insolvency Act 1986 (avoidance of certain floating charges) shall not apply (if it would otherwise do so) to any charge created or otherwise arising under a security financial collateral arrangement.

(3) Where the collateral arrangement includes a close-out netting provision, it will be possible to bring into account sums which became due after the commencement of the winding up (unless

---

[14] SI 2003/3226

[15] 2002/47/EC.

[16] Regulation 10.

the other party was aware or should have been aware that the liquidation had already commenced).[17]

(4) The Regulations also provide that the specific provisions in a financial collateral arrangement regarding the currency in which obligations are to be calculated and the rate of any currency conversions will displace the Rules in the Insolvency (Scotland) Rules 1986, on the calculation of debts in a liquidation in the UK unless the rate set through the arrangement is unreasonable,[18] in which case the rate in the Insolvency (Scotland) Rules 1986 will be applied.

---

[17] Regulation 12.
[18] Regulation 15.

CHAPTER 21

LIMITED LIABILITY PARTNERSHIPS

21.1 General

The provisions of the Insolvency Act 1986 are applied with modifications to Limited Liability Partnerships.[1]

21.2 Amendments to Companies Regime

(1) The corporate regime of the 1986 Act is extended to Limited Liability Partnerships but with references to directors or officers also including members of the LLP — including shadow members.

(2) Schedules 2 and 3 to the 2001 LLP Regulations set out the provisions of the Act which apply to LLPs and the changes which are required to those provisions to take account of the particular circumstances of LLPs.

(3) However the import of the regulation is to place LLPs on an almost identical footing from an insolvency perspective to Companies, and for that reason, the detailed amendments are not reproduced here.

---

[1] Limited Liability Partnerships (Scotland) Regulations 2001 (SI 2001/128).

CHAPTER 22

SPECIAL SECTORS

22.1 General

In addition to the overarching insolvency regime set out in the 1986 Act, it is unfortunately the position that successive governments have seen fit to amend the general rules for particular sectors, sometimes for industry reasons, sometimes for political reasons. Whilst most practitioners will rarely come across any of these specialties, the Handbook has sought to include some of them. The list is unlikely to be exhaustive and if one of these sectors is involved (or indeed if the industry is subject to any industry specific regulation, further investigation should be undertaken.

22.2 Agricultural Marketing Boards

By virtue of section 3(3) of and Schedule 2, Part 4 of the Agricultural Marketing Act 1958, an agricultural marketing scheme may, in it constitution provide for winding up of the board. From a Scottish perspective, the only extant scheme is the Wool Marketing Scheme which applies to the whole of Scotland (except Shetland).[1]

22.3 Foreign Companies

(1) Notwithstanding the provisions of the EC Regulation, the Secretary of State may by order provide for the Insolvency Act 1986 to apply, with or without modification, in relation to a company incorporated outwith the United Kingdom.[2]

(2) This power is presumably in addition to the rules in relation to overseas companies under Part V of the Act and, in particular section 225 thereof.

22.4 Railway Companies

(1) Pursuant to section 61 of the Railways Act 1993, where a petition is presented for the winding up of a protected railway company[3] (other than by the Secretary of State), no winding-up order shall be made unless notice of the petition has been served on the Secretary of State and (where the company holds a passenger licence) the Strategic Rail Authority, and a period of at least 14 days has elapsed since service.

---

[1] SI 1950/1326
[2] Enterprise Act 2002, s.254(1)
[3] A private sector operator which is the holder of a passenger licence, a network licence, a station licence or a light maintenance depot licence in terms of the Railways Act 1993.

(2) At any time before the winding-up order is made, the Secretary of State, or (where the company holds a passenger licence) the Strategic Rail Authority, may instead apply to the court for the making of a railway administration order.

(3) No resolution for voluntary winding up may be made by a railway company without leave of the court and only after notice to the Secretary of State and (where the company holds a passenger licence) the Strategic Rail Authority and a period of at least 14 days has elapsed since service.

(4) At any time before leave is granted, the Secretary of State, or (where the company holds a passenger licence) the Strategic Rail Authority, may instead apply to the court for the making of a railway administration order.

22.5 Coal Industry

(1) In the insolvency of a company which is a licensed operator under the Coal Industry Act 1994, the licence itself (and the obligations arising thereunder) are not to be considered as property for the purposes of the Insolvency Act 1986.[4]

(2) Where the liquidator sends to the Registrar of Companies any notice under sections 94(3), 106(3), 172(8), 202(2), 204(4) or 205(1)(b) of the Insolvency Act — basically returns in relation to the completion of the winding up — he is also required contemporaneously to send a copy of the same material/form to the Coal Authority.[5]

22.6 Air Traffic Services

(1) No company holding an air traffic services licence may be wound up voluntarily.[6]

(2) No application for the winding up of a company holding an air traffic services licence may be made by a person other than the Secretary of State unless he and the Civil Aviation Authority have been given at least 14 days notice of the intention to make the application.

(3) In any petition, the Secretary of State and the CAA are entitled to be heard by the court.[7]

(4) The court must not make a winding-up order or appoint a provisional liquidator.

(5) Where the court is satisfied that it would be appropriate to make a winding-up order it shall instead make an air traffic administration order. The Secretary of State and the CAA may propose a person to manage the business in the administration and the court must appoint that person.[8]

---

[4] Section 36(1) of the Coal Industry Act 1994.
[5] Section 36(2) of the Coal Industry Act 1994.
[6] Section 26 of the Transport Act 2000.
[7] Section 27 of the Transport Act 2000.
[8] Sections 27(4), 27(5) of the Transport Act 2000.

22.7   Heavy Goods and Passenger Vehicle Operators

(1) In the event that the liquidation is that of the holder of a Heavy Goods Licence or a Passenger Vehicle Licence, the local Traffic Commissioner requires to be informed, in terms of the licence conditions of such a change in the conduct of the business.

(2) The Commissioner is empowered to permit the insolvency practitioner to continue to trade for a period of up to 18 months.

22.8   Any other company holding any form of licence/authorisation

Where the company going into liquidation (or already in liquidation) holds or it is believed might hold any form of licence or authorisation required to enable it to carry out its operations, it is imperative that investigations of the position be made before the commencement of the winding up to ensure that the business can be continued/sold if required.

22.9   Scottish Partnerships

(1) A Scottish partnership may not (save as aftermentioned) be wound up under the Insolvency Act 1986. The correct procedure is a petition under the Bankruptcy (Scotland) Act 1985.

(2) The exception to this rule is where the Scottish partnership is an authorised person/appointed representative/is carrying on (or has carried on) a regulated activity in contravention of a general prohibition under the Financial Services and Markets Act 2000, in which case the Financial Services Authority may present a petition either on the grounds of inability to pay its debts or if it is just and equitable that a winding-up order be made.[9] In those cases, the Scottish partnership is treated as an unregistered company as defined in section 220 of the Insolvency Act 1986.

22.10   European Economic Interest Groupings

(1) European Economic Interest Groupings ("EEIGs") were established by a 1985 EU Regulation.[10] However, certain matters required to be determined by the individual Member States and, in the UK, this was achieved by the European Economic Interest Grouping Regulations 1989.[11]

(2) An EEIG may be wound up by the Court on application of the Secretary of State pursuant to art.32 of the EEIG Regulation, or on just and equitable grounds pursuant to regulation 7(2) of the 1989 EEIG Regulations.

(3) Additionally, it is provided by regulation 19 of the 1989 EEIG Regulations that the Insolvency Act 1986 applies to EEIGs as if they were companies incorporated under the Companies Acts.

---

[9] Section 367(2) of the FSMA.
[10] Council Regulation (EEC) No. 2137/85 OF 25th July 1985 on the European Economic Interest Grouping (EEIG).
[11] SI 1989/638.

(4) Curiously it appears that the Sheriff Court has concurrent jurisdiction to wind up an EEIG with the Court of Session in that it is provided in regulation 19(2) that:

> "Section 120 of the Insolvency Act 1986 shall apply to an EEIG, and its establishments, registered under these Regulations in Scotland, as if it were a company registered in Scotland the paid-up or credited as paid-up share capital of which did not exceed £120,000 and as if in that section any reference to the Company's registered office were a reference to the official address of the EEIG."

(5) Regulation 20 applies the Company Directors Disqualification Act 1986 to EEIGs "where the EEIG is wound up as an unregistered company under Part V [*unregistered companies*] of the Insolvency Act 1986", with the EEIG Manager (or past manager) being treated as a director.

(6) It is not clear why reference is only made to section 120 where the remaining references are to unregistered companies, but it appears that the only reason that reference is made to section 120 may be to deal with Sheriff Court jurisdiction.

22.11   Energy Companies

(1) The Energy Act 2004 introduces a new category of entity, a "protected energy company", defined in section 154(5) as a company which holds an electricity transmission and distribution licence or a gas transporter licence.

(2) By virtue of section 160, the court may not exercise its powers (under sections 125 or 135 of the Insolvency Act 1986) on a winding-up petition for a protected energy company unless notice of the petition has been served on the Secretary of State for Energy and on the Gas and Electricity Markets Authority and at least 14 days has elapsed.

(3) A protected energy company may not pass a resolution for voluntary winding-up without the consent of the court and the court may not give consent unless notice of the petition has been served on the Secretary of State for Energy and on the Gas and Electricity Markets Authority and at least 14 days has elapsed.

CHAPTER 23

EMPLOYMENT ISSUES IN LIQUIDATION[1]

23.1 Introduction

The purpose of this Chapter is to introduce the insolvency practitioner to the key employment issues which impact on the role of liquidator and affect the transactions that are made as they go through the process of realising a company's assets and distributing the proceeds to creditors.[2]

23.2 Why is Employment Law so Important?

A contract of employment is a contract just like any other and is therefore governed by normal contractual principles. However, it is also governed by extensive statutory provisions, which give an umbrella of "employment protection" through implied terms and a corresponding framework by which employees can bring claims in the employment tribunal system. Although the process of a liquidation and winding up may differ as between England and Wales on the one hand, and Scotland, on the other, the employment provisions generally apply UK wide.

We will examine what issues the liquidator can expect to deal with once he has taken control of the company and assumed the mantle of "employer" until such time as it is either liquidated or the assets of the business are sold. We will look at the effect a liquidation has on the contracts of employment and also at the employee rights which impact upon the liquidator's role, principally the right of employees not to be unfairly dismissed and to be consulted about major decisions like redundancy and transfer. It should be noted that employees enjoy many additional rights such as the wide-ranging provisions against discrimination on the grounds of sex, race, disability, sexual orientation or religious beliefs. Compensation in discrimination cases is potentially unlimited and can include an award for injury to feelings. Detailed examination of these rights is outside the scope of this book, but the liquidator should still be alert to any overt practices which could give rise to claims and seek advice on how to minimise liabilities where appropriate.

In considering what might amount to an unfair dismissal, we will look at the definition of "redundancy". The liquidator needs to be aware of the law on redundancy, not only because he may have to handle claims brought by disgruntled employees but also because he may have to dismiss more employees by reason of redundancy.

---

[1] Prepared in conjunction with the Employment Group at MacRoberts.
[2] It should be noted that employment law, probably more than any other area of law in this Handbook, changes rapidly and therefore specialist advice should always be sought when a problem or issue arises as the law may well have changed from that stated here.

Although the liquidator's primary function is to realise the assets of the company to the benefit of creditors, by doing so he may manage to achieve the sale of all or part of the business as a going concern. Where there is a transfer of any asset, there is the risk that the TUPE Regulations will apply. We will consider what impact the TUPE Regulations have on the liquidator's discretion to take decisions in the best interest of the company's creditors. We will look at the background to TUPE, the current trends in interpretation by the courts and the likely structure of the new TUPE Regulations which are expected to come into force in late 2004.

In reviewing these issues, we will adopt a practical perspective. We will also look briefly at those additional liabilities which might require the close attention of the insolvency practitioner from time to time.

Throughout this Chapter, the word "employer" is used to cover all circumstances. The liquidator must consider the employment law obligations not only because he has control over the employer company, but also because the duties of the employer may have been breached before his appointment.

23.3   Effect of Liquidation on the Contract of Employment

The legal consequences of a winding-up order have been the subject of considerable academic debate because the nature of insolvency means the employer's identity has changed so significantly that it cannot continue with the employment relationship that existed before. At common law, the consequence is that the employees' contracts of employment are automatically terminated.[3]

However, the liquidator may waive the discharge of the contract of employment which would otherwise apply automatically and the employee may consent to that by continuing to work or by accepting a new term. This might be for the purpose of continuing reduced trading arrangements, including informal arrangements to continue work on an *ad hoc* basis.

Section 136(5)(b) of the Employment Rights Act 1996 provides that where there is "an event affecting an employer . . . "this operates to terminate a contract under which an employee is employed by him".

This means that if the employees do not wish to continue their employment, they will be treated as having been dismissed for the purpose of claiming a redundancy payment from the business if they have two years service (although there is no "dismissal" for the purpose of claiming unfair dismissal. So if the employee wishes to leave the company and claim their entitlement to a redundancy payment, they can do so by virtue of section 136(5)(b) even where the liquidator would prefer them to stay on. This may impact on the liquidator's attempts to salvage any existing trading arrangements.

Further details regarding the redundancy payments scheme are set out later in this Chapter.

---

[3] *Re Oriental Bank Corporation* (1886) 32 Ch.D. 336 (a decision of the Chancery Division in England and Wales)

If the liquidator wishes to keep employees on, the effects of the winding-up order can be avoided through the formal renewal or re-engagement of the employee under a new contract of employment, pursuant to section 138 of the 1996 Act. For this to apply, the employee must have been offered the employment before the end of his employment under the previous contract and, given the timeframe which applies in winding-up situations, this provision will only be of use to the liquidator in exceptional circumstances.

Section 138 also preserves the employee's right to a redundancy payment during a statutory "trial period". This applies where the contract is renewed (the employee having elected to stay on in his old job) or where the employee has been engaged on new terms and conditions. If the trial period does not work out, then the employee may terminate the contract. There is a corresponding right for the employer to terminate the contract during this period with the employee's right to a redundancy payment preserved. For these provisions to apply, the employee must have received the offer of renewal or re-engagement before the end of his employment under the previous contract. This may not often apply in situations of insolvency.

If an employee decides to take his redundancy payment at the point that the winding-up order is made (because, as we have seen, this amounts to a dismissal for that part of the Employment Rights Act), this will break continuity of service for future claims to a redundancy payment. If the employee is re-engaged (within the four-week period but having already received a redundancy payment) then he or she would not receive a second redundancy payment if they were dismissed in the two years thereafter.

23.4 Handling Dismissals

23.4.1 Unfair Dismissal

It is important for the liquidator to be aware of the framework by which employees can lodge claims for unfair dismissal. This is not only because of past claims which may affect the value of the Company (particularly where there have been allegations of discrimination for which compensation is potentially unlimited) but also from the perspective of the liquidator's own decisions to maximise the value of the Company following appointment. Employees are one of the assets of the business but where the decision is taken to dispense with their services then if the claim cannot be defended, they will quickly become a liability.

Section 98 of the Employment Rights Act 1996 provides as follows:

"(1) In determining for the purposes of this Part whether the dismissal of an employee is fair or unfair, it is for the employer to show:

 (a) the reason (or, if more than one, the principal reason) for the dismissal; and
 (b) that it is either a reason falling within subsection (2) or some other substantial reason of a kind such as to justify the dismissal of an employee holding the position which the employee held.

(2) A reason falls within this subsection if it:

> (a) relates to the capability or qualifications of the employee for performing work of the kind which he was employed by the employer to do;
>
> (b) relates to the conduct of the employee;
>
> (c) is that the employee was redundant; or
>
> (d) is that the employee could not continue to work in the position which he held without contravention (either on his part or on that of his employer) of a duty or restriction imposed by or under an enactment.
>
> (3) ...
>
> (4) Where the employer has fulfilled the requirements of subsection (1) the determination of the question whether the dismissal is fair or unfair (having regard to the reason shown by the employer):
>
>> (a) depends on whether in the circumstances (including the size and administrative resources of the employer's undertaking) the employer acted reasonably or unreasonably in treating it as a sufficient reason for dismissing the employee; and
>>
>> (b) shall be determined in accordance with equity and the substantial merits of the case."

In short, the Company must have a potentially fair reason for dismissal and they must also ensure that the dismissal is fair in all the circumstances (taking into account the administrative resources). This requires an examination of the procedure followed in relation to that employee. The Tribunal cannot substitute its own decision for that of the employer but will instead consider whether the decision to dismiss fell within the band of reasonable responses which a reasonable employer would adopt.

Employees who have one year's continuous employment can claim for unfair dismissal. However, if they have a service of less than one year, they will still be able to bring a claim if the basis for that claim is that they have been discriminated against (on grounds of sex, race, disability, sexual orientation or religious beliefs) or that they have relied on a statutory right, for example where the Employee has refused to give up the rights conferred by the Working Time Regulations 1998, as amended.

Claims for unfair dismissal are brought in the Employment Tribunal and are usually listed to be heard within six months to one year of being lodged (unless there are multiple claims, in which case listing may take much longer).

If the claim is successful then the Tribunal will make a basic award of compensation, unless the reason for dismissal is redundancy in which case the Employee should already have received the equivalent of a basic award (calculated the same as the statutory redundancy entitlement for which see below on handling redundancies).

The Tribunal will also make a compensatory award. For dismissals which take effect on or after February 1, 2004 the maximum compensatory award that can be awarded by the Employment Tribunal is £55,000 per employee (this is generally increased on an annual basis). Where the case involves discrimination, compensation is unlimited. Compensation for unfair dismissal is not designed to "penalise" the employer, but is aimed at putting the employee in the same position as if they had not been unfairly dismissed. This means that a Tribunal will not only assess the employee's losses between the date of the dismissal and the date of the hearing, but will also attempt to forecast the likely losses for an appropriate period into the future. An employee is obliged to mitigate his losses by searching for alternative work.

If the decision to dismiss an employee (whether for redundancy or otherwise) is taken on one of the following grounds, then the dismissal will be automatically unfair, regardless of the length of service or the procedure followed in relation to that employee:

- Pregnancy or pregnancy related reasons;
- Health and safety reasons;
- That the employee is an Employee Representative or a candidate to be such representative;
- That the employee is a Trustee of the Occupational Pension Scheme;
- That the employee is a Trade Union Member or has been seeking to rely on their rights as a Trade Union Representative;
- That the employee has made a "whistleblowing disclosure" or has otherwise sought to rely on their rights under the Public Interest Disclosure Act 1998.

23.4.2   Contractual Claims

In addition to making sure any dismissal is "fair" the company must also ensure that termination is in accordance with the individual's contract of employment or in the case of directors, their service agreement. If the termination is not in accordance with the contract then the employee will have a claim for breach of contract, otherwise known as "wrongful dismissal".

This can be brought in the employment tribunal only to the value of £25,000; otherwise it must be brought in the civil courts. Where the contract is silent on the notice period, then the minimum notice prescribed by the Employment Rights Act 1996 will apply.

For employees with up to two years' service this is one week's notice. For employees with two years' to twelve years' service, this is one week for every complete year of service (up to a maximum of 12 weeks).

23.5   Redundancy

23.5.1   Introduction

As well as understanding the liabilities which will be met by the Secretary of State for Trade and Industry, the liquidator needs to be aware of the law on redundancy. This is firstly so that he understands redundancy as a fair reason for dismissal in the statutory framework for unfair dismissal claims, which was introduced earlier in this Chapter. Although redundancy is a potentially fair reason for dismissal and in circumstances giving rise to a liquidation a liquidator may not have a great deal of difficulty in satisfying the appropriate test, the decision to dismiss must still be shown to be fair in relation to that particular employee.

This means the liquidator must be aware of the need for individual consultation and the requirement to search for alternative employment for that employee.

Although a Tribunal will acknowledge the duty that the liquidator must discharge, the mere fact of a liquidation will not automatically mean that the dismissal is "fair" or that a fair procedure need not be followed. The Tribunal will instead assess the fairness of the procedure in the context of the liquidation as a whole so the liquidator will be expected to take fair and proper steps in relation to employees in the time available to him, even if that time is of necessity short.

Secondly, a liquidator should understand the operation of the statutory redundancy scheme.

The third area where the liquidator must be aware of the legal obligations is in relation to collective redundancies and the requirement to notify the Department of Trade and Industry and to consult with employee representatives about the forthcoming redundancies. We will look at these obligations in detail and again consider whether the unique circumstances in insolvency provide a defence for the liquidator against any claims.

23.5.2   *Dismissals for Redundancy*

Section 139 of the Employment Rights Act provides as follows:

(1) For the purpose of this Act an employee who is dismissed shall be taken to be dismissed by reason of redundancy if the dismissal is wholly or mainly attributable to:

(a) the fact that his employer has ceased or intends to cease:

(i) to carry on the business for the purposes of which the employee was employed by him; or

(ii) to carry on that business in the place where the employee was so employed; or

(b) the fact that the requirements of that business:

(i) for employees to carry out work of a particular kind; or

(ii) for employees to carry out work of a particular kind in the place where the employee was employed by the employer;

have ceased or diminished or are expected to cease or diminish.

It is not for the Tribunal to decide whether there was a redundancy situation — that is a business decision. However, the Tribunal should be satisfied overall that there was a need to reduce numbers of jobs or a requirement for less people to carry out the same work. This should of course be self-evident in a situation where a liquidator has been appointed.

Once it has been established that redundancy was the reason for dismissal, the employer must go on to show that the dismissal itself was fair, taking into account the size and administrative resources of the employer's undertaking. The test is whether the employer acted reasonably or unreasonably in treating the redundancy as a sufficient reason for dismissing the employee. There should be consultation with the employee to try to find ways of mitigating or avoiding redundancies (for example, by seeking volunteers at an early stage). Where the redundancy situation requires employee numbers to be reduced, the employer must consider the appropriate pool from which to select those employees who will be dismissed as redundant. The employer should consult with the employees about the selection criteria to be applied and the selection criteria themselves must be fair, objective and non-discriminatory. Before dismissing any employees, the employer must carry out a search for alternative employment and this would include employment with associated companies.

23.5.3   Redundancy Payments

Where an employee is to be dismissed by reason of redundancy, he is entitled to work out his notice period or receive payment in lieu. They will also receive a statutory redundancy payment if he has continuous service of two years or more as at the date of termination. He may also have the right to an enhanced contractual payment. The statutory redundancy payment is calculated as follows:

Ready Reckoner for calculating the number of weeks' pay due

Read off the employee's age and number of complete years' service. You will then see to how many weeks' pay the employee is entitled.

The table starts at 20 because no-one below this age can qualify for a redundancy payment.

If the employees aged between 64 and 65, the amount due will be reduced by one-twelfth for every complete month over 64.

There is a limit on the amount of a week's pay that can be taken into account in working out entitlement. The limit changes annually in line with the Retail Prices Index. The limit was raised from £260 to £270 on February 1, 2004. Calculation of entitlement where the reckonable period of service ended before February 1, 2004 should therefore be at the lower rate. Please see **Ready Reckoner** overleaf.

Age (years)	Service (years)																		
	2	3	4	5	6	7	8	9	10	11	12	13	14	15	16	17	18	19	20
20	1	1	1	1	-														
21	1	1½	1½	1½	1½	-													
22	1	1½	2	2	2	2	-												
23	1½	2	2½	3	3	3	3	-											
24	2	2½	3	3½	4	4	4	4	-										
25	2	3	3½	4	4½	5	5	5	5	-									
26	2	3	4	4½	5	5½	6	6	6	6	-								
27	2	3	4	5	5½	6	6½	7	7	7	7	-							
28	2	3	4	5	6	6½	7	7½	8	8	8	8	-						
29	2	3	4	5	6	7	7½	8	8½	9	9	9	9	-					
30	2	3	4	5	6	7	8	8½	9	9½	10	10	10	10	-				
31	2	3	4	5	6	7	8	9	9½	10	10½	11	11	11	11	-			
32	2	3	4	5	6	7	8	9	10	10½	11	11½	12	12	12	12	-		
33	2	3	4	5	6	7	8	9	10	11	11½	12	12½	13	13	13	13	-	
34	2	3	4	5	6	7	8	9	10	11	12	12½	13	13½	14	14	14	14	-
35	2	3	4	5	6	7	8	9	10	11	12	13	13½	14	14½	15	15	15	15
36	2	3	4	5	6	7	8	9	10	11	12	13	14	14½	15	15½	16	16	16
37	2	3	4	5	6	7	8	9	10	11	12	13	14	15	15½	16	16½	17	17
38	2	3	4	5	6	7	8	9	10	11	12	13	14	15	16	16½	17	17½	18
39	2	3	4	5	6	7	8	9	10	11	12	13	14	15	16	17	17½	18	18½
40	2	3	4	5	6	7	8	9	10	11	12	13	14	15	16	17	18	18½	19
41	2	3	4	5	6	7	8	9	10	11	12	13	14	15	16	17	18	19	19½
42	2½	3½	4½	5½	6½	7½	8½	9½	10½	11½	12½	13½	14½	15½	16½	17½	18½	19½	20½
43	3	4	5	6	7	8	9	10	11	12	13	14	15	16	17	18	19	20	21
44	3	4½	5½	6½	7½	8½	9½	10½	11½	12½	13½	14½	15½	16½	17½	18½	19½	20½	21½
45	3	4½	6	7	8	9	10	11	12	13	14	15	16	17	18	19	20	21	22

Service (years) Age (years)	2	3	4	5	6	7	8	9	10	11	12	13	14	15	16	17	18	19	20
46	3	4½	6	7½	8½	9½	10½	11½	12½	13½	14½	15½	16½	17½	18½	19½	20½	21½	22½
47	3	4½	6	7½	9	10	11	12	13	14	15	16	17	18	19	20	21	22	23
48	3	4½	6	7½	9	10½	11½	12½	13½	14½	15½	16½	17½	18½	19½	20½	21½	22½	23½
49	3	4½	6	7½	9	10½	12	13	14	15	16	17	18	19	20	21	22	23	24
50	3	4½	6	7½	9	10½	12	13½	14½	15½	16½	17½	18½	19½	20½	21½	22½	23½	24½
51	3	4½	6	7½	9	10½	12	13½	15	16	17	18	19	20	21	22	23	24	25
52	3	4½	6	7½	9	10½	12	13½	15	16½	17½	18½	19½	20½	21½	22½	23½	24½	25½
53	3	4½	6	7½	9	10½	12	13½	15	16½	18	19	20	21	22	23	24	25	26
54	3	4½	6	7½	9	10½	12	13½	15	16½	18	19½	20½	21½	22½	23½	24½	25½	26½
55	3	4½	6	7½	9	10½	12	13½	15	16½	18	19½	21	22	23	24	25	26	27
56	3	4½	6	7½	9	10½	12	13½	15	16½	18	19½	21	22½	23½	24½	25½	26½	27½
57	3	4½	6	7½	9	10½	12	13½	15	16½	18	19½	21	22½	24	25	26	27	28
58	3	4½	6	7½	9	10½	12	13½	15	16½	18	19½	21	22½	24	25½	26½	27½	28½
59	3	4½	6	7½	9	10½	12	13½	15	16½	18	19½	21	22½	24	25½	27	28	29
60	3	4½	6	7½	9	10½	12	13½	15	16½	18	19½	21	22½	24	25½	27	28½	29½
61	3	4½	6	7½	9	10½	12	13½	15	16½	18	19½	21	22½	24	25½	27	28½	30
62	3	4½	6	7½	9	10½	12	13½	15	16½	18	19½	21	22½	24	25½	27	28½	30
63	3	4½	6	7½	9	10½	12	13½	15	16½	18	19½	21	22½	24	25½	27	28½	30
64	3	4½	6	7½	9	10½	12	13½	15	16½	18	19½	21	22½	24	25½	27	28½	30

This table is intended only as a guide to show how statutory redundancy pay is calculated for people who are entitled to receive it. Guidelines as to the correct calculation of a week's pay should also be followed and further details are available on the DTI website.

Where the company is legally insolvent, the DTI will make the redundancy payments to affected employees through its statutory scheme (the liquidator will be required to assist with the administration of this through various forms). Prior to insolvency, the DTI will only make the payments for the employer if the employer cannot afford to make them without risking going out of business. However, the employer must agree to repay the money as soon as the business can afford it, so it is on a loan-only basis.

23.5.4 *Consultation in Relation to Collective Redundancies*

Where 20 or more employees are to be made redundant within a 90-day period at one establishment, statutory consultation procedures apply.

23.5.5 *Relevant Law*

- The EC Collective Redundancies Directive (No. 75/129/EEC)
- Trade Union and Labour Relations (Consolidation) Act 1992 ("TULRCA")
- Collective Redundancies and Transfers of Undertakings (Protection of Employment) (Amendment) Regulations 1995 ("the 1995 Regulations")
- Collective Redundancies and Transfer of Undertakings (Protection of Employment) (Amendment) Regulations 1999 ("the 1999 Regulations")

23.5.6 *Obligation to Consult*

Section 188 of the TULRCA as amended by the regulations imposes an obligation on all employers to consult with "appropriate representatives", where the employer is proposing to dismiss 20 or more employees at one establishment over a 90-day period.

23.5.7 *"Proposing to Dismiss"*

This is a key phrase in the timing of consultation. It contemplates that matters have reached a stage where a specific proposal has been formulated not just the diagnosis of a problem and an appreciation that redundancies are one way of dealing with it.

It is essential to note that there are minimum periods of consultation laid down in section 188 of the TULRCA. This section states that consultation must take place in "good time" and at least:

- 90 days before the first of the dismissals is due to take effect where the employer is proposing to dismiss 100 or more employees at one establishment within a period of 90 days or less; and
- 30 days before the first dismissal takes effect where the employer

proposes to dismiss at least 20 but less than 100 employees, at one establishment within 90 days or less.

23.5.8   Establishment

The fact that a business is carried on at different sites does not necessarily mean that each of those sites is a separate establishment for the purposes of the consultation requirements. The European Court of Justice ruled in *Rockfon A/S v Specialarbejderforbunet i Danmark*[4] that the term "establishment" must be understood as describing "the unit to which the workers made redundant are assigned to carry out their duties". This means that geographically dispersed units of a company may not necessarily have to be aggregated for the purposes of determining the threshold for collective redundancy consultation. However, in each case it will depend upon the circumstances and is a matter of judgement whether any given "establishment" is itself a "unit" or merely a component part of a larger unit.

23.5.9   Intimation to the Secretary of State

Intimation of the proposed redundancies must be given to the Secretary of State for Trade and Industry using Form HR1, in the case of 20 to 99 employees, 30 days before the first of the dismissals take effect and in the case of 100 or more employees, at least 90 days before the first of the dismissals takes effect.

Form HR1 is available from the Department of Education and Employment.

The National Redundancy Helpline telephone number is 0845 145 000.

The penalty for a failure to intimate timeously is a fine of up to £5,000.

23.5.10   Appropriate Representatives

Consultation must be with appropriate representatives.

"Appropriate representatives" are:

- "employee representatives" elected by the employees; or
- if the employees are of a description in respect of which an independent Trade Union is recognised by the employer, representatives of that Union.

23.5.11   Union Recognition

Recognition in this context means recognition to any extent for the purposes of collective bargaining, that being negotiations relating to or connected with one or more of the matters set out in section 178(2) of the TULRCA. A recognised union is therefore one which has negotiating rights over matters such as terms and conditions of employment, hiring, dismissal and suspension of workers, the allocation of work, discipline, Union membership, Union facilities and negotiating or consultative machinery or other procedures. Partial negotiating rights on any one of these matters, covering any class, grade or number of workers, will amount to recognition.

---

[4]   *C-449/93* [1996] I.R.L.R. 168.

23.5.12   Elected Employee Representatives

In organisations where a Trade Union is not recognised, "employee representatives" do not generally exist automatically. Employee representatives are:

- Persons who have been specifically elected by employees for the purpose of being consulted about proposed dismissals; or
- Persons who were elected by employees (whether before or after dismissals have been proposed) otherwise than for that specific purpose, but where it is appropriate (having regard to the purposes for which they were elected) for the employer to consult with them about the proposed dismissals.

Representatives must be employed by the employer at the time when they are elected. At present, representatives may be elected under "ad hoc" procedures as and when collective redundancies are proposed or under standing arrangements, which may or may not relate specifically to redundancy.

A representative could for example be an elected member of an existing works or staff council or a joint consultative committee, provided that consultation for these purposes is "appropriate". The DTI guidance states that it would not be sufficient for example to consult members of an elected canteen committee, about redundancies but it might be appropriate to consult a committee, which is regularly informed or consulted more generally about the employers financial position and personnel matters.

The 1999 Regulations specify that employee representatives have to be both capable (suitably mandated) and independent of the employer. In the event of a dispute, the onus would be on the employer to prove to an Employment Tribunal that both of these requirements have been met.

23.5.13   Invitation to Elect Representatives

The 1999 Regulations require the employer to consult with representatives of all those employees who may be affected, directly or indirectly, by the dismissals and not just those who may be dismissed by reason of redundancy.

Where no recognised union exists and no other existing employee representatives are available, the employer must make suitable arrangements for the election of employee representatives. The employer is obliged to take all reasonable steps to ensure that it does so sufficiently early to allow for information to be given and consultation to take place in "good time". Given the statutory minimum dictated by the number of proposed redundancies the employer must take steps to meet its responsibilities well in advance of these deadlines. The employer should invite the employees to elect representatives. If no representatives are elected following the employer having invited the employees to do so, the employer has a defence so long as he has ensured that the requirements as set out in section 188(7A) of the TULRCA are met. These are:

- that an invitation has been issued to all those employees who may be affected by the dismissals to elect representatives; and
- the invitation was issued long enough before the time when consul-

tation is required to begin, to allow them to elect representatives by that time.

23.5.14   The Ballot

The 1999 Regulations introduced requirements for the election of representatives for the first time.

- The number of representatives to be elected and the term for which they are to be elected are matters for the employer to determine, so long as the numbers are sufficient to properly represent all relevant employees, and the representatives stay in office long enough to complete the necessary consultation.
- The candidates for election must be members of the affected workforce on the date of the election.
- Anyone who is a member of the affected workforce on the date of the election cannot be unreasonably excluded from standing as a candidate.
- All those who are members of the affected workforce on the date of the election must be entitled to vote and may cast as many votes as there are representatives to be elected e.g. where there are three representatives to be elected to represent a unit or department, each employee will have three votes.
- The election is to be conducted so as to ensure that those voting do so in secret and the votes given at the election are fairly and accurately counted.

In the event of a dispute about whether the procedure has been followed, the employees may complain to a Tribunal and it shall be for the employer to prove that all of the election requirements have been met. It is recommended that careful notes should be kept of the meetings, which form part of this process, and of all communications and documents, which are issued, in order to prove compliance.

If the employer genuinely provides the opportunity for elections but the employees fail to respond, the employer will be held to have discharged its responsibility to consult if it informs the general body of employees in the workplace, in the same way as it would have informed the Employee representatives had they been available.

Employees can complain to an Employment Tribunal if pressure is put on them to not take part in an election.

23.5.15   Elected Representatives and a Recognised Union

As a result of the 1999 Regulations, the employer is obliged to consult with the Union if one is recognised. The employer no longer has the right to choose who to consult.

23.5.16   Representatives — Access to Facilities and Time Off

Once the employee representatives have been elected or where Trade Union representatives are being consulted, the representatives must be given accommodation and facilities including secretarial facilities, in order to carry out their duties.

In addition, they have the right to reasonable time off with pay during their normal working hours to carry out their duties as representatives.

The dismissal of an elected representative (or a candidate for election) for a reason wholly or mainly related to the employee's status or activities as a representative will be automatically unfair. It is also unlawful to take action short of dismissal against a representative or a candidate for election on those grounds, just as it is unlawful to take similar action against a Trade Union representative.

23.5.17   *Consultation with the Representatives*

The consultation carried out must be fair and meaningful and must include consultation about ways of:

(1) avoiding the dismissals;
(2) reducing the number of employees to be dismissed; and
(3) mitigating the consequences of the dismissals.

Consultation must be undertaken by the employer with a view to reaching agreement with the representatives. However, while consultation needs to be meaningful, it is not a requirement that the representatives should be able, through consultation, to prevent the redundancies. Accordingly, while consultation is undertaken with a view to reaching an agreement, agreement need not necessarily be reached.

As soon as the necessary representatives are established, the consultation exercise may begin. The representatives in such a situation have a statutory right in terms of TULRCA, section 188(4) to be given certain information regarding the reasons for the dismissals and the selection procedure proposed. As the information must be in writing, this is best given in the form of a written brief, volunteered at the outset of the consultation process. The information to be given to the representatives must be disclosed by being given to each of the appropriate representatives by delivering to them or sending it by post to an address notified by them to the employer or in the case of Union representatives, by post to the Union at the address of its head or main office.

This information *must* include the following:

A copy of Form HR1, (the intimation to the Secretary of State for Trade and Industry) together with the following information in writing:

- the reasons for the redundancy proposals;
- the numbers and descriptions of the employees whom it is proposed to dismiss as redundant, and of those employees who will be affected by the dismissals;
- the total number of employees of any such descriptions employed by the employer establishment in question;
- the proposed method of selecting the employees who may be dismissed;
- the proposed method of carrying out the dismissals with due regard to any agreed procedure, including the period over which the dismissals are to take effect; and

- the proposed method of calculating redundancy payments to individual employees, where this differs from the statutory scheme.

While the information does not have to be provided in a single document, that is the preferred approach. The representatives should not have to attempt to glean the information from the surrounding circumstances and any existing documents.

It should be noted that it is no longer the case that consultation will only be deemed to have begun with the disclosure of the specified information.[5] However it is good practice to supply the information at the outset before the consultation begins otherwise representatives may not be in a position to make constructive proposals, which are an essential feature of the consultation process. The point at which the provision of information becomes sufficient to enable meaningful consultation to begin is a question of fact and circumstances, hence the suggested provision of a detailed brief addressing all the information required by statute. There is no rule that full and specific information under each of the heads listed in section 188(4) must be provided before consultation can begin. However, it is prudent, in every case, to attempt to provide the information required under these headings.

23.5.18 The Aims of the Consultation Process

While it is not necessary to reach agreement with the representatives nor to avoid any redundancies, the consultation exercise must not be a sham and must be meaningful. Accordingly, consultation cannot begin *after* the date on which redundancy notices are issued to individual employees, as that cannot satisfy the relevant conditions. There must be sufficient time for meaningful consultation before notices of dismissal are sent out and for the representatives to properly consider the proposals which are being put to them. Issuing redundancy notices is clearly incompatible with inviting consultation.

The employer's duty to consult with a view to reaching agreement does not require the joint regulation of the redundancy process but it goes beyond simply listening to and responding to representations. Where representations or counterproposals are made, these must be carefully considered and a genuine attempt made to reach some form of accommodation or understanding. Fair consultation means consultation at a point where proposals are still at a formative stage and by definition capable of being adjusted or changed completely. That means that the employee representatives consulted, have to have a fair and proper opportunity to understand fully the matters about which they are being consulted and to express their views on those matters. The employer must then consider the responses to the consultation properly, genuinely and conscientiously. Employers should endeavour in such circumstances to answer and distinguish the various points raised, which do not accord with the employer's aim or intentions.

---

[5] *Securicor Omega Express Ltd v GMB* [2004] I.R.L.R. 9.

23.5.19   Call for Volunteers

Before proceeding to the stage of mandatory redundancies, employers should always issue a call for volunteers. Volunteers need not be accepted if they are necessary to the employer's operation and would have to be replaced. Nor in ordinary circumstances need a volunteer be accepted if the cost of that particular redundancy would be disproportionately high. This may be of particular importance where a contractual redundancy scheme is in force. Not to call for volunteers for redundancy is potentially to adopt an unfair procedure and consideration should always be given to doing so.

23.5.20   Criteria for Selection

Once the number of employees to be made redundant has been established, taking into account any volunteers, criteria should be determined for use in the selection of the employees to be made redundant. Where consultation with representatives is required, as part of the consultation process, the two sides should seek to agree the selection criteria and the pools from which the employees are to be selected. Organisations have often applied historically agreed criteria, *e.g.* Last In First Out ("LIFO") but that is no longer binding on employers. However, existing agreed arrangements should only be departed from for good reason, in circumstances which dictate that the agreed procedure would not achieve the required result.

Once the criteria have been agreed and applied, the representatives should be told (subject to undertakings as to confidentiality at that stage) who has been identified as a candidate for selection. Any submissions by the representatives on a candidate's behalf should be considered. The representatives should be instructed not to disseminate the information regarding selection to the workforce pending consultation with the individual employees.

23.5.21   Consultation with the Employees Selected

Once consultation with the Trade Union has proceeded to the stage where the likely candidates for selection for redundancy have been identified, consultation with the affected individuals should commence.

Consultation meetings should be arranged with the individuals concerned. Each should have the opportunity to be accompanied by a representative, where one is available or alternatively by a fellow employee of their choosing. Employees should be aware of the nature of the meetings when requested to attend.

At the individual consultation meeting, management should work to a prepared order of events or a script. The employee should be advised that he (or she) is a potential candidate for redundancy, the selection pool into which he falls, why he has been selected as a candidate, the criteria used in the selection process and his score against the criteria. He should be advised in general how that places him in relation to the others in the same pool. Any criticism of the scoring should be considered and where necessary investigated and a response given. Detailed notes should be kept of the meeting. The employee should be advised of the financial implications of being selected for redundancy and invited to make any comment on his selection.

Where the employee does not dispute his selection, management may move to confirm the selection at the meeting or alternatively may advise any decision will be made later. Where further consultation is required due to points raised by the employee, the meeting should be adjourned to enable that to be undertaken. The position may then be confirmed at the adjourned meeting.

23.5.22   Failure to Consult

Where there is a failure to comply with the requirement for collective consultation, a complaint may be presented to an Employment Tribunal. A complaint may be presented:

- In the case of a failure relating to elected employee representatives, by any of the employee representatives to whom the failure related;
- In the case of a failure relating to Trade Union representatives, by the Trade Union;
- In any other case, by any of the employees who have been or may be dismissed as redundant.

However, where a Trade Union is recognised or there are properly elected employee representatives and they have failed to act, an individual employee may not bring an application to a Tribunal.

Complaints may be presented:

- Before the date on which the last of the dismissals to which the complaint relates takes effect; or
- During the period of three months beginning with that date; or
- Such further period as the Tribunal considers reasonable.

23.5.23   Protective Awards

If the Tribunal finds the claim well founded, it must make a declaration to that effect and it may make a protective award.

A protective award is an award in respect of one or more employees, who has been dismissed or whom it is proposed to dismiss as redundant and in respect of whose dismissal or proposed dismissal the employer has failed to comply with the requirement of section 188, ordering the employer to pay remuneration to those employees for a protected period.

23.5.24   "Protected Period"

The protected period begins with the date on which the first of the dismissals to which the complaint relates takes effect or the date of the Tribunal award, whichever is the earlier.

The length of the protected period is a matter for the Tribunal to determine as just and equitable in the circumstances having regard to the seriousness of the employers default, subject to a maximum of 90 days.

The entitlement is calculated on the basis of an actual weeks pay for each week of the protected period and remuneration in respect of a period of less than a week is calculated by proportionately reducing the amount of a weeks pay. The award is compensatory and not penal.

The maximum protective award is accordingly 90 days actual pay per employee affected. In a closure situation that equates to potentially one quarter of the annual wage bill.

23.6 TUPE

The Transfer of Undertakings (Protection of Employment) Regulations 1981 as amended ("the TUPE Regulations") implement the Acquired Rights Directive 77/187/EEC ("the ARD"). Before the TUPE Regulations came into force, there was no special protection for employees in the event of a change of employer including the appointment of a liquidator or a series of transactions by which the liquidator disposes of the business. Instead the liquidator could reach agreement with the acquiring party to allow it to pick and choose which employees were taken on and on what terms.

The TUPE Regulations now provide that all rights and obligations under contracts of employment transfer automatically to the new employer on the transfer of an undertaking or business and that the transfer of the undertaking shall not in itself constitute grounds for dismissal by either the transferor or the transferee. They also provide that any changes to an employee's terms and conditions of employment post-transfer are void. Employees must be consulted with in advance of the transfer as prescribed by the Regulations.

The TUPE Regulations are designed to apply by operation of law, so it is not possible to contract out of the protection they offer.

23.6.1 *When do the TUPE Regulations apply to Transactions?*

The TUPE Regulations apply when an undertaking or part of an undertaking is transferred from one employer to another, also known as a "TUPE transfer". European jurisprudence on the the ARD has developed over the years to assist the tribunals and courts in applying the relevant test. An undertaking includes "any trade or business" and a "stable economic entity" which generally means there must be an identifiable and cohesive management structure which pursues one or more specific economic aims.[6] The economic entity should retain its identity post-transfer which is why not every disposal by a liquidator will be a TUPE transfer.

The word "transfer" is not restricted to formal transfer in the legal sense (although in corporate sales the applicability of the TUPE Regulations may be explicitly acknowledged and sale documentation will often be the best evidence of the relevant date that the entity has transferred). Examples of transfers under the TUPE Regulations are as follows:

- The outsourcing of an economic entity

---

[6] *Sanchez Hidalgo v Asociacion de Servicios Aser and Sociedad Cooperativa Minerva* [1999] I.R.L.R. 136.

- The bringing of contract work back in-house
- Sale of all or part of a business or partnership
- Where a company or part of it is acquired through the transferee buying or acquiring the assets and then running the business (*although* the TUPE Regulations do *not* apply to a pure share sale)
- Where a group is reorganised so that two companies cease to exist and combine to form a third
- Business transfers between group companies
- A change of management through the acquisition of a licence or assignment of a lease

As the application of the TUPE Regulations is a matter of fact to be determined by the employment tribunal applying the relevant test, it is impossible to give a definitive answer prior to the transfer taking place. The prudent liquidator will seek advice from an employment lawyer (and the prudent advice will often be to assume that TUPE will apply). The key factors that the liquidator should be aware of are those set out in the European Court of Justice decision in *Spijkers v Gebroeders Benedik Abattoir CV*.[7] The ECJ held in that case that the following factors should be taken into account in determining whether or not there has been a TUPE transfer:

- The type of undertaking or business
- Whether or not the tangible assets of the business, such as buildings or stock, transfer
- The value of the intangible assets at the time of the transfer
- Whether the majority of employees are taken over by the new employer
- Whether the customers are transferred
- The degree of similarity between the activities carried on before and after the transfer
- The periods (if any) of interruption to the business activities

Although the UK courts have reached varied decisions about the weight to be given to each of these factors (for example, in the case of *Betts v Brintel Helicopters Limited*,[8] the Court of Appeal in England and Wales applied the approach taken by the ECJ in *Suzen v Zehnacker Gebäudereinigung GmbH Krankenhausservice*[9] that, in a labour intensive business, if no employees or assets transfer, there may be no TUPE transfer on a mere change of contractor).

In the case of *Oy Liikenne AB v Liskojärvi and Juntunen*[10] there was no TUPE transfer when the transferee took over bus routes previously operated by the transferor but did not acquire any of the buses themselves. The ECJ held that, because of the reliance of the activity upon the fleet itself, the failure to transfer those assets meant that there was no TUPE transfer. However, in the case of *McLeod & Another v Ingram t/a Phoenix Taxis and*

---

[7] 24/85 [1986] E.C.R. 1119.
[8] [1997] I.R.L.R. 361.
[9] C-13/95 [1997] I.R.L.R. 255.
[10] [2001] I.R.L.R. 171.

Rainbow Cars Limited[11] the Scottish Employment Appeal Tribunal held that there was a TUPE transfer when one taxi firm took over another and acquired the name of the business, client list and goodwill but did not acquire any assets or employees.

23.6.2   What happens to Employees?

Regulation 5(1) of the TUPE Regulations provides that (except where the employee informs the transferor that he objects to becoming employed by the transferee) "a relevant transfer shall not operate so as to terminate the contract of employment of any person employed by the transferor in the undertaking or part transferred but any such contract which would otherwise have been terminated by the transfer shall have effect after the transfer as if originally made between the persons so employed and the transferee".

Regulation 5(2) goes on to say that, on the completion of the relevant transfer:

> "(a) all transferor's rights, powers, duties and liabilities under or in connection with any such contract, shall be transferred by virtue of this regulation to the transferee; and
> (b) anything done before the transfer is completed by or in relation to the transferor in respect of that contract or a person employed in that undertaking or part shall be deemed to have been done by or in relation to the transferee."

To determine who transfers this means that there are three separate tests to be met:

- The employee must be employed by the transferor.
- The employee must be employed in the undertaking or part of the undertaking transferred.
- The employee must be so employed "immediately before" the transfer.

Regulation 5(3) provides that the reference to a person employed in an undertaking or part of an undertaking transferred by a relevant transfer "is a reference to a person so employed immediately before the transfer, including, where the transfer is affected by a series of two or more transactions, a person so employed immediately before any of those transactions."

Regulation 8(1) provides as follows:

> "Where either before or after a relevant transfer, any employee of the transferor or transferee is dismissed, that employee shall be treated . . . as unfairly dismissed if the transfer or a reason connected with it is the reason or principal reason for his dismissal."

---

[11] EAT/1344/01 April 22, 2002.

However, the dismissal will not be unfair if the reason or principal reason is "an economic, technical or organisational reason entailing changes in the workforce of either the transferor or the transferee before or after a relevant transfer", in which case the dismissal will be held to be of a "substantial reason of a kind such as to justify the dismissal of an employee holding the position which that employee held" (regulation 8(2)).

In the key case of *Litster v Forth Dry Dock & Engineering Company Limited*,[12] a liquidator dismissed employees in order to slim down the business and achieve a sale. On a strict interpretation of regulation 5(3), the employment protection conferred by the TUPE Regulations could easily be defeated and the liquidator would be able to offer the business to the purchaser in a slimmed down state or allow the purchaser to choose which employees he would rather not take on and then dismiss them prior to sale. So, in *Litster*, the House of Lords stated that the definition in regulation 5(3) must extend to a person who "would have been so employed if he had not been unfairly dismissed in the circumstances described in regulation 8(1)".

Where the employee informs the transferor or the transferee that he objects to becoming employed by the transferee, regulation 4(a) of the TUPE Regulations provides that there will be no transfer of the contract of employment and the associated liabilities. Regulation 4(b) goes on to say that in those circumstances the employee "shall not be treated for any purpose, as having been dismissed by the transferor".

Regulation 5(5) also preserves the right of an employee to terminate his contract of employment without notice if a substantial change is made in his working conditions to his detriment (although the employee would not be able to resign merely in response to a change of the identity of his employer unless it is to his detriment). An employee in these circumstances must still show that the detriment would be substantial.[13]

The effect of these provisions was explored by the decision of the Court of Appeal in England and Wales in *University of Oxford v Humphries*.[14] It was held in that case that where the transfer will involve the substantial and detrimental change in an employee's terms and conditions of employment within the meaning of Regulation 5(5) then the employee is entitled to treat his contract as terminated by the (then) employer and seek compensation. In those circumstances any liabilities for wrongful and (constructive) unfair dismissal will remain with the transferor.

23.6.3 *How do the TUPE Regulations apply to an Insolvency Situation?*

"It is the primary duty of a liquidator to engather and dispose of assets for the maximum benefit of creditors. It seems to us that, if he has to look over his shoulder at the TUPE Regulations, this might well fetter to the extent to which he might perform his duty. We do, however, recognise that, in receivership or administration, there may be an opportunity for the Regulations to apply if the business is sold

[12] [1989] I.R.L.R. 161.
[13] *Rossiter v Pendragon plc* [2002] I.R.L.R. 483–EWCA.
[14] [2000] I.R.L.R. 1H3.

on. Provided it is so done as a going concern, then this is very important."[15]

The extent to which the TUPE Regulations may or may not apply to insolvency situations has been subject to some judicial debate but remains unresolved. It was acknowledged in the European Court of Justice in the case of *Abels v Administrative Board of the Bedrijfsvereniging voor de Metaalindustries en de Electrotechnische Industrie*[16] that the ARD, on which the Regulations are based, "does not apply to transfers taking place in the context of insolvency proceedings instituted with a view to the liquidation of the assets of the transferor under the supervision of the competent judicial authority". The absence of any express provision in the Directive to deal with liquidation led in *D'Urso v Ercole Marelli Elettromeccanica Generale SpA (in special administration)*[17] to a finding that the ARD did not apply to a transfer which was intended to realise the assets of the undertaking for the benefit of its creditors, in the context of insolvency proceedings.

In the *Perth & Kinross* case it was submitted that the TUPE Regulations must be interpreted in accordance with the ARD only and should not be given any broader consideration. The EAT agreed that, if the TUPE Regulations had previously been interpreted as bringing irretrievable insolvency and cessation of business within the scope of the ARD, then that was incorrect. They stated that the issue should be addressed by primary legislation and they declined to refer the issue to the ECJ for further guidance on the grounds that the European position with regard to absolute insolvency was clear.

In that case the EAT found that the *ad hoc* arrangements of a contract for housing maintenance, which the liquidators of the company had arranged to continue, could not be considered as a stable entity capable of transfer, given that the "day to day effective handout of work . . . could be terminated or ceased at any time". The EAT also concluded that as the liquidator was bringing the business to an end because there was no more work for it to do, this meant that "there was simply nothing to transfer". This was the case even though the work continued after the Council brought the maintenance contract back in-house. As this is one of the situations in which TUPE would normally apply, it is perhaps not surprising that this decision is likely to be the subject of a further appeal in due course.

The broad rule to be taken from these cases might be said to be that what is important is the purpose of the procedure. If it is solely to liquidate the company's assets TUPE will probably not apply, but if it is to allow the business to continue to trade or if that is the effect then there may well be a TUPE transfer.

---

[15] Lord Johnston in the Employment Appeal Tribunal (Scotland) in *Perth & Kinross Council v Tony Donaldson & 14 Others (1); New Town Construction Scotland Limited (2) and Meldrums (3)* – Decision of October 30, 2003.

[16] [1985] E.C.R. 469.

[17] C-362/89 [1992] I.R.L.R. 136.

The law in this area is changing and even though in a "pure" liquidation the liquidator may feel justified in distancing himself from the Regulations, the liquidator must assume that the TUPE Regulations may still apply and take advice accordingly.

Despite the judicial uncertainty, the unique nature of insolvency situations is recognised by regulation 4 which is designed to cover the "hiving down" process. Hiving Down allows the liquidator time to assess the business and make it viable for a potential purchaser by forming a wholly owned subsidiary of the insolvent company and transferring to that subsidiary the ownership of the parent company's business. At the same time the liquidator maintains the employees' contracts of employment with the parent company and simply hires them out to the subsidiary company in order to carry on the business. The subsidiary is therefore unencumbered by the employment contracts and their corresponding liabilities. Regulation 4 operates to suspend the transfer of the undertaking (to the subsidiary company) which would ordinarily occur straight away, taking all the employees with it. It will only become a "relevant transfer" within the meaning of the TUPE Regulations when the undertaking or part of it is sold *on* to a purchaser, in which case those employees assigned to that undertaking will then transfer.

23.6.4 Effects of TUPE

We have already seen how regulation 5(2) provides for the transfer of contracts of employment and the corresponding rights, powers, duties and liabilities. The practical effect of this is that the transferee will inherit:

- All existing contractual terms, whether express or implied (including terms as to remuneration, notice and terms incorporated from any collective agreement)
- Liability for past breaches of contract, *e.g.* arrears of wages
- Statutory liability (such as liability to meet any unfair dismissal claim, claims for redundancy pay and claims under discrimination legislation)
- Continuous employment
- Delictual liabilities

The transfer of liabilities does not include occupational pension rights (although this does not include any contractual arrangements for sums payable on early retirement, which do transfer).

23.6.5 Information and Consultation

The second main obligation arising under the TUPE Regulations is to inform and consult in relation to the effect of the transfer on both the employees of the transferor and the transferee.

As we have seen in relation to redundancy, the primary requirement to consult with a recognised trade union where there is one, was laid down by the Collective Redundancies and Transfer of Undertakings (Protection of Employment) (Amendment) Regulations 1999.

The TUPE Regulations were amended by the Collective Redundancies & Transfer of Undertakings (Protection of Employment) (Amendment)

Regulations 1995 to provide for the election of employee representatives where there is no recognised trade union with whom the employer can consult.

Regulation 10 of TUPE states that "long enough" before a relevant transfer to enable the employer of any affected employee to consult all the persons who are appropriate representatives of any of those affected employees, the employer must inform those representatives in writing of:

- the fact that the relevant transfer is to take place, when appropriate approximately it is to occur and the reasons for it;
- the legal, economic and social implications of the transfer for the affected employees;
- the measures which it envisages it will take in connection with the transfer in relation to those employees (and if it envisages that no measures will be taken, it must state that);
- if the employer is the transferor, the measures which the transferee envisages it will take, in connection with the transfer, in relation to those of the transferor's employees who become by virtue of regulation 5 of TUPE, employees of the transferee after the transfer (and if it envisages that no measures will be taken, it must state that).

The transferee must give the transferor such information at such time as will enable the transferor to perform its duty to inform those employees who are to be transferred about the measures envisaged by the transferee (regulation 10(3)). This information must be provided by the transferee to the transferor to enable him to perform that duty and cannot be supplied under cover of commercial confidentiality thereby preventing the transferor performing that duty.

"Measures Envisaged" means visualised or foreseen. Reference to measures which a transferee "will" take rather than "may" take, excludes mere hopes or possibilities. A definite plan or proposal has to be formulated. Consultation should be with a view to seeking agreement and representations made by the representatives should be considered and responded to.

23.6.6 *Appropriate Representatives*

The information is to be given to appropriate representatives. "Appropriate representatives" are:

- "employee representatives" elected by the employees; or
- if the employees are of a description in respect of which an independent Trade Union is recognised by the employer, representatives of that Union.

Where no recognised union exists and no other existing employee representatives are available, the employer must ensure that the workforce has the opportunity to elect the necessary representatives to enable consultation to take place in good time. The numbers of representatives must be sufficient to properly represent all relevant employees, and the representatives must stay in office long enough to complete the necessary consultation.

The employer should invite the employees to elect representatives as and when required. If no representatives are elected after the employer has invited the employees to do so, the employer has a defence so long as he has ensured that the requirements as set out in section 188(7A) are met. These are:

- that an invitation has been issued to the employees who may be dismissed to elect representatives; and
- the invitation was issued long enough before the time when consultation is required to begin, to allow them to elect representatives by that time.

The employees will have the right to complain if pressure had been put on them not to take part in an election.

If this defence is to be used, the employer is still obliged to give such information to the individual employees, which he would have given to the representatives had they been elected.

23.6.7 Remedies for the Failure to Consult

Where there is a failure to comply with any requirement of regulation 10, a complaint may be presented to an Employment Tribunal. A complaint may be presented:

- In the case of a failure relating to elected employee representatives, by any of the employee representatives to whom the failure related;
- In the case of a failure relating to Trade Union representatives, by the Trade Union;
- In any other case, by any of the employees who have been or may be dismissed as redundant.

However, where a Trade Union is recognised or there are properly elected employee representatives and they have failed to act, an individual employee may not bring an application to a Tribunal.

Complaints may be brought both before and after the date of transfer.

Complaints of failure to consult are brought against the transferor. However where the transferor has failed to disclose information about measures envisaged by the transferee, the transferor can give the transferee notice that it intends to show that the reason for its failure was the transferee's failure to supply the requisite information at the requisite time in accordance with regulation 10(3). The giving of that notice makes the transferee a party to the proceedings and the protective awards may be made against the transferee in that situation.

Where the successful sale of an undertaking is achieved and a business transfer occurs, liability for failure to consult by a transferor will pass to the transferee (*Kerry Foods Limited v Creber*)[18] as upheld by the EAT in *Alamo Group (Europe) Limited v Tucker*.[19] This is on the basis that the duty to consult is a right, which arises from the individual contracts

---

[18] [2000] I.R.L.R. 10.
[19] [2003] I.R.L.R. 266.

between each worker and his employer, and the remedy for failure to consult belongs to the individual and is regarded as part of his contractual entitlement. Protective awards made by an employment tribunal for failure to consult are a liability "in connection with" a contract of employment and liability for the protective award transfers to the transferee. This is obviously of importance to the liquidator who can dispose of the business cleanly but it should be noted that previous cases have held the opposite and it is important to seek up to date advice on the position before assuming that liability will transfer.

23.6.8   The Protective Award

A complaint for failure to consult should be lodged with the Employment Tribunal within three months of the transfer but time may be extended if it was not reasonably practicable to lodge. If a complaint is well founded, the Tribunal must make a declaration to that effect and may order the payment of appropriate compensation. Appropriate compensation is such a sum not exceeding 13 weeks pay for each of the specified employees.

23.6.9   Redundancies in the Context of a Transfer of an Undertaking

In a situation where there is both a relevant transfer and there are to be redundancies, which will exceed 19 in number, there is a concurrent obligation to consult in respect of both.

Any protective awards made in relation to a failure to consult regarding the transfer cannot be offset against protective awards made under the redundancy consultation provisions and vice versa.

23.6.10   Future Legislative Developments

The Acquired Rights Directive was revised in 1998 and consolidated in 2001 (Council Directive 2001/23/EC) and Member States have been given some flexibility to tailor implementation of the new measures to national circumstances. The TUPE Regulations will soon be updated to not only implement the new Directive, but also to modernise the Regulations in accordance with current employment and business practice. As well as extending the provisions which apply to service contracting operations which are labour intensive and providing for more information about employees' terms and conditions to be transferred to the new employer, the new Regulations will also improve the way TUPE operates when insolvent businesses are sold.

When the liquidator transfers an insolvent business (which includes wound up businesses but not those placed in receivership) there will be more flexibility for the transferee to agree changes to terms and conditions with the workforce. As it currently stands, all changes to terms and conditions amount to a breach of the TUPE Regulations and are therefore void even if they favour the employee.

Article 5 of the 2001 Directive provides as follows:

1. Unless Member States provide otherwise, Articles 3 and 4 shall not apply to any transfer of an undertaking, business or part of an undertaking or business where the transferor is the subject of

bankruptcy proceedings or any analogous insolvency proceedings which have been instituted with a view to the liquidation of the assets of the transferor and are under the supervision of a competent public authority (which may be an insolvency practitioner authorised by a competent public authority).

2. Where Articles 3 and 4 apply to a transfer during insolvency proceedings which have been opened in relation to a transferor (whether or not those proceedings have been instituted with a view to the liquidation of the assets of the transferor) and provided that such proceedings are under the supervision of a competent public authority (which may be an insolvency practitioner determined by national law) a Member State may provide that:

   (a) notwithstanding Article 3(1), the transferor's debts arising from any contracts of employment or employment relationships and payable before the transfer or before the opening of the insolvency proceedings shall not be transferred to the transferee, provided that such proceedings give rise, under the law of that Member State, to protection at least equivalent to that provided for in situations covered by Council Directive 80/987/EEC of October 20, 1980 on the approximation of the laws of the Member States relating to the protection of employees in the event of the insolvency of their employer, and, or alternatively, that,

   (b) the transferee, transferor or person or persons exercising the transferor's functions, on the one hand, and the representatives of the employees on the other hand may agree alterations, in so far as current law or practice permits, to the employees' terms and conditions of employment designed to safeguard employment opportunities by ensuring the survival of the undertaking, business or part of the undertaking or business.

3. A Member State may apply paragraph 20(b) to any transfers where the transferor is in a situation of serious economic crisis, as defined by national law, provided that the situation is declared by a competent public authority and open to judicial supervision, on condition that such provisions already existed in national law on July 17, 1998.

4. Member States shall take appropriate measures with a view to preventing misuse of insolvency proceedings in such a way as to deprive employees of the rights provided for in this Directive.

It is thought that the new Regulations will, where a company meets the definition of insolvency proceedings in the revised Directive namely if it is "under the supervision of competent public authority (which may be an insolvency practitioner determined by national law)" provide for any outstanding debts towards employees to either:

• Be met from the national insurance fund, if they are within the categories and statutory upper limits on amounts guaranteed under the

Insolvency Payments Provisions of the Employment Rights Act 1996 (see below); or
- Pass to the transferee (if they fall outwith the statutory limits).

The second main provision (in insolvency proceedings as defined) will allow for changes to terms and conditions of employment to be made by reason of the transfer itself so long as:

- They are agreed between either the transferor or the transferee and appropriate representatives of those employees;
- They are designed to safeguard employment opportunities by ensuring the survival of the undertaking or business or part of the undertaking or business; and
- They are not otherwise contrary to UK law (*e.g.* the National Minimum Wage Act 1998).

The provisions as to hive-down are thought to be unnecessary and are likely to be abolished.

23.7. Failure to Consult — The "Special Circumstances" Defence

23.7.1 Defence

The law recognises that in some circumstances it will be impossible for an Employer to carry out lengthy consultation with Employees. However, in a claim for a protective award (either for failure to consult in respect of collective redundancies or failure to consult in connection with a TUPE Transfer) the insolvent employer is by no means exempt from the duties to consult.

This part of the Chapter will look at the approach the courts have taken to the "special circumstances" defence in insolvency situations.

23.7.2 Redundancy Consultation

The fact that an employer is insolvent does not exempt the employer from complying with the statutory consultation requirements. No concessions are made to the difficulties which may arise in insolvencies. Section 188(7) of TULRCA does provide a defence in that the employer can plead that there are "special circumstances" which render it not reasonably practicable for an employer to comply with any of the statutory requirements in relation to the timing, duration and substance of consultation or with the provisions regulating the disclosure of information. An employer seeking to rely on this defence has the burden of proving both the existence of special circumstances and that it took the necessary steps towards compliance.

Section 188(7) was amended by TURERA 1993 (section 34(2)) to make it clear that, where the decision leading to the proposed dismissals is that of the person controlling the employer (directly or indirectly) a failure on the part of that person to provide information to the employer shall not constitute special circumstances.

Even if there are special circumstances, the employer (and therefore the liquidator) must still take such steps towards compliance as are reasonably practicable. If the statutory time limits for collective consultation cannot be adhered to, consultation should start as soon as possible before redundancies are declared.

Given that the liquidator has 14 days from the date of appointment within which to determine whether or not he wishes to adopt employees' contracts of employment, it is unsurprising that he may take a swift decision to reduce the workforce. If this is done without the requisite notice and consultation, claims for protective awards and unfair dismissal may follow.

23.7.3   What are Special Circumstances?

In protective award proceedings it will also be open to an employer to plead that there were "special circumstances" which rendered it not reasonably practicable for him to comply with the consultation requirements. Even if such circumstances are present, the employer must still take all such steps towards compliance with the requirements as are reasonably practicable in the circumstances (section 188(7)).

A broad interpretation of "special circumstances" would have the potential of rendering the entire protection mechanism a dead letter. Therefore, it is not surprising to see that the courts have taken a restrictive approach. Insolvency, *per se*, has been said not to amount to a special circumstance.[20] The appointment of a Receiver is similarly not a special circumstance[21] nor is the fact that there may have been a pending application for Government Aid.[22]

"Special circumstances" are something out of the ordinary, something uncommon. Whether insolvency will be accepted by a Tribunal as a special circumstance will depend entirely on the cause of the insolvency. Sudden disaster, which makes it necessary to close a concern, would be a matter which was capable of being a special circumstance whether the disaster was physical, *e.g.* a fire, or financial, *e.g.* the collapse of the sole or principal customer. However, insolvency due to a gradual run down of the company, does not constitute special circumstances. The shedding of employees in order to make the sale of a business more attractive does not constitute a special circumstance. Similarly, the failure to sell a business or the loss of orders are also common incidents of insolvencies and do not constitute special circumstances. The sudden withdrawal of credit facilities may constitute a special circumstance.

Even when there was a shedding of labour as part of a receivership followed by a closure, that was held not to amount to special circumstances in the absence of any element of sudden disaster or unexpected insolvency.[23]

In *Amalgamated Society of Boilermarkers v George Wimpey*[24] it was said that the difficulty of predicting the end of a building contract might amount to a special circumstance.

---

[20] *Clarks of Hove Limited v Bakers' Union* [1978] I.R.L.R. 366.
[21] *Association of Pattern Makers v Kirvin* [1978] I.R.L.R. 318.
[22] *Hamish Armour v Association of Scientific, Technical and Managerial Staffs* [1979] I.R.L.R. 24.
[23] *GMB v Rankin & Harrison* [1992] I.R.L.R. 514.
[24] [1977] I.R.L.R. 95.

When there was a collapse of negotiations for the sale of a business followed immediately by the bank appointment of a receiver that was held to be special circumstances.[25]

23.7.4   TUPE Consultation in Insolvency

Regulation 10(7) of the TUPE Regulations provides that if there are "special circumstances which render it not reasonably practicable for an employer to perform a duty imposed on him . . . he shall take all such steps towards performing that duty as are reasonable practicable in the circumstances". The TUPE Regulations do not themselves contain any definition of "special circumstances" but guidance may be found by referring to the case law on "special circumstances" in relation to collective redundancies as set out above. As with the TUPE Regulations generally, the test must be applied to the individual circumstances of the case and the courts will usually take a purposive approach to the employment protection which the Regulations are designed to give.

23.7.5   Liabilities for Protective Award

Where protective awards are made in relation to employees of an insolvent employer, they will fall to be met as arrears of pay by the National Insurance Fund under Part XII of the Employment Rights Act 1996 and will not lie in the first instance against the insolvent employer nor are they a personal liability of the insolvency practitioner. By subrogation they rank as part of an employee's preferred claim and otherwise as an ordinary claim. The basic award for unfair dismissal is also treated in this way.

23.8   Miscellaneous Liabilities

We have looked at the employment law provisions that impact most on the liquidator's duty whilst he is in control of the company as employer. In addition to the claims for breach of contract, unfair dismissal, redundancy payment and claims for a protective award for failure to consult, there are other general duties which could have serious consequences for the company and to which the liquidator should therefore have regard.

23.8.1   Stigma Damages

The first concerns the implied contractual obligation of mutual trust and confidence between employer and employees. In the case *of Malik v Bank of Credit and Commerce International SA*,[26] the House of Lords recognised the importance of this term for senior employees. Mr Malik and a colleague were dismissed by the provisional liquidators of the BCCI by reason of redundancy. They sought damages for breach of the implied trust and confidence on the basis that the wide publicity regarding the alleged fraudulent practices of the BCCI had affected their ability to search for work in the employment market (even though they were not directly involved). The House of Lords upheld the claim although stated

---

[25] *Union of Shop Distributive and Allied Workers v Leancut Bacon Limited* [1981] I.R.L.R. 295

[26] [1997] I.R.L.R. 462.

that the employer's conduct in such cases must have been "without reason and proper cause". Because the implied duty of trust and confidence is widely founded upon in other claims (*e.g.*, where an employer's conduct is said to give rise to a constructive dismissal for the purposes of claiming unfair dismissal) the award of damages for breach of this term is likely to have a wide impact.

23.8.2 Negligent Misstatement

Another case of which liquidators should be aware is *Hagen v ICI Chemicals and Polymers Limited*[27] where employees brought claims for negligent misstatement regarding information they had been provided with about the pension arrangements, which were to apply after the TUPE transfer. This case confirms that the usual delictual duties apply and the liquidator will require to act in good faith when passing information to be given to employees to satisfy the consultation requirements. Employees must not be misled, so care should be taken not to exaggerate or misrepresent terms of conditions of employment or other implications which a decision by the liquidator will have for employees.

23.8.3 Reasonableness

The third general duty is one of overall "reasonableness". The liquidator should bear in mind that any term of the contract of employment must be exercised reasonably and not "capriciously" in any way. This is especially true of terms relating to fiscal payments like those that might operate as part of a bonus scheme. If one employee is treated differently from another, there may be a claim that the term in question has been exercised unreasonably. If it is sufficiently serious then the employee may resign and claim (constructive) unfair and wrongful dismissal. Differential treatment can also give rise to discrimination claims.

23.9   The National Insurance Fund

The Employment Rights Act 1996 lays down an additional framework for employment rights where an employer is insolvent. For the rights to apply, the employee must make an application to the Secretary of State in writing. The Secretary of State must be satisfied that the employee's employer has become insolvent and this includes where a winding-up order has been made, or resolution for voluntary winding up has been passed. It also applies where a voluntary arrangement has been proposed in the case of the company for the purposes of Part I of the Insolvency Act 1986. Similar provisions apply for limited liability partnerships.

The employee can only apply under the scheme if his employment has been terminated and he is owed, on a defined date, the categories of debt to which Part XII of the 1996 Act applies.

The Secretary of State will require the liquidator's co-operation in administering these payments. Section 187 provides that the Secretary of State shall not make a payment to the employee in respect of a debt until he has received a statement from the relevant officer "of the amount of

---

[27] [2002] I.R.L.R. 31.

that debt which appears to have been owed to the employee on the appropriate date and to remain unpaid". This will not be necessary in all cases, but the liquidator should respond to the Secretary of State with that statement on request.

The debts are set out in section 184(1) as follows:

(a) any arrears of pay in respect of one or more (but not more than eight) weeks;

(b) any amount which the employer is liable to pay the employee for the period of notice required by section 86(1) or (2) or for any failure of the employer to give the period of notice required by section 86 (1);

(c) any holiday pay:

   (i) in respect of a period or periods of holiday not exceeding six weeks in all; and

   (ii) to which the employee became entitled during the twelve month ending with the appropriate date;

(d) any basic award of compensation for unfair dismissal . . .;

(e) any reasonable sum by way of reimbursement of the whole or part of any fee or premium paid by an apprentice or articled clerk.

So far as notice is concerned, the provisions of section 86 are the minimum statutory period of notice required to be given to an employee on termination of employment. These are as follows:

23.10   What are arrears of pay?

Section 184(2) of the 1996 Act defines arrears of pay as follows:

Length of Service	Length of Notice
Less than two years	One week's notice
Two years, but less than twelve years	One week's notice for each year of continuous employment
Twelve years or more	Twelve weeks

(a) a guarantee payment;

(b) payments for time off prescribed by statute (including time off for trade union duties, time off for ante-natal care and other rights prescribed by Part VI of the Act);

(c) remuneration on suspension on medical grounds or on maternity grounds prescribed by the Act; and

(d) remuneration under a protective award (for failure to properly consult in connection with collective redundancies).

The appropriate date is laid down by section 185 as follows:

(a) in relation to arrears of pay (but not the protective award) and holiday pay — the date on which the employer became insolvent;

(b) in relation to a basic award of compensation for unfair dismissal and to the protective award, whichever is the later of the date of insolvency, the date of termination of employment and the date on which the award was made;

(c) in relation to any other date, whichever is later of the date of insolvency and the date of termination of employment.

All of the debts are subject to the statutory limit on a week's pay which, as at February 1, 2004, is £270. Any liabilities in excess of this (for example the protective award for failure to consult in respect of collective redundancies which will not have been capped at source) will remain with the company.

A person who does not receive his payment or receives less than that to which he believes he is entitled, having applied under section 182 of the Act, can present a claim to the Employment Tribunal.

23.11 Redundancy Payment Scheme

Eligibility for redundancy payments is dealt with in Part XI or the Employment Rights Act 1996. Section 166 provides as follows:

(1) where an employee claims that his employer is liable to pay to him an "employer's payment" and either:

(a) that the employee has taken all reasonable steps, other than legal proceedings, to recover the payment from the employer and the employer has refused or failed to pay it, or has paid part of it and has refused or failed to pay the balance; or

(b) that the employer is insolvent and the whole or part of the payment remains unpaid,

the employee may apply to the Secretary of State for a payment under this section.

Subsection (2) provides that an "employer's payment" can mean not only a statutory redundancy payment as prescribed by the Act, but also a redundancy payment which is liable to be made under a collective agreement with a trade union.

23.12 Change of Employer

In addition to the provisions of the TUPE Regulations, the Employment Rights Act 1996 expressly recognises that there may be a transfer between employers and preserves continuity of employment accordingly. The two periods of employment will be amalgamated and the change of employer will not itself break the continuity of the period of employment (section 218). This will apply not only where there is a transfer of an undertaking to a third party, but also where there is a transfer between associated employers.

23.12.1 *Why is this Important?*

If an employee wants to claim unfair dismissal then, in most cases, they must show continuous employment of one year. For redundancy payments, they must show continuous employment of two years (although years in employment below the age of 18 do not count for this purpose).

For all other purposes, the liquidator should be aware that the continuous employment will not necessarily be broken merely because the sale of a business results in employees being dismissed at different times and then re-engaged. There is a general presumption of continuity contained in section 210 of the 1996 Act, although this relates to whole weeks of employment. The problem arises where there is a full week which elapses between the employment with the old employer coming to an end and the commencement of the employment with a new employer. The courts have required to consider this in the context of a transfer of undertaking and what is meant by section 218(2)(a) "the period of employment of an employee in the trade or business or undertaking **at the time of the transfer**" (emphasis added). Such period will count as a period of employment with the transferee and the transfer will not break the continuity of the period of employment.

The courts have given a loose interpretation to this by holding that the words "at the time of the transfer" should not be construed as meaning a moment of time in the same way as it would be construed in the TUPE Regulations which consider whether an employee was employed "immediately before the transfer" (regulation 5(3) see above).

In *Macer v Abafast Limited*,[28] the Employment Appeal Tribunal in England and Wales found that the requisite continuous employment of (then) two years for claiming unfair dismissal was established in circumstances where:

- the liquidator terminated contracts of employment on December 31;
- a new company offered to purchase the assets and goodwill on January 18;
- the offer was accepted on February 19 with completion almost a year thereafter;
- the offer to employees to begin work with the new company was backdated to January 12, (the actual offer of employment being made on January 21).

Such gaps in time will not necessarily defeat the application of the statutory test for calculating continuity of employment and therefore no assumption should be made as to an employee not having sufficient continuity to bring a claim for unfair dismissal or a claim for redundancy payment.

The subsequent case of *Celtec Limited v Astley*[29] took a slightly different approach but did not disregard the approach followed in *Macer*. The test of continuity must be determined as a matter of fact.

---

[28] [1990] I.R.L.R. 137.
[29] [2001] I.R.L.R. 788.

CHAPTER 24

TAXATION ISSUES IN LIQUIDATION[1]

24.1 Direct Taxes

24.1.1 *Corporation Tax on Profits*

(1) Profits which arise in the winding up of a company are chargeable to Corporation Tax in the normal way. Assessments are made on the company and not on the liquidator.

(2) A company in liquidation is normally a close investment-holding company. This is because a company in liquidation exists for the purpose of winding up its affairs and distributing its assets to shareholders. Although during the winding up the company might continue to carry on the trade or business that it had carried on previously, it is unlikely that this will be other than incidental to its main purpose of winding up its affairs.

(3) A trading company does not necessarily cease to trade for tax purposes on the commencement of winding up, however, and each case must be considered on its own facts, to ensure that the company's tax affairs are correctly dealt with. It is fair to say that the Inland Revenue are likely to assume that trading has ceased on the commencement of the winding up, and evidence would have to be available to support a claim that the company in liquidation had continued to trade.

24.1.2 *Administrative Matters*

(1) The liquidator is under no statutory duty to advise the Inland Revenue of his appointment, but would normally do so as a matter of courtesy.

(2) The liquidator is the proper officer of a company in liquidation and so is responsible for preparing and submitting the corporation tax self assessment returns of the company in liquidation. The liquidator must sign the declaration on the corporation tax self assessment form that the return is correct and complete to the best of his knowledge and belief.

(3) Special rules allow liquidators to work out tax liabilities based on the previous year's tax rates, so that they can make self assessments earlier and settle the tax affairs of the company quickly.

(4) Corporation tax arising during the winding up of a company is treated as an expense of the liquidation.

---

[1] Prepared in conjunction with the Corporate Tax Group at MacRoberts

(5) The liquidator has no personal liability for the corporation tax of the company, although he should take care to retain sufficient funds to meet the corporation tax liabilities before making distributions. Liquidators will normally seek a clearance from the Inland Revenue that all tax liabilities have been dealt with before finalising the winding up. As a result of the introduction of corporation tax self assessment, however, the Inland Revenue may only be prepared to state that they do not intend to make any enquiries into the corporation tax self assessment returns which have been lodged.

24.1.3   *Preferential Claim for Tax*

(1) The preferential claim for assessed taxes such as corporation tax and income tax was abolished by IA 1986.
(2) Until September 15, 2003, there was a preferential claim for PAYE and deductions under the Construction Industry Sub-Contractors Scheme relating to the 12 month period ending on the "relevant date" set out in IA 1986, section 387. The relevant date depended on the type of winding up involved.
(3) The Enterprise Act 2002 abolished preferential claims for PAYE and Construction Industry Sub-Contractors Scheme, and are now ordinary claims in the liquidation.

24.1.4   *Pre-liquidation Corporation Tax Liabilities*

(1) The liquidator has a duty to agree and settle the corporation tax liabilities of the periods prior to commencement of the liquidation in the same way as other liabilities.
(2) The liquidator should normally liaise with existing tax advisors, and if possible, the pre-commencement returns should be signed by the directors.
(3) If there are no funds for unsecured creditors, the Inland Revenue may be prepared to agree a no/gain no/loss position for the pre-commencement periods without the need for submission of outstanding returns.

24.1.5   *Accounting Periods*

(1) An accounting period ends and a new one begins on the commencement of the winding up of a company. After that an accounting period ends only at:

   • the expiry of twelve months from its beginning, or
   • the completion of the winding up

   unless the company ceases to be in liquidation without being wound up, in which case the 12-month rule ceases to apply.
(2) For this purpose a winding up is to be taken to commence on the passing by the company of a resolution for the winding up of the company, or on the presentation of a winding-up petition if no such resolution has previously been passed and a winding-up

order is made on the petition, or on the doing of any other act for a like purpose in the case of a winding up otherwise than under the Insolvency Act 1986.

(3) The fact that an accounting period ceases means that capital losses incurred after the appointment of the liquidator cannot be set against post appointment capital gains. Capital losses in the pre-liquidation period can be carried forward and set against post liquidation gains.

24.1.6 Ownership of Assets

(1) For tax purposes, a company in liquidation retains legal ownership of its assets, but not beneficial ownership.

(2) This means that the company is not treated as disposing of its assets on the commencement of a liquidation.

(3) A company is not treated as leaving a capital gains tax group when it goes into liquidation (TCGA 1992, section 170(11)).

(4) When winding-up commences, a company loses its beneficial interest in its assets. This includes shares owned in other companies.[2]

(5) This means that where the provisions of the Corporation Tax Acts depend on such shareholdings, they can no longer be taken into account when the company owning the shares commences winding up.

(6) For example group income elections may be invalidated when the beneficial ownership of shares on which the election depends is forfeited as a result of winding up.

(7) The loss of beneficial ownership at the start of winding up also means that it is not possible to carry out a hive down of the company's assets to a subsidiary company after the commencement of liquidation.

(8) When a company is in liquidation it is the liquidator, not the company or its members, who has control of the assets of the company. This may also affect the application of other tax provisions.

24.1.7 Disposal of Assets by the Liquidator

(1) As explained above, the appointment of a liquidator does not mean that the company disposes of its assets for capital gains tax purposes.

(2) A charge to Corporation Tax on chargeable gains may arise if the liquidator disposes of assets of the company. This applies whether the disposal is by sale or on a distribution to shareholders.

(3) If the liquidator disposes of assets to the shareholders, the company is deemed to dispose of the assets and the shareholder is deemed to acquire the assets at market value.

---

[2] See *Ayerst v C and K (Construction) Ltd*, 50 T.C. 651

(4) The shareholders are also deemed to make a disposal or part disposal of their shares, the proceeds being the market value of the assets received by the shareholders.

(5) The fact that an accounting period ceases on the commencement of a winding up means that capital losses incurred after the appointment of the liquidator cannot be set against post appointment capital gains. Capital losses in the pre-liquidation period can be carried forward and set against post liquidation gains.

24.1.8   *Shareholders — Capital Gains Tax*

(1) The appointment of a liquidator does not give rise to the disposal of shares by the shareholders.

(2) A distribution by a company to its shareholders in the course of a winding up is not treated as an income distribution for tax purposes.

(3) On receipt of a capital distribution, the shareholders are treated as making a capital disposal of their shares, and if a number of capital distributions are made, there will be a series of part disposals.

(4) To establish the capital gains tax arising on each part disposal, the residual value of the shares would have to be ascertained. To avoid delays in agreeing the valuation of the residual value of shares in such cases, for unquoted companies, the Board of Inland Revenue have authorised Inspectors to accept any valuation of the residual value of the shares, provided it is reasonable, and provided that the liquidation is expected to be completed within two years (Inland Revenue Statement of Practice D8).

(5) If the liquidator disposes of assets to the shareholders, then there is:

- a disposal of the assets at market value by the company;
- an acquisition of the assets at market value by the shareholders; and
- a part disposal by the shareholders of their shares.

(6) In an insolvent liquidation, shareholders are likely to incur a capital loss, and a negligible value claim may be possible in advance of the final winding up of the company (see below).

24.1.9   *Capital Gains Tax Treatment of Shareholders — Business Assets Taper Relief*

(1) Where distributions are made in the course of a solvent liquidation, shareholders who are individuals will be subject to capital gains tax on the amount received less the base cost of the shares. If the company was a qualifying trading company, business assets taper relief may be available to reduce the rate of capital gains tax payable.

(2) The availability of business assets status for shares is not determined by whether or not a company is in liquidation and being formally wound up. The important factor is whether the company

has ceased trading. If the company ceases to trade before the distribution, it will cease to be a qualifying company for business assets taper relief purposes and a time apportionment calculation may be necessary to determine the amount of business assets taper relief which will be available.

(3) Where a liquidator is appointed to wind up a company which at the time was not carrying on a business of holding investments, the company will not be regarded as commencing such a business for the purposes of business assets taper relief by reason of a temporary investment which the liquidator makes pending a distribution to creditors and/or shareholders of funds arising in the winding up.

(4) As mentioned above, if capital gains tax assets are disposed of to shareholders, this may also give rise to corporation tax on chargeable gains for the company.

24.1.10 *Capital Distribution without a Winding-up — Extra Statutory Concession C16*

(1) A company may wish to achieve the capital treatment of distributions to shareholders without the costs of a formal winding up.

(2) Provided that various conditions are met, the Inland Revenue is prepared, under Extra Statutory Concession C 16, to accept distributions made to shareholders as if they had been made in the course of a formal winding up.

(3) In that case, the shareholders would be subject to capital gains tax on the distribution received.

(4) The company has to satisfy the Inspector that:

- it does not intend to trade or carry on business in future;
- it intends to collect its debts, pay off its creditors in full and distribute any balance of its assets to its shareholders (or has already done so); and
- it intends to seek or accept striking off and dissolution.

(5) The company and its shareholders have to agree that:

- they will supply such information as is necessary to determine, and will pay, any Corporation Tax liability on income or capital gains; and
- the shareholders will pay any Capital Gains Tax liability (or Corporation Tax in the case of a corporate shareholder) in respect of any amount distributed to them in cash or otherwise as if the distributions had been made during a winding up.

24.1.11 *Capital Gains Tax Treatment of Shareholders in Insolvent Liquidation*

(1) The commencement of the formal insolvency of a company does not give rise to a disposal by shareholders of their shares in the company. Instead, there is a disposal of the shares when the company is finally wound up.

(2) In practice, if the company is insolvent, shareholders will be able to claim a capital loss before the company is finally wound up on the grounds that the shares have become of negligible value (TCGA 1992, section 24(2)).

(3) In certain circumstances, shareholders may also be able to make a claim to set off the capital loss against income. The company has to be a qualifying trading company and the shareholder must have subscribed for the shares in order for the relief to be available.

24.1.12   Shareholders — Inheritance Tax Business Property Relief

(1) Shares in or securities of a company do not qualify for inheritance business property relief if, at the time of the transfer:

  (a) a winding-up order has been made, or
  (b) the company has passed a resolution for voluntary winding up, or
  (c) the company is otherwise in process of liquidation1.

(2) However, if the business is to continue and:

  (a) the purpose of the winding up or liquidation was to enter into a reconstruction or amalgamation, or
  (b) a reconstruction or amalgamation takes place within a year of the transfer, the shares or securities will still qualify as relevant business property, and business property relief will still be available.

24.1.13   Enterprise Investment Scheme

The liquidation of a company does not of itself cause the whole of any EIS relief to be withdrawn. But if the investor receives value in respect of his ordinary shares in the liquidation, there is a withdrawal of relief by reference to the amount of that value if it is received for shares issued in his period of restriction.

24.1.14   Corporate Shareholders — Substantial Shareholdings Exemption

(1) There is an exemption from corporation tax on chargeable gains for the disposal by a trading company of a substantial shareholding in another trading company which has been held for a qualifying period.

(2) Although the assets of a company in liquidation vest in the liquidator, special provisions in the substantial shareholdings legislation provide that where the investing company or a member of its group is in liquidation, the relevant company is treated as being the beneficial owner of shares held by it for the purposes of establishing whether the substantial shareholding requirement is met.

24.1.15 Loan Relationship Rules

(1) Where a company has borrowed money from a connected company, special rules mean that the lender cannot claim a corporation tax deduction for the amount of any loan. The special rules for loan relationships between connected companies are overridden when a company goes into liquidation.

(2) The special rules only cease to apply while the company is in liquidation.

24.1.16 Stamp Duty and Stamp Duty Land Tax

(1) There is no stamp duty on the transfer of shares owned by a company to its shareholders in the course of a winding up.

(2) Stamp duty land tax (SDLT) replaced stamp duty on land and buildings in the UK from December 1, 2003.

(3) No SDLT is payable on the transfer of land and buildings to shareholders in the course of the winding up of a company, except where the assets have previously been transferred between group companies and the clawback rules apply.

24.2 Value Added Tax ("VAT")

24.2.1 General

(1) VAT causes many difficulties in relation to liquidation due to the lack of a coherent framework in the VAT legislation.

(2) Guidance can be obtained from VAT Leaflet No 700/56/02 Vat: Insolvency, and reference should also be made to the Society of Practitioners of Insolvency Technical Release 2: VAT in Insolvency.

24.2.2 Notification of the Appointment of a Liquidator

(1) A liquidator must notify Customs and Excise of his appointment within 21 days of commencing to act. In most cases the liquidator should use Form VAT 769.

(2) The Form 769 is not used where a liquidator is appointed after an administrative receiver. In that case, the liquidator should notify Customs.[3]

(3) The Form 769 is also not required for the appointment of a provisional liquidator. In that case, the appointment should be notified to the VAT Business Advice centre which deals with the insolvent company.

---

[3] Currently by letter to HM Customs and Excise, Insolvency Branch, Legal Recovery Unit, Queens Dock, Liverpool, L74 4AA.

24.2.3   *VAT registration and returns*

(1) The business of a company does not cease automatically on the commencement of liquidation, and it is likely that the company will continue to make taxable supplies during the winding-up period. When the company ceases to make taxable supplies, deregistration may be necessary (see below).

(2) The VAT registration of the company is not normally affected by the appointment of a liquidator.

(3) Regulation 30 of the VAT Regulations 1995 applies where a person becomes incapacitated (which in the case of a company includes the appointment of a liquidator) and control of his assets passes to inter alia a receiver or liquidator. Where the Commissioners so require, the liquidator or receiver has to comply with the requirements of the VAT Regulations in relation to those assets over which he has control.

(4) Assuming that the Commissioners have made a requirement under regulation 30, this means that the liquidator must deal with all VAT administrative requirements in relation to the period after the commencement of the winding up of the company, including completion of VAT returns and accounting to Customs and Excise for any VAT due.

(5) Regulation 25 of the VAT Regulations provides that where a requirement under regulation 30 has been made, the VAT accounting period of the company ceases on the day before the appointment of the liquidator, and a VAT return has to be submitted in respect of that period within 30 days.

(6) In some cases, a receiver appointed before the liquidator may continue to make the company's VAT returns notwithstanding the appointment of the liquidator, if the receiver has control of the assets.

(7) It should be noted that Customs have the power under regulation 9 of the VAT Regulations 1995 to treat as a taxable person any person carrying on the business of a taxable person who has become incapacitated. In practice Customs do not normally invoke this provision, and continue to treat the company as being the registered person, so that returns are submitted under the company's VAT registration number.

(8) In some cases, where both a receiver and a liquidator are in place, Customs may use their powers under regulation 9 to treat the receiver as a separate taxable person and to require him to make returns.

24.2.4   *Pre-liquidation Returns*

(1) If any VAT returns are outstanding for the period before the appointment of the liquidator, Customs and Excise may issue an assessment to recover the VAT due. If the liquidator submits an adequate VAT return for the period, however, Customs are likely to accept that return.

(2) The liquidator should submit unsigned returns bearing the legend "Completed from the books and records of the company".

24.2.5 *Preferential Claim for VAT*

(1) Until September 15, 2003, there was a preferential claim for VAT due in relation to the six month period prior to the winding up.
(2) The Enterprise Act 2002 has abolished all preferential claims in relation to VAT.

24.2.6 *Disposal of Assets*

(1) The liquidator should ensure that VAT is properly charged on the disposal of individual assets of the business, including land and buildings where the election to waive exemption has been exercised.
(2) Where the business of the company is sold as a going concern, however, the disposal will not attract VAT. This is because transactions that satisfy the requirements for a transfer of a going concern (as set out in section 49 of the VATA 1994 and Value Added Tax (Special Provisions) Order 1995 (SI 1995/1268), are outside the scope of VAT and are treated as neither the supply of goods or a supply of services.
(3) Careful consideration should be given as to whether the business being sold is a going concern, and advice may be necessary.

24.2.7 *Election to Waive Exemption*

(1) If the company in liquidation has elected to waive exemption from VAT over any land or buildings the election binds a liquidator appointed to carry on the business. This means that if the liquidator sells the land or buildings, he must charge VAT on that sale and account for the VAT to HM Customs & Excise.
(2) If the liquidator is not certain whether the company in liquidation has elected to waive exemption over any property, it is usual to approach the company's local VAT office and request confirmation as to whether the option to tax applies. However, the responses from HM Customs & Excise are not always conclusive and often just confirm whether or not HM Customs & Excise have a record of any election being in place over any particular property. It is hoped that responses will become more conclusive in future years, following the establishment of a national central unit in Glasgow administering all elections to waive exemptions over all property across the UK.
(3) A liquidator can elect to waive exemption in respect of any land or buildings over which he has control (subject to the usual requirements regarding whether permission to elect to waive the exemption from VAT is required for HM Customs & Excise).

24.2.8 *Repayments and Set-off*

(1) As a general rule under sections 81(3) and (3A) of the VATA 1994, any amounts due from HM Customs & Excise to a VAT registered trader are set off against sums due from that person to HM Customs & Excise. Section 81(4A) of the VATA 1994 states that this does not apply where an "insolvency procedure" is underway, and the sum due from HM Customs becomes due after the relevant date, and the sum due to HM Customs before the relevant date. An "insolvency procedure" includes a solvent liquidation.

(2) If there is any repayment to be made, a claim for this should be submitted in the normal way on the VAT return. The repayment will be made, normally within 30 days, if there are no problems with the VAT 769 (Customs and Excise form for Notification of Insolvency Details) and no delay in the notification of the appointment of an insolvency office holder. The repayment will be made to the VAT registered business, care of the office holder. However, under VATA 1994, section 81, where there is interest ("amount due by way of credit") to be repaid which becomes due after the relevant date but the liability to pay the debt or the period which the debt relates to was before the relevant date that cannot be set off against that debt.

24.2.9 *Cash Accounting Scheme*

(1) The Cash Accounting Scheme allows a company to account for VAT on the basis of payments made and received rather than by reference to the invoices issued or received. A number of criteria must be met before the scheme can be implemented. It is open to businesses whose taxable supplies in the period of any one year do not exceed £600,000.

(2) If a company operating the cash accounting scheme becomes insolvent, then the liquidator must make a cash accounting scheme adjustment, *i.e.* must account for VAT on all supplies made and received up to the date of the insolvency which has not previously been accounted for.

(3) Any VAT due under this adjustment should be accounted for on a pre-insolvency return.

(4) By concession, the liquidator may continue to use the cash accounting scheme after the commencement of liquidation if the company was entitled to use the scheme before the commencement of the liquidation.

24.2.10 *Deregistration for VAT*

(1) As explained above, a company does not cease to make taxable supplies on the commencement of winding up, and so is not automatically liable to deregister.

(2) Indeed the company may continue to make taxable supplies after it ceases carrying on business, as anything done in connection with the termination of a business is treated as being done in the furtherance of the business, and so may attract VAT.

(3) If the company does cease to make taxable supplies, or to have the intention of making taxable supplies, it must notify Customs and Excise within 30 days and its registration will be cancelled (as will any separate registration of a liquidator or receiver).

(4) There is also a discretionary deregistration procedure, whereby the registration will be cancelled if Customs and Excise are satisfied that the value of taxable supplies in the next twelve months will not exceed £50,000.

(5) In practice, Customs & Excise generally issue a de-registration questionnaire at the same time as they submit their claim in the insolvency. The form will be followed up by a warning, after five weeks, that if there is no response in seven days, the company will be deregistered without further warning on the 8th day. If deregistration at this time is inappropriate, then Customs and Excise should be informed without delay. The process will then be suspended until it is agreed that deregistration is appropriate.

(6) Once it has been decided that deregistration would be appropriate, then a final VAT return (a Form VAT193) will be issued for the period from the last accounting day to the day before deregistration. VAT must be accounted for on goods in stock and assets on which input tax had previously been reclaimed. No tax is payable if the amount of VAT payable does not exceed £1,000.

24.2.11   *VAT Groups and Deregistration*

If the insolvent company is a member of a VAT group, further issues arise. If the representative member of the group is deregistered, all members of the VAT group are automatically de-registered, and each solvent member of the group which continues to trade is automatically re-registered for VAT. A request can be made for group treatment to continue — but this needs to be requested as soon as possible to ensure that members of the group are not re-registered with individual registrations. Any such request should be made by letter to the Legal Recovery Unit at HM Customs & Excise.

24.2.12   *Accounting for and Reclaiming VAT Post Deregistration*

(1) If there is any VAT to be accounted for or reclaimed after deregistration, then Forms VAT 833 and VAT 426 should be used (VAT 833 for accounting for output tax and VAT 426 for reclaiming input tax) and should be submitted to the Legal Recovery Unit.

(2) There is guidance in Public Notice 700/15 on what can and cannot normally be claimed . Claims can generally be made for bad debt relief, and for input tax on any realisation fees, on services supplied after deregistration but relating to business carried on before deregistration, on agents fees, and on any goods or services supplied and invoiced before deregistration but not yet claimed on a VAT return.

CHAPTER 25

DATA PROTECTION AND DATA DISPOSAL ISSUES[1]

25.1 Introduction

(1) It has long been recognised that information is an asset. Recently (and unfortunately), for some companies in the UK, information has been virtually their only asset. That, indeed, could be said to be a defining characteristic of soft companies trading exclusively over the web.

(2) Information assets can take many forms from employee know how to customer lists. An insolvency practitioner's interest will be in the latter as it is customer lists and databases that are capable of being transferred for profit.

(3) However, in addition to traditional legal rules protecting information (such as the law of confidential information) a liquidator must also acquaint himself with data protection rules which operate to restrict the manner in which information about an individual can be used and, in particular, its onward disclosure.

25.2 General Principles of Data Protection

(1) Data protection rules are intended to provide balance between, on the one hand, the interests of business (public or private) in using information relating to individuals to achieve its legitimate aims and, on the other, the interests of the individual in ensuring that his privacy is not unduly intruded upon.

(2) The Data Protection Act 1998 ("the Act") is the legislation currently in force in the UK. That Act implements the Data Protection Directive[2] and repealed the previous legislation (the Data Protection Act 1984) in its entirety.

(3) The main features of the legislation are that:

- A wider category of information is covered by the Act (including some paper records);
- Individuals have rights;
- Data controllers have obligations;
- These rights and obligations only extend to "personal data"; and
- There is an enforcement regime.

---

[1] Prepared in conjunction with the Technology, Media and Communications Group at MacRoberts

[2] Directive 95/46/EC of the European Parliament and of the Council of October 24, 1995 on the protection of individuals with regard to the processing of personal data and on the free movement of such data.

25.3 Information Covered by the Act

(1) There is a fairly complex definition of the information to which the Act applies. Basically it extends to information:

- stored on computer;
- recorded with the intention that it be stored on computer;
- forming part of a relevant filing system;
- recorded with the intention that it form part of a relevant filing system; or
- contained in an accessible record

which relates to an individual to the extent that it could be said to be biographical of that individual to a significant degree and has that individual as its focus (**personal data**[3]).

(2) Accordingly, whether information is held on computer or in paper form, it must have the requisite degree of proximity to the individual to whom it refers in order for it to be personal data regulated by the Act.

(3) A **relevant filing system** is the Act's definition of the particular paper records intended to be regulated. Not all paper records are caught. Recent case law has indicated that only highly structured files are caught.[4]

(4) An **accessible record** is one which does not possess the high level of structure required to be a relevant filing system but which is held by a public authority and contains certain health, social work and education records.

(5) The Freedom of Information Act 2000 will, in due course, amend the definition of data to include recorded information, not already covered within the definition of personal data, which is held by a public authority.[5]

(6) The importance of these points is that a liquidator need only concern himself with data protection rules if the information he is seeking to sell or otherwise dispose of constitutes personal data.

(7) If personal data does exist then it is impossible to transact with the asset comprised of that personal data without having regard to the terms of the Act. All "**processing**" of personal data is regulated and this term is incredibly wide spanning obtaining, holding (and doing nothing else), perusing, consulting, deleting and destroying).[6] Unless an exemption applies all processing must be done in compliance with the Act.[7]

---

[3] Defined at s.1(1) of the 1998 Act. See also paras 21 to 31 of *Durant v Financial Services Authority* [2003] EWCA Civ 1746, *per* Lord Justice Auld.

[4] *Durant v Financial Services Authority* [2003] EWCA Civ 1746, para.50, *per* Lord Justice Auld.

[5] Section 68(2) of the Freedom of Information Act 2000.

[6] Section 1(a) of the Data Protection Act 1998.

[7] Various exemptions exist from some or all of the provisions of the 1998 Act. The main exemptions can be found in Pt IV and Sch.7 of the 1998 Act.

25.4   Individual's Rights

(1) Individuals have a number of rights under this Act. In order to exercise these rights the person must be alive. An individual can exercise rights through an agent. Legal entities (such as limited companies) are not "**data subjects**" under the Act and so do not benefit from these rights.

(2) The main rights are:

- a right of access to personal data[8];
- a right to prevent processing likely to cause unwarranted damage or distress[9];
- a right to seek compensation for damage arising from a breach of the Act[10];
- a right to require cessation of direct marketing[11];
- a right to seek an order requiring rectification, blocking, erasure or destruction of inaccurate data[12]; and
- a right to be told the logic of any decision taken about himself on an automated basis.[13]

25.5   Is a Liquidator a Data Controller?

(1) A **data controller** is the legal entity which determines the purposes for which and the manner in which personal data are processed.[14] While a company may have delegated that responsibility to an individual manager, it is the company that retains the legal status of data controller. It is the data controller that is fixed with the vast majority of legal obligations created by the Act.

(2) From a liquidator's perspective, the company recently put into liquidation is likely to have been the data controller in respect of personal data that the company has in its possession (for instance, employee information and any customer or supplier databases) as at the date of his appointment.

(3) It is possible that the company in liquidation was not a data controller in respect of all the personal data that it held. This could possibly be the case where the information is held by the company on behalf of and on the instructions of a third party. Where this occurs the company would be a **data processor** and its responsibilities in relation to that information should be (but rarely are) set out in some form of written agreement. A liquidator's ability to transact with information of that nature is likely to be limited.

(4) The question of whether a liquidator is a data controller in respect of the personal data held by the company is a difficult one. To an extent it transcends questions of ownership of the data

---

[8] Section 7 of the 1998 Act.
[9] Section 10 of the 1998 Act.
[10] Section 13 of the 1998 Act.
[11] Section 11 of the 1998 Act.
[12] Section 14 of the 1998 Act.
[13] Section 12 of the 1998 Act.
[14] Section 1(1) of the 1998 Act.

and whether a liquidator stands as principal in respect of that data or as agent. Rather, the issue is likely to be determined by reference to the degree of control exercised by the liquidator over the personal data in question.[15]

(5) The fundamental point is that, to be a data controller, you must exercise control over the purposes for which and the manner in which personal data are processed. Upon entering into liquidation (with the possible exception of a scenario where the company in liquidation continues to trade) it is almost certainly the case that a company ceases to exercise the requisite degree of control. Accordingly, a company may be the owner of personal data but not the data controller in respect thereof.

(6) Whilst a liquidator may act as agent for the company in liquidation it is (notwithstanding that a liquidator is subject to some of the same rules as a normal agent[16]) not a classic agent/principal relationship. Rather, it is a quasi-agency relationship in which the liquidator is, by statute, entitled to transact in assets belonging to the company. Of particular importance is the fact that the former management of the company exercises no control over the liquidator who has a wide discretion (within the boundaries of the law and the terms of his appointment) to act in such manner as he sees fit.

(7) For example, if a customer list (consisting of information amounting to personal data) exists as an asset then it is the liquidator who decides whether this is to be sold and, if so, to whom and for how much. If a third party is interested in purchasing assets of the company in relation to which a TUPE issue may arise then it is the liquidator that will decide whether or not to disclose employment records and, if so, to whom and to what extent. The ability of the company to exert influence in these areas has disappeared.

(8) Accordingly, even though the company remains the owner of the various assets of the company (the liquidator merely transacts with these on the company's behalf) it is the liquidator that is likely to exercise that degree of control over the purposes for which and the manner in which personal data forming part of those assets are processed which is necessary to achieve the status of data controller under the Act.

(9) It is possible that the company remains a data controller in respect of the personal data that it holds either in common with the liquidator or jointly. Joint data controllers decide the purposes and manner of processing equally together. Data controllers in common share the same pool of information but make decisions about its processing independently of each other. However, the main point to make here is that the liquidator may, having conducted an initial risk analysis, wish to transact with

---

[15] Recent correspondence with the Office of the Information Commissioner supports this analysis.

[16] For instance, the obligation not to make a secret profit, to avoid conflicts of interest and to exercise a high standard of skill and care.

assets comprised of personal data on the basis that he is the data controller fixed with the obligations under the Act.

(10) The Information Commissioner (in his previous guise as the Data Protection Registrar) issued Guidance on Registration and Compliance for Insolvency Practitioners in England and Wales under the Data Protection Act 1984.[17] Whilst that legislation has been repealed, the analysis contained in that guidance note is still of assistance to practitioners north and south of the border in assessing whether or not an insolvency practitioner is a Data Controller. For instance, at paragraph 7.4.2 the Data Protection Registrar (as she was then) stated that:

> "In circumstances where the business is carried on or personal data is used or processed after the appointment of a liquidator, it will be a question of fact as to whether his control has been exercised on behalf of the company (in which case the company will be the data user) or on his own behalf, (in which case the liquidator must register separately as a data user)."

(11) That analysis probably still holds true today, however, it is possible that too much emphasis is put on the existence or otherwise of a quasi-agency relationship and too little on the actual level of control exercised by the company and by the liquidator post-appointment.

(12) A Data Controller's obligations are many. The main obligations are set out in Schedule 1 to the Act and are expressed as 8 Principles. These are:

1. personal data shall be processed fairly and lawfully;
2. personal data shall be obtained for one or more lawful purposes and shall not be further processed in any manner incompatible with that purpose or those purposes;
3. personal data shall be adequate relevant and not excessive in relation to those purposes;
4. personal data shall be accurate and, where necessary, kept up to date;
5. personal data shall not be kept for longer than is necessary for those specified purposes;
6. personal data shall be processed in accordance with data subject's rights;
7. appropriate technical and organisational measures must be taken to protect against the unauthorised or unlawful processing of personal data; and
8. personal data should not be transferred to a country outwith the EEA unless that country has laws in place which ensure an adequate level of protection.

(13) If the liquidator is a data controller then he will become responsible for ensuring that these principles are complied with.

---

[17] Guidance Note 26, March 1996.

incorporate standard terms approved by the European Commission into the contract of sale.[24]

(3) Accordingly, if sales of information assets incorporating personal data to a third party located outwith the EEA are contemplated the liquidator may decide to seek advice before concluding the sale or transferring the data.

25.7 Penalties for Non-compliance

Many of the issues set out above are evidence of a very onerous and bureaucratic piece of legislation ill-suited to the role of the liquidator. While it is hoped that the Information Commissioner may clarify some of these issues over time it is unlikely that he will do so without a degree of lobbying by the industry itself. In the meantime, the following arise as issues associated with breaches of the 1998 Act:

25.7.1 Complaint by an Individual

(1) An individual can complain to the Information Commissioner in the event that a liquidator has breached the 1998 Act. Typically, the Information Commissioner is likely to treat a complaint as a request for an assessment of the processing undertaken by the data controller involved. The nature and extent of such an assessment is largely at the discretion of the Information Commissioner.

(2) An individual who can establish that that have sustained damage as a result of a breach of the provisions of the 1998 Act can seek compensation in the courts.

25.7.2 Action by the Information Commissioner

The Information Commissioner can initiate investigations on his own account but, more often, does so in response to complaints. The Commissioner's two main tools of enforcement are the **Information Notice** and the **Enforcement Notice**.

25.7.3 Information Notice

The Commissioner can require a data controller to provide such information as it reasonably requires to ascertain whether processing has been undertaken in compliance with the 1998 Act.

25.7.4 Enforcement Notice

The Commissioner can require that a data controller stop processing in an infringing manner. Breach of an Enforcement Notice is a criminal offence.

---

[24] Standard Clauses are, by virtue of Commission Decisions 2001/497/EC and 2002/16/EC, available for transfers to either a Data Controller or a Data Processor outwith the EEA. The Standard Clauses can be accessed at: *http://www.europa.eu.int/comm/internal_market/privacy/modelcontracts_en.htm*

25.7.5   Liquidator's Immunity

It is, of course, a well-established principle that, in the absence of negligence, a liquidator does not attract personal liability for the obligations of the company.[25] Other exemptions from liability also exist, however, it has yet to be seen whether these principles would necessarily extend to liabilities or prosecutions arising from breaches of the 1998 Act. It may be relevant that if a liquidator is a data controller then these obligations are his own and not those of the company at all.

25.8   Subject Access Requests

(1) If the liquidator is data controller in respect of the personal data held by the company at the point he was appointed then it will fall to the liquidator to respond to access requests made from that point onwards, either as agent of the company or on his own account as data controller.

(2) Recent case law has had the effect of restricting the right of access in the UK. The court in *Durant v Financial Services Authority*[26] indicated that the right of access is restricted to personal data, that is, information which:

- is biographical of the individual making the request to a significant degree;
- has the individual making the request as its focus;
- has a sufficient degree of proximity to the person making the access request; and
- affects that individuals informational privacy in some way.[27]

(3) In relation to information held on paper files there is an additional test (which may logically be conducted before the above analysis) whereby the paper files in which the information is contained must amount to a relevant filing system.[28]

(4) While this decision will have the effect of reducing the administrative burden on all data controllers a liquidator should still be prepared to follow the statutory process in response to properly made access requests.

(5) Accordingly, where a request is made in writing (or email) and is accompanied by the statutory fee (where this has been requested) then a liquidator should:

---

[25] Palmer's Company Insolvency in Scotland, para.496.

[26] *infra* No. 2

[27] This is not a very helpful statement. It is not information that affects privacy but what is done with that information; this would mean that the use made of data (or the processing purposes) would be relevant to defining what personal data actually is. That would appear to be unworkable. Notwithstanding this, the Information *Commissioner's* Guidance following the *Durant* case goes further and suggests that the effect on privacy must be an "adverse" effect in order for data to be persona data. There does not seem to be any basis for this and this issue is likely to develop further.

[28] *infra* No. 3

(a) confirm whether or not that person's personal data is being processed by the liquidator or by any person on that Data Controller's behalf;

(b) If so, to give a *description* of:

(i) what that personal data is;

(ii) what it is being used for; and

(iii) the people, or type of people to whom that personal data may be disclosed.

(c) To provide a communication in one permanent form or another of:

(i) the information that constitutes that personal data:

(ii) any information available to the liquidator as to the source of that personal data:

(6) Where a data subject makes an access request for any one of the pieces of information set out in (5) above then that is to be regarded as a request for all of that information.

(7) This response should be made promptly and, in any event within 40 days of receipt. To provide a further level of complexity, there are detailed rules to be followed in situations where responding to an access request would involve disclosing information about a third party.

25.9 Conclusion

(1) At the time of writing, the Office of the Information Commissioner has confirmed that, in responding to requests for assessment which involve liquidators, it has previously, in the particular circumstances of the case in question, come to the view that a liquidator is a data controller. However, this question has not yet come before the courts and it may be that a different conclusion could be reached at that time.

(2) Similarly, the question of what personal data actually is and the extent of the right of access have only recently been adjudicated on and *Durant* in particular may be appealed or distinguished in the future.

(3) What is clear is that data protection has now become an issue of importance for all insolvency practitioners and advice should be taken at appropriate times.

CHAPTER 26

PENSION SCHEMES OF COMPANIES IN LIQUIDATION AND THEIR TRUSTEES[1]

26.1 Pension Schemes of Insolvent Companies

(1) A company in liquidation may have arrangements in place for providing pensions in retirement for its directors and employees. Such arrangements can take a variety of forms ranging from contractual promises to pre-funded retirement benefits schemes established under trust. They can be Revenue approved or unapproved. The most typical pension arrangements an insolvency practitioner is likely to encounter will involve the company contributing to its employees' personal pension scheme or to an occupational pension scheme in which the company acts as the main sponsoring employer or a participating employer.

(2) Benefits provided via pension arrangements are usually categorised as money purchase (defined contribution) or salary related (defined benefit). In a money purchase arrangement the recipient's pension will be calculated by reference to the value of his own fund built up from his own and his employer's contributions together with investment growth. In a salary related arrangement the recipient's pension will be calculated by reference to a formula (*e.g.* a percentage of final pensionable salary based on pensionable service or an accumulation of percentages of career average salaries). The critical difference is in the nature of the promise underlying the arrangement. In money purchase schemes the employer, in financial terms, usually promises nothing beyond contributing at a certain percentage level of salary. In salary related schemes the employer guarantees the scheme will deliver a pension based on the formula and acts as financial underwriter of these benefits. This requires the employer to pre-fund the scheme and to ascertain the contribution level by reference to actuarial funding assumptions. Depending on how these assumptions (including investment growth and income assumptions) work out in practice, a scheme can vary from being fully funded to being over-funded (surplus) or under-funded (deficit).

Hybrid schemes are ones which provide both money purchase and salary related benefits.

Personal pension schemes invariably provide money purchase benefits but occupational pension schemes can be designed to provide either money purchase or salary related benefits. Some

---

[1] Prepared in conjunction with the Pensions and Employee Benefits Group at MacRoberts.

occupational pension schemes provide both types of benefits and there are a variety of hybrid arrangements. It is crucial that the insolvent company's pension arrangements are properly reviewed to determine what type of arrangement one is dealing with.

Although death in service benefits can be calculated by reference to a formula linked to salary, this does not, of itself, create a salary related scheme. Employers often provide lump sum death in service benefits for employees either as a stand-alone benefit or in tandem with a pension scheme.

(3) In the context of liquidations, money purchase schemes are relatively straightforward for insolvency practitioners to deal with: although for occupational money purchase schemes there may be surplus funds that could be made available to creditors. The principal issues are likely to relate to payment of contributions and expenses. Conversely, salary related schemes and hybrid schemes providing salary related benefits involve additional considerations including whether there is a surplus that could be made available to creditors? Due to the substantial regulation of salary related schemes, considerable hurdles have to be surmounted before surplus can be refunded [s.76 of the Pensions Act 1995]. However, if they are surmountable an insolvency practitioner will normally want to recover the surplus for the creditors.

(4) Any unpaid employer contributions to a company's occupational pension scheme will create a debt due by the company to the trustees [sections 59 and 88 of the Pensions Act 1995] and may involve notifications to members and the Occupational Pensions Regulatory Authority (OPRA) in addition to possible fines against the employer. Deficits on a winding up of salary related occupational pension schemes create debts due from the participating employers [section 75 of the Pensions Act 1995]. It is conceivable that there may also be claims against the employer under indemnity provisions in governing trust documentation for breaches of trust. All these will result in the trustees of a trust based scheme ranking as ordinary creditors. Pursuant to section 386 and Schedule 6 of Insolvency Act 1986 up to four months employees' contributions, deducted by the employer but not paid to the trustees of an occupational pension scheme, and up to 12 months of certain employer's contributions to contracted-out schemes will rank as preferential debts. An insolvency practitioner may be asked to produce a statement or certificate to enable unpaid employer and employee contributions to an occupational or personal pension scheme to be recovered from the National Insurance Fund [sections 124 and 125 of the Pension Schemes Act 1993] and may be asked to co-operate with the trustees of an occupational pension scheme to assist them in applying for compensation from the Pensions Compensation Board where there has been a reduction in the value of a scheme's assets and there are reasonable grounds for attributing this to dishonesty (including an intention to defraud) [sections 81 to 86 of the Pensions Act 1995].

(5) The Pensions Bill 2004, once enacted, will impact on the pension schemes of companies in liquidation and the duties of an insolvency practitioner in relation to them. Under the Bill the functions of OPRA are to be transferred to a new Pensions Regulator and the Board of the Pension Protection Fund will be established. The Board will administer a Pension Protection Fund and a Fraud Compensation Fund. The Pension Protection Fund is designed to enhance the protection afforded to members of under-funded salary related schemes by providing them with compensation where the sponsoring employer becomes insolvent. The Fraud Compensation Fund will assume the functions of the Pensions Compensation Board and will be relevant to both money purchase and salary related schemes where the value of a scheme's assets has been diminished due to an act or omission constituting a criminal offence and the scheme employer is insolvent.

(6) The principal statutory duties of an insolvency practitioner in respect of pension schemes of companies in liquidation are in relation to (i) the independent trustee requirements under the Pensions Act 1995 [see paragraphs 26.2 to 26.8] and (ii), once the Pensions Bill 2004 is enacted, certain duties connected with the role of the Board of the Pension Protection Fund [see paragraph 26.9].

26.2 Insolvency Practitioners and the Requirement for an Independent Trustee

(1) Where an insolvency practitioner is appointed to act in relation to a company that is a participating employer in its own or a group's pension scheme, the insolvency practitioner must ensure there is an independent trustee in place.

(2) The independent trustee requirements are contained in sections 22 to 26 of the Pensions Act 1995 and are relevant where section 22 applies to a pension scheme. Section 22 will apply if a person begins to act as an insolvency practitioner in relation to a company which is an employer in relation to a trust scheme [section 22(1)(a) of the Pensions Act 1995].

(3) A trust scheme is an occupational pension scheme established under trust: [section 124(1) of the Pensions Act 1995]. Certain schemes are exempted (see 26.3 below). An occupational pension scheme does not include a personal pension scheme and one would normally identify a trust scheme by the existence of a trust deed.

(4) Section 22 can apply even where a company has an old frozen or paid-up pension scheme in respect of former employees that has never been wound up. References to employer include the person who last employed persons in the description or category of employment to which the scheme in question relates [Regulation 6 of the Occupational Pension Schemes (Independent Trustee) Regulations 1997].

(5) The independent trustee requirements which flow from the insolvency practitioner beginning to act in relation to a company will

only cease to apply if another person is substituted as scheme employer for the company or the insolvency practitioner stops acting as such in relation to the company [section 22(2) of the Pensions Act 1995].

26.3 Exemptions from Independent Trustee Requirements and their Effect

(1) By reason of regulation 5 of the Occupational Pension Schemes (Independent Trustee) Regulations 1997 certain types of trust scheme are exempt from the independent trustee requirements. These comprise:

(a) a scheme in which each of the members is a trustee;
(b) a money purchase scheme (including one which has liabilities to provide guaranteed minimum pensions for service prior to April 1997);
(c) a scheme which solely provides death benefits (*e.g.* on death in service);
(d) a scheme under which all the promised benefits have been secured by the purchase of policies of insurance or annuity contracts which have been specifically allocated to individual members or other beneficiaries to provide them with their benefits;
(e) a scheme which provides relevant benefits (*i.e.* basically any pension benefit on retirement or death) which is neither an approved scheme nor a relevant statutory scheme; and
(f) a scheme with such a superannuation fund as is mentioned in section 615(6) of the Income and Corporation Taxes Act 1988 (*i.e.* basically schemes providing benefits in connection with business and employment outside the UK).

(2) The effect of the foregoing is that the main type of trust scheme to which the independent trustee requirements apply are pension schemes providing salary related benefits unless they fall within one of the exemptions.

(3) Another effect is that a company, in relation to which an insolvency practitioner has begun to act, may be sole trustee of a pension scheme which, apart from falling within one of the exemptions, would have been subject to the independent trustee requirements. In the absence of those involved in the administration of the scheme receiving an employer's assurance that there is no reason why it cannot continue to act as trustee, they must inform OPRA [section 26B of the Pensions Act 1995].

26.4 Duties of Insolvency Practitioner in respect of Independent Trustee

(1) While section 22 applies in relation to a pension scheme, the insolvency practitioner must satisfy himself that at least one of the scheme trustees is independent and if he is not so satisfied must appoint, or secure the appointment of, an independent person as scheme trustee [section 23(1) of the Pensions Act 1995].

(2) The duty to appoint an independent trustee must be performed by the insolvency practitioner within three months beginning from (i) the date on which he first becomes aware that section 22 applies in relation to the pension scheme in question, or (ii) the date on which the duty arises, whichever is the later [section 23(2) of the Pensions Act 1995 and regulation 3(1) of the Occupational Pension Schemes (Winding up Notices and Reports etc) Regulations 2002].

(3) Several organisations, including actuarial firms and solicitors specialising in pensions law, offer independent trustee services either through individuals or corporate trustees. Once the insolvency practitioner has identified a person to act as independent trustee their appointment will normally be effected by a deed of appointment executed by the insolvency practitioner and the independent trustee. It is good practice for any such deed to specify that the insolvency practitioner is contracting solely as agent for the company and not in any personal capacity and to disclaim any liability in connection with the pension scheme attributable to the acts or omissions of the independent trustee.

(4) An independent trustee must continue to be independent for so long as section 22 applies in relation to the pension scheme. If a trustee's independent status is lost then the duty of the insolvency practitioner to appoint an independent person as scheme trustee will revive.

(5) Where the duties imposed by section 23(1) fall to be discharged at the same time by two or more persons acting in different capacities, the duties require to be discharged by the person or persons acting as the company's liquidator, provisional liquidator or administrator [section 23(4)(a) of the Pensions Act 1995].

(6) If an insolvency practitioner neglects or refuses to discharge any duty imposed on him by section 23(1), any member of the pension scheme may apply for a court order requiring him to discharge his duties. Where a winding-up order has been made or a provisional liquidator appointed, the court is the court which made the order or appointed the liquidator, otherwise it is any court having jurisdiction to wind up the company [section 24 of the Pensions Act 1995].

(7) It is good practice for an insolvency practitioner to ensure that the existing trustees of a pension scheme to which section 22 applies are informed, either that he is satisfied that one of their number is independent or that he intends to appoint an independent trustee within the requisite statutory period. A failure to do so may result in the existing trustees notifying OPRA of the lack of an independent trustee which they are duty bound to do within one month of concluding the insolvency practitioner has not satisfied himself of independence unless it appears to them on reasonable grounds that it is the insolvency practitioner's intention to effect an appointment timeously [sections 26A(1) and (3) of the Pensions Act 1995]. In certain circumstances OPRA may appoint an independent trustee [section 7 of the Pensions Act 1995].

26.8 Duties on appointment of Independent Trustee

(1) An independent trustee appointed under section 23, apart from having the enhanced powers conferred by the legislation, will be invested with all the powers conferred on trustees in law and by the scheme's documentation and be subject to the usual duties imposed on trustees.

(2) On appointment, as part of the general trustee duty of ingathering the trust estate, as good practice an independent trustee will usually perform a thorough due diligence and investigation exercise on the pension scheme (including, for example, reviewing the documentation, obtaining information from the scheme's advisers and checking the state of the scheme's assets and investments). Where relevant, a non-compliance report may have to be made to OPRA. Any claims against the insolvency practitioner for debts due from the employer will have to be lodged as will any claim on the National Insurance Fund or the Pensions Compensation Board. The pre-appointment activities of trustees and former trustees will inevitably be scrutinised to ensure there have been no breaches of trust committed. In fulfilling its duties the independent trustee may require access to records held by and request a measure of assistance from the insolvency practitioner.

(3) The trustees of a pension scheme to which section 22 applies, are subject to disclosure requirements imposed by regulation 7 of the Occupational Pension Schemes (Independent Trustee) Regulations 1997. These comprise:

    (a) informing every member or relevant trade union in writing of the name and address of an independent trustee appointed by the insolvency practitioner within two months of the appointment;

    (b) where an insolvency practitioner is satisfied that one of the existing trustees is independent, informing every member or relevant trade union in writing of the name and address of the independent person as soon as practicable but by no later than two months from being so advised by the insolvency practitioner; and

    (c) as soon as practicable and by no later than two months from any written request of a member, prospective member or relevant trade union (provided such request is made no more than once in a 12-month period by such person), the trustees are obliged to furnish information on the name and address of a scheme's independent trustee, the scale of fees chargeable by such and the amounts charged to the scheme within the preceding twelve months.

The terms member, prospective member and relevant trade union are defined in the Regulation.

Failure to comply with the above duties without reasonable excuse can result in OPRA imposing fines on the trustees.

26.9   Duties of Insolvency Practitioners under the Pensions Bill 2004 and the role of the Board of the Pension Protection Fund

(1) If the Pensions Bill 2004, introduced in the House of Commons on February 11, 2004, is enacted in its original form it will impose additional duties on an insolvency practitioner. These derive from Part 2 of the Bill that relates to the Board of the Pension Protection Fund (the Board) and its role and responsibilities [see paragraph 26.1(5) above].

(2) Where an insolvency event occurs in relation to an employer of an occupational pension scheme, the insolvency practitioner acting in respect of the employer is under two main duties. The duty to notify the occurrence of an insolvency event [see 26.9(3)] and the duty to issue a notice confirming the status of the scheme [see 26.9(4)].

An occupational pension scheme, for these purposes, is defined by reference to the wide definition contained in section 1 of the Pension Schemes Act 1993 [clause 241(1) Pensions Bill 2004].

An insolvency event in relation to companies is defined in clause 95(3) Pensions Bill 2004 but for the purposes of companies in liquidation it comprises a resolution being passed for the voluntary winding up of a company without a declaration of solvency under section 89 of the Insolvency Act 1986 and an order for the winding up of a company being made by the court under Parts IV or V of that Act [clause 95(3)(e) and (f) Pensions Bill 2004]. Regulations may prescribe additional events as an insolvency event [clause 95(5) Pensions Bill 2004].

(3) The duty to notify the occurrence of an insolvency event requires an insolvency practitioner to notify the Board, the new Pensions Regulator (the Regulator) which will replace OPRA and the trustees or managers of the scheme. This duty must be discharged within the notification period to be prescribed in regulations. The notification period commences the later of the date on which the insolvency event occurs and the date the insolvency practitioner becomes aware of the existence of the pension scheme. The form and content of the notice will be prescribed in regulations [clause 94, Pensions Bill 2004].

(4) The duty to issue a notice confirming the status of the scheme requires an insolvency practitioner to confirm either that a scheme rescue is not possible or that a scheme rescue has occurred. What constitutes the foregoing will be prescribed in regulations.

One would anticipate that a scheme rescue would include a new employer being substituted for and assuming the responsibilities of the insolvent employer in relation to the pension scheme.

Where an insolvency practitioner is able to confirm that a scheme rescue is not possible or that a scheme rescue has occurred he is obliged to issue a notice to that effect.

In circumstances to be prescribed in regulations (including where insolvency proceedings in relation to an employer have been stayed or come to an end), if a person who was formerly acting as an insolvency practitioner has not been able to confirm that a scheme rescue is not possible or that a scheme rescue has occurred he is obliged to issue a notice to that effect.

Copies of notices must be given to the Board, the Regulator and the trustees or managers of the scheme as soon as reasonably practicable [clause 96, Pensions Bill 2004].

The failure of an insolvency practitioner or former insolvency practitioner to issue notices confirming the status of the scheme will oblige the Board to issue such notice and, as soon as reasonably practicable, to give a copy to the Regulator, the trustees or managers of the scheme and any insolvency practitioner in relation to the employer or, if none, the employer. The issue of such notice by the Board takes effect as if it were a notice issued by an insolvency practitioner or a former insolvency practitioner [clause 97, Pensions Bill 2004].

(5) Where a qualifying insolvency event has occurred in relation to the employer of an eligible scheme, the issuing of a notice by an insolvency practitioner as discussed in 26.9(4), where such notice confirms that a scheme rescue is not possible, may result in the Board assuming responsibility for the pension scheme under the Pension Protection Fund (PPF). It will be obliged to do this where the scheme's assets (excluding those relating to money purchase benefits) are less than the amount of its protected liabilities (*i.e.* principally, those in respect of which the PPF will provide compensation) and provided the Board has not ceased to be involved with the scheme in the period commencing the time immediately preceding the occurrence of a qualifying insolvency event and the issuing of the notice by an insolvency practitioner [clause 99].

A qualifying insolvency event is an insolvency event in relation to the employer provided it does not fall within an assessment period which began before the occurrence of the event (*i.e.* a period during which the Board is already assessing whether or not it is under a duty to assume responsibility for the pension scheme of the employer in question).

A pension scheme will be an eligible scheme if it is an occupational pension scheme which is not a money purchase scheme or one prescribed in regulations or a scheme which commenced winding up prior to an appointed day [clause 98, Pensions Bill 2004]. Eligible schemes will, in effect, be salary related schemes and hybrid schemes containing defined benefit promises.

The Board will cease to have been involved with the scheme if it has previously encountered the scheme and assessed that it is not under a duty to assume responsibility for it under the PPF, for example, because the pension scheme is not an eligible scheme or is one created to replace an old scheme which was not an eligible scheme and was established with the main purpose (or one of the main purposes) of bringing it within the compensation provisions of the PPF [clause 117, Pensions Bill]. In the foregoing examples the Board will have been obliged to issue a withdrawal notice in respect of the scheme and copied this to the Regulator, the trustees or managers of the scheme and any insolvency practitioner in relation to the employer or, if none, the employer [clauses 115 and 116, Pensions Bill 2004].

The Board may have previously assessed the pension scheme or be in the process of doing so on application by the trustees or on notice from the Regulator that the scheme employer is unlikely to continue as a going concern [clause 102, Pensions Bill 2004].

(6) During any assessment period the Board stands in place of the trustees as creditor of the employer in respect of any debt (including contingent debt) owed by the employer to the pension scheme under section 75 of the Pensions Act 1995 or otherwise. All rights and powers of the trustees in respect of such debts are exercisable exclusively by the Board who are obliged to account for any payments to the trustees [clause 109, Pensions Bill 2004].

(7) The Board is obliged to notify insolvency practitioners of certain matters in relation to the pension scheme.

A copy of the actuarial valuation of the pension scheme obtained by the Board in assessing whether it must assume responsibility for the scheme must be copied to the insolvency practitioner [clause 113, Pensions Bill 2004] who must also be notified when the valuation becomes binding and copied the binding valuation [clause 114, Pensions Bill 2004].

Where the Board is obliged to assume responsibility for the pension scheme under the PPF it must give the trustees or managers of the scheme a transfer notice and copy this to the insolvency practitioner [clause 122, Pensions Bill 2004]. On issuing a transfer notice the Board assumes responsibility for the pension scheme and in consequence the assets and liabilities of the scheme transfer to the Board, the trustees or managers are discharged from their obligations and the Board is responsible for securing that compensation is paid to members from the PPF [clause 123, Pensions Bill 2004].

Where the Board determines to make a payment from the Fraud Compensation Fund to the trustees or managers of a pension scheme notice of this must be given to an insolvency practitioner [clause 146, Pensions Bill 2004].

(8) In order to facilitate the exercise its statutory functions the Board has extensive powers to gather information. These include power to require certain persons to produce documents and provide information and power to enter premises to collect information or documents and to examine persons who may be able to furnish relevant information. These powers are exercisable in relation to an insolvency practitioner and his premises [clauses 153 and 154, Pensions Bill 2004]. A failure without reasonable excuse to comply with the Board's requirements can result in a fine being imposed and a person who intentionally and without reasonable excuse alters, suppresses, conceals or destroys documents which must be produced is liable to a fine and/or imprisonment [clause 155, Pensions Bill 2004]. To knowingly or recklessly furnish information to the Board which is false or misleading in a material

particular can result in a fine and/or imprisonment [clause 157, Pensions Bill 2004].

(9) A determination by the Board that an insolvency practitioner or former insolvency practitioner has failed in his duty to issue a notice confirming the status of the scheme [see 26.9(4)] can, on written application, be the subject of a review by the Reconsideration Committee of the Board [clauses 167 and 168 Pensions Bill 2004] and a subsequent referral to the PPF Ombudsman [clause 173, Pensions Bill 2004]. Appeals on points of law from determinations of the PPF Ombudsman may be made to the Court of Session [clause 175, Pensions Bill 2004].

26.10   MacRoberts Trustees Limited

MacRoberts Trustees Limited (incorporated in Scotland under the Companies Acts (No. 241503) and having its registered office at 152 Bath Street, Glasgow, G2 4TB) is an independent company offering services as an independent trustee to insolvency practitioner. Its directors are all solicitors, and has considerable experience in insolvency situations.

CHAPTER 27

LIQUIDATORS AND THE ENVIRONMENT[1]

27.1 Waste Management Licences

(1) Waste Management Licences can be as much of a liability as an asset to a liquidator.

   With landfill sites for example, costly and onerous post closure obligations normally coincide with the loss of the income stream from the site and it is perhaps unsurprising that some licence holders get into financial difficulties while others declare bankruptcy in an attempt to circumvent licence obligations.

   Liquidators should be aware of the potential difficulties concerning companies which hold a waste management licence (WML).

(2) In terms of section 39 of the Environmental Protection Act 1990 (the EPA 1990) a WML continues in force until it is either revoked or accepted for surrender. As surrender can be almost impossible to achieve especially for landfill sites, there has in England been a number of recent cases involving insolvency practitioners attempting to "disclaim" WMLs as "onerous property" in terms of section 178 of the Insolvency Act 1986.

(3) Following a number of early cases in which the courts struggled with the apparent inconsistency between the protection of the environment and the safe and orderly winding up of companies, *i.e.* the provisions of the Insolvency Act 1986 and the EPA 1990 the law is now settled.

(4) In *Official Receiver as Liquidator of Celtic Extraction Limited and Bluestone Chemicals Limited v Environment Agency* [2] the Court of Appeal found that the WML's of two companies which had gone into liquidation could be "disclaimed" as "onerous property" under section 178 of the Insolvency Act 1986 (the 1986 Act) as there were no assets to meet the costs of remedying the breaches of the licence conditions. The court held that WMLs were "property" within the meaning of s.436 of the 1986 Act or alternatively an "interest . . . incidental to property" (that is incidental to the land to which the licence related as contained in the definitions set out in section 436 of the Insolvency Act 1986) and they could therefore be considered as "onerous property" in terms of section 178.

   The court considered the question of inconsistency between the 1986 Act and the EPA 1990, however, it noted that the "pol-

[1] Prepared in conjunction with the Environmental and Planning Law Group at MacRoberts.

[2] 2000 Env. L.R.86.

luter pays principle" did not extend to making unsecured creditors pay where the polluter could not.[3]

(5) Other implications of disclaiming WMLs were considered in late 2003 in the case of *Environment Agency v Hillridge Limited.*[4]

The Environment Agency made an application under section 112 of the 1986 Act in relation to monies held in a Trust Fund, the purpose of which was to ensure restoration and after care of a landfill site owned by Waste Point and run by its subsidiary Hillridge Limited. The problems began when both companies were placed in liquidation.

The joint liquidators disclaimed the interest of each company in the site licence and WML. The court considered the question of ownership of the trust monies and found that the liquidators were held to have disclaimed any interest in disclaiming the licences. Similarly, the Environment Agency were not held not to be entitled to access funds to carry out site restoration as there was no longer any WML setting out restoration obligations. Accordingly, the fund was declared to vest in the Crown as *bona vacantia* on the basis that there was no-one available to assert a claim to it.

This case may prompt a review of the law relating to trust instruments for financial provision backing WMLs if a disclaimer means that the money is no longer available for clean up; however the inability for a Scottish liquidator to disclaim should avoid this situation arising in Scotland.

27.2 Contaminated Land

(1) Part IIA of the Environmental Protection Act 1990 (the EPA 1990) introduced statutory liability for contaminated land, *i.e.* land the condition of which was likely to cause significant harm or pollution of water courses.

(2) The basic liability premise of Part IIA is "polluter pays". Often however, the polluter cannot pay. Companies responsible for contamination will either already have become bankrupt when the problem is discovered or have made no financial provision for the legacy of contamination and be unable to pay for remediation.

(3) Section 78X(3) of the EPA 1990 provides protection for persons acting in insolvency situations with respect to contaminated land. The person acting is defined in section 78(4) to include liquidators, official receivers, etc.

---

[3] Interestingly for insolvency practitioners in Scotland, one of the arguments raised by the Environment Agency in supporting its view that the EPA 1990 prevailed over the 1986 Act was that s.178 of the 1986 Act did not extend to Scotland whereas s.39 of the EPA 1990 covering surrender of WML's did. The court was not persuaded by this argument and commented that the common law in Scotland concerning disclaimers by liquidators was similar to the statutory regime in England. There appears to be no justification in Scots law for this proposition and therefore cannot be considered as a statement of the position in relation to a Scottish company.

[4] [2003] EWHC 3023.

The protection of section 78(3) is two-fold:

(a) It removes any personal liability for remediation costs unless those costs are referable to an act or omission on the part of the person acting; and

(b) The person acting will not be guilty of an offence or failing to comply with a remediation notice unless it is something for which he is responsible for in (a).

(4) While any contamination is unlikely to be as a result of the act of a liquidator, it might be argued that its presence could be as a result of an omission on his part, *i.e.* a failure to remove it or to take steps to prevent it occurring. This raises the question of what it is reasonable to expect the liquidator to do and in light of the less than absolute statutory exemption, it would be prudent for liquidators to consider carefully all due diligence available. However, should the liquidator be served with a remediation notice seeking to make him personally liable for the costs of remediation, the statutory exemption would normally provide a valid ground of appeal against its terms.

27.3 Pollution Prevention and Control

(1) The area of pollution prevention and control (PPC) like waste management licensing, has implications for liquidation practitioners.

(2) The PPC regime regulated under the Pollution, Prevention and Control (Scotland) Regulations 2000 regulates many major process industries and landfill sites formerly regulated under the waste management licensing regulations. These are known as part A installations.

(3) One aspect of the PPC regime is that it requires sites to be returned to a satisfactory state on the closure of the installation. Significantly, before obtaining a permit, an applicant will require to show that he will be capable of restoring the site as well as meeting other obligations and this may lead to the lodging of a bond or insurance policy.

(4) As with waste management licences, PPC permits for part A installations can be surrendered if the Scottish Environment Protection Agency is satisfied that there is no pollution risk from the site and that no further steps are needed to return the site to a satisfactory state.

(5) Although there are no reported cases as yet, on the basis of *Re Celtic Extraction*,[5] there would appear to be nothing to prevent an English liquidator disclaiming a PPC permit as "onerous property" leaving the issue of site restoration to be tackled possibly through the contaminated land regime. However a Scottish liquidator does not have any ability to disclaim.

---

[5] 2000 Env L.R. 86.

(6) There has recently been consultation in England by the Department for the Environment, Food and Rural Affairs on possible legislative changes to prevent permits being disclaimed as "onerous property". However, this would raise other policy issues particularly regarding whether the "polluter pays principle" should extend to making unsecured creditors pay where the polluter could not do so.

APPENDIX

STYLES[1]

---

[1] Prepared in conjunction with the Dispute Resolution Group at MacRoberts and with the Corporate Recovery Department of Grant Thornton.

A – COURT LIQUIDATION

A1. Petition by Creditor (Section 123(1)(a))

<u>SHERIFFDOM OF GLASGOW AND STRATHKELVIN AT GLASGOW</u>

PETITION

of

GALAXY PRODUCTS LIMITED
incorporated under the Companies Acts and
having its Registered office at Heavenly
Mansions, Pitlochry ("the Petitioners")

for

ORDER to WIND UP ROCOCO COCOA
CO LIMITED having its Registered Office at
1 Main Street, Glasgow

The Petitioners crave the Court:

To appoint this application to be intimated on the Walls of Court and to be advertised once in the *Edinburgh Gazette* and once in "*The Herald*" newspaper and to be served on the said Rococo Cocoa Co Limited (hereinafter referred to as "the Company") and to appoint the Company and all other persons having an interest to lodge answers hereto if so advised within eight days after such intimation, service and advertisement and in the meantime to appoint David Flint, Solicitor, 152 Bath Street, Glasgow G2 4TB or such other person as the Court may think fit to be Provisional Liquidator of the Company upon his finding such caution or security as the Court may deem proper and to authorise such Provisional Liquidator to exercise the powers contained in Parts II and III of Schedule 4 to the Insolvency Act 1986 (as amended) (hereinafter referred to as "the Act"); and on resuming consideration hereof, with or without answers, to order that the Company be wound-up by the Court under the provisions of the Act, and to appoint the said David Flint or such other person as the Court may think fit to be Interim Liquidator of the Company; to authorise the Interim Liquidator to advertise his appointment in the *Edinburgh Gazette* and *The Herald* newspaper in lieu of sending notices to creditors and others in terms of rule 4.18(4) of the Insolvency (Scotland) Rules 1986; to find the Petitioners entitled to the expenses of this application and to direct the same to be expenses in the liquidation; to find any party opposing this application liable in the expenses occasioned by such opposition; or to do further or otherwise in the premises as to the Court may seem proper.

CONDESCENDENCE

1. The Petitioners are designed in the Instance. Rococo Cocoa Co Limited (hereinafter referred to as "the Company") was incorporated on May 13, 1988 under the Companies Acts as a company limited by shares. The Registered Office of the Company is at 1 Main Street, Glasgow. The Company has had no other registered office within the period of six months immediately before the presentation of this petition. This Court accordingly has jurisdiction in terms of section 120 of the Act. The Company conducts the administration

of its affairs from its registered office on a regular basis. The Company does not conduct the administration of its affairs from any other office. The Company's registered office is its centre of main interests. This Court accordingly has jurisdiction in terms of Council Regulation (EC) No 1346/2000.

2.   The Company carries on business as Entertainment Consultants all as more fully set out in the Company's Memorandum of Association. A copy of the Company's Memorandum and Article of Association is produced herewith.

3.   The share capital of the Company is £100 divided into 100 shares of £1 each, of which two are issued and are fully paid. The amount of the assets of the Company is not known to the Petitioners.

4.   The Company was due and resting owing to the Petitioners as at March 1, 2004 in the sum of £10,000 in respect of goods and services provided. Copies of invoices rendered by the Petitioners to the Company are produced herewith.

5.   On June 1, 2004, in terms of subsection (1)(a) of section 123 of the Act the Petitioners served upon the Company by Sheriff Officer a Form 4.1 (Scotland), being the prescribed form of Statutory Demand for Payment of Debt, calling on the Company to make payment of the said sum of £10,000 to the Petitioners within 21 days of the said date of service. A copy of the said Form 4.1 (Scotland) together with the Execution of Service thereof are produced herewith.

6.   The said period of 21 days has expired and no payment has been received from the Company by the Petitioners and no attempt has been made by the Company to secure or compound for the said sum of £10,000. The Company has not disputed that the said sum is currently due by the Company to the Petitioners. Section 122(1)(f) of the Act provides that a company may be wound-up by the court if it is unable to pay its debts. Section 123(1)(a) of the Act provides that a company is deemed unable to pay its debts if a creditor to whom a company is indebted in a sum exceeding £750 then due has served upon the company's registered office a written demand (in the prescribed form) requiring the company to pay the sum so due and the company has thereafter for three weeks neglected to pay the sum or secure or compound for it to the reasonable satisfaction of the creditor. Accordingly, the Petitioners respectfully submit that the Company is unable to pay its debts in terms of s122(1)(f) and s123(1)(a) of the Act and should be wound-up by the Court and an Interim Liquidator appointed for that purpose

7.   The Petitioners respectfully suggest that David Flint, Solicitor, 152 Bath Street, Glasgow, who is a qualified insolvency practitioner within the meaning of Part XIII of the Act, is a suitable person for the office of Interim Liquidator. Copies of his consent to act, Insolvency Permit and Insolvency Practitioner Licence Bond are produced herewith.

8.   [The Petitioners understand that there are a considerable number of other creditors seeking payment from the Company. There are currently five unsatisfied judgements against the Company. The Petitioners are therefore concerned that the Company is in considerable financial difficulties and may attempt to conceal or dissipate certain of its assets upon service and advertisement of this Petition.] In order to secure the position of the Company's creditors and safeguard the Company's assets, the Petitioners submit that it is expedient that a Provisional Liquidator be appointed in terms of section 135 of the Act and that authority be given to him to exercise the powers craved. The said David Flint is also a suitable person to be Provisional Liquidator and consents so to act. Copies of his consent to act, Insolvency Permit and Insolvency Practitioner Licence Bond are produced herewith.

9. To the knowledge of the Petitioners, no receiver has been appointed to the Company, nor is it in administration, nor has a liquidator been appointed for the voluntary winding-up of the Company.

10. This Petition is presented in terms of the Insolvency Act 1986 and, in particular, sections 122, 123, and 135 thereof and Schedule 4 thereto, and in terms of the Insolvency (Scotland) Rules 1986 and in terms of Part IV of the Act of Sederunt (Sheriff Court Company Insolvency Rules) 1986.

PLEAS-IN-LAW

1. The Company, being unable to pay its debts, should be wound-up by the Court and an Interim Liquidator appointed.

2. In the meantime, a Provisional Liquidator should be appointed and authority granted to him to exercise the powers craved.

IN RESPECT WHEREOF

(sgd) A Wiseman

Solicitor
152 Bath Street
Glasgow G2 4TB

PETITIONERS' AGENT

A2. Advertisement of First Order (with Provisional Liquidator)

<u>ROCOCO COCOA CO LIMITED</u>

Notice is hereby given that on [*date*] a petition was presented to the Sheriff at Glasgow by Galaxy Products Ltd, Heavenly Mansions, Pitlochry, craving the Court *inter alia*, that Rococo Cocoa Co Limited having their Registered Office at 1 Main Street, Glasgow ("the Company") be wound-up by the Court and that an interim liquidator be appointed; in which petition the Sheriff at Glasgow by inter-locutor dated [*date*] appointed all persons having an interest to lodge answers in the hands of the Sheriff Clerk, Glasgow within eight days after intimation, adver-tisement or service, and *eo die* appointed David Flint, Solicitor, 152 Bath Street, Glasgow G2 4TB to be provisional liquidator of the Company with the powers specified in Parts II and III of Schedule 4 of the Insolvency Act 1986 (as amended), of all of which notice is hereby given.

MacRoberts
Solicitors
152 Bath Street
Glasgow G2 4TB

<u>Agents for the Petitioners</u>

A3. Petition by Creditor (Section 123(1)(c))

PETITION

of

GALAXY   PRODUCTS   LIMITED
incorporated under the Companies Acts and
having its Registered office at Heavenly
Mansions, Pitlochry ("the Petitioners")

for

ORDER to WIND UP ROCOCO COCOA
CO LIMITED having its Registered Office at
1 Main Street, Glasgow

To appoint this application to be intimated on the Walls of Court and to be advertised once in the *Edinburgh Gazette* and once in "*The Herald*" newspaper and to be served on the said Rococo Cocoa Co Limited and to appoint the said Rococo Cocoa Co Limited and all other persons having an interest to lodge answers hereto if so advised within eight days after such intimation, service and advertisement and in the meantime to appoint David Flint, Solicitor, 152 Bath Street, Glasgow G2 4TB or such other person as the Court may think fit to be Provisional Liquidator of the said Company upon his finding such caution or security as the Court may deem proper and to authorise such Provisional Liquidator to exercise the power contained in Parts II and III of Schedule 4 to the Insolvency Act 1986 (hereinafter referred to as "the Act"); and on resuming consideration hereof, with or without answers, to order that said Rococo Cocoa Co Limited be wound-up by the Court under the provisions of the Act, and to appoint the said David Flint or such other person as the Court may think fit to be Interim Liquidator of the said Company; to authorise the Interim Liquidator to advertise his appointment in the *Edinburgh Gazette* and *The Herald* newspaper in lieu of sending notices to creditors and others in terms of rule 4.18(4) of the Insolvency (Scotland) Rules 1986; to find the Petitioners entitled to the expenses of this application and to direct the same to be expenses in the liquidation; to find any party opposing this application liable in the expenses occasioned by such opposition; or to do further or otherwise in the premises as to the Court may seem proper.

CONDESCENDENCE

1.   The Petitioners are designed in the Instance. Rococo Cocoa Co Limited (hereinafter referred to as "the Company") was incorporated on May 13, 1988 under the Companies Acts as a company limited by shares. The Registered Office of the Company is at 1 Main Street, Glasgow. The Company has had no other registered office within the period of six months immediately before the presentation of this petition. This Court accordingly has jurisdiction in terms of section 120 of the Act. The Company conducts the administration of its affairs from its registered office on a regular basis. The Company does not conduct the administration of its affairs from any other office. The Company's registered office is its centre of main interests. This Court accordingly has jurisdiction in terms of Council Regulation (EC) No 1346/2000.

2.   The Company carries on business as Entertainment Consultants all as more fully set out in the Company's Memorandum of Association. A copy of the Company's Memorandum and Article of Association is produced herewith.

3. The share capital of the Company is £100 divided into 100 shares of £1 each, of which two are issued and are fully paid. The amount of the assets of the Company is not known to the Petitioners.

4. The Company was due and resting owing to the Petitioners as at March 1, 2004 in the sum of £8,400 in respect of goods and services provided. Copies of invoices rendered by the Petitioners to the Company are produced herewith.

5. In an action in the Sheriff Court of Glasgow and Strathkelvin at Glasgow at the instance of the Petitioners against the Company the Sheriff decerned the Company to pay to the Petitioners the sum of £8,400 with interest thereon at the rate of 8 per centum per annum from January 10, 2004 until payment with expenses. An Extract of such Decree dated [*date*] together with a Charge for Payment were served on the Company by Sheriff Officers on [*date*] charging the Company to make payment of the sum then due to the Petitioners within fourteen days of such service. The said Extract Decree together with Charge for Payment are produced herewith.

6. The said period of 14 days referred to in the said Charge for Payment has expired and no payment has been received from the Company by the Petitioners. Section 122(1)(f) of the Act provides that a company may be wound-up by the court if it is unable to pay its debts. Section 123(1)(c) of the Act provides that a company is deemed unable to pay its debts if the *induciae* of a charge for payment on an extract decree has expired without payment being made. Accordingly, the Company is unable to pay its debts in terms of sections 122(1)(f) and 123(1)(c) and should be wound-up by the Court and an Interim Liquidator appointed for that purpose.

7. The Petitioners respectfully suggest that David Flint, Solicitor, 152 Bath Street, Glasgow, who is a qualified insolvency practitioner within the meaning of Part XIII of the Act is a suitable person for the office of Interim Liquidator. Copies of his consent to act, Insolvency Permit and Insolvency Practitioner Licence Bond are produced herewith.

8. [The Petitioners understand that there are a considerable number of other creditors seeking payment from the Company. There are currently five unsatisfied judgements against the Company. The Petitioners are therefore concerned that the Company is in considerable financial difficulties and may attempt to conceal or dissipate certain of its assets upon service and advertisement of this Petition.] In the meantime, therefore in order to secure the position of the Company's creditors and safeguard the Company's assets, the Petitioners submit that it is expedient that a Provisional Liquidator be appointed in terms of section 135 of the Act and that authority be given to him to exercise the powers craved. The said David Flint is also a suitable person to be Provisional Liquidator and consents so to act. Copies of his consent to act, Insolvency Permit and Insolvency Practitioner Licence Bond are produced herewith. To the knowledge of the Petitioners, no receiver has been appointed to the Company, nor is it in administration, nor has a liquidator been appointed for the voluntary winding-up of the Company.

9. This Petition is presented in terms of the Insolvency Act 1986 and, in particular, sections 122, 123, 135 thereof and Schedule 4 thereto, and in terms of the Insolvency (Scotland) Rules 1986 and in terms of Part IV of the Act of Sederunt (Sheriff Court Company Insolvency Rules) 1986.

PLEAS-IN-LAW

1. The Company, being unable to pay its debts, should be wound-up by the Court and an Interim Liquidator appointed.

2. In the meantime, a Provisional Liquidator should be appointed and authority granted to him to exercise the powers craved.

IN RESPECT WHEREOF

(sgd) A Wiseman

Solicitor
152 Bath Street
Glasgow G2 4TB

<u>PETITIONERS' AGENT</u>

A4.   Advertisement of First Order (without Provisional Liquidator)

ROCOCO COCOA CO LIMITED

Notice is hereby given that on [date] a petition was presented to the Sheriff at Glasgow by Galaxy Products Ltd, Heavenly Mansions, Pitlochry, craving the Court *inter alia*, that Rococo Cocoa Co Limited having their Registered Office at 1 Main Street, Glasgow ("the Company") be wound-up by the Court and that an interim liquidator be appointed; in which petition the Sheriff at Glasgow by interlocutor dated [date] appointed all persons having an interest to lodge answers in the hands of the Sheriff Clerk, Glasgow within eight days after intimation, advertisement or service of all of which notice is hereby given.

MacRoberts
Solicitors
152 Bath Street
Glasgow G2 4TB

Agents for the Petitioners

A5. Petition by Receiver

SHERIFFDOM OF GLASGOW AND STRATHKELVIN AT GLASGOW

PETITION

by

ALAN CATCHER, Solicitor, Excel House, 30 Semple Street, Edinburgh, EH3 8BL, Receiver of the property and under taking of ROCOCO COCOA CO LIMITED ("the Petitioner")

for

ORDER to WIND UP ROCOCO COCOA CO LIMITED, having its Registered Office at 1 Main Street, Glasgow

The Petitioner craves the Court:

To appoint this application to be intimated on the Walls of Court and to be advertised once in the *Edinburgh Gazette* and once in *The Herald* newspaper, and to appoint all persons having an interest to lodge answers hereto if so advised within eight days after such intimation and advertisement; and on resuming consideration hereof, with or without answers, to order that the said Rococo Cocoa Co Limited be wound-up by the Court under the provisions of the Insolvency Act 1986 (hereinafter referred to as "the Act"), and to appoint David Flint, Solicitor, 152 Bath Street, Glasgow, G2 4TB or such other person as the Court thinks fit to be Interim Liquidator of the said Company; and to determine what security or caution is to be given by such Interim Liquidator; to find the Petitioner entitled to the expenses of this application and to direct the same to be expenses in the liquidation; to find any party opposing this application liable in the expenses occasioned by such opposition, or to do further or otherwise in the premises as to the Court may seem proper.

CONDESCENDENCE

1. Rococo Cocoa Co Limited (hereinafter referred to as "the Company") was incorporated on May 13, 1988 under the Companies Acts as a company limited by shares. The Registered Office of the Company is at 1 Main Street, Glasgow. The Company has had no other registered office within the period of six months immediately before the presentation of this petition. This Court accordingly has jurisdiction in terms of section 120 of the Act. The Company conducts the administration of its affairs from its registered office on a regular basis. The Company does not conduct the administration of its affairs from any other office. The Company's registered office is its centre of main interests. This Court accordingly has jurisdiction in terms of Council Regulation (EC) No 1346/2000.

2. The Company carries on business as Entertainment Consultants all as more fully set out in the Company's Memorandum of Association. A copy of the Company's Memorandum and Article of Association is produced herewith.

3. The share capital of the Company is £100 divided into 100 shares of £1 each, of which two are issued and are fully paid. The amount of the assets of the Company is not known to the Petitioners.

4. On May 1, 1999 the Petitioner was appointed Receiver of the whole property and undertaking of the Company by Instrument of Appointment made by

Galaxy Products Limited the holders of a Floating Charge granted by the Company in their favour. A copy of the said Instrument of Appointment is produced. Since the date of his appointment the Petitioner has carried out the duties of Receiver and continues to act in that capacity. No administrator has been appointed to the Company. No liquidator has been appointed voluntarily to wind up the Company.

5. Section 122(1)(f) of the Act provides that a company may be wound-up by the Court if *inter alia* "the company is unable to pay its debts". Section 123(1)(e) of the Act provides that a company shall be deemed to be unable to pay its debts if *inter alia* "it is proved to the satisfaction of the Court that the Company is unable to pay its debts". Section 123(2) of the Act further provides that a company is deemed unable to pay its debts if it is proved to the satisfaction of the court that the value of the Company's assets is less than the amount of its liabilities, taking into account its contingent and prospective liabilities.

6. The Petitioner has prepared an approximate Statement of Affairs as at June 30, 1999 which shows assets of £125,012 and liabilities of £762,923. The Company's liabilities therefore exceed its assets. The Company is accordingly insolvent and unable to pay its debts and should be wound-up by the Court and an Interim Liquidator appointed for that purpose. The Petitioner is empowered by section 55 of and Schedule 2 to the Act to present this Petition.

7. The Petitioner respectfully submits that David Flint, Solicitor, 152 Bath Street, Glasgow G2 4TB who is a qualified insolvency practitioner within the meaning of Part XIII of the Act is a suitable person to be appointed Interim Liquidator of the Company and the said David Flint consents so to act. Copies of his consent to act, Insolvency Permit and Insolvency Practitioner Licence Bond are produced herewith.

8. This Petition is presented in terms of the Insolvency Act 1986 and, in particular, sections 55, 122 and 123 thereof and Schedule 2 thereto, and in terms of the Insolvency (Scotland) Rules 1986 and in terms of Part IV of the Act of Sederunt (Sheriff Court Company Insolvency Rules) 1986.

PLEAS-IN-LAW

The Company, being unable to pay its debts, should be wound-up by the Court and an Interim Liquidator appointed.

IN RESPECT WHEREOF

(sgd) A Wiseman

Solicitor
152 Bath Street
Glasgow G2 4TB

PETITIONER'S AGENT

A6. Advertisement of First Order (Receiver's Petition)

<u>ROCOCO COCOA CO LIMITED (In Receivership)</u>

Notice is hereby given that on [*date*] a petition was presented to the Sheriff at Glasgow by Alan Catcher, Solicitor, Excel House, 30 Semple Street, Edinburgh, EH3 8BL, Receiver of the property and undertaking of Rococo Cocoa Co Limited having their Registered Office at 1 Main Street, Glasgow ("the Company") craving the Court *inter alia*, that the Company be wound-up by the Court and that an interim liquidator be appointed; in which petition the Sheriff at Glasgow by interlocutor dated [*date*] appointed all persons having an interest to lodge answers in the hands of the Sheriff Clerk, Glasgow, within eight days after intimation, advertisement or service, of all of which notice is hereby given.

MacRoberts
Solicitors
152 Bath Street
Glasgow G2 4TB

<u>Agents for the Petitioners</u>

A7. Petition by Administrator – Creditor Rejection of Proposals[2]

<u>SHERIFFDOM OF GLASGOW AND STRATHKELVIN AT GLASGOW</u>

PETITION

by

JAMES FULWELL, Solicitor, Excel House, 30 Semple Street, Edinburgh, EH3 8BL, Administrator of ROCOCO COCOA CO LIMITED ("the Petitioner")

for

ORDER to WIND UP ROCOCO COCOA CO LIMITED, having its Registered Office at 1 Main Street, Glasgow

The Petitioner craves the Court:

To appoint this application to be intimated on the Walls of Court and to be advertised once in the *Edinburgh Gazette* and once in *The Herald* newspaper, and to appoint all persons having an interest to lodge answers hereto if so advised within eight days after such intimation and advertisement; and on resuming consideration hereof, with or without answers, to order that the said Rococo Cocoa Co Limited be wound-up by the Court under the provisions of the Insolvency Act 1986 (hereinafter referred to as "the Act"), and to appoint David Flint, Solicitor, 152 Bath Street, Glasgow, or such other person as the Court thinks fit, to be Interim Liquidator of the said Company; and to determine what security or caution is to be given by such Interim Liquidator; to find the Petitioner entitled to the expenses of this application and to direct the same to be expenses in the liquidation; to find any party opposing this application liable in the expenses occasioned by such opposition, or to do further or otherwise in the premises as to the Court may seem proper.

CONDESCENDENCE

1. Rococo Cocoa Co Limited (hereinafter referred to as "the Company") was incorporated on [*date*] under the Companies Acts as a company limited by shares. The Registered Office of the Company is at 1 Main Street, Glasgow. The Company has had no other registered office within the period of six months immediately before the presentation of this petition. This Court accordingly has jurisdiction in terms of section 120 of the Act. The Company conducts the administration of its affairs from its registered office on a regular basis. The Company does not conduct the administration of its affairs from any other office. The Company's registered office is its centre of main interests. This Court accordingly has jurisdiction in terms of Council Regulation (EC) No 1346/2000.

2. The Company carries on business as Entertainment Consultants all as more fully set out in the Company's Memorandum of Association. A copy of the Company's Memorandum and Article of Association is produced herewith.

---

[2] There are no reported cases on the transfer from post Enterprise Act administration to liquidation, and accordingly, amendments may be required to this style

3. The share capital of the Company is £100 divided into 100 shares of £1 each, of which two are issued and are fully paid. The amount of the liabilities of the Company is £2,345,678 as per the attached statement of affairs.

4. On [*date*] the Petitioner was appointed Administrator of the whole property and undertaking of the Company. A copy of the said order is produced. Since the date of his appointment the Petitioner has carried out the duties of Administrator and continues to act in that capacity. No liquidator has been appointed voluntarily to wind up the Company.

5. In terms of paragraph 55 of Schedule B1 to the Act, the court may make any order it thinks appropriate in the event that the Administrator of a company reports that a meeting of creditors held under paragraphs 50–53 of Schedule B1 to the Act has failed to approve the Administrator's proposals presented to it.

6. At a meeting of creditors of the Company held on [*date*] the creditors of the company rejected the Petitioner's proposals for achievement of the purpose of administration. The Petitioner accordingly believes the requirements of paragraph 55(1) (and in particular sub-paragraph (a) thereof) to be met.

7. In the circumstances condescended upon, the appointment of the Petitioner as administrator should cease to have effect.

8. The Company being insolvent, the Petitioner considers that a winding-up order be made in relation to the Company. The court is empowered to make such an order pursuant to paragraph 55(2)(e) of Schedule B1 to the Act and rule 14 of the Act of Sederunt (Sheriff Court Company Insolvency Rules) 1986.

9. The Petitioner respectfully submits that David Flint, Solicitor, 152 Bath Street, Glasgow G2 4TB who is a qualified insolvency practitioner within the meaning of Part XIII of the Act is a suitable person to be appointed Interim Liquidator of the Company and the said David Flint consents so to act. Copies of his consent to act, Insolvency Permit and Insolvency Practitioner Licence Bond are produced herewith.

10. This Petition is presented in terms of the Insolvency Act 1986 and, in particular paragraph 55 of Schedule B1 thereto, and in terms of the Insolvency (Scotland) Rules 1986 (as amended) and in terms of Parts II and IV of the Act of Sederunt (Sheriff Court Company Insolvency Rules) 1986.

PLEAS-IN-LAW

The Administrator's proposals for the achievement of the purpose for which the Company entered into administration having been rejected by the creditors of the company, and the Company being insolvent, the appointment of the Petitioner as administrator should cease to have effect, the Company should be wound-up by the Court and an Interim Liquidator appointed.

IN RESPECT WHEREOF

(sgd) A Wiseman

Solicitor
152 Bath Street
Glasgow G2 4TB

PETITIONERS' AGENT

A8.   Petition by Administrator – Proposals unachievable[3]

<u>SHERIFFDOM OF GLASGOW AND STRATHKELVIN AT GLASGOW</u>

PETITION

by

JAMES FULWELL, Solicitor, Excel House, 30 Semple Street, Edinburgh, EH3 8BL, Administrator of ROCOCO COCOA CO LIMITED ("the Petitioner")

for

ORDER to WIND UP ROCOCO COCOA CO LIMITED, having its Registered Office at 1 Main Street, Glasgow

The Petitioner craves the Court:

To appoint this application to be intimated on the Walls of Court and to be advertised once in the *Edinburgh Gazette* and once in *The Herald* newspaper, and to appoint all persons having an interest to lodge answers hereto if so advised within eight days after such intimation and advertisement; and on resuming consideration hereof, with or without answers, to order that the said Rococo Cocoa Co Limited be wound-up by the Court under the provisions of the Insolvency Act 1986 (hereinafter referred to as "the Act"), and to appoint David Flint, Solicitor, 152 Bath Street, Glasgow, or such other person as the Court thinks fit, to be Interim Liquidator of the said Company; and to determine what security or caution is to be given by such Interim Liquidator; to find the Petitioner entitled to the expenses of this application and to direct the same to be expenses in the liquidation; to find any party opposing this application liable in the expenses occasioned by such opposition, or to do further or otherwise in the premises as to the Court may seem proper.

CONDESCENDENCE

1.   Rococo Cocoa Co Limited (hereinafter referred to as "the Company") was incorporated on [*date*] under the Companies Acts as a company limited by shares. The Registered Office of the Company is at 1 Main Street, Glasgow. The Company has had no other registered office within the period of six months immediately before the presentation of this petition. This Court accordingly has jurisdiction in terms of section 120 of the Act. The Company conducts the administration of its affairs from its registered office on a regular basis. The Company does not conduct the administration of its affairs from any other office. The Company's registered office is its centre of main interests. This Court accordingly has jurisdiction in terms of Council Regulation (EC) No 1346/2000.

2.   The Company carries on business as Entertainment Consultants all as more fully set out in the Company's Memorandum of Association. A copy of the Company's Memorandum and Article of Association is produced herewith.

---

[3] There are no reported cases on the transfer from post Enterprise Act administration to liquidation, and accordingly, amendments may be required to this style.

3. The share capital of the Company is £100 divided into 100 shares of £1 each, of which two are issued and are fully paid. The amount of the liabilities of the Company is £2,345,678 as per the attached statement of affairs.

4. On [*date*] the Petitioner was appointed Administrator of the whole property and undertaking of the Company. A copy of the said order is produced. Since the date of his appointment the Petitioner has carried out the duties of Administrator and continues to act in that capacity. No liquidator has been appointed voluntarily to wind up the Company.

5. At a meeting of creditors of the Company held on [*date*] the creditors of the company approved the Petitioner's proposals for achievement of the purpose of administration, namely the disposal of the Company's business to Orinoco Cocoa Co Limited, a leading business in the performer management sector.

6. Unfortunately, a number of the Company's artistes have indicated that they are not willing to be managed by the said Orinoco Cocoa Co Limited and have terminated their management arrangements with the Company. The Company is therefore unable to dispose of its business, now largely non-existent, to Orinoco Cocoa Co Limited or any other party.

7   In terms of paragraph 79(2) of Schedule B1 to the Act, the Administrator of a company can make application to the court for a winding-up order if he believes that the purpose of the administration cannot be achieved in relation to the Company.

8. In the circumstances condescended upon, the appointment of the Petitioner as administrator should cease to have effect.

9. In these circumstances, the Company being insolvent, the Petitioner considers that a winding-up order be made in relation to the Company. The court is empowered to make such an order pursuant to paragraph 79(4)(d) of Schedule B1 to the Act and rule 14 of the Act of Sederunt (Sheriff Court Company Insolvency Rules) 1986.

10. The Petitioner respectfully submits that David Flint, Solicitor, 152 Bath Street, Glasgow G2 4TB who is a qualified insolvency practitioner within the meaning of Part XIII of the Act is a suitable person to be appointed Interim Liquidator of the Company and the said David Flint consents so to act. Copies of his consent to act, Insolvency Permit and Insolvency Practitioner Licence Bond are produced herewith.

11. This Petition is presented in terms of the Insolvency Act 1986 and, in particular paragraph 79 of Schedule B1 thereto, and in terms of the Insolvency (Scotland) Rules 1986 (as amended) and in terms of Parts II and IV of the Act of Sederunt (Sheriff Court Company Insolvency Rules) 1986.

PLEAS-IN-LAW

The purposes for which the Company entered into administration being unable to be achieved, the appointment of the Petitioner as administrator should cease to have effect, the Company should be wound-up by the Court and an Interim Liquidator appointed.

IN RESPECT WHEREOF

(sgd) A Wiseman

Solicitor
152 Bath Street
Glasgow G2 4TB

PETITIONERS' AGENT

A9.   Petition by Administrator – Proposals achieved[4]

<u>SHERIFFDOM OF GLASGOW AND STRATHKELVIN AT GLASGOW</u>

PETITION
by

JAMES FULWELL, Solicitor, Excel House, 30 Semple Street, Edinburgh, EH3 8BL, Administrator of ROCOCO COCOA CO LIMITED ("the Petitioner")

for

ORDER to WIND UP ROCOCO COCOA CO LIMITED, having its Registered Office at 1 Main Street, Glasgow

The Petitioner craves the Court:

To appoint this application to be intimated on the Walls of Court and to be advertised once in the *Edinburgh Gazette* and once in *The Herald* newspaper, and to appoint all persons having an interest to lodge answers hereto if so advised within eight days after such intimation and advertisement; and on resuming consideration hereof, with or without answers, to order that the said Rococo Cocoa Co Limited be wound-up by the Court under the provisions of the Insolvency Act 1986 (hereinafter referred to as "the Act"), and to appoint David Flint, Solicitor, 152 Bath Street, Glasgow, or such other person as the Court thinks fit, to be Interim Liquidator of the said Company; and to determine what security or caution is to be given by such Interim Liquidator; to find the Petitioner entitled to the expenses of this application and to direct the same to be expenses in the liquidation; to find any party opposing this application liable in the expenses occasioned by such opposition, or to do further or otherwise in the premises as to the Court may seem proper.

CONDESCENDENCE

1.   Rococo Cocoa Co Limited (hereinafter referred to as "the Company") was incorporated on [*date*] under the Companies Acts as a company limited by shares. The Registered Office of the Company is at 1 Main Street, Glasgow. The Company has had no other registered office within the period of six months immediately before the presentation of this petition. This Court accordingly has jurisdiction in terms of section 120 of the Act. The Company conducts the administration of its affairs from its registered office on a regular basis. The Company does not conduct the administration of its affairs from any other office. The Company's registered office is its centre of main interests. This Court accordingly has jurisdiction in terms of Council Regulation (EC) No 1346/2000.

2.   The Company carries on business as Entertainment Consultants all as more fully set out in the Company's Memorandum of Association. A copy of the Company's Memorandum and Article of Association is produced herewith.

3.   The share capital of the Company is £100 divided into 100 shares of £1 each, of which two are issued and are fully paid. The amount of the liabilities of the Company as at the date of this petition is estimated by the Petitioner to be £1,234,567 as per the attached statement of affairs.

---

[4] There are no reported cases on the transfer from post Enterprise Act administration to liquidation, and accordingly, amendments may be required to this style.

4. On [*date*] the Petitioner was appointed Administrator of the whole property and undertaking of the Company. A copy of the said order is produced. Since the date of his appointment the Petitioner has carried out the duties of Administrator and continues to act in that capacity. No liquidator has been appointed voluntarily to wind up the Company.

5. At a meeting of creditors of the Company held on [*date*] the creditors of the company approved the Petitioner's proposals for achievement of the purpose of administration, namely the disposal of the Company's business to Orinoco Cocoa Co Limited, a leading business in the performer management sector.

6. In terms of an agreement dated [*date*] the Administrator concluded the sale of the Company's business to the said Orinoco Cocoa Co Limited in accordance with the proposals presented to and approved by the creditors of the company.

7. As a result of the said sale, the Company no longer has a business nor any material assets.

8. In the circumstances condescended upon, the appointment of the Petitioner as administrator should cease to have effect.

9. In terms of paragraph 79(3)(b) of Schedule B1 to the Act, the Administrator of a company can make application to the court for a winding-up order if he believes that the purpose of the administration has been sufficiently achieved in relation to the Company.

10. In these circumstances, the purposes for which the Administration Order having been granted having been achieved, and the Company remaining insolvent, the Petitioner considers that a winding-up order be made in relation to the Company. The court is empowered to make such an order pursuant to paragraph 79(4)(d) of Schedule B1 to the Act and rule 14 of the Act of Sederunt (Sheriff Court Company Insolvency Rules) 1986.

11. The Petitioner respectfully submits that David Flint, Solicitor, 152 Bath Street, Glasgow G2 4TB who is a qualified insolvency practitioner within the meaning of Part XIII of the Act is a suitable person to be appointed Interim Liquidator of the Company and the said David Flint consents so to act. Copies of his consent to act, Insolvency Permit and Insolvency Practitioner Licence Bond are produced herewith.

12. This Petition is presented in terms of the Insolvency Act 1986 and, in particular paragraph 79 of Schedule B1 thereto, and in terms of the Insolvency (Scotland) Rules 1986 (as amended) and in terms of Parts II and IV of the Act of Sederunt (Sheriff Court Company Insolvency Rules) 1986.

PLEAS-IN-LAW

The purposes for which the Company entered into administration being unable to be achieved, the appointment of the Petitioner as administrator should cease to have effect, the Company being insolvent, the Company should be wound-up by the Court and an Interim Liquidator appointed.

IN RESPECT WHEREOF

(sgd) A Wiseman

Solicitor
152 Bath Street
Glasgow G2 4TB

PETITIONERS' AGENT

A10.   Advertisement of First Order (Administrator's Petition)

ROCOCO COCOA CO LIMITED

Notice is hereby given that on [*date*] a petition was presented to the Sheriff at Glasgow by James Fulwell, Solicitor, Excel House, 30 Semple Street, Edinburgh, EH3 8BL, Administrator of the property and undertaking of Rococo Cocoa Co Limited having their Registered Office at 1 Main Street, Glasgow ("the Company") craving the Court *inter alia*, that the Company be wound-up by the Court and that an interim liquidator be appointed; in which petition the Sheriff at Glasgow by Interlocutor dated [*date*] appointed all persons having an interest to lodge answers in the hands of the Sheriff Clerk, Glasgow, within eight days after intimation, advertisement or service, of all of which notice is hereby given.

MacRoberts
Solicitors
152 Bath Street
Glasgow G2 4TB

Agents for the Petitioners

A11. Petition by Company together with Excerpt Minute of Meeting of Directors

SHERIFFDOM OF GLASGOW AND STRATHKELVIN AT GLASGOW

PETITION

by

Rococo Cocoa Co Limited incorporated under the Companies Acts and having its Registered Office at 1 Main Street, Glasgow ("the Petitioners")

for

ORDER to WIND UP ROCOCO COCOA CO LIMITED

To appoint this application to be intimated on the Walls of Court and to be advertised once in the *Edinburgh Gazette* and once in *"The Herald"* newspaper and to appoint all persons having an interest to lodge answers hereto if so advised within eight days after such intimation, service and advertisement and in the meantime to appoint David Flint, Solicitor, 152 Bath Street, Glasgow G2 4TB or such other person as the Court may think fit to be Provisional Liquidator of the said Company upon his finding such caution or security as the Court may deem proper and to authorise such Provisional Liquidator to exercise the powers contained in Parts II and III of Schedule 4 to the Insolvency Act 1986 (hereinafter "the Act"); and on resuming consideration hereof, with or without answers, to order that said Rococo Cocoa Co Limited be wound-up by the Court under the provisions of the Act, and to appoint the said David Flint or such other person as the Court may select to be Interim Liquidator of the said Company; to authorise the Interim Liquidator to advertise his appointment in the *Edinburgh Gazette* and *The Herald* newspaper in lieu of sending notices to creditors and others in terms of rule 4.18(4) of the Insolvency (Scotland) Rules 1986; to find the Petitioners entitled to the expenses of this application and to direct the same to be expenses in the liquidation; to find any party opposing this application liable in the expenses occasioned by such opposition; or to do further or otherwise in the premises as to the Court may seem proper.

CONDESCENDENCE

1. Rococo Cocoa Co Limited (hereinafter referred to as "the Company") was incorporated on May 13, 1988 under the Companies acts as a company limited by shares. The Registered Office of the Company is at 1 Main Street, Glasgow. The Company has had no other registered office within the period of six months immediately before the presentation of this petition. This Court accordingly has jurisdiction in terms of s.120 of the Act. The Company conducts the administration of its affairs from its registered office on a regular basis. The Company does not conduct the administration of its affairs from any other office. The Company's registered office is its centre of main interests. This Court accordingly has jurisdiction in terms of Council Regulation (EC) No 1346/2000.

2. The Company carries on business as Entertainment Consultants all as more fully set out in the Company's Memorandum of Association. A copy of the Company's Memorandum and Article of Association is produced herewith.

3. The share capital of the Company is £100 divided into 100 shares of £1 each, of which two are issued and are fully paid.

4. The directors of the Company prepared a Statement of Affairs as at [*date*] with a view to ascertaining the financial position of the Company. A copy of the said Statement of Affairs is produced herewith and referred to for its terms.

5. At a Meeting of the Directors of the Company held at Glasgow on [*date*] the Directors considered the financial position of the Company as disclosed by the Statement of Affairs. The Statement of Affairs disclosed that the value of the Company's assets is less than the amount of its liabilities and that it is unable to pay its debts. An Excerpt Minute of the said Meeting of the Directors is produced herewith and referred to for its terms.

6. By section 122(1)(f) of the Act it is provided that a Company may be wound-up by the Court if the Company is unable to pay its debts, and by section 123(1)(e) it is provided that a company shall be deemed to be unable to pay its debts if it is proved to the satisfaction of the Court that the Company is unable to pay its debts as they fall due. Section 123(2) of the Act further provides that a company is deemed unable to pay its debts if it is proved to the satisfaction of the court that the value of the Company's assets is less than the amount of its liabilities, taking into account its contingent and prospective liabilities. The Company is therefore unable to pay its debts and should be wound-up by the Court.

7. The Petitioners respectfully suggest that David Flint, Solicitor, 152 Bath Street, Glasgow, G2 4TB who is a qualified insolvency practitioner within the meaning of Part XIII of the Act is a suitable person for the office of Interim Liquidator. Copies of his consent to act, Insolvency Permit and Insolvency Practitioner Licence Bond are produced herewith.

8. The Company has ceased trading; however the Petitioners submit that, in the meantime, in order to ingather any sums due by debtors of the company and to secure and subsequent dispose of any stock, and furthermore to secure an orderly and maximum realisation of assets for the creditors of the Company, it is expedient that a Provisional Liquidator be appointed in terms of section 135 of the Act and that authority be given to him to exercise the powers craved. The said David Flint is also a suitable person to be Provisional Liquidator and consents so to act. Copies of his consent to act, Insolvency Permit and Insolvency Practitioner Licence Bond are produced herewith.

9. No receiver has been appointed to the Company, nor is it in administration.

10. This Petition is presented in terms of the Act and, in particular, sections 122 and 123 thereof and Schedule 4 thereto, and in terms of the Insolvency (Scotland) Rules 1986 and in terms of Part IV of the Act of Sederunt (Sheriff Court Company Insolvency Rules) 1986.

PLEAS-IN-LAW

1. The Company, being unable to pay its debts, should be wound-up by the Court and an Interim Liquidator appointed.

2. In the meantime, a Provisional Liquidator should be appointed and authority granted to him to exercise the powers craved.

IN RESPECT WHEREOF

(sgd) A Wiseman

Solicitor
152 Bath Street
Glasgow G2 4TB

PETITIONERS' AGENT

A12.   Minute of Directors resolving to Wind-up

EXCERPT MINUTE OF MEETING of the DIRECTORS of ROCOCO COCOA CO LIMITED held at Glasgow on [*date*] at 12 noon

Present: I B Broke
U R Broke

Mr I B Broke presided.

The Chairman tabled a Statement of Affairs of the Company as at [*date*] and pointed out that in terms of the said Statement of Affairs the Company was insolvent.

The Directors agreed that the Company was insolvent, unable to continue to trade and concluded that it should be wound-up.

It was resolved that MacRoberts, Solicitors, 152 Bath Street, Glasgow G2 4TB be instructed to present in the appropriate Court a Petition for the winding-up of the Company as soon as practicable.

In order to secure an orderly and maximum realisation of assets for the Company's creditors, it was further resolved that it would be in the interests of the creditors as a whole if a Provisional Liquidator were appointed to the Company in the meantime and it was resolved that MacRoberts should be instructed to seek the appointment of David Flint, Solicitor, 152 Bath Street, Glasgow G2 4TB or such other person as the Court may consider appropriate to that office.

This was all the business.

(sgd) I. B. Broke
....
Chairman

A13. Advertisement of First Order (with Provisional Liquidator) – Company Petition

<u>ROCOCO COCOA CO LIMITED</u>

Notice is hereby given that on [*date*] a petition was presented to the Sheriff at Glasgow by Rococo Cocoa Co Limited, roc having their Registered Office at 1 Main Street, Glasgow ("the Company") craving the Court *inter alia*, that the Company be wound-up by the Court and that an interim liquidator be appointed, in which petition the Sheriff at Glasgow by interlocutor dated [*date*] appointed all persons having an interest to lodge answers in the hands of the Sheriff Clerk, Glasgow, within eight days after intimation, advertisement or service, and *eo die* appointed David Flint, Solicitor, 152 Bath Street, Glasgow G2 4TB to be provisional liquidator of the Company with the powers specified in Parts II and III of Schedule 4 of the Insolvency Act 1986, of all of which notice is hereby given.

MacRoberts
Solicitors
152 Bath Street
Glasgow G2 4TB

<u>Agents for the Petitioners</u>

A14.   Petition by Members (Section 122(1)(g))

<u>SHERIFFDOM OF GLASGOW AND STRATHKELVIN AT GLASGOW</u>

PETITION

by

IAN   BARRY   BROKE,   "Duntradin",
Kilmacolm, and URIAH RODNEY BROKE,
"Tumbledown Cottage", Bridge of Weir ("the
Petitioners")

for

ORDER to WIND UP ROCOCO COCOA
CO LIMITED

To appoint this application to be intimated on the Walls of Court and to be advertised once in the *Edinburgh Gazette* and once in *"The Herald"* newspaper and to appoint all persons having an interest to lodge answers hereto if so advised within eight days after such intimation, service and advertisement; and on resuming consideration thereof, with or without answers, to order that said Rococo Cocoa Co Limited be wound-up by Court Order under the Provisions of the Insolvency Act 1986 (hereinafter referred to as "the Act"), and to appoint David Flint, Solicitor, 152 Bath Street, Glasgow G2 4TB or such other person as the Court may elect to be Provisional Liquidator of the said Company; to authorise the Interim Liquidator to advertise his appointment in the *Edinburgh Gazette* and *The Herald* newspaper in lieu of sending notices to creditors and others in terms of rule 4.18(4) of the Insolvency (Scotland) Rules 1986; to find the Petitioners entitled to the expenses of this application and to direct the same to be expenses in the liquidation; to find any party opposing this application liable in the expenses occasioned by such opposition; or to do further or otherwise in the premises as to the Court may seem proper.

CONDESCENDENCE

1.   Rococo Cocoa Co Limited (hereinafter referred to as "the Company") was incorporated on May 13, 1988 under the Companies Acts as a company limited by shares. The Registered Office of the Company is at 1 Main Street, Glasgow.

2.   The objects for which the Company was incorporated were to carry on the business of *inter alia* Entertainment Consultants as the Memorandum of Associated more fully provides. A copy of the Memorandum and Articles of Association of the Company is produced herewith and referred to for their terms.

3.   The share capital of the Company is £100 divided into 100 shares of £1 each, of which two are issued and are fully paid. The Petitioners hold one of these shares each.

4.   The Petitioners believe that the Company's business is not being conducted in accordance with [the Companies Act 1985] [the Articles of Association of the Company] in respect that [*e.g.* fraudulent element in running of the Company, no proper books kept, no auditors appointed, deadlock situation between shareholders][*Insert substantial reasoning here*].

5. By section 122(1)(g) of the Act it is provided that a Company may be wound-up by the Court, if the Court is of the opinion that it is just and equitable that the Company should be wound-up.

6. In the circumstances set forth the Petitioners submit that it is just and equitable that the Company should be wound-up. No receiver has been appointed to the Company, nor is it in administration.

7. The Petitioners respectfully suggest that David Flint, Solicitor, 152 Bath Street, Glasgow, G2 4TB who is a qualified insolvency practitioner within the meaning of Part XIII of the Act, is a suitable person for the office of Interim Liquidator. Copies of his consent to act, Insolvency Permit and Insolvency Practitioner Licence Bond are produced herewith.

8. This Petition is presented in terms of the Act and, in particular, section 122 thereof, in terms of the Insolvency (Scotland) Rules 1986 and in terms of Part IV of the Act of Sederunt (Sheriff Court Company Insolvency Rules) 1986.

PLEA-IN-LAW

It being just and equitable, the Company should be wound-up by the Court and an Interim Liquidator appointed.

IN RESPECT WHEREOF

(sgd) A Wiseman

Solicitor
152 Bath Street
Glasgow G2 4TB

PETITIONERS' AGENT

A15.   Advertisement of First Order (Members' Petition)

<u>ROCOCO COCOA CO LIMITED</u>

Notice is hereby given that on [*date*] a petition was presented to the Sheriff at Glasgow by Ian Barry Broke, "Duntradin", Kilmacolm and Uriah Rodney Broke, "Tumbledown Cottage", Bridge of Weir, carving the Court *inter alia*, that Rococo Cocoa Co Limited, having their Registered Office at 1 Main Street, Glasgow ("the Company") be wound-up by the Court and that an interim liquidator be appointed, in which petition the Sheriff at Glasgow by interlocutor dated [*date*] appointed all persons having an interest to lodge answers in the hands of the Sheriff Clerk, Glasgow, within eight days after intimation, advertisement or service, of all of which notice is hereby given.

MacRoberts
Solicitors
152 Bath Street
Glasgow G2 4TB

<u>Agents for the Petitioners</u>

A16.   Note for Recall of the Provisional Liquidator

SHERIFFDOM OF GLASGOW AND STRATHKELVIN AT GLASGOW

NOTE

relative to

PETITION

by

GALAXY PRODUCTS LIMITED ("the Petitioners")

for

Order to Wind up

ROCOCO COCOA CO LIMITED, 1 Main Street, Glasgow ("the Company")

for

Recall of the appointment of a provisional liquidator in terms of sections 172 and 174 of the Insolvency Act 1986 (as amended)

WISEMAN for the Petitioners states that a settlement of the claim by the Petitioners against the Company has been reached extra-judicially and craves the Court to grant Decree of Dismissal WHEREAS any fee due to the Provisional Liquidator has been or will be paid, the Petitioners crave the Court in terms of section 172 and section 174 of the Insolvency Act 1986 to recall the appointment of the Provisional Liquidator granted on [*date*], no expenses being found due to or by either party, AND WHEREAS the Petitioners have not yet advertised the import of the Petition and Deliverance dated [*date*] in the *Edinburgh Gazette* and *The Herald* newspaper, the Petitioners crave the Court to dispense with such advertisement and the advertisement of this Note and the Interlocutor to follow hereon or to do further or otherwise in the premises as to the Court may seem proper.

IN RESPECT WHEREOF

(sgd) A Wiseman

Solicitor
152 Bath Street
Glasgow G2 4TB

PETITIONERS' AGENT

A17. Note for Substitute Petitioner

<u>SHERIFFDOM OF GLASGOW AND STRATHKELVIN AT GLASGOW</u>

NOTE

for

ORINOCO COCOA CO LIMITED, having its Registered Office at 15 London Road, Paisley PA1 1NT ("the Noters") relative to Petition

by

GALAXY PRODUCTS LIMITED ("the Petitioners")

for

ORDER TO WIND UP ROCOCO COCOA CO LIMITED, having its Registered Office at 1 Main Street, Glasgow

for

an order to sist the Noters in place of the Petitioners in terms of rule 21 of the Act of Sederunt (Sheriff Court Company Insolvency Rules) 1986.

The Noters crave the Court:

To make an order sisting the Noters in place of the Petitioners in respect of the Petition for the winding-up of Rococo Cocoa Co Limited dated [*date*] in accordance with the provisions of rule 21 of the Act of Sederunt (Sheriff Court Company Insolvency Rules) 1986; to find any party opposing this application liable in the expenses occasioned by such opposition; to do further or otherwise in the premises as to the Court shall seem proper.

CONDESCENDENCE

1. On [*date*] a petition was presented to the Sheriff of Glasgow and Strathkelvin at Glasgow by Galaxy Products Limited craving the Court *inter alia* for an order to wind up Rococo Cocoa Co Limited, a private company incorporated under the Companies Acts and having its Registered Office at 1 Main Street, Glasgow (hereinafter called "the Company") under sections 122 and 123 of the Insolvency Act 1986 (hereinafter referred to as "the Act") and for the appointment of, firstly, a Provisional Liquidator and, subsequently, an Interim Liquidator.

2. The Petitioners have been found not entitled to present the petition. In an action in the Sheriff Court of Glasgow and Strathkelvin at Glasgow at the instance of the Noters against the Company the Sheriff decerned against the Company to pay to the Noters the sum of £10,000 with interest thereon at the rate of 15 per centum per annum from [*date*] until payment with expenses. An Extract of such Decree dated [*date*] together with a Charge for Payment were served on the Company by Sheriff Officers on [*date*] charging the Company to make payment of the sum then due to the Noters within 14 days of such service. The said Extract Decree together with Charge for Payment is produced herewith. The said period of fourteen days referred to in the said Charge for Payment has expired and no payment has been received from the

Company by the Noters. Section 122(1)(f) of the Act provides that a company may be wound-up by the court if it is unable to pay its debts. Section 123(1)(c) of the Act provides that a company is deemed unable to pay its debts if the *induciae* of a charge for payment on an extract decree has expired without payment being made. Accordingly, the Noters would therefore have been entitled to petition the Court for a winding-up order. The Noters, are entitled to be sisted as petitioners in room of Galaxy Products Limited in terms of rule 21 of the Act of Sederunt (Sheriff Court Company Insolvency Rules) 1986.

PLEA-IN-LAW

The Noters being creditors of the Company, the appropriate order should be granted as craved.

IN RESPECT WHEREOF

(sgd) A Wiseman

Solicitor
152 Bath Street
Glasgow G2 4TB

Agent for the Noters

A18. Notice of Winding-Up Order with Appointment of Interim Liquidator

<u>ROCOCO COCOA CO LIMITED (IN LIQUIDATION)</u>

Notice is hereby given that by interlocutor of the Sheriff at Glasgow dated [*date*], David Flint, Solicitor, 152 Bath Street, Glasgow G2 4TB was appointed interim liquidator of Rococo Cocoa Co Limited, having their Registered Office at 1 Main Street, Glasgow; it is the intention of the interim liquidator to summon a meeting of creditors for the purpose of establishing a liquidation committee of all of which intimation is hereby given.

> MacRoberts
> Solicitors
> 152 Bath Street
> Glasgow G2 4TB
>
> <u>Agents for the interim liquidator</u>

A19. Consent to Act by Liquidator – Following Court Order

<u>ROCOCO COCOA CO LIMITED (IN LIQUIDATION)</u>

I, DAVID FLINT of, MacRoberts, 152 Bath Street, Glasgow G2 4TB, hereby declare that I am an insolvency practitioner duly qualified under the Insolvency Act 1986 (as amended) to be the liquidator of the above company and that, in terms of rule 4.18(2) of the Insolvency (Scotland) Rules 1986, I consent so to act.

[*Signature*]

(Sgd) David Flint

**A20.   Letter to Directors with request for Statement of Affairs –
Provisional Appointment**

Your ref................................
Our ref ....

[*Date*]

Name and address

Dear Sir/Madam

Rococo Cocoa Co Limited – In Provisional Liquidation

In terms of rule 4.2(1)(b) of the Insolvency (Scotland) Rules 1986, I enclose formal notification of my appointment as Provisional Liquidator of Rococo Cocoa Co Limited with powers as specified in the attached copy Interlocutor of the Sheriff of Glasgow and Strathkelvin at Glasgow.

Pursuant to section 131 of the Insolvency Act 1986, I require from you a Statement as to the Affairs of the Company on the prescribed Form 4.4(Scotland) within 21 days after receipt of this notice, and I enclose From 4.3(Scotland) giving formal notice to that effect. This Statement should be verified by your Affidavit and both initialled and dated on each page.

Under rule 4.9(1) of the Insolvency (Scotland) Rules 1986, you may be entitled to be reimbursed by me out of the assets under my control in respect of any reasonable and proper professional fees which you incur in preparation of the Statement but, before any fees are incurred, you must advise me of the expected costs and receive my permission to proceed in writing.

Yours faithfully

David Flint
Provisional Liquidator

A21. Statement of Time and Trouble – Provisional Liquidator

ROCOCO COCOA CO LIMITED – IN PROVISIONAL LIQUIDATION

1. An analysis of the appropriate time records of MacRoberts, Solicitors, from [*date*] to [*date*] is as follows:

	Hours	£
Partner		
Associate		
Assistant		
Clerk		

Such time as is necessary for administering the termination of my appointment will be additional and is estimated as £_____.

2. A petition, at the instance of Galaxy Products Limited, was presented to the Sheriff of Glasgow and Strathkelvin at Glasgow for an order to wind up the Company on the ground specified in section 122(1)(f) of the Insolvency Act 1986.

3. My appointment as provisional liquidator was made by Interlocutor dated [*date*].

4. I forthwith gave notice of my appointment to:

    (a) the Registrar of Companies;

    (b) the Accountant in Bankruptcy;

    (c) the Company;

    [(d) the Receiver.]

5. I complied with the directions of the Court as to:

    (a) _____

    (b) _____

    (c) _____

6. Investigations were made as to the value of the realisable assets of the Company and an appropriate Certificate of Specific Penalty requested from my insurers.

7. The outstanding debt of the petitioning creditor has been paid.

8. I completed my statutory duties before requesting the law agent of the petitioning creditor to petition the Sheriff of Glasgow and Strathkelvin at Glasgow for:

(a)   the fixing of my remuneration expenses;

(b)   the termination of my appointment in terms of section 174(5) of the Insolvency Act 1986;

(c)   the dismissal of the winding-up petition.

(Sgd) David Flint
Provisional Liquidator

A22. **Sederunt Book – Contents**

in terms of rule 7.33(1) of the Insolvency (Scotland) Rules 1986

PROVISIONAL LIQUIDATION

ROCOCO COCOA CO LIMITED

Copy of petition
Copy of Interlocutor
Notice of Appointment
Copies of relevant *Edinburgh Gazettes*
Copies of relevant newspapers
Certificates of posting and related circulars
Certificate of specific penalty (pre 1 April 93)   Insolvency Practitioner
Regulations 13(1) ("IP")
Copy of bordereaux (post 1 April '93)   IP15
Statements of Affairs received from directors   Rule 4.8(2)
Reports on administration
Professional valuations of assets   Rule 4.22(1)(b)
Periodic accounts
Approval of fee
Release

Any other document necessary to give a correct view of the administration of the
Provisional Liquidation.

Note 1

When any document is of a confidential nature
(such as opinion of counsel on any matter
affecting the interests of the creditors), the
Liquidator shall not be bound to insert it, or
exhibit it to any person

                                             IR 7.27(1)

Note 2

The Sederunt Book shall be retained by the
Liquidator for a period of ten years
from the date of dissolution of the company.   IR 7.33(5)
                                             IP18

A23.   Letter to Directors requesting attendance at Creditors' Meeting and Statement of Affairs

Your ref ....
Our ref ....

[date]

Name and address

Dear Sir/Madam

Rococo Cocoa Co Limited – In Liquidation

I write to inform you that I was appointed Interim Liquidator of the above Company by Interlocutor of the Sheriff of Glasgow and Strathkelvin at Glasgow on *[date]*. I am authorised by The Law Society of Scotland to act as an insolvency practitioner.

In order to comply with sections 138 and 142 of the Insolvency Act 1986, I enclose a copy of the Statutory Notice convening a Meeting of Creditors.

In accordance with rule 4.14(2) of the Insolvency (Scotland) Rules 1986 and in your capacity as a director, your attendance at this meeting is required and failure to co-operate without reasonable excuse may lead to an application to the Court to require your attendance under section 157 or to prosecution under section 235 of the said Act.

Pursuant to section 131 of the Insolvency Act 1986, I require from you a Statement as to the Affairs of the Company on the prescribed Form 4.4(Scotland) within 21 days after receipt of this notice, and I enclose From 4.3(Scotland) giving formal notice to that effect. This Statement should be verified by your Affidavit and both initialled and dated on each page.

Under rule 4.9(1) of the Insolvency (Scotland) Rules 1986, you may be entitled to be reimbursed by me out of the assets under my control in respect of any reasonable and proper professional fees which you incur in preparation of the Statement but, before any fees are incurred, you must advise me of the expected costs and receive my permission to proceed in writing.

Yours faithfully

David Flint
Interim Liquidator

A24. Notice of Creditors' Meeting

INSOLVENCY ACT 1986

ROCOCO COCOA CO LIMITED – IN LIQUIDATION

Registered Office: 1 Main Street, Glasgow
Trading Address: Paradise Way, Ibrox, Glasgow

I, DAVID FLINT of MacRoberts, Solicitors, 152 Bath Street, Glasgow G2 4TB give notice that I was appointed Interim Liquidator of Rococo Cocoa Co Limited by Interlocutor of that Sheriff of Glasgow and Strathkelvin at Glasgow on [*date*].

NOTICE IS HEREBY GIVEN that, in terms of section 138(4) of the Insolvency Act 1986 a Meeting of Creditors of the above Company will be held at Trades Hall, Glasgow on [*date*] at 12 noon for the purpose of choosing a person (who may be the Interim Liquidator) to be liquidator of the above company, and of determining whether to establish a liquidation committee in terms of section 142 of the Insolvency Act 1986.

The attention of Creditors is drawn to the following:

1. A Creditor is entitled to vote only if he has submitted his claim (Form 4.7(Scotland)) and his claim has been accepted in whole or in part.

2. A Resolution at the meeting is passed if a majority in value of those voting vote in favour of it.

3. Proxies may be lodged at or before the meeting at the offices of MacRoberts, Solicitors, 152 Bath Street, Glasgow G2 4TB marked for the attention of Mr David Flint.

4. Claims may be lodged by those who have not already done so at or before the meeting at the said offices.

5. The provisions of rules 4.15–4.17 (as amended by Schedule 1) and of rule 7 of the Insolvency (Scotland) Rules 1986.

For the purpose of formulating claims, creditors should note that the date of liquidation is [*date*].

If you are in any doubt as to any of these matters, you should consult your Solicitor immediately.

....
(Sgd) David Flint
Interim Liquidator

[*date*]

MacRoberts
Solicitors
152 Bath Street
Glasgow G2 4TB

A25.   Agenda for First Statutory Meeting of Creditors

AGENDA FOR FIRST STATUTORY MEETING OF CREDITORS

ROCOCO COCOA CO LIMITED – IN LIQUIDATION

held at Trades Hall, Glasgow

on [*date*] at 12 noon

in terms of section 38 of the Insolvency Act 1986

[Quorum:	One creditors in person or by proxy	Rule 7.7, 7.16]
	entitled to vote	
[Chairman:	The Interim Liquidator	Rule 7.5(4)]

1.   Introduction

Explanation of Purpose of Meeting:

To choose a Liquidator	Section 138(3); 4.12(3)(a)
To establish a Liquidation Committee	Section 142(1); 4.12(3)(b)
To specify the terms on which the Liquidator is to be remunerated if no Liquidation Committee is established	Rule 4.12(3)(c)
To adjourn the meeting if no quorum is present and for the chairman to give notice of the date and time of the adjourned meeting	Rule 7.8(5)
To take any other resolution which the Chairman considers it right to allow for special reason	Rule 4.12(3)(e)

Documents Laid on Table:

By Statute:	None	
By Habit:	Notice of Meeting	Rule 7.3(2)(d)
	Related Certificate of Posting	Rule 7.23(1)
	Edinburgh Gazette	
	One newspapers	Rule 7.3(3)
	Directors' Statement of Affairs, if available	Section 131

2.   Report based on Company History, Deficiency Statement, Estimated Statement of Affairs and Directors' Statement of Affairs   Rule 4.10(1) + (3)

Questions

3.   Appointment of Liquidator

(a)   Interim Liquidator as sole nominee:

Elect another chairman of meeting for this purpose only	Rule 7.5(4)
Exhibit Consent to Act and certify appointment	Rule 4.19(2)

(b)   Another insolvency practitioner as sole nominee:

Exhibit Consent to Act and certify appointment		Rule 4.19(2)

(c) Interim Liquidator and one or more other insolvency practitioners as nominees:

Elect another Chairman of meeting for this purpose only	Rule 7.5(4)

Exhibit Consent to Act and certify appointment	Rule 4.19(2)

One vote is required if one nominee has a clear majority in value of claim over all the other nominees	Rule 7.12(3)(a) + (b)

Several votes are required if no one nominee has a clear majority, the nominee with the least support withdrawing at each subsequent vote	Rule 7.12(3)(c)

(d) No nominee:

Report to Court which shall appoint as Liquidator either the Interim Liquidator or another insolvency practitioner	Section 138(5)

4. Establishment of Liquidation Committee

Explanation of Composition and powers:

Composition:	At least three and not more than five creditors or their	Rule 4.41(1)(a)
	representatives plus up to three contributories or their representatives if the Company is solvent and a separate Meeting of Contributories has been held under s 138(3), (plus the Deposit Protection Board if the Company in liquidation is a Bank and the DPB exercises its right to	Rule 4.41(1)(b)
	join the Committee)	Rule 4.41(1)(b)
Powers:	to assist the Liquidator in the winding-up	
	to audit the intromissions of the Liquidator	Rule 4.32(1)
	to determine the outlays and remuneration of the Liquidator	Rule 4.32 (2)
	to review the adequacy of caution obtained by Liquidator	Rule 7.28(2)(b)
[Note:	Except with the prior leave of the Court or of the Liquidation Committee, a member, or any person who has been a member within the	Rule 4.58

last twelve months, shall not
enter into any transaction
whereby he receives any
payment for services given or
goods supplied, or obtains
profit, or acquires any part
of the liquidated assets.
A member shall be reimbursed   Rule 4.57(1)
for any reasonable travelling
expenses incurred in
attending meetings of the
Liquidation Committee
excepting those in respect of a
meeting held within three
months of a previous
meeting]   Rule 4.57(2)

Obtain written Consents to Act, with full names,
addresses and telephone numbers. If formed,
then hold first meeting after close of this meeting.

5. If no Liquidation Committee is established the   Rule 4.12(3)(c)
   liquidator shall:

   (a) advise creditors that until or unless a
        liquidation committee is later established
        applications shall be made, at the
        appropriate times, to the Court for
        approval of the liquidator's remuneration
        and expenses based on the time records
        of his firm.

   (b) put resolutions to the meeting for approval:

        ■ to dispense in whole with the
           settlement of a list of contributories.

        ■ to fix as the date on or before which
           all creditors are to prove their debts or
           claims or be excluded from the benefit
           of distribution made before those
           debts are proved.

        ■ to appoint Solicitors in the Liquidation
           to assist the Liquidator in the
           performance of his duties.

6. Close of Meeting

A26. Minute of Statutory meeting of Creditors (Section 138)

MINUTE OF STATUTORY MEETING OF CREDITORS OF ROCOCO COCOA CO LIMITED – IN LIQUIDATION, held at Trades Hall, Glasgow on [*date*] at 12 noon in terms of section 38 of the Insolvency Act 1986

Present:

In Attendance:

1. The meeting was deemed to be properly constituted.

2. The Interim Liquidator reported on the History and the Statement of Affairs of the Company, and answered the questions of the creditors.

3. [B Smith (an employee of the Interim Liquidator)] was elected as Chairman of the meeting for the purpose of choosing the Liquidator.

4. It was resolved to appoint as Liquidator, David Flint, Solicitor, 152 Bath Street, Glasgow G2 4TB and a Certificate of Appointment was duly issued after the Chairman had been provided with a written statement to the effect that Mr Flint was a duly qualified insolvency practitioner and that he consented so to act.

5. It was resolved that the Liquidator be remunerated for his time and trouble by reference to the time records of his firm

6. A Liquidation Committee to act with the Liquidator was elected, comprising:

[*name*]

[*name*]

[*name*]

Its members agreed to act and the Liquidator issued a Certificate of Constitution.

OR

6. A Liquidation Committee to act with the Liquidator was not elected and it was resolved:

(a) to dispense in whole with the settlement of a list of contributories;

(b) to fix [*date*] as the date on or before which all creditors are to prove their debts or claims or to be excluded from the benefit of any distribution made before those debts are proved.

(c) to appoint MacRoberts, Solicitors, 152 Bath Street, Glasgow G2 4TB as solicitors in the liquidation to assist the liquidator in the performance of his duties.

OR

1. The meeting was adjourned until _____ at _____ at _____.

....

Chairman

A27. Letter of Consent from the Liquidator – Following Creditors Meeting

ROCOCO COCOA CO LIMITED

(In Liquidation)

I, DAVID FLINT of MacRoberts, Solicitors, 152 Bath Street, Glasgow G2 4TB, hereby declare that I am an insolvency practitioner duly qualified under the Insolvency Act 1986 to be the liquidator of the above company and that, in terms of Rule 4.19(2) of the Insolvency (Scotland) Rules 1986, I consent so to act.

....(Sgd) David Flint

A28.   **Sederunt Book**

in terms of rule 7.33(1) of the Insolvency (Scotland) Rules 1986

COURT LIQUIDATION

ROCOCO COCOA CO LIMITED

Copy of winding-up petition
Copy of Interlocutor
Certificate of Appointment
External notices of appointment
Copies of relevant *Edinburgh Gazettes*
Copies of relevant newspapers
Certificates of posting and related circulars   Insolvency Practitioner
                                                          Regulations 1990, regulation
                                                          13(1)
Certificate of Constitution of Liquidation Committee
Claims endorsed with date of receipt
Notice of change of Registered Office
Statements of Affairs received from directors   Rule 4.8(2)
Reports on administration
Minutes of meetings of creditors   Rule 7.13(3)
Proxies used for voting at meetings   Rule 7.17(3)
Minutes of meetings of liquidation committee   Rule 4.55(5)
Professional valuations of assets   Rule 4.22(1)(*b*)
Reports on conduct of directors
Periodic accounts
Dividends paid
Approval of fee   Rule 4.32
Release

Any other document necessary to give correct
view of the administration of the liquidation.

Note 1   When any document is of a confidential nature (such as opinion of coun-
          sel on any matter affecting the interests of the creditors), the Liquidator
          shall not be bound to insert it, or exhibit it to any person other than a
          court official or a member of the Liquidation Committee.

                              Rule 7.27(1)

Note 2   The Sederunt Book shall be retained by the Liquidator for a period of ten
          years from the date of dissolution of the Company.

                              Rule 7.33(5)

A29. Minutes of First Meeting of the Liquidation Committee

MINUTES OF THE FIRST MEETING OF THE LIQUIDATION COMMIT-
TEE APPOINTED TO ASSIST THE LIQUIDATOR OF ROCOCO COCOA
CO LIMITED HELD AT GLASGOW ON [*date*].

Present: ....

In Attendance: ....

It was:

1. resolved to ask the Court to fix _____ as the date on or
    before which all creditors are to prove their debts or claims or to be excluded
    from the benefit of any distribution made before those debts are proved;

2. reported that the Liquidator had appointed MacRoberts, Solicitors, 152 Bath
    Street, Glasgow G2 4TB, as Solicitors in the Liquidation to assist the
    Liquidator in the performance of his duties, such report conforming to sec-
    tion 167(2)(b) of the Insolvency Act 1986;

3. resolved to meet as required within the terms of rule 4.45(1) of the Insolvency
    (Scotland) Rules 1986 and to waive written notice thereof under rule 4.45(3);

4. resolved that the Liquidator sends to every member of the Liquidation
    Committee a written report setting out the position generally as regards the
    progress of the winding-up and matters arising in connection with it, all in
    terms of rule 4.56(2) of the Insolvency (Scotland) Rules 1986 as and when the
    Liquidator considers it appropriate;

5. resolved that the Liquidator will give notice to the Committee of any inten-
    tion to dispose of any property of the Company to a person who is connected
    with the Company under section 167(2) of the Insolvency Act 1986;

6. resolved that the Liquidator investigates the following:

    a.
    b.
    c.

7. resolved that the Liquidator be remunerated by reference to the time records
    of his firm and that the Liquidator be authorised to draw remuneration on
    account.

Norman E Bodie (Liquidator's Representative)
Chairman

A30. Letter agreeing to act as Member of the Liquidation Committee

David Flint Esq ....*[signature]*
Liquidator,
Rococo Cocoa Co Limited

Dear Sir

I write to confirm that I am agreeable to acting as a member of the Liquidation Committee of Rococo Cocoa Co Limited – in Liquidation which was elected on *[date]*.

Yours faithfully

Name: ....

Representing: ....

Address: ....

                        ....

                        ....

Telephone: ....

A31. Letter Nominating Chairman of Meeting of the Liquidation Committee

<u>ROCOCO COCOA CO LIMITED</u> – In Liquidation

MEETING OF LIQUIDATION COMMITTEE
Held at Glasgow on [*date*]

I, DAVID FLINT, Solicitor, Liquidator of Rococo Cocoa Co Limited, nominate Norman E Bodie, my employee who is experienced in insolvency matters, to be Chairman of the above meeting in terms of Rule 4.46(2)(b) of the Insolvency (Scotland) Rules 1986.

(Sgd) David Flint

A32. Notice of Statutory Meeting

INSOLVENCY ACT 1986

ROCOCO COCOA CO LIMITED – IN LIQUIDATION

NOTICE IS HEREBY GIVEN that, in terms of rule 4.13(1) of the Insolvency (Scotland) Rules 1986, a meeting of the creditors of the above company will be held within the offices of MacRoberts, Solicitors, 152 Bath Street, Glasgow G2 4TB at 12 noon on [date], for the purpose of receiving an account of the Liquidator's acts and dealings and of the conduct of the winding-up for the year ended [date].

The attention of creditors is drawn to the following:

1. A Creditor is entitled to vote only if he has submitted his claim (Form 4.7(Scotland)) and his claim has been accepted in whole or in part.

2. A Resolution at the meeting is passed if a majority in value of those voting vote in favour of it.

3. Proxies may be lodged at or before the meeting at the office of MacRoberts, Solicitors, 152 Bath Street, Glasgow G2 4TB marked for the attention of Mr David Flint.

4. Claims may be lodged by those who have not already done so at or before the meeting at the said offices.

5. The provisions of rules 4.15–4.17 (as amended by Schedule 1) and of rule 7 of the Insolvency (Scotland) Rules 1986.

For the purpose of formulating claims, creditors should note that the date of liquidation is [date].

If you are in any doubt as to any of these matters, you should consult your Solicitor immediately.

....
Liquidator

MacRoberts
Solicitors
152 Bath Street
Glasgow
G2 4TB
[date]

A33.   Minute of Statutory Meeting of Creditors

> MINUTE OF STATUTORY MEETING
> OF CREDITORS OF ROCOCO COCOA
> CO LIMITED – IN LIQUIDATION held
> at 152 Bath Street, Glasgow G2 4TB on
> [*date*] at 12 noon in terms of rule 4.13(1) of
> the Insolvency (Scotland) Rules 1986

Present:

In Attendance:

1. The meeting was deemed to be properly constituted.

2. The Chairman gave an account of the Liquidator's acts and dealings and of the conduct of the winding-up for the year ended [*date*] which was accepted by the Meeting.

OR

1. The meeting was deemed to be properly convened.

2. It was noted that there was no quorum.

3. An account of the Liquidator's acts and dealings and of the conduct of the winding-up for the year ended [*date*] was deemed to have been tabled.

....

Chairman

A34. Minute of Meeting of Liquidation Committee

MINUTE of a MEETING of the Liquidation Committee appointed to assist the Liquidator of ROCOCO COCOA CO LIMITED held at 152 Bath Street, Glasgow G2 4TB on [*date*] at 10 am

Present:

In Attendance:

1. The meeting was held to be properly constituted.

2. The Liquidator gave an account of the winding-up to date which was accepted by the meeting.

3. The amount of caution obtained by the Liquidator was reviewed and was deemed adequate.

4. It was agreed that the following dividends be paid to the various ranking creditors:

5. It was agreed that the Liquidator should receive an interim fee of £_____ plus VAT. (Basis of Calculation)

[6. It was agreed that the Liquidator could be released from his office subject to the concurrence of the final meeting of creditors held pursuant to section 146 of the Insolvency Act 1986.]

....

Chairman

A35.   Notice of Meeting for Release of Liquidator (Resignation)

INSOLVENCY ACT 1986

ROCOCO COCOA CO LIMITED – IN LIQUIDATION

NOTICE IS HEREBY GIVEN that, pursuant to rule 4.28(1) of the Insolvency (Scotland) Rules 1986, a meeting of the creditors of the above Company will be held at 152 Bath Street, Glasgow G2 4TB on [*date*] at 12 noon for the purpose of considering resolutions in relation to the resignation as liquidator of [*name*] and which shall include a determination under section 174(4)(c) of the Insolvency Act and rule 4.29(4) of the said Rules.

In the event that the resignation of [*name*] is approved, the meeting will need to determine whether or not he is granted his release and may also resolve to appoint another liquidator to fill the vacancy.

The attention of creditors is drawn to the following:

1.   A Creditor is entitled to vote only if he has submitted his claim (Form 4.7 (Scotland)) to the address mentioned below and his claim has been accepted in whole or in part.

2.   A Resolution at the meeting is passed if a majority in value of those voting vote in favour of it.

3.   Proxies may be lodged at or before the meeting at the office of MacRoberts, Solicitors, 152 Bath Street, Glasgow G2 4TB marked for the attention of Mr David Flint.

4.   Claims may be lodged by those who have not already done so at or before the meeting at the said offices.

5.   The provisions of rules 4.15–4.17 (as amended by Schedule 1) and of rule 7 of the Insolvency (Scotland) Rules 1986.

For the purpose of formulating claims, creditors should note that the date of liquidation is [*date*].

If you are in any doubt as to any of these matters, you should consult your Solicitor immediately.

....
Liquidator

MacRoberts
Solicitors
152 Bath Street
Glasgow
G2 4TB
[*date*]

A36.   Agenda for Release of Liquidator

<u>AGENDA FOR MEETING OF CREDITORS OF</u>

<u>ROCOCO COCOA CO LIMITED – IN LIQUIDATION</u>

<u>held at [*address*]</u>

<u>on [*date*] at [*time*]</u>

<u>in terms of rule 4.28 of the Insolvency (Scotland) Rules 1986</u>

[Quorum:	One creditors in person or by proxy entitled to vote	Rule 7.7, 7.16]
[Chairman:	The Interim Liquidator]	Rule 7.5(4)]
[Note:	If no quorum is present, the meeting is deemed to have been held, the resignation of the liquidator being immediately effective	Rule 4.29(6) and (7)]

1.   Introduction

Explanation of Purpose of Meeting:

To accept the resignation of the Liquidator due to: Rule 4.28(3)

    (a)   ill health; or
    (b)   intention to cease practice as an insolvency
         practitioner; or
    (c)   conflict of interest having arisen; or
    (d)   such a change of personal circumstances as to
         make continuation in office impracticable

To choose a succeeding Liquidator   Rule 4.29(5)
To specify the terms on which the former liquidator
be remunerated

Documents Laid on Table:

By Statute:	None	

By Habit:	Notice of meeting	Rule 7.6(3)
	Related certificate of posting	Rule 7.23(1)
	Edinburgh Gazette	-
	Two newspapers	Rule 7.3(3)
	Letter of resignation	-

2.   Elect another Chairman, who will:

    (a)   determine the release f the Liquidator, who will
         lodge with the Registrar of Companies Form
         4.16(Scotland)   Section 171(5)
    (b)   invite nominations for a succeeding Liquidator
         under procedures given in Rules 4.19, 4.20,
         4.27 and 7.12 of the Insolvency (Scotland)
         Rules 1986   Rule 4.29(5)

3,   The succeeding Liquidator will take the Chair and:

    (a)   invite proposals for the determination of the fee
         and outlays of the former Liquidator
    (b)   discuss any other relevant business
    (c)   close meeting

A37. Notice of Meeting for Removal of Liquidator

INSOLVENCY ACT 1986

<u>ROCOCO COCOA CO LIMITED – IN LIQUIDATION</u>

NOTICE IS HEREBY GIVEN that, in terms of section 172(2) of the Insolvency Act 1986, a meeting of the creditors of the above Company will be held at 152 Bath Street, Glasgow G2 4TB on [date] at 12 noon to consider the resolutions for the removal of [name] as Liquidator which shall include a determination under section 174(4)(a) or (b) of the said Act.

In the event that the removal of [name] is approved, the meeting will need to determine whether or not he is granted his release and may also resolve to appoint another liquidator to fill the vacancy.

The attention of creditors is drawn to the following:

1. a creditor is entitled to vote only if he has submitted his claim (Form 4.7(Scotland)) to the address mentioned below and his claim has been accepted in whole or in part;

2. a resolution at the meeting is passed if a majority in value of those voting vote in favour of it;

3. proxies may be lodged at or before the meeting at the undernoted offices marked for the attention of Mr David Flint;

4. claims may be lodged by those who have not already done so at or before the meeting at the said offices;

5. the provisions of rule 4.15–4.17 (as amended by Schedule 1) and of rule 7 of the Insolvency (Scotland) Rules 1986.

For the purpose of formulating claims, creditors should note that the date of liquidation is [date].

If you are in any doubt as to any of these matters, you should consult your Solicitor immediately.

....
Liquidator

MacRoberts
Solicitors
152 Bath Street
Glasgow
G2 4TB

[date]

A38. Notice of Meeting of Creditors

INSOLVENCY ACT 1986

ROCOCO COCOA CO LIMITED – IN LIQUIDATION

NOTICE IS HEREBY GIVEN that, in terms of section 172(3) of the Insolvency Act 1986, a meeting of the creditors of the above Company will be held at 152 Bath Street, Glasgow G2 4TB on [date] at 12 noon to consider the resolutions which shall include a determination under section 173(2)(a) or (b) of the said Act.

The attention of creditors is drawn to the following:

1. a creditor is entitled to vote on if he has submitted his claim (Form 4.7(Scotland)) to the address mentioned below and his claim has been accepted in whole or in part;

2. a resolution at the meeting is passed if a majority in value of those voting vote in favour of it;

3. proxies may be lodged at or before the meeting at the undernoted offices marked for the attention of Mr David Flint;

4. claims may be lodged by those who have not already done so at or before the meeting at the said offices;

5. the provisions of rules 4.15–4.17 (as amended by Schedule 1) and of rule 7 of the Insolvency (Scotland) Rules 1986.

If you are in any doubt as to any of these matters, you should consult your Solicitor immediately.

....
Liquidator

MacRoberts
Solicitors
152 Bath Street
Glasgow
G2 4TB

[date]

A39.   Sederunt Book

CONTENTS

in terms of rule 7.33(1) of the Insolvency (Scotland) Rules 1986

INTERIM LIQUIDATION

ROCOCO COCOA CO LIMITED

Copy of winding-up petition
Copy of Interlocutor
Notice of Appointment
External notices of appointment
Copies of relevant *Edinburgh Gazettes*
Copies of relevant newspapers
Certificates of posting and related circulars
Certificate of specific penalty   Insolvency Practitioner
                                                     Regulations 1990, regulation
                                                     13(1)

Notice of change of Registered Office
Statements of Affairs received from directors   Rule 4.8(2)
Reports on administration
Minute of meetings of creditors   Rule 7.13(3)
Proxies used for voting at meetings   Rule 7.17(3)
Professional valuations of assets   Rule 4.22(1)(b)
Periodic accounts
Approval of fee   Rule 4.32
Release

Any other document necessary to give a correct view of the administration of the
Interim Liquidation.

Note 1   When any document is of a confidential
          nature (such as opinion of counsel on any
          matter affecting the interests of the
          creditors), the Liquidator shall not be
          bound to insert it, or exhibit it to any
          person other than a court official.
                                                     Rule 7.27(1)

Note 2   The Sederunt Book shall be retained
          by the Interim Liquidator for a period
          of ten years from the date of the
          dissolution of the Company.
                                                     Rule 7.33(5)

A40. Note for Dispensing with List of Contributories / Fixing a Date for Claims

<u>SHERIFFDOM OF GLASGOW AND STRATHKELVIN AT GLASGOW</u>

NOTE

for

DAVID FLINT, Solicitor, 152 Bath Street, Glasgow, G2 4TB, the Liquidator of Rococo Cocoa Co Limited, incorporated under the Companies Acts and having its Registered Office at 1 Main Street, Glasgow ("the Noter")

relative to

Winding-up of

ROCOCO COCOA CO LIMITED, 1 Main Street, Glasgow ("the Company")

for

(1)   Dispensation with the settlement of a list of contributories;

(2)   Fixing a date for proving claims.

The Noter craves the Court:

(1)   to dispense with the settlement of a list of contributories in pursuance of section 148(2) of the Insolvency Act 1986 ("the Act");

(2)   to fix [*date*] in pursuance of section 153 of the Act as the date on or before which all creditors of the Company are to prove their debts or claims, or to be excluded from the benefit of any distribution made before the said debts are proved, and to appoint the Petitioner to advertise such date once in the *Edinburgh Gazette* and once in *The Herald* newspaper or to do further and otherwise in the premises as to the Court shall seem proper.

CONDESCENDENCE

1.   On [*date*] a Petition was presented to the Sheriff of Glasgow and Strathkelvin at Glasgow by Galaxy Products Limited for an order to Wind up Rococo Cocoa Co Limited (hereinafter called "the Company") a private company incorporated under the Companies Acts and having its Registered Office at 1 Main Street, Glasgow under sections 122 and 123 of the Act and for the appointment of first a Provisional Liquidator and subsequently an Interim Liquidator. On [*date*] the Sheriff of Glasgow and Strathkelvin at Glasgow pronounced an Interlocutor nominating and appointing the Noter to be Provisional Liquidator of the Company. On [*date*] the Sheriff of Glasgow and Strathkelvin at Glasgow pronounced an Interlocutor ordering that the said Rococo Cocoa Co Limited be wound-up in pursuance of the Act on the ground that the Company was unable to pay its debts and nominated and appointed the Noter to be the Interim Liquidator of the Company. Notice of this Interlocutor was inserted in the *Edinburgh Gazette* on [*date*].

2.   At a meeting of the creditors of the Company convened in accordance with the provisions of sections 138 and 142 of the Act and held on [ ] it was resolved that:

    (a) The Noter be appointed as Liquidator of the Company; and

    (b) [no/a] Liquidation Committee should be appointed to act with such Liquidator.

3.   All the shares of the Company being fully paid up and the prospects of any distribution being made to the holders thereof being exceedingly remote, application is made to the Court for the Court to dispense with the settlement of a list of contributories in terms of section 148 of the Act.

4.   As it is desirable to have a date fixed for the proving of claims in the liquidation, application is made to the Court to fix the [*date*] as the date on or before which all creditors of the Company must prove their debts or be excluded from the benefit of any distribution made before the said debts are proved and to advertise such date as craved.

5.   This Note is presented in terms of the Act and in particular sections 148 and 153, and in terms of the Insolvency (Scotland) Rules 1986 and in terms of Part IV of the Act of Sederunt (Sheriff Court Company Insolvency Rules) 1986.

PLEAS-IN-LAW

1.   All the shares of the Company being fully paid up and the likelihood of there being a surplus available for the contributories being extremely remote, the Court should dispense with the settlement of a list of contributories.

2.   It be desirable to fix a date for proving of claims in the liquidation, the Court should fix such a date.

           IN RESPECT WHEREOF

           (sgd) A Wiseman

           Solicitor
           152 Bath Street
           Glasgow G2 4TB

           NOTER'S AGENT

A41. Note for Approval of Interim Accounts – Change of Liquidator, where no Committee and Accounts cannot be agreed.

SHERIFFDOM OF GLASGOW AND STRATHKELVIN AT GLASGOW

NOTE

for

DAVID FLINT, Solicitor, 152 Bath Street, Glasgow, G2 4TB the Liquidator of Rococo Cocoa Co Limited, incorporated under the Companies Acts and having its Registered Office at 1 Main Street, Glasgow ("the Noter")

relative to

Winding-up of

ROCOCO COCOA CO LIMITED, 1 Main Street, Glasgow ("the Company")

for

Approval of his Accounts to [*name*]; Authority to have his Solicitors' Business Account taxed and payment made thereof; and Authority to make payment of his remuneration

The Noter craves the court:

(1) to dispense with advertisement hereof in the *Edinburgh Gazette* and *The Herald* newspaper;

(2) to remit the business account incurred by the Noter as Provisional Liquidator and as Interim Liquidator to his solicitors for the period from the commencement of the Liquidation to [*name*] to the Auditor of Court for taxation and to authorise the Liquidator to pay the taxed amount thereof;

(3) to remit the account of intromissions of the Noter as Provisional Liquidator and as Interim Liquidator for the period from the commencement of the Liquidation to [ ] to Ivor Winner, CA, Counting House Lane, Glasgow G1 4SS or to such other person as to the Court shall seem proper and to direct such person to report what in his opinion is a suitable remuneration for the Noter as Provisional and as Interim Liquidator;

(4) on the result of such examination and audit being reported to the Court to fix and declare the amount of the remuneration to be paid to the Noter as Provisional and as Interim Liquidator and to authorise A N Other, Solicitor, Excel House, 30 Semple Street, Edinburgh, EH3 8BL, the Liquidator of the Company (hereinafter called "the Liquidator") to make payment thereof;

or to do further and otherwise in the premises as to the Court shall seem proper.

CONDESCENDENCE

1. On [*date*] a Petition was presented to the Sheriff of Glasgow and Strathkelvin at Glasgow by Galaxy Products Limited for an order to Wind up Rococo Cocoa Co Limited (hereinafter called "the Company") a private company incorporated under the Companies Acts and having its Registered Office at 1 Main Street, Glasgow under sections 122 and 123 of the Insolvency Act 1986 (as amended) (hereinafter referred to as "the Act") and for the appointment of first a Provisional Liquidator and subsequently an Interim Liquidator. On

[*date*] the Sheriff of Glasgow and Strathkelvin at Glasgow pronounced an Interlocutor nominating and appointing the Noter to be Provisional Liquidator of the Company. On [*date*] the Sheriff of Glasgow and Strathkelvin at Glasgow pronounced an Interlocutor ordering that the Company be wound-up in pursuance of the Act on the ground that the Company was unable to pay its debts and nominated and appointed the Noter to be the Interim Liquidator of the Company. Notice of the this Interlocutor was inserted in the *Edinburgh Gazette* on [*date*].

2. At a meeting of the creditors of the Company convened in accordance with the provisions of sections 138 and 142 of the Act 1986 and held on [*date*] it was resolved that:

    (a) A N Other, Solicitor, Excel House, 30 Semple Street, Edinburgh, EH3 8BL be appointed as Liquidator of the Company; and

    (b) no Liquidation Committee should be appointed to act with such Liquidator.

3. In view of the appointment of A N Other as Liquidator aforesaid, the Noter considers it appropriate that his intromissions as Provisional Liquidator and as Interim Liquidator be audited and payment made in respect of his remuneration.

4. The Noter has prepared a Statement of his Intromissions for the period from the commencement of the liquidation to [*name*] and is desirous that said Statement should be audited and a payment in respect of his remuneration fixed. The Noter respectfully submits that Ivor Winner, Chartered Accountant, 1 Counting House Lane, Glasgow G1 4SS is a suitable person to examine and audit said Statement. The Noter is also desirous of having the Business Account incurred by him to his solicitors for the period from [*date*] to date remitted to the Auditor of Court for taxation and of the Liquidator being authorised to pay the taxed amount thereof.

5. This Notice is presented in terms of the Act and in terms of the Insolvency (Scotland) Rules 1986 and in terms of Part IV of the Act of Sederunt (Sheriff Court Company Insolvency Rules) 1986.

PLEA-IN-LAW

The Noter being entitled to have the Court fix his remuneration, the appropriate orders should be granted as craved.

IN RESPECT WHEREOF

(sgd) A Wiseman

Solicitor
152 Bath Street
Glasgow G2 4TB

NOTER'S AGENT

A42. Note for Approval of Final Accounts – Change of Liquidator

SHERIFFDOM OF GLASGOW AND STRATHKELVIN AT GLASGOW

NOTE

for

ALAN NEIL OTHER, Solicitor, Excel House, 30 Semple Street, Edinburgh, EH3 8BL, Liquidator of ROCOCO COCOA CO LIM ITED, incorporated under the Companies Acts and having its Registered Office at 1 Main Street, Glasgow ("the Noter")

relative to

Winding-up of

ROCOCO COCOA CO LIMITED, 1 Main Street, Glasgow ("the Company")

for

Approval of his Accounts from [*name*]; Authority to have Solicitors' Business Account taxed and payment made thereof; and Authority to take payment of his remunera tion

The Noter craves the Court:

(1) to dispense with advertisement hereof in the *Edinburgh Gazette* and *The Herald* newspaper;

(2) to remit the business account incurred by the Noter as Liquidator to his Solicitors for the period from [*date*] to the close of the liquidation to the Auditor of Court for taxation and to authorise the Liquidator to pay the taxed amount thereof;

(3) to remit the account of intromissions of the Noter as Liquidator for the period from [*date*] to date to Ivor Winner, CA, Counting House Lane, Glasgow G1 4SS, or such other person as to the Court shall seem proper and to direct such person to report what, in his opinion, is a suitable remuneration for the Noter as Liquidator as aforesaid;

(4) on the result of such examination and audit being reported to the Court to fix and declare the amount of the remuneration to be paid to the Noter as Liquidator and to authorise him to take credit therefor;

(5) to approve the Noter's whole intromissions in the said liquidation and to approve of the accounts of his intromissions;

or to do further and otherwise in the premises as to the Court shall seem proper.

CONDESCENDENCE

1. On [*date*] a Petition was presented to the Sheriff of Glasgow and Strathkelvin at Glasgow by Galaxy Products Limited for an order to wind up Rococo Cocoa Co Limited (hereinafter called "the Company"), a private company incorporated under the Companies Acts and having its Registered Office at 1 Main Street, Glasgow under sections 122 and 123 of Insolvency Act 1986 (as amended) (hereinafter referred to as "the Act") and for the appointment of first a Provisional Liquidator and subsequently an Interim Liquidator. On

[*date*] the Sheriff of Glasgow and Strathkelvin at Glasgow pronounced an Interlocutor nominating and appointing David Flint, Solicitor, 152 Bath Street, Glasgow G2 4TB as Provisional Liquidator of the Company. On [*date*] the Sheriff of Glasgow and Strathkelvin at Glasgow pronounced an Interlocutor ordering that the Company be wound-up in pursuance of the Act on the ground that the Company was unable to pay its debts and nominated and appointed the said David Flint to be Interim Liquidator of the Company. Notice of this Interlocutor was inserted in the *Edinburgh Gazette* on [*date*].

2.   At a meeting of the creditors of the Company convened in accordance with the provisions of sections 138 and 142 of the Act and held on [*date*] it was resolved that:

    (a) the Noter be appointed as Liquidator of the Company; and

    (b) no Liquidation Committee should be appointed to act with such Liquidator.

3.   On [*date*] the Court remitted to Ivor Winner, Chartered Accountant, Counting House Lane, Glasgow, G1 4SS, to examine and audit the Accounts of the said David Flint's intromissions as Provisional and as Interim Liquidator from [*date*] to [*date*] and to report what would be suitable payment of the Provisional and Interim Liquidator's remuneration for the said period and remitted the Business Account incurred by the Provisional and Interim Liquidator to his solicitors in respect of such period to the Auditor of Court for taxation. By Interlocutor dated [*date*] the Court approved the Report of the said Ivor Winner on the intromissions of the said David Flint and fixed his remuneration as Provisional and Interim Liquidator at the sum of £100,000 and authorised payment to be made thereof.

4.   The Noter as Liquidator has now ingathered all the assets of the Company and has adjudicated on all the claims of Creditors. He is accordingly desirous of having the Business Account incurred by him to his Solicitors for the period from [*date*] to the close of the liquidation remitted to the Auditor of Court for taxation and that he should be authorised to pay the taxed amount thereof. The Noter as Liquidator has also completed the Accounts of his Intromissions in the Liquidation for the period from [*date*] to [*date*] which show that at the latter date the balance in his hands as Liquidator amounted to £909,227 which sum will be available to meet his remuneration as Liquidator, the Business Account incurred by him for said period to the Liquidator's Solicitors and the expenses of and incidental to the close of Liquidation. The said Accounts of his Intromissions are produced herewith. The Liquidator is now desirous therefore that the said Accounts of Intromissions, together with the said Business Account, be remitted for examination, audit and taxation and thereafter that he should be authorised to pay the amount thereof.

5.   This Note is presented in terms of the Act and in terms of the Insolvency (Scotland) Rules 1986 and in terms of Part IV of the Act of Sederunt (Sheriff Court Company Insolvency Rules) 1986.

PLEA-IN-LAW

The Liquidator being entitled to have the Court fix his remuneration, the appropriate orders should be granted as craved.

IN RESPECT WHEREOF

(sgd) A Wiseman

Solicitor
152 Bath Street
Glasgow G2 4TB

<u>NOTER'S AGENT</u>

A43. Note for Interim Account – No change of Liquidator where no Committee

<u>SHERIFFDOM OF GLASGOW AND STRATHKELVIN AT GLASGOW</u>

NOTE

for

DAVID FLINT, Solicitor, 152 Bath Street, Glasgow, G2 4TB, Liquidator of ROCOCO COCOA CO LIMITED, incorporated under the Companies Acts and having its Registered Office at I Main Street, Glasgow ("the Noter")

relative to

Winding-up of

ROCOCO COCOA CO LIMITED, 1 Main Street, Glasgow ("the Company")

for

Approval of his Accounts to [*name*]; Authority taxed and payment made thereof; and Authority to make payment of his remuneration

The Noter craves the Court:

(1) to dispense with advertisement hereof in the *Edinburgh Gazette* and *The Herald* newspaper;

(2) to remit the business account incurred by the Noter as Liquidator to his Solicitors for the period from the commencement of the Liquidation to [*name*] to the Auditor of Court for taxation and to authorise the Liquidator to pay the taxed amount thereof;

(3) to remit the account of intromissions of the Noter as Liquidator for the period from the commencement of the Liquidation to [*name*] to Ivor Winner, CA, Counting House Lane, Glasgow G1 4SS, or to such other person as to the Court shall seem proper and to direct such person to report what in his opinion is suitable remuneration for the Noter as Liquidator for the period in question;

(4) on the result of such examination and audit being reported to the Court to fix and declare the amount of the remuneration to be paid to the Noter as Liquidator and to authorise him to take credit therefor;

or to do further and otherwise in the premises as to the Court shall seem proper.

CONDESCENDENCE

1. On [*date*] a Petition was presented to the Sheriff of Glasgow and Strathkelvin at Glasgow by Galaxy Products Limited for an order to wind up Rococo Cocoa Co Limited (hereinafter called "the Company"), a private company incorporated under the Companies Acts and having its Registered Office at 1 Main Street, Glasgow under sections 122 and 123 of the Insolvency Act 1986 (hereinafter referred to as "the Act") and for the appointment of, first, a Provisional Liquidator and, subsequently, an Interim Liquidator. On [*date*] the Sheriff of Glasgow and Strathkelvin at Glasgow pronounced an

Interlocutor nominating and appointing the Noter as Provisional Liquidator of the Company. On [*date*] the Sheriff of Glasgow and Strathkelvin at Glasgow pronounced an Interlocutor ordering that the Company be wound-up in pursuance of the Act and on the ground that the Company was unable to pay its debts and nominated and appointed the Noter to be Interim Liquidator of the Company. Notice of this Interlocutor was inserted in the *Edinburgh Gazette* on [*date*].

2. At a meeting of the creditors of the Company convened in accordance with the provisions of sections 138 and 142 of the Act and held on [*date*] it was resolved that:

    (a) the Noter be appointed as Liquidator of the Company; and

    (b) no Liquidation Committee should be appointed to act with such Liquidator.

3. The Noter has prepared a Statement of his intromissions for the period from the commencement of the liquidation to [*name*]. The Noter is desirous that said Statement should be audited and a payment in respect of his remuneration fixed. Rule 4.32 of the Insolvency (Scotland) Rules 1986 provides that a liquidator may at any time before the end of an accounting period, submit to the liquidation committee (if any) an interim claim in respect of that period for the outlays reasonably incurred by him and for his remuneration. Section 142(5) of the Act provides that where there is no liquidation committee the functions of such a committee are vested in the court except to the extent that the rules otherwise provide. The Noter respectfully submits that Ivor Winner, Counting House Lane, Glasgow, G1 4SS, is a suitable person to examine and audit said Statement. The Noter is also desirous of having the Business Account incurred by him to his Solicitors for the period from [*date*] to date remitted to the Auditor of Court for taxation and of the Liquidator being authorised to pay the taxed amount thereof.

4. This Note is presented in terms of the Act and in terms of the Insolvency (Scotland) Rules 1986 and in terms of Part IV of the Act of Sederunt (Sheriff Court Company Insolvency Rules) 1986.

PLEA-IN-LAW

The Noter, being entitled to have the Court fix his remuneration, the appropriate orders should be granted as craved.

IN RESPECT WHEREOF

(sgd) A Wiseman

Solicitor
152 Bath Street
Glasgow G2 4TB

NOTER'S AGENT

A44. Note for Leave to bring Proceedings against the Company (Section 130(2))

SHERIFF OF GLASGOW AND STRATHKELVIN AT GLASGOW

NOTE

for

I M HURT, residing at 30 Park Lane, Glasgow ("the Noter")

relative to

Winding-up of

ROCOCO COCOA CO LIMITED, 1 Main Street, Glasgow ("the Company")

for

Leave to bring proceedings against the Company in terms of section 130(2) of the Insolvency Act 1986 (as amended)

The Noter craves the Court:

To appoint intimation of this application to be made on David Flint, Solicitor, 152 Bath Street, Glasgow, G2 4TB, the Liquidator of Rococo Cocoa Co Limited ("the Company") and to order such further intimation and advertisement as to the Court shall seem proper and to allow the said Liquidator and all others having an interest to lodge answers hereto if so advised within such time as the Court may appoint; and, on resuming considering hereof, with or without answers, to grant leave to the Noters in terms of section 130(2) of the Insolvency Act 1986 (as amended) to bring proceedings against the Company; to find the Noter entitled to the expenses of this application and to direct the same to be expenses in the liquidation; or to do further or otherwise in the premises as to the Court may seem proper.

CONDESCENDENCE

1. On [*date*] a Petition was presented to the Sheriff of Glasgow and Strathkelvin at Glasgow by Galaxy Products Limited for an order to wind up Rococo Cocoa Co Limited (hereinafter called "the Company"), a private company incorporated under the Companies Acts and having its Registered Office at 1 Main Street, Glasgow under sections 122 and 123 of the Insolvency Act 1986 and for the appointment of first a Provisional Liquidator and subsequently an Interim Liquidator. On [*date*] the Sheriff of Glasgow and Strathkelvin at Glasgow pronounced an Interlocutor nominating and appointing David Flint, Solicitor, 152 Bath Street, Glasgow G2 4TB as Provisional Liquidator of the Company. On [*date*] the Sheriff of Glasgow and Strathkelvin at Glasgow pronounced an interlocutor ordering that the Company be wound-up in pursuance of the Insolvency Act 1986 on the ground that the company was unable to pay its debts and nominated and appointed the said David Flint to be interim Liquidator of the Company. Notice of this interlocutor was inserted in the *Edinburgh Gazette* on [*date*].

2. At a meeting of the creditors of the Company convened in accordance with the provisions of sections 138 and 142 of the Insolvency Act 1986 (as amended) and held on [*date*] it was resolved that:

(a) the said David Flint be appointed as Liquidator of the Company; and

(b) no liquidation committee should be appointed to act with such liquidator.

3. On or about [*date*] the Company's vehicle registration A1 RCC collided with the rear of a vehicle being driven by the Noter. The Company's said vehicle was being driven by an employee of the Company and acting in the course of his employment with the Company. The Company is therefore vicariously liable for the said accident. The Noter sustained loss, injury and damage as a result of the said collision. The Noter holds the Company's said employee responsible for the said collision. The Company is vicariously liable for its employee's acts and omissions in the course of his employment with the Company. The Company is therefore liable for the Noter's loss, injury and damage.

4. The Company's motor insurers at the material time were [*name and address*]. The Company, and its insurers, deny liability for the said collision. The Noters therefore wish to raise proceedings against the Company in order that the matter may be determined, and that the rights of the Noters in terms of the Third Parties (Rights Against Insurers) Act 1930 may be thereby preserved.

5. Application is accordingly made in terms of section 130(2) of the Insolvency Act 1986 (as amended) for leave to bring proceedings against the Company.

6. This Note is presented in terms of the Insolvency Act 1986 and, in particular, section 130(2) thereof, and in terms of the Insolvency (Scotland) Rules 1986 and in terms of Part IV of the Act of Sederunt (Sheriff Court Company Insolvency Rules) 1986.

PLEA-IN-LAW

The Company being liable to the Noter for the said loss, injury and damage sustained by him, leave should be granted to the Noter to bring proceedings against the Company.

IN RESPECT WHEREOF

(sgd) A Wiseman

Solicitor
152 Bath Street
Glasgow G2 4TB

NOTER'S AGENT

A45.   Note for Public Examination of Officers etc. (Section 133)

<u>SHERIFF OF GLASGOW AND STRATHKELVIN AT GLASGOW</u>

NOTE

for

> DAVID FLINT, Solicitor, 152 Bath Street, Glasgow, G2 4TB, Liquidator of ROCOCO COCOA CO LIMITED, having its Registered Office at 1 Main Street, Glasgow ("the Noter")

relative to

Winding-up of

> ROCOCO COCOA CO LIMITED, 1 Main Street, Glasgow ("the Company")

for

> Order requiring public examination of an officer in terms of section 133 of the Insolvency Act 1986 (as amended)

The Noter craves the Court:

To fix a diet for the public examination of Ian Barry Broke, "Duntradin", Kilmacolm, relative to the affairs, business and property of Rococo Cocoa Co Limited ("the Company") and to order the said person to attend for examination at the diet so fixed and to bring with him and produce at said diet all books and papers in his custody relating to the affairs, business and property of Rococo Cocoa Co Limited ("the Company") and to order the said person to attend for examination at the diet so fixed and to bring with him and produce at said diet all books and papers in his custody relating to the affairs, business and property of the Company all in terms of section 133(1) of the Insolvency Act 1986 and to find the said person liable in expenses; or to do further or otherwise in the premises as to the Court shall seem proper.

CONDESCENDENCE

1.   The Company is a company incorporated under the Companies Acts and having its Registered Office at 1 Main Street, Glasgow.

2.   David Flint, Solicitor, 152 Bath Street, Glasgow G2 4TB is the liquidator of the Company appointed by resolution of the creditors dated [*date*].

3.   The said Ian Barry Broke, "Duntradin", Kilmacolm, is a director of the Company.

4.   The Noter, having taken over the assets of the Company, has discovered certain irregularities in the affairs, business and records of the Company for all of which the Noter has been unable to receive satisfactory answers from the books and records in his possession. The Noter is of the belief that further information, records and papers in connection with these matters is obtainable from the said Ian Barry Broke. It is accordingly necessary for a public examination of the said person to obtain the information sought by the Noter and to have any records and papers in the possession of the said person relating to the Company produced.

5.   Application is accordingly made in terms of section 133(1) of the Insolvency Act 1986 for an order directing the public examination of the said Ian Barry Broke by the court.

6.   This Note is presented in terms of the Insolvency Act 1986 and, in particular, section 133 thereof, and in terms of the Insolvency (Scotland) Rules 1986 and in terms of Part IV of the Act of Sederunt (Sheriff Court Company Insolvency Rules) 1986.

PLEA-IN-LAW

The person specified, being able to afford information to the affairs, business and property of the Company, the necessary order should be granted as craved.

IN RESPECT WHEREOF

(sgd) A Wiseman

Solicitor
152 Bath Street
Glasgow G2 4TB

NOTER'S AGENT

A46. Information relating to Directors

NAME OF COMPANY: Rococo Cocoa Co Limited

DATE OF PRESENTATION OF WINDING-UP PETITION:

[ ]

DATE OF APPOINTMENT OF INTERIM LIQUIDATOR:

[ ]

DATE OF APPOINTMENT OF LIQUIDATOR:

[ ]

FULL NAME OF DIRECTOR: [ ]

PRIVATE ADDRESS: [ ]

DATE OF BIRTH: [ ]

DATES OF DIRECTORSHIP – From: [ ]

           To: [ ]

OTHER DIRECTORSHIPS HELD IN LAST THREE YEARS:
(please indicate which, if any, are in respect of holding, associated or subsidiary companies)   [ ]

OCCUPATION, TRADE OR PROFESSION: [ ]

QUALIFICATIONS: [ ]

POSITION(S) HELD IN COMPANY: [ ]
(please describe responsibilities)

PLEASE STATE YOUR SHAREHOLDING (if any)
IN THIS COMPANY: [ ]

IN ANY OTHER COMPANY: [ ]

Signed: [ ]
Date: [ ]

PLEASE LIST YOUR REMUNERATION AND OTHER BENEFITS
DURING EACH OF THE LAST THREE YEARS:

Period ended	Remuneration received £	Remuneration voted £	Cash expenses £	Benefits in kind £

PLEASE GIVE DETAILS OF ANY GUARANTEES GIVEN OR LOANS
MADE BY YOU THAT ARE OUTSTANDING:

[ ]

WHEN DID YOU FIRST SEE THE LAST:
Audited Accounts?   [ ]
Draft Accounts?   [ ]
Management Accounts?   [ ]

HOW DID YOU KEEP YOURSELF INFORMED OF THE COMPANY'S
FINANCIAL POSITION?   [ ]

WHAT DO YOU BELIEVE WERE THE CAUSES OF THE COMPANY'S
FAILURE?   [ ]

WHEN AND HOW DID YOU BECOME AWARE OF THE COMPANY'S
INSOLVENCY?   [   ]

WHAT STEPS DID YOU THEN TAKE?   [   ]

HAVE YOU EVER BEEN BANKRUPT OR CONVICTED OF AN
OFFENCE IN RELATION TO A COMPANY? IF SO, PLEASE GIVE
DETAILS.   [   ]

PLEASE NAME ANY PERSON WHO, IN YOUR OPINION, WAS A
SHADOW DIRECTOR (*i.e.* a person in accordance with whose instructions you
were accustomed to act)   [   ]

THE INFORMATION GIVEN ABOVE IS CORRECT TO THE BEST OF
MY KNOWLEDGE AND BELIEF.

Signed:
Date:
[Please ensure that you have attested the preceding pages]

A47. Matters to Consider in determining the Unfitness of Directors

ROCOCO COCOA CO LIMITED – IN LIQUIDATION

DIRECTOR: IAN BARRY BROKE

MATTERS TO CONSIDER IN DETERMINING THE UNFITNESS OF DIRECTORS

1.   Has the Director received money or other gifts from the Company other than his remuneration?

2.   Has the Director authorised any payments or gifts by the Company to persons connected with him?

3.   Has the Director been responsible for non-disclosure to the Company of any contracts in which he had any interest?

4.   Has the Director been responsible for any material loss resulting from the sale or disposal of any of the Company's assets?

5.   Has the Director been responsible for any misapplication of the Company's monies or property?

6.   Has the Director been responsible for the transfer or disposal of the Company's property at an undervalue in order to place assets beyond the reach of the Company's creditors?

7.1 Did the Company keep proper books of account with full details of transactions, assets and liabilities?

7.2 If not, to what extent was the Director responsible?

8.   Are there any material omissions or deficiencies in the books of account and statutory records?

9.   Are there any qualifications relating to the adequacy of the records in the auditors report?

10. Are the necessary statutory registers maintained?

11. Have the annual returns for the last three years been completed, and on what date have they been submitted to the Registrar?

12. How up to date are the audited accounts?

13. Are there any relevant qualifications to the accounts in the auditor's report?

14. What other accounts since that date are available?

15. When did the Company first become insolvent?

16. What events led to the Company's insolvency?

17. What evidence is available of the commencement of the insolvency and the Director's knowledge of the situation? (*e.g.* returned cheques, draft accounts, writs, three-week notices, etc.)

18.1 Did the business continue after the insolvency commenced?

18.2 If so, what justification did the Director have for the continuation of business?

19.1 Are there any deposits relating to non-supply of goods?

19.2 Over what period have these been received?

20. Have the following statutory requirements relating to creditors' meetings been complied with:

    (a) date of winding-up resolution:

    (b) date of creditors' meeting:

    (c) were creditors informed of the main address of Insolvency Practitioner dealing?

    (d) has notice of meeting then published in *Gazette* and two local newspapers?

21.1 Have the Directors submitted a signed statement of affairs?

21.2 If submitted, are there any material omissions or deficiencies?

22. Has the Director failed to deliver any property, books or records of the Company?

23. What is the scale and nature of inter-company transactions?

A48.   Note for Warrant to Arrest (Section 134)

SHERIFF OF GLASGOW AND STRATHKELVIN AT GLASGOW

NOTE

for

DAVID FLINT, Solicitor, 152 Bath Street, Glasgow, G2 4TB Liquidator of Rococo Cocoa Co Limited, having its Registered Office at 1 Main Street, Glasgow ("the Noter")

relative to

Winding-up of

ROCOCO COCOA CO LIMITED, 1 Main Street, Glasgow ("the Company")

for

ORDER for Warrant to Arrest IAN BARRY BROKE

The Noter craves the Court:

To grant warrant to all judges, magistrates, sheriffs, justices of the peace and officers of the law, to apprehend, arrest and transmit Ian Barry Broke, residing at "Duntradin", Kilmacolm, to the place of his examination and to enforce the same; to grant authority for the detention and imprisonment of the said Ian Barry Broke, if necessary; to find the said person liable in expenses; or to do further or otherwise in the premises as to the Court shall seem proper.

CONDESCENDENCE

1.   The Company is a company incorporated under the Companies Acts and having its Registered Office at 1 Main Street, Glasgow.

2.   The Noter is the Liquidator of the Company appointed by resolution of the creditors dated [*date*].

3.   Ian Barry Broke residing at "Duntradin", Kilmacolm, is a director of the Company within the meaning of section 741 of the Companies Act 1985.

4.   By Interlocutor dated [*date*] the Sheriff of Glasgow and Strathkelvin at Glasgow ordered the said Ian Barry Broke to appear at Glasgow Sheriff Court on [*date*] at 10 am for public examination relative to the affairs, business and property of the Company in terms of section 133(1) of the Insolvency Act 1986 (hereinafter referred to as "the Act").

5.   The said Ian Barry Broke failed to appear at the said public examination as ordered and, accordingly, this application is made in terms of section 134 of the Act for an order for warrant to arrest the said Ian Barry Broke.

6.   This Note is presented in terms of the Act 1986 and, in particular, sections 133 and 134 thereof, and in terms of the Insolvency (Scotland) Rules 1986 and in terms of Part IV of the Act of Sederunt (Sheriff Court Company Insolvency Rules) 1986.

PLEA-IN-LAW

The said person, having failed to attend his public examination in terms of section 133 of the Act 1986, as ordered, a Warrant for his arrest should be granted as craved, with expenses, in terms of section 134 of the Act.

IN RESPECT WHEREOF

(sgd) A Wiseman

Solicitor
152 Bath Street
Glasgow G2 4TB

NOTER'S AGENT

A49.   Note for Inspection of Books by Creditors/Contributories (Section 155)

<u>SHERIFFDOM OF GLASGOW AND STRATHKELVIN AT GLASGOW</u>

NOTE

by

ORINOCO COCOA CO LIMITED, 15
London Road, Paisley PA1 1NT ("the Noter")

relative to

Winding-up of

ROCOCO COCOA CO LIMITED, 1 Main
Street, Glasgow ("the Company")

for

Order for inspection of the Company's books
and papers in terms of section 155 of the
Insolvency Act 1986 (as amended)

The Noter craves the Court:

To appoint intimation of this application to be made on David Flint, Solicitor, 152
Bath Street, Glasgow, G2 4TB the Liquidator of Rococo Cocoa Co Limited ("the
Company") and to order such further intimation and advertisement as to the
Court shall seem proper and to allow the said Liquidator and all others having an
interest to lodge answers hereto if so advised within such time as the Court may
appoint; and, on resuming considering hereof, with or without answers, to order,
in terms of section 155 of the Insolvency Act 1986 (hereinafter referred to as "the
Act") that all books and papers of the Company be made available for inspection
by all creditors and contributories of the Company; to find the Noter entitled to
the expenses of this application and to direct the same to be expenses in the liquidation; or to do further or otherwise in the premises as to the Court may seem
proper.

CONDESCENDENCE

1.   The Company is a company incorporated under the Companies Acts and
     having its Registered Office at 1 Main Street, Glasgow.

2.   David Flint, Solicitor, 152 Bath Street, Glasgow G2 4TB is the
     Liquidator of the Company appointed by resolution of the creditors
     dated [*date*].

3.   The Noter is a creditor of the Company. The Noter is not satisfied with
     the contents of the Liquidator's Report/Statement of Affairs in respect
     that it omits to value the Company's property at Gray Towers, Shangri
     La Bay, Grand Cayman.

4.   The Noter believes that, in the best interests of the liquidation, all the
     books and records of the Company should be made available for inspec-
     tion by the creditors and contributories. As the liquidator refuses to do
     so the present proceedings are accordingly necessary.

5.   This Note is presented in terms of the Act and, in particular, section 155
     thereof, and in terms of the Insolvency (Scotland) Rules 1986 and in
     terms of the Part IV of the Act of Sederunt (Sheriff Court Company
     Insolvency Rules) 1986.

PLEA-IN-LAW

In respect that for the benefit of the winding-up the books and records of the Company should be made available for inspection, the necessary order should be pronounced as craved in terms of section 155 of the Act.

IN RESPECT WHEREOF

(sgd) A Wiseman

Solicitor
152 Bath Street
Glasgow G2 4TB

NOTER'S AGENT

A50.   Special Manager (Section 177)

SHERIFFDOM OF GLASGOW AND STRATHKELVIN AT GLASGOW

NOTE

for

DAVID FLINT, Solicitor, 152 Bath Street, Glasgow, G2 4TB Liquidator of Rococo Cocoa Co Limited, having its Registered Office at 1 Main Street, Glasgow ("the Noter")

relative to

Winding-up of

ROCOCO COCOA CO LIMITED, 1 Main Street, Glasgow ("the Company")

for

Appointment of Special Manager in terms of section 177 of the Insolvency Act 1986 (as amended)

The Noter craves the Court:

To appoint Dwayne Z Minosc, residing at 15 Long Acre, Covent Garden, London, or such other person as the Court may think fit to be Special Manager of the Company for an indefinite period of time in terms of section 177 of the Insolvency Act 1986 (hereinafter referred to as "the Act") upon his finding such caution or security ad the Court may deem proper and to authorise such Special Manager to exercise the powers contained in Parts II and III of Schedule 4, to the Act; to find the Noter entitled to the expenses of this application and to direct the same to be expenses in the liquidation; or to do further or otherwise in the premises as to the Court may seem proper.

CONDESCENDENCE

1.   The Company is a company incorporated under the Companies Acts and having its Registered Office at 1 Main Street, Glasgow. The Company carries on business as Entertainment Consultants.

2.   The Noter is the Liquidator of the Company appointed by resolution of the creditors dated [*date*].

3.   Having regard to the nature of the business and the property of the Company, the Noter considers that, in order to secure the position of the Company's creditors and to safeguard the Company's assets, it is advantageous that a Special Manager be appointed to the Company and that authority be given to him to exercise the powers craved.

4.   The Noter has prepared a Report setting out in detail the reason for this application and the value of the proposed assets to be entrusted to the Special Manager, a copy of which is produced herewith and referred to for its terms.

5.   The said Dwayne Z Minosc is a suitable person to be appointed Special Manager to the Company and consents so to act.

6.   This application is made in accordance with section 177 of the Act and Part IV of the Act of Sederunt (Sheriff Court Company Insolvency Rules) 1986.

PLEA-IN-LAW

Having regard to the specialised nature of the business of the Company, a Special Manager should be appointed as craved in terms of section 177 of the Act and the necessary powers be given to the said Special manager as craved .

IN RESPECT WHEREOF

(sgd) A Wiseman

Solicitor

152 Bath Street
Glasgow G2 4TB
NOTER'S AGENT

A51. Note for Examination (Section 198)

<u>SHERIFFDOM OF GLASGOW AND STRATHKELVIN AT GLASGOW</u>

NOTE

for

DAVID FLINT, Solicitor, 152 Bath Street, Glasgow, G2 4TB, Liquidator of ROCOCO COCOA LIMITED having its Registered Office at 1 Main Street, Glasgow ("the Noter ")

relative to

Winding-up of

ROCOCO COCOA CO LIMITED, 1 Main Street, Glasgow ("the Company")

for

Order for examination in terms of section 198 of the Insolvency Act 1986 (as amended).

The Noter craves the Court:

To fix a diet for the public examination of Rebecca Unwin Broke, 1 Chancer Drive, Pollokshields, Glasgow in the presence of the Sheriff Principal of Glasgow and Strathkelvin relative to the trade, dealings, affairs or property of the Company, and to order the said person to attend for examination at the diet so fixed and to bring with him and produce at said diet all books and papers in his custody relative to the trade, dealings, affairs or property of the Company all in terms of section 198 of the Insolvency Act 1986 (hereinafter referred to as "the Act") and to find the said person liable in expenses; or to do further or otherwise in the premises as to the Court shall seem proper.

CONDESCENDENCE

1.   The Company is a company incorporated under the Companies Acts and having its Registered Office at 1 Main Street, Glasgow

2.   David Flint is the liquidator of the Company appointed by resolution of the creditors dated [*date*].

3.   The said Rebecca Unwin Broke is a contributory of the Company. She is resident at 1 Chancer Drive, Pollokshields, Glasgow and is therefore resident within the Sheriffdom of Glasgow and Strathkelvin.

4.   The Noter having taken over the assets of the Company has discovered certain irregularities in the trade, dealings, affairs and property of the Company for all of which the Noter has been unable to receive satisfactory answers from the books and records in his possession. The Noter is of the belief that further information, records and papers in connection with these matters is obtainable from the said Rebecca Unwin Broke. It is accordingly necessary for an examination of the said person on oath in the presence of the Sheriff Principal of Glasgow and Strathkelvin to obtain the information sought by the Noter and to have any books and papers in the possession of the said person relating to the Company produced.

5. Application is accordingly made in terms of section 198 of the Act for an order directing the examination of the said Rebecca Unwin Broke in the presence of the Sheriff Principal of Glasgow and Strathkelvin.

6. This application is made in accordance with section 198 of the Act and Part IV of the Act of Sederunt (Sheriff Court Company Insolvency Rules) 1986.

PLEA-IN-LAW

The person specified being able to afford information relative to the trade, dealings, affairs and property of the Company, the necessary order should be granted as craved.

IN RESPECT WHEREOF

(sgd) A Wiseman
Solicitor
152 Bath Street
Glasgow G2 4TB

Noter's Agent

A52. Note for Early Dissolution (Section 204)

<u>SHERIFFDOM OF GLASGOW AND STRATHKELVIN AT GLASGOW</u>

NOTE

for

DAVID FLINT, Solicitor, 152 Bath Street, Glasgow, G2 4TB, the Liquidator for Rococo Cocoa Co Limited, having its Registered Office at 1 Main Street, Glasgow ("the Noter"

relative to

Winding-up of

ROCOCO COCOA CO LIMITED, 1 Main Street, Glasgow ("the Company")

for

Order for early dissolution of the Company in terms of section 204 of the Insolvency Act 1986 (as amended) and Approval of his Accounts to [*name*]; Authority to have his Solicitors' Business Account taxed and pay ment made thereof; and Authority to make payment of his remuneration.

The Noter craves the Court:

(1)   to order such intimation, advertisement and service as to the Court shall seem proper;

(2)   to order dissolution of the said Rococo Cocoa Co Limited;

(3)   to remit the accounts of Intromissions of the Noter as (a) Provisional Liquidator and (b) Interim Liquidator in respect of the affairs of the Company for examination and audit to Ivor Winner, Chartered Accountant, 1 Counting House Lane, Glasgow, G1 4SS, or to such other person as to the Court shall seem proper and to direct such person to report what in his opin-ion is a suitable remuneration for the Noter;

(4)   on the result of such examination and audit being reported to the Court to fix and declare the amount of the remuneration to be paid to the Noter as (a) Provisional Liquidator and (b) Interim Liquidator; and to authorise the Noter to take credit therefor and also for the outlays incurred by the Noter including the accounts of the Noter's solicitors after taxation thereof by the Auditor of Court.

(5)   to declare the expenses of this Note and any proceedings to follow hereon to be expenses of the Liquidation and authorise the Liquidator to make pay-ment thereof; or to do further or otherwise as to the Court may seem proper.

or to do further or otherwise in the premises as to the Court shall seem proper.

CONDESCENDENCE

1.   On [*date*] a Petition was presented to the Sheriff of Glasgow and Strathkelvin at Glasgow by Galaxy Products Limited for an order to Wind up Rococo Cocoa Co Limited (hereinafter called "the Company"), a private company incorporated under the Companies Acts and having its Registered Office at 1 Main Street, Glasgow, under sections 122 and 123 of the Insolvency Act 1986

(as amended) (hereinafter referred to as "the Act") and for the appointment of first a Provisional Liquidator and subsequently an Interim Liquidator.

2. On [*date*] the Sheriff of Glasgow and Strathkelvin at Glasgow pronounced an Interlocutor nominating and appointing the Noter as Provisional Liquidator of the Company. On [*date*] the Sheriff of Glasgow and Strathkelvin at Glasgow pronounced an Interlocutor ordering that the Company be wound-up in pursuance of the Act on the ground that the Company was unable to pay its debts and nominated and appointed the Noter to be Interim Liquidator of the Company.

3. At a meeting of the creditors of the Company convened in accordance with the provisions of sections 138 and 142 of the Act and held on [*date*] the Noter tabled a Statement of Affairs of the Company as at [*date*] which shows that the total assets of the Company amount to £1358. A copy of the Statement of Affairs is produced herewith and referred to for its terms. A statement of the Noter's acts and dealings and of his conduct of the winding-up to the [*date*] is produced. The Noter's fees and expenses up to the said date amount to £1200. It is reasonably estimated that the Noter's final fees and expenses shall amount to £3000. It is clear to the Noter that in these circumstances the realisable assets of the Company are insufficient to cover the expenses of the winding-up. Accordingly, it appears to the Noter that it is appropriate that the Company be dissolved in accordance with section 204 of the Act.

4. In the event of such an Order being made, the Noter considers it appropriate that his intromissions as Provisional Liquidator and Interim Liquidator be audited and payment made in respect of his remuneration.

5. The Noter has prepared a Statement of his Intromissions for the said period form the Commencement of the Liquidation to [*date*] and is desirous that said Statement should be audited and a payment in respect of his remuneration fixed. The Noter respectfully submits that Ivor Winner, Chartered Accountant, 1 Counting House Lane, Glasgow G1 4SS, is a suitable person to examine and audit the said statement. The Noter is also desirous having the Business Account incurred by him to his solicitors for the period from [*date*] to date remitted to the Auditor of Court for taxation and of the Noter being authorised to pay the taxed amount thereof.

6. This application is made in terms of the Act and in particular section 204 thereof and in terms of the Insolvency (Scotland) Rules 1986 and in terms of Part IV of the Act of Sederunt (Sheriff Court Company Insolvency Rules) 1986.

PLEA-IN-LAW

1. In respect that the realisable assets of the Company are insufficient to cover the expenses of the winding-up, the Company should be dissolved in terms of section 204 of the Act and decree should be pronounced as craved.

2. The Noter being entitled to have the Court fix his remuneration, the appropriate orders should be granted as craved.

IN RESPECT WHEREOF

(sgd) A Wiseman

Solicitor
152 Bath Street
Glasgow G2 4TB

Noter's Agent

A53.   Note for Misfeasance (Section 212)

<u>SHERIFFDOM OF GLASGOW AND STRATHKELVIN AT GLASGOW</u>

NOTE

for

DAVID FLINT, Solicitor, 152 Bath Street, Glasgow, G2 4TB, Liquidator of Rococo Cocoa Co Limited having its Registered Office at 1 Main Street, Glasgow ("the Noter")

relative to

Winding-up of

ROCOCO COCOA CO LIMITED, 1 Main Street, Glasgow ("the Company")

for

Order in terms of section 212 of the Insolvency Act 1986 (as amended)

The Noter craves the Court:

To appoint intimation of this application to be made on Ian Barry Broke residing at "Duntradin", Kilmacolm, and to order such further intimation and advertisement as to the Court shall seem proper, and to allow the said named person and all others having an interest to lodge answers hereto if so advised within such time as the Court may appoint; and, on resuming consideration hereof, with or without answers, to order, in terms of section 212 of the Insolvency Act 1986, that the said Ian Barry Broke taking part in the management of the Company misapplied the sum of £22,150 being monies of the Company, and to grant decree against the said Ian Barry Broke for payment to the Petitioner as Liquidator foresaid of the said sum of £22,150 or such other sum as may be ascertained to be the amount misapplied or retained by the said person, with interest thereon from the date of decree to follow hereon until payment; and to find the said Ian Barry Broke liable in expenses; or to do further or otherwise in the premises as to the Court shall seem proper.

CONDESCENDENCE

1.   The Company is a company incorporated under the Companies Acts and having its Registered Office at 1 Main Street, Glasgow

2.   The Noter is the Liquidator of the Company appointed by resolution of the creditors dated [*date*].

3.   Ian Barry Broke was a director of the Company within the meaning of section 741 of the Companies Act 1985.

4.   The Noter having taken over the assets of the Company has discovered certain irregularities in the affairs of the Company, and certain monies of the Company, and certain monies of the Company misapplied or misappropriated, including:

(a)   personal expenses paid;
(b)   unaccounted for cash payments.

These irregularities arose while the person named was involved in the management of the Company. The person named refuses or delays to state how these irregularities arose or where appropriate how the money was disposed of. Although here exist within the records of the Company letters and memoranda from the person named, acknowledging that he had taken the money concerned and acknowledging that it was for his own use. It is believed by the Noter that these sums were misapplied or misappropriated by the person named. Accordingly, the present proceedings are necessary in terms of section 212 of the Insolvency Act 1986 (as amended) to examine the conduct of the said named person and to obtain compensation for the Company in respect of the misfeasance. [note: this will need expanded to show why evidence exists of misfeasance, or breach of statutory or other fiduciary duty].

5. This Note is presented in terms of the Insolvency Act 1986 and in particular section 212 thereof and in terms of the Insolvency (Scotland) Rules 1986 and in terms of Part IV of the Act of Sederunt (Sheriff Court Company Insolvency Rules) 1986.

PLEA-IN-LAW

In respect that the said person, who took part in the management of the Company, has misapplied or misappropriated money of the Company, his conduct should be examined in terms of section 212 of the Insolvency Act 1986 and decree should be pronounced as craved.

IN RESPECT WHEREOF

(sgd) A Wiseman

Solicitor
152 Bath Street
Glasgow G2 4TB

Noter's Agent

A54.   Note for Fraudulent Trading (Section 213)

SHERIFFDOM OF GLASGOW AND STRATHKELVIN AT GLASGOW

NOTE

for

DAVID FLINT, Solicitor, 152 Bath Street, Glasgow, G2 4TB, Liquidator of Rococo Cocoa Co Limited having its Registered Office at 1 Main Street, Glasgow ("the Noter")

relative to

Winding-up of

ROCOCO COCOA CO LIMITED, 1 Main Street, Glasgow ("the Company")

for

Order in terms of section 213 of the Insolvency Act 1986

The Noter craves the Court:

To appoint intimation of this application to be made on Uriah Rodney Broke residing at "Tumbledown Cottage", Bridge of Weir and to order such further intimation and advertisement as to the Court shall seem proper, and to allow the same named person and all others having an interest to lodge answers hereto if so advised within such time as the Court may appoint; and, on resuming consideration hereof, with or without answers, to order, in terms of section 213 of the Insolvency Act 1986, that the said Uriah Rodney Broke was knowingly a party to the carrying on of the business of the Company with the intent to defraud creditors, and to grant decree against the said Uriah Rodney Broke for payment to the Noter as Liquidator foresaid of the sum of £39,000 or such other sum as the Court thinks proper, with interest thereon from the date of decree to follow hereon until payment; and to find the said Uriah Rodney Broke liable in expenses; or to do further or otherwise in the premises as to the Court shall seem proper.

CONDESCENDENCE

1.   The Company is a company incorporated under the Companies Acts and having its Registered Office at 1 Main Street, Glasgow.

2.   The Noter is the liquidator of the Company appointed by resolution of the creditors dated [*date*].

3.   Uriah Rodney Broke was a director of the Company within the meaning of section 741 of the Companies Act 1985.

4.   The Noter having taken over the assets of the Company has discovered that the said Uriah Rodney Broke was fraudulently involved in the management of the Company between [*date*] and [*date*] with intent to defraud creditors in that he was a party to the following transaction, namely, taking deposits for events which he knew would not take place. [Note: additional specification required]

5.   It is believed by the Noter that because of the actings of the said Uriah Rodney Broke the creditors of the Company were defrauded of £39,000. Accordingly, the present proceedings are necessary in terms of section 213 of the Insolvency Act 1986 to examine the conduct of the said named person and obtain compensation for the creditors of the Company.

6. This Note is presented in terms of the Insolvency Act 1986 (as amended) and in particular section 213 thereof, and in terms of the Insolvency (Scotland) Rules 1986 and in terms of Part IV of the Act of Sederunt (Sheriff Court Company Insolvency Rules) 1986.

PLEA-IN-LAW

In respect that the said person, who took part in the management of the Company, was knowingly a party to the carrying on of the business of the Company with intent to defraud creditors his conduct should be examined in terms of section 213 of the Insolvency Act 1986 and decree should be pronounced as craved.

IN RESPECT WHEREOF

(sgd) A Wiseman

Solicitor
152 Bath Street
Glasgow G2 4TB

Noter's Agent

A55.   Note for Wrongful Trading (Section 214)

<u>SHERIFFDOM OF GLASGOW STRATHKELVIN AT GLASGOW</u>

NOTE

for

DAVID FLINT, Solicitor, 152 Bath Street, Glasgow, G2 4TB, Liquidator of Rococo Cocoa Co Limited having its Registered Office at 1 Main Street, Glasgow ("the Noter")

relative to

Winding-up of

ROCOCO COCOA CO LIMITED, 1 Main Street, Glasgow ("the Company")

for

Order in terms of section 214 of the Insolvency Act 1986

The Noter craves the Court:

To appoint intimation of this application to be made on Ian Barry Broke residing at "Duntradin", Kilmacolm, and to order such further intimation and advertisement as to the Court shall seem proper, and to allow the said named person and all others having an interest to lodge answers hereto of so advised within such time as the Court may appoint; and, on resuming consideration hereof, with or without answers, to order, in terms of section 214 of the Insolvency Act 1986, that the said Ian Barry Broke while a Director of the Company was a party to the carrying on of the business of the Company when he knew or ought to have known that there was no reasonable prospect of the Company avoiding going into insolvent liquidation, and to grant decree against the said Ian Barry Broke for payment to the Petitioner as Liquidator foresaid of the sum of £18,725 or such other sum as may be ascertained to be the amount of the debts of the Company from the date on which the said person should have realised that the Company would go into insolvent liquidation until the Noter was appointed liquidator of the Company, with interest thereon from the date of decree to follow hereon until payment; and to find the said Ian Barry Broke liable in expenses; or to do further or otherwise in the circumstances as to the Court shall seem proper.

CONDESCENDENCE

1.   The Company is a company incorporated under the Companies Acts and having its Registered Office at 1 Main Street, Glasgow.

2.   The Noter is the liquidator of the Company appointed by resolution of the creditors dated [*date*].

3.   Ian Barry Broke was a director of the Company within the meaning of section 741 of the Companies Act 1985.

4.   The Petitioner having taken over the assets of the Company has discovered that on [*date*] the Company was insolvent with no reasonable prospect of avoiding going into insolvent liquidation, as demonstrated by the attached management accounts of the Company, at that time, prepared by Big4 Audit plc. The said Ian Barry Broke was a Director of the Company and allowed the Company to continue trading at a time when he should have concluded that the Company could not avoid going into insolvent liquidation.

5. Between [*date*] and the Company going into liquidation, the Company incurred further debts totalling £18,725. It is believed by the Noter that by continuing to trade during this period the said Ian Barry Broke is guilty of wrongful trading. Accordingly the present proceedings are necessary in terms of section 214 of the Insolvency Act 1986 (as amended) to examine the conduct of the said named person and obtain compensation for the Company in respect of the wrongful trading. [Note: further specification should be inserted]

6. This Note is presented in terms of the Insolvency Act 1986 (as amended) and in particular section 214 thereof, and in terms of the Insolvency (Scotland) Rules 1986 and in terms of Part IV of the Act of Sederunt (Sheriff Court Company Insolvency Rules) 1986.

PLEA-IN-LAW

In respect that the said person was guilty of wrongful trading in relation to the business of the Company, his conduct should be examined in terms of section 214 of the Insolvency Act 1986 and decree should be pronounced as craved.

IN RESPECT WHEREOF

(sgd) A Wiseman

Solicitor,
152 Bath Street,
Glasgow G2 4TB

Noter's Agent

A56.   Note for Leave to be a Director of Company with Prohibited Name (Section 216)

SHERIFFDOM OF GLASGOW AND STRATHKELVIN AT GLASGOW

NOTE

of

URIAH RODNEY BROKE, Tumbledown Cottage, Bridge of Weir ("the Noter")

relative to

Winding-up of

ROCOCO COCOA CO LIMITED, 1 Main Street, Glasgow ("the Company")

For

Leave of the Court to be a Director of a Compant with a prohibited name in terms of section 216 of the Insolvency Act 1986 (as amended)

The Noter craves the Court:

To appoint intimation of this application to be made on David Flint, Solicitor, 152 Bath Street, Glasgow, G2 4TB the Liquidator of Rococo Cocoa Co Limited and to order such further intimation and advertisement as to the Court shall seem proper and to allow the said David Flint and all others having an interest to lodge answers hereto if so advised within such time as the Court may appoint; and, on resuming consideration hereof, with or without answer, to grant leave to the Noter to be involved in the management of Rococo Coffee Company Limited, a company with a prohibited name in relation to the Noter in terms of section 216 of the Insolvency Act 1986; to find any party opposing this application liable in the expenses occasioned by such opposition, or to do further or otherwise in the premises as to the Court may seem proper.

CONDESCENDENCE

1.   Rococo Cocoa Co Limited is a company incorporated under the Companies Act and having its Registered Office at 1 Main Street, Glasgow. The Company carried on business as Entertainment Consultants. The Company went into liquidation on [*date*] and the said David Flint, Solicitor, 152 Bath Street, Glasgow, G2 4TB was appointed Liquidator.

2.   The Noter was a director of the Company throughout the 12–month period preceding the commencement of the winding-up.

3.   The Noter wishes to re-commence trading and in particular to form and manage a company with the name Rococo Coffee Company Limited, carrying on business as food importers. Such name is a prohibited name in terms of section 216 of the Insolvency Act 1986 in relation to the Noter. The Noter believes that the name Rococo is of itself of no value and that as the proposed new company to be formed and managed by the Noter is to trade in a different geographical area and product range from Rococo Cocoa Co Limited the Noter believes that he should be granted leave to commence trading using the name Rococo.

4.   The present proceedings are accordingly necessary in terms of section 216 of the Insolvency Act 1986 (as amended).

5. This Note is presented in terms of the Insolvency Act 1986 (as amended) and in particular section 216 thereof, and in terms of the Insolvency (Scotland) Rules 1986 and in terms of Part IV of the Act of Sederunt (Sheriff Court Company Insolvency Rules) 1986.

PLEA-IN-LAW

In respect that the said person wishes to be involved in the management of a company using a name which is prohibited in relation to him decree should be granted in terms of section 216 of the Insolvency Act 1986 as craved.

IN RESPECT WHEREOF

(sgd) A Wiseman

Solicitor,
152 Bath Street,
Glasgow G2 4TB

Noter's Agent

A57.   Note for Delivery of Property (Section 234)

<u>SHERIFFDOM OF GLASGOW AND STRATHKELVIN AT GLASGOW</u>

NOTE

for

David Flint, Solicitor, 152 Bath Street,
Glasgow, G2 4TB, Liquidator of Rococo
Cocoa Co Limited, having its Registered
Office at 1 Main Street, Glasgow ("the
Noter")

relative to

Winding-up of

ROCOCO COCOA CO LIMITED, 1 Main
Street, Glasgow ("the Company")

for

Delivery of Property of the Company in terms
of section 234 of the Insolvency Act 1986

The Noter craves the Court:

To appoint intimation of this application to be made on Ian Fixit, Chartered
Accountant, 10 Times Avenue, Bishopton and to order such further intimation
and advertisement as to the Court shall seem proper, and to allow the said Ian
Fixit and all others having an interest to lodge answers hereto if so advised within
such time as the Court may appoint; and, on resuming consideration hereof, with
or without answers, to order that the said Ian Fixit deliver to the Noter as liquidator foresaid all property, books, papers and records in his possession or control to which the Company is entitled in terms of section 234 of the Insolvency Act
1986; to find the Noter entitled to the expenses of this application and to direct the
same to be expenses in the liquidation; to find any party opposing this application
liable in the expenses occasioned by such opposition, or to do further or otherwise
in the premises as to the Court may seem proper.

CONDESCENDENCE

1.   The Company is a company incorporated under the Companies Acts and hav-
     ing its Registered Office at 1 Main Street, Glasgow.

2.   The Noter is the liquidator of the Company appointed by resolution of the
     creditors dated [*date*].

3.   The said Ian Fixit was Chief Accountant of the Company from incorporation
     to [*date*].

4.   The Noter having taken over the assets of the Company has reason to believe
     that the said Ian Fixit has in his possession or control certain property, books,
     papers and records to which the Company is entitled including: purchase and
     sales ledgers and cash books.

5.   The Noter believes that in order to assist him in the winding-up of the
     Company these items and all others in the possession or control of the said
     Ian Fixit to which the Company is entitled should be delivered to him as
     Liquidator. The said Ian Fixit refuses to do so and the present proceedings are
     accordingly necessary.

6. This Note is presented in terms of the Insolvency Act 1986 and in particular section 234 thereof, and in terms of the Insolvency (Scotland) Rules 1986 and in terms of Part IV of the Act of Sederunt (Sheriff Court Company Insolvency Rules) 1986.

PLEA-IN-LAW

In respect that the person specified has in his possession or control property, books, papers and records to which the Company is entitled, decree should be pronounced as craved in terms of section 234 of the Insolvency Act 1986.

IN RESPECT WHEREOF

(sgd) A Wiseman

Solicitor,
152 Bath Street,
Glasgow G2 4TB

Noter's Agent

A58.   Note for Inquiry into Company's Dealings (Section 236)

<u>SHERIFFDOM OF GLASGOW AND STRATHKELVIN AT GLASGOW</u>

NOTE

for

DAVID FLINT, Solicitor, 152 Bath Street, Glasgow, G2 4TB, Liquidator of Rococo Cocoa Co Limited having its Registered Office at 1 Main Street, Glasgow ("the Noter")

relative to

Winding-up of

ROCOCO COCOA CO LIMITED, 1 Main Street, Glasgow ("the Company")

for

Order requiring inquiry into Company's dealings in terms of section 236 of the Insolvency Act 1986 to summon and examine Ian Barry Broke, "Duntradin", Kilmacolm.

The Noter craves the Court:

To fix a diet for the examination of Ian Barry Broke, "Duntradin", Kilmacolm, relative to the affairs, business and property of the Company, and to order the said person to attend for examination at the diet so fixed and to submit to the Court an affidavit containing an account of his dealings with the Company and to produce all books, papers and records in his possession or control relating to the Company all in terms of section 236 of the Insolvency Act 1986 and to find the said person liable in expenses; or to do further or otherwise in the premises as to the Court shall seem proper.

CONDESCENDENCE

1.   Rococo Cocoa Co Limited ("the Company") is a company incorporated under the Companies Acts and having its Registered Office at 1 Main Street, Glasgow.

2.   The Noter is the liquidator of the Company appointed by resolution of the creditors dated [*date*].

3.   The said Ian Barry Broke is a director of the Company in terms of section 741 of the Companies Act 1985.

4.   The Noter having taken over the assets of the Company requires all property of the Company and certain information relating to the business and affairs of the Company to be delivered to him. The Noter is of the belief that the said Ian Barry Broke has certain property of the Company in his possession and is capable of giving the information in relation to the business and affairs of the Company required by the Noter. [Note: Further details should be given as to belief and documents etc.]

5.   It is accordingly necessary for an examination of the said person to obtain the information sought by the Noter, to have an affidavit containing an account of his dealings with the Company submitted to the Court by the said person and to have any books, papers and records in his possession produced.

6. This application is made in terms of section 236 of the Insolvency Act 1986 and the Act of Sederunt (Sheriff Court Company Insolvency Rules) 1986.

PLEA-IN-LAW

The person named being able to afford information relative to his dealings with the Company, the necessary orders should be granted as craved.

IN RESPECT WHEREOF

(sgd) A Wiseman

Solicitor,
152 Bath Street,
Glasgow G2 4TB

Noter's Agent

A59.   Note for Reduction of Gratuitous Alienation (Section 242)

SHERIFFDOM OF GLASGOW AND STRATHKELVIN AT GLASGOW

NOTE

for

DAVID FLINT, Solicitor, 152 Bath Street, Glasgow, G2 4TB, Liquidator of ROCOCO COCOA CO LIMITED, having its Registered Office at 1 Main Street, Glasgow (the "Noter")

relative to

Winding-up of

ROCOCO COCOA CO LIMITED, 1 Main Street, Glasgow ("the Company")

for

Reduction of Gratuitous Alienation in terms of section 242 of the Insolvency Act 1986

The Noter craves the Court:

To appoint intimation of this application to be made on Ann Broke, "Duntradin", Kilmacolm, and to order such further intimation and advertisement as to the Court shall seem proper, and to allow the said Ann Broke and all others having an interest to lodge answers hereto if so advised within such time as the Court may appoint; and, on resuming consideration hereof, with or without answers, to order, in terms of section 242 of the Insolvency Act 1986, that on [*date*] the Company unlawfully alienated property of the Company to the said Ann Broke for no adequate consideration; to grant decree of reduction of the alienation and an order restoring the property the subject of the alienation to the Company, or failing which for payment to the Noter as liquidator foresaid of such sum as may be ascertained to be the amount of the gratuitous alienation; to find the Noter entitled to the expenses of this application and to direct the same to be expenses in the liquidation; to find any party opposing this application liable in the expenses occasioned by such opposition; or to do further or otherwise in the premises as to the Court may seem proper.

CONDESCENDENCE

1.   The Company is a company incorporated under the Companies Acts and having its Registered Office at 1 Main Street, Glasgow.

2.   The Noter is the liquidator of the Company appointed by resolution of the creditors dated [*date*].

3.   The Noter having taken over the assets of the Company has discovered that on [*date*] (*i.e.* within five years of the commencement of the winding-up), at a time when the Company was absolutely insolvent, the Company transferred the following asset of the Company, namely, a Ferarri Testarossa Registration No. IBB 7, to the said Ann Broke, being an Associate of the Company within the meaning of the Bankruptcy (Scotland) Act 1985.

4.   The financial records of the Company do not disclose any payment having been received by the Company from the said Ann Broke in respect of such

transfer, Accordingly, it is the belief of the Noter that such transfer was not for adequate consideration. The said Ann Broke has declined to return the asset to the Company and the present proceedings are accordingly necessary in order that the alienation be set aside.

5. This application is made in terms of section 242 of the Insolvency Act 1986 and Part IV of the Act of Sederunt (Sheriff Court Company Insolvency Rules) 1986.

PLEA-IN-LAW

In respect that the Company disposed of property to an Associate for no adequate consideration at a time when its liabilities exceeded its assets, decree should be pronounced as craved in terms of section 242 of the Insolvency Act 1986.

IN RESPECT WHEREOF

(sgd) A Wiseman

Solicitor,
152 Bath Street,

Glasgow G2 4TB
Noter's Agent

A60.   Note for Reduction of Unfair Preference (Section 243)

<u>SHERIFFDOM OF GLASGOW AND STRATHKELVIN AT GLASGOW</u>

NOTE

for

DAVID FLINT, Solicitor, 152 Bath Street, Glasgow, G2 4TB, Liquidator of ROCOCO COCOA CO LIMITED, having its Registered Office at 1 Main Street, Glasgow ("the Noter")

relative to

Winding-up of

ROCOCO COCOA CO LIMITED, 1 Main Street, Glasgow ("the Company")

for

Reduction of Unfair Preference in terms of section 243 of the Insolvency Act 1986

The Noter craves the Court:

To appoint intimation of this application to be made on Orinoco Cocoa Co Limited, 15 London Road, Paisley, and to order such further intimation and advertisement as to the Court shall seem proper, and to allow the said Orinoco Cocoa Co Limited and all others having an interest to lodge answers hereto if so advised within such time as the Court may appoint; and, on resuming consideration hereof, with or without answers, to order, in terms of section 243 of the Insolvency Act 1986, that on [*date*] the Company created a preference in favour of the said Orinoco Cocoa Co Limited which preference prejudiced the general body of creditors; to grant decree of reduction of the preference and an order restoring the property the subject of the preference to the Company, or failing which for payment to the Noter as liquidator foresaid of such sum as may be ascertained to be the amount of the preference; to find the Noter entitled to the expenses of this application and to direct the same to be expenses in the liquidation; to find any party opposing this application liable in the expenses occasioned by such opposition; or to do further or otherwise in the premises as to the Court may seem proper.

CONDESCENDENCE

1.   The Company is a company incorporated under the Companies Acts and having its Registered Office at 1 Main Street, Glasgow.

2.   The Noter is the liquidator of the Company appointed by resolution of the creditors dated [*date*].

3.   The Noter having taken over the assets of the Company has discovered that on [*date*] (*i.e.* six months of the commencement of the winding-up) the Company transferred the following assets of the Company, namely, a debt due to the Company by Entertainment Impressario Inc, 1526 Fifth Avenue, Chicago to Orinoco Cocoa Co Limited (who were a creditor of the Company) to the prejudice of the general body of creditors.

4.   The Noter is of the belief that the transfer of this asset to Orinoco Cocoa Co Limited constitutes an unfair preference and prejudices the general body of

creditors. The present proceedings are accordingly necessary in order that the preference be set aside.

5. This application is made in accordance with section 243 of the Insolvency Act 1986 and Part IV of the Act of Sederunt (Sheriff Court Company Insolvency Rules) 1986.

PLEA-IN-LAW

In respect that the Company disposed of an asset of the Company to one creditor to the prejudice of the general body of creditors within six months of winding-up, decree should be pronounced as craved in terms of section 243 of the Insolvency Act 1986.

IN RESPECT WHEREOF

(sgd) A Wiseman

Solicitor,
152 Bath Street,
Glasgow G2 4TB

Noter's Agent

A61. Note for Reduction of Extortionate Credit Transaction (Section 244)

<u>SHERIFFDOM OF GLASGOW AND STRATHKELVIN AT GLASGOW</u>

NOTE

for

DAVID FLINT, Solicitor, 152 Bath Street, Glasgow, G2 4TB, Liquidator of ROCOCO COCOA CO LIMITED having its Registered Office at 1 Main Street, Glasgow ("the Noter")

relative to

Winding-up of

ROCOCO COCOA CO LIMITED, 1 Main Street, Glasgow ("the Company")

for

Reduction of an Extortionate Credit Transaction in terms of section 244 of the Insolvency Act 1986

The Noter craves the Court:

To appoint intimation of this application to be made on Galaxy Product Limited, Heavenly Mansions, Pitlochry and to order such further intimation and advertisement as to the Court shall seem proper, and to allow the said Galaxy Products Limited and all others having an interest to lodge answers hereto if so advised within such time as the Court may appoint; and, on resuming consideration hereof, with or without answers, to order, in terms of section 244 of the Insolvency Act 1986, that the Company is a party to the transaction on extortionate credit terms with the said Galaxy Products Limited; to grant decree of reduction of the whole obligations incumbent on the Company in terms of the credit agreement; to find the Noter entitled to the expenses of this application and to direct the same to be expenses in the Liquidation; to find any party opposing this application liable in the expenses occasioned by such opposition; or to do further or otherwise in the premises as to the Court may seem proper.

CONDESCENDENCE

1. The Company is a company incorporated under the Companies Acts and having its Registered Office at 1 Main Street, Glasgow.

2. The Noter is the Liquidator of the Company appointed by resolution of the creditors dated [*date*].

3. The Noter having taken over the assets of the Company has discovered that on [*date*] (*i.e.* within three years of the winding-up) the Company became party to a transaction with Galaxy Products Limited, Heavenly Mansions, Pitlochry, for the provision of credit to the Company. In terms of the transaction the Company is bound to pay interest and charges amounting to twenty-two per centum per month. [*Note: insert details*]

4. The Noter is of the opinion that the terms on which the credit was made available to the Company under this transaction are extortionate. The present proceedings are accordingly necessary in order that the terms of the credit transaction should be set aside.

5.   This application is made in accordance with section 244 of the Insolvency Act 1986 (as amended) and the Act of Sederunt (Sheriff Court Company Insolvency Rules) 1986.

PLEA-IN-LAW

In respect that the Company is a party to a transaction involving the provision of credit to the Company on extortionate terms, decree of reduction should be granted as craved in terms of section 244 of the Insolvency Act 1986.

IN RESPECT WHEREOF

(sgd) A Wiseman

Solicitor,
152 Bath Street,
Glasgow G2 4TB

Noter's Agent

A62.   Note for Contribution Order (Section 15 of the CDDA 1986)

SHERIFFDOM OF GLASGOW AND STRATHKELVIN AT GLASGOW

NOTE

for

DAVID FLINT, Solicitor, 152 Bath Street, Glasgow, G2 4TB, Liquidator of ROCOCO COCOA CO LIMITED, having its Registered Office at 1 Main Street, Glasgow ("the Noter")

relative to

Winding-up of

ROCOCO COCOA CO LIMITED, 1 Main Street, Glasgow ("the Company")

for

Order in terms of section 15 of Company Directors Disqualification Act 1986

The Noter craves the Court:

To appoint intimation of this application to be made on Ian Barry Broke residing at "Duntradin", Kilmacolm, and to order such further intimation and advertisement as to the Court shall seem proper, and to allow the said Ian Barry Broke and all others having an interest to lodge answers hereto if so advised within such time as the Court may appoint; and, on resuming consideration hereof, with or without answers, to order, in terms of section 15 of the Company Director Disqualification Act 1986, that the said Ian Barry Broke was involved in the management of the Company and acted on the instructions of Vera Broke residing at "Shangri La Cottage", Kilwinning between [*date*] and [*date*] in the knowledge that such person was an undischarged bankrupt during which period the Company incurred debts and other liabilities totalling £26,213; and to grant decree against the said Ian Barry Broke with the Company for payment to the Noter as liquidator foresaid of the said sum of £26,213 or such other sum as may be ascertained to be the amount of the debts and other liabilities of the Company incurred during the said period, with interest thereon from the date of decree to follow hereon until payment; and to find the said Ian Barry Broke liable with the Company in expenses; or to do further or otherwise in the premises as to the Court shall seem proper.

CONDESCENDENCE

1.   The Company is a company incorporated under the Companies Acts and having its Registered Office at 1 Main Street, Glasgow.

2.   The Noter is the liquidator of the Company appointed by resolution of the creditors dated [*date*].

3.   Ian Barry Broke was a director of the Company within the meaning of section 741 of the Companies Act 1985.

4.   The Noter having taken over the assets of the Company has discovered that during the period from [*date*] to [*date*] while the said Ian Barry Broke was involved in the management of the Company, the Company incurred debts and other liabilities totalling £25,000 including:

Galaxy Products Limited   £12,850

Orinoco Cocoa Co Limited   £ 6,329

It is believed by the Noter that during the said period the said Ian Barry Broke acted on the instructions of Vera Broke, "Shangri La Cottage", Kilwinning, being a person who he knew at that time to be an undischarged bankrupt.

5.   The said Ian Barry Broke, being liable jointly and severally with the Company for the said sum, refuses to pay to the Noter as Liquidator foresaid the said sum and accordingly the present proceedings are necessary.

6.   This application is made in terms of section 15 of the Company Directors Disqualification Act 1986.

PLEA-IN-LAW

In respect that the said person was involved in the management of the Company on the instructions of a person who he knew to be an undischarged bankrupt decree should be pronounced as craved for the debts and other liabilities of the Company in terms of section 15 of the Company Directors Disqualification Act 1986.

IN RESPECT WHEREOF

(sgd) A Wiseman

Solicitor,
152 Bath Street,
Glasgow G2 4TB

Noter's Agent

A63.   Note for Calls on Contributories (Section 161)

<u>SHERIFFDOM OF GLASGOW AND STRATHKELVIN AT GLASGOW</u>

NOTE

for

DAVID FLINT, Solicitor, 152 Bath Street, Glasgow, G2 4TB, Liquidator of Rococo Cocoa Co Limited having its Registered Office at 1 Main Street, Glasgow ("the Noter")

relative to

Winding-up of

ROCOCO COCOA CO LIMITED, 1 Main Street, Glasgow ("the Company")

for

Order in terms of section 161 of the Insolvency Act 1986

The Noter craves the Court:

To grant decree in terms of section 161 of the Insolvency Act 1986 (as amended) against Uriah Rodney Broke, residing at "Tumbledown Cottage", Bridge of Weir for payment to the Noter as Liquidator foresaid of the sum of £2,000 being the amount due by the said Uriah Rodney Broke to the Company in respect of unpaid calls, with interest thereon from the date of decree to follow hereon until payment at the rate of five per centum per annum; and to find the said Uriah Rodney Broke liable in expenses; or to do further or otherwise in the premises as to the Court shall seem proper.

CONDESCENDENCE

1.   The Company is a company incorporated under the Companies Acts and having its Registered Office at 1 Main Street, Glasgow.

2.   The Noter is the Liquidator of the Company appointed by resolution of the creditors dated [*date*].

3.   The Noter having taken over the books and records of the Company has discovered that the said Uriah Rodney Broke is liable to pay to the Company £2,000 in respect of unpaid calls for the Shares held by him as set out in the certified list prepared by the Noter and produced herewith. [*Note: if a list of Contributories has been fixed by the Court reference should be made to it.*]

4.   The said Uriah Rodney Broke refuses or delays to make payment of such sum and, accordingly, the present proceedings are necessary in terms of section 161 of the Insolvency Act 1986 to obtain payment for the Company in respect of the unpaid calls.

5.   This Note is presented in terms of the Insolvency Act 1986 and in particular section 161 thereof and in terms of the Insolvency (Scotland) Rules 1986 and in terms of the Act of Sederunt (Sheriff Court Company Insolvency Rules) 1986.

PLEA-IN-LAW

In respect that the said person is liable to make payment to the Company in respect of unpaid calls, decree should be pronounced as craved.

IN RESPECT WHEREOF

(sgd) A Wiseman

Solicitor,
152 Bath Street,

Glasgow G2 4TB
Noter's Agent

A64. Notice for Final Meeting of Creditors

INSOLVENCY ACT 1986

<u>ROCOCO COCOA CO LIMITED – IN LIQUIDATION</u>

NOTICE IS HEREBY GIVEN that, in terms of section 146(1) of the Insolvency Act 1986 a final meeting of the creditors of the above Company will be held within the offices of MacRoberts, 152 Bath Street, Glasgow G2 4TB at 12 noon on [*date*] for the purpose of receiving an account of the Winding-up from the Liquidator together with any explanations that may be given by him.

The attention of creditors is drawn to the following:

1. A Creditor is entitled to vote only if he has submitted his claim (Form 4.7 (Scotland)) to the above address and his claim has been accepted in whole or in part.

2. A Resolution at the meeting is passed if a majority in value of those voting vote in favour of it.

3. Proxies may be lodged at or before the meeting at the above offices marked for the attention of Mr David Flint.

4. Claims may be lodged by those who have not already done so at or before the meeting at the said offices.

5. The provisions of rules 4.15–4.17 (as amended by Schedule 1) and of rule 7 of the Insolvency (Scotland) Rules 1986.

For the purpose of formulating claims, creditors should note that the date of liquidation is [*date*].

If you are in any doubt as to any of these matters, you should consult your Solicitor immediately.

....
Liquidator

MacRoberts
Solicitors
152 Bath Street
Glasgow
G2 4TB

......................................(Date)

A65. Agenda for Final Meeting of Creditors

<u>AGENDA FOR FINAL MEETING OF CREDITORS OF</u>

<u>ROCOCO COCOA CO LIMITED – IN LIQUIDATION</u>

held at 152 Bath Street, Glasgow

on [*date*] at [*time*]

in terms of section 146 of the Insolvency Act 1986

[Quorum:	one creditor in person or by proxy entitled to vote	Rule 7.7, 7.16
Chairman:	The Liquidator or his appointed nominee]	Rule 7.5(1)

1. Introduction

Explanation of Purpose of Meeting:

To lay the Liquidator's Report before the meeting	Section 146(1)(a) Rule 4.31(2)
To provide an opportunity for creditors to question the Liquidator with respect to any matter contained in his Report	Rule 4.31(3)
To determine the mode of the release of the Liquidator	Section 146(1)(b)
To close the meeting if no quorum is present and report same to the Court and the Registrar of Companies	Rule 4.31(5)

Documents laid on table

By Statute:	Report of Liquidator	Section 146(1)(a) Rule 4.31(2)
By Habit:	Notice of Meeting Related Certificate of Posting *Edinburgh Gazette*	Rule 7.3(1) Rule 7.23(1)

2. Report of Liquidator	Section 146(1)(a) Rule 4.31(2)
Questions	Rule 4.31(3)
3. To determine mode of release of Liquidator	Section 146(1)(b)

    (a) *With agreement of creditors*

Upon notification to Court and the Registrar of Companies	Section 172(8), 164(d)(ii) Rule 4.31(6)

    (b) *Without agreement of creditors*

Upon receipt of release from Accountant in Bankruptcy	Section 172(8), 174(4)(d)(i) Rule 4.25(2) and (3), 4.31(6)

    (c) *In absence of quorum of creditors*

Upon notification to Court and the Registrar of Companies	Section 172(8), 174(d)(ii) Rule 4.31(5)

4. Close meeting.

A66.   Minutes of Final Meeting of Creditors

MINUTES OF FINAL MEETING OF CREDITORS OF ROCOCO COCOA CO LIMITED – IN LIQUIDATION held at 152 Bath Street, Glasgow G2 4TB on [*date*] at [*time*] in terms of section 146 of the Insolvency Act 1986.

Present:

In Attendance:

1.   The meeting was held to be properly constituted.

2.   The Report of the Liquidator was presented to the meeting.

3.   The following responses were given by the Liquidator in answer to questions from creditors.

4.   The Report of the Liquidator was ** accepted/not accepted.

5.   The creditors resolved that the Liquidation should ** have/not have his release.

OR

1.   It was resolved that no quorum was present, and that rule 4.31(5) of the Insolvency (Scotland) Rules 1986 would accordingly apply.

....

Chairman

** delete as appropriate

A67. Adjudication of Claim and Form of Receipt

Adjudication of the claim of:

[*Creditor Name & Address*]

In the Liquidation of ROCOCO COCOA CO LIMITED

Preferential ranking	£
Ordinary ranking	£
Total Claim	£

I hereby agree the above adjudication of my claim and confirm my acceptance of the sum of £[ ] as a final dividend on my [ ] claim, being a dividend of [ ]p in the £

Signature ....

Name ....
(in block letters)

On behalf of .... [Creditor]

Stamp:

A68.   Note for Removal of Liquidator (Section 172)

SHERIFFDOM OF GLASGOW AND STRATHKELVIN AT GLASGOW

NOTE

by

ORINOCO COCOA CO LIMITED, 15 London Road, Paisley PA1 1NT ("the Noter")

relative to

Winding-up of

ROCOCO COCOA CO LIMITED, 1 Main Street, Glasgow ("the Company")

For

The removal of David Flint as liquidator in terms of section 172 Insolvency Act 1986

The Noter craves the Court:

To appoint intimation of this application to be made on David Flint, Solicitor, 152 Bath Street, Glasgow, G2 4TB, the Liquidator of Rococo Cocoa Co Limited ("the Company") and to order such further intimation and advertisement as to the Court shall seem proper and to allow the said Liquidator and all others having an interest to lodge answers hereto if so advised within such time as the Court may appoint; and, on resuming consideration hereof, with or without answers, to remove the said David Flint from the office of Liquidator of the Company and to appoint Alan Neil Other, Solicitor, Excel House, 30 Semple Street, Edinburgh, EH3 8BL or such other person as the Court may think fit to be Liquidator in his place with the powers contained in Part II and III of Schedule 4 to the Insolvency Act 1986; to find the Noter entitled to the expenses of this application and to direct the same to be expenses in the Liquidation; or to do further or otherwise in the premises as to the Court may seem proper.

CONDESCENDENCE

1.   The Company is a company incorporated under the Companies Acts and having its Registered Office at 1 Main Street, Glasgow.

2.   David Flint, Solicitor, 152 Bath Street, Glasgow G2 4TB was appointed Liquidator of the Company by resolution of the creditors dated [*date*].

3.   The Noter is a creditor of the Company. The Noter believes that as the said Liquidator has various business relations with the directors of the Company prior to the Company going into Liquidation there is a potential conflict of interest and that accordingly the removal of the said Liquidator from office and the appointment of another Liquidator in his place would be for the beneficial winding-up of the Company.

4.   The Noter respectfully suggests that Alan Neil Other, Solicitor, Excel House, 30 Semple Street, Edinburgh, EH3 8BL, who is a qualified Insolvency Practitioner within the meaning of Part XIII of the Insolvency Act 1986 (as amended) is a suitable person for the office of Liquidator.

PLEA-IN-LAW

In respect that for the benefit of the winding-up the Liquidator should be removed by the Court and a substitute Liquidator appointed in his place, the orders should be pronounced as craved in terms of section 172 of the Insolvency Act 1986.

IN RESPECT WHEREOF

(sgd) A Wiseman

Solicitor,
152 Bath Street,
Glasgow G2 4TB

Noter's Agent

A69. Note for Court's Approval of Liquidator's Fees

SHERIFFDOM OF GLASGOW AND STRATHKELVIN AT GLASGOW

NOTE

by

DAVID FLINT, Solicitor, 152 Bath Street, Glasgow G2 4TB ("the Noter")

relative to

Winding-up of

ROCOCO COCOA CO LIMITED, 1 Main Street, Glasgow ("the Company")

for

Approval of his Accounts; Authority to have his Solicitor's business account taxed and payment made thereof; and Authority to make payment of his remuneration.

The Noter craves the Court:

To appoint the note to be intimated on the Walls of Court and to be served on the Liquidation Committee and to allow all parties having an interest to lodge Answers hereto within fourteen days after such intimation and service; and on resuming consideration hereof, with or without Answers:

1. to remit the accounts of Intromissions of the Noter as (a) Provisional Liquidator; (b) Interim Liquidator and (c) since [*date*] in respect of the affairs of the Company for examination and audit to Ivor Winner, Chartered Accountant, 1 Counting House Lane, Glasgow G1 4SS, or to such other person as to the Court shall seem proper and to direct such person to report what in his opinion is a suitable remuneration for the Noter.

2. on the result of such examination and audit being reported to the Court to fix and declare the amount of the remuneration to be paid to the Petitioner as (a) Provisional Liquidator; (b) Interim Liquidator; and (c) thereafter; and to order the amount to be paid to the Noter out of the assets of the Liquidation.

3. to authorise the Liquidator of the Company to make such payments and also to pay the amount of the outlays incurred by the Petitioner including the accounts of the Noter's solicitors after taxation thereof by the Auditor of Court.

4. to declare the expenses of this Note and any proceedings to follow hereon to be expenses of the Liquidation and authorise the Liquidator to make payment thereof; or to do further or otherwise as to the Court may seem proper.

CONDESCENDENCE

1. By Interlocutor dated [*date*], the Sheriff at Glasgow nominated and appointed the Noter to be Interim Liquidator of the Company, he having previously been appointed Provisional Liquidator on [*date*].

2. The Noter in accordance with the provisions of section 138 of the Insolvency Act 1986 and Part 7 of the Insolvency (Scotland) Rules 1986 ("the Rules") convened a Meeting of Creditors of the Company for [*date*].

3. At said Meeting Alan Neil Other, Solicitor, Excel House, 30 Semple Street, Edinburgh, EH3 8BL, was appointed Liquidator of the Company.

4. In accordance with rule 4.5 of the Rules, the remuneration of the Noter as Provisional Liquidator is to be fixed by the Court.

5. In accordance with the provisions of rule 4.32 of the Rules the Noter on [*date*] made a claim in respect of the period from [*date*] to date for the outlays incurred by him and for his remuneration to the Liquidation Committee.

6. The said Committee declined to accept the quantum of the Noter's claim as being appropriate. Accordingly the Noter wishes to apply to the Court for an order fixing the amount of his remuneration in accordance with rule 4.34 of the Rules.

7. Ivor Winner, Chartered Accountant, 1 Counting House Lane, Glasgow G1 4SS, is an experienced insolvency practitioner with considerable experience in preparing report for the Court on the appropriate amount of remuneration for *inter alia* liquidators. He is therefore a suitable person to report on the appropriate amount of remuneration due to the Noter.

8. The Noter has incurred outlays and expenses to *inter alia* his law agents. The Noter therefore also wishes these outlays and expenses to be determined and authority given to the Liquidator of the Company to pay these forthwith.

9. Notice of this application was given to the Liquidation Committee in accordance with rule 4.34(2) of the Rules on [*date*]. A copy of the Notice is attached.

10. This application is made in accordance with rule 4.34 of the Insolvency (Scotland) Rules 1986 and rule 28 of the Act of Sederunt (Sheriff Court Company Insolvency Rules) 1986.

PLEA-IN-LAW

The Liquidator being entitled to have the Court fix his remuneration, the appropriate orders should be granted as craved.

IN RESPECT WHEREOF

(sgd) A Wiseman

Solicitor,
152 Bath Street,
Glasgow G2 4TB

Noter's Agent

A70.   Letter to Creditors

Our Ref

Your Ref

[Date]

Dear Sirs

ROCOCO COCOA CO LIMITED – IN LIQUIDATION

I was appointed Liquidator of the above named company on [*date*]. All goods and services supplied by the company during the liquidation will only be supplied on condition that they will be paid for in full, by the due date, without deduction or set off against any monies you may be owed by the company. Your acceptance of goods or services will constitute acceptance of these terms and conditions of sale. You should note that I am not in a position to give any guarantees or warranties in a personal capacity for goods or services supplied.

Please remit to me any amounts which are owed to the above company.
I look forward to hearing from you as soon as possible.

Yours faithfully

Liquidator

[Notes:
i   To be sent to all customers.

ii   Where set off is known to be a potential problem, this letter is to be specifically addressed and sent by recorded delivery and an acknowledgement obtained.

iii   Where the company's terms and conditions are inadequate, consideration should be given to attaching new terms and conditions drafted by liquidator's solicitors.]

A71. Memorandum regarding Powers of Provisional Liquidator

ROCOCO COCOA CO LIMITED (IN PROVISIONAL LIQUIDATION)

POWERS GRANTED BY INTERLOCUTOR AS HIGHLIGHTED

INSOLVENCY ACT 1986

SCHEDULE 4

POWERS OF LIQUIDATOR IN A WINDING-UP

Part I

Powers Exercisable with Sanction

i   Power to pay any class of creditors in full.

ii   Power to make any compromise or arrangement with creditors or persons claiming to be creditors, or having or alleging themselves to have any claim (present or future, certain or contingent, ascertained or sounding only in damages) against the Company, or whereby the Company may be rendered liable.

iii   Power to compromise, on such terms as may be agreed:

     a   all calls and liabilities to calls, all debts and liabilities capable of resulting in debts, and all claims (present or future, certain or contingent, ascertained or sounding only in damages) subsisting or supposed to subsist between the Company and a contributory or alleged contributory or other debtor or person apprehending liability to the Company, and

     b   all questions in any way relating to or affecting the assets or the winding-up of the Company

and take any security for the discharge or any such call, debt, liability or claim and give a complete discharge in respect of it.

Part II

Powers Exercisable Without Sanction in Voluntary Winding-up, With Sanction in Winding-up By The Court

i   Power to bring or defend any action or other legal proceeding in the name of and on behalf of the Company.

ii   Power to carry on the business of the Company so far as may be necessary for its beneficial winding-up.

Part III

Powers Exercisable Without Sanction In Any Winding-up

i   Power to sell any of the Company's property by public auction or private contract with power to transfer the whole of it to any person or to sell the same in parcels.

ii   Power to do all acts and execute, in the name and on behalf of the Company, all deeds, receipts and other documents and for that purpose to use, when necessary, the Company's seal.

iii   Power to prove, rank and claim in the bankruptcy, insolvency or sequestration of any contributory for any balance against his estate and to receive dividends in the bankruptcy, insolvency or sequestration in respect of that balance, as a separate debt due from the bankrupt or insolvent, and rateably with the other separate creditors

iv   Power to draw, accept, make and indorse any bill of exchange or promissory note in the name and on behalf of the Company, with the same effect with respect to the Company's liability as if the bill or note had been drawn accepted, made or indorsed by or on behalf of the Company in the course of its business.

v   Power to raise on the security of the assets of the Company any money requisite.

vi   Power to take out in his official name letters of administration to any deceased contributory, and to do in his official name any other act necessary for obtaining payment of any money due from a contributory or his estate which cannot conveniently be done in the name of the Company.

In all such cases the money due is deemed, for the purpose of enabling the liquidator to take out the letters of administration or recover the money, to be due to the liquidator himself.

vii   Power to appoint an agent to do any business which the liquidator is unable to do himself.

viii   Power to do all such other things as may be necessary for winding-up the Company's affairs and distributing its assets.

A72.   Section 204 Early Dissolution Checklist

1   Although not a statutory requirement, it is good
    practice to send to all known creditors as an
    estimated statement of affairs and a brief
    circular indicating that the company assets are
    insufficient to cover the expenses of the winding-
    up and that it is the Liquidator's intention to
    apply to the court for early dissolution in terms
    of section 204 of the Insolvency Act.

2   Send letter to law agent requesting application   s.204
    to the relevant court under section 204. (The
    relevant court being the court where the
    company was wound-up). Law agent will
    require:
    - Copy interlocutor of appointment
    - Estimated statement of affairs
    - Minute of the section 138 meeting

3   Send court order to Companies House for   s.204(4)
    registration accompanied by Form   s.172(7)
    4.28 (Scotland) within 14 days from date of
    order. The company will be dissolved three
    months from the date of registration of order.

4   Submit Form 4.12 (Scotland) to the Accountant   s.174(4)
    of Court requesting release of the Liquidator,   IR4.25
    enclosing sederunt book of liquidator's
    documents.

5   Accountant of Court will issue Forms 4.13 &   IR4.25
    4.14 (Scotland), the certificate and notice of
    release.

6   Copies of Forms 4.13 & 4.14 (Scotland) should
    then be submitted to Companies House
    forthwith.

B – CREDITORS' VOLUNTARY LIQUIDATION

B1. Minute of Meeting of Directors

MINUTES of a MEETING of the DIRECTORS of ROCOCO COCOA CO LIMITED held at 152 Bath Street, Glasgow G2 4TB on [*date*] at 12 noon

PRESENT: I B Broke

U R Broke

ATTENDING

1. The financial position of the Company was discussed and it was resolved that an Extraordinary General Meeting of the Members of the Company be convened in accordance with the Insolvency Act 1986, section 84(1)(c), to take place at Trades Hall, Glasgow on [*date*] at 12 noon at which the following resolutions, respectively extraordinary and ordinary, be proposed:

   1.1 That it has been proved to the satisfaction of the meeting that the Company cannot, be reason of its liabilities, continue its business and that the Company be wound-up voluntarily.

   1.2 That David Flint, Solicitor, of MacRoberts, Solicitors, 152 Bath Street, Glasgow, G2 4TB be appointed as Liquidator for the purposes of such winding-up.

2. It was noted that the aforesaid David Flint is an insolvency practitioner qualified under the Insolvency Act 1986, section 230 to be the Liquidator and that, in terms of rule 4.19(2) of the Insolvency (Scotland) Rules 1986, he, on the passing of the resolution for his appointment, will consent so to act.

3. It was further resolved that:

   3.1 The Company Secretary be instructed to convene a Meeting of the Creditors of the Company, in accordance with the Insolvency Act 1986, section 98(1)(a), to take place at Trades Hall, Glasgow on [*date*] at 12 noon.

   3.2 David Flint of MacRoberts, Solicitors, on behalf of the Company Secretary, be requested to send to the Members and Creditors of the Company Notice of the respective Meetings and to cause the same to be published in the *Edinburgh Gazette* and two newspapers, namely *The Herald* and *The Evening Times*, all in accordance with the Insolvency Act 1986, sections 98(1) and 98(2).

   3.3 Ian B Broke be the Director to preside at he Statutory Meeting of Creditors in accordance with section 99(1)(c) of the Insolvency Act 1986.

4. It was further resolved that, during the period between the date hereof and the date of the passing of the resolutions described in the foregoing paragraphs 1.1 and 1.2:

   4.1 MacRoberts, Solicitors, be requested to assist the Directors in the preparation of the Statement of Affairs required by the Insolvency Act 1986, section 99(1)(a) and of other information required to be laid before the Meeting of Creditors.

4.2 Big4 Audit plc, Chartered Accountants, be requested to advise the Directors in the financial control and supervision of the business.

4.3 A Trust Account be opened at the [*name*] Branch of the [*name*] Bank, to be operated on behalf of the Company by MacRoberts, Solicitors, to preserve income for the benefit of the creditors of the Company.

4.4 The funds held in Trust and the assets of the Company be used to meet the proper charges and disbursements arising, including ongoing operating expenses, the cost of public notice and fees charges for professional valuations; also including the professional fees and attendant costs of MacRoberts, Solicitors, it being clearly understood that their related services are both requested and given for the benefit of the creditors of the Company.

[   ] I B Broke

[   ] U R Broke

Directors

[*date*]

B2.   Letter to Directors

[*date*]

The Board of Directors
Rococo Cocoa Co Limited
1 Main Street
Glasgow

Dear Sirs

We hereby acknowledge receipt of a signed copy of the Minutes of the Meeting of Directors held at Trades Hall, Glasgow on [*date*] at which we were present and at which information was supplied to which indicated that the Company was insolvent, and confirm that we will act in accordance with the Resolutions therein adopted.

We now write to summarise the advice which we gave, in the clear understanding that you remain entirely responsible for the control of your Company until a Liquidator is appointed.

As you have agreed that immediate steps be taken to place the Company into liquidation, it is particularly important that you comply strictly with the advice hereinafter described.

1.   Statutory Meetings of Members and Creditors must be convened, and a Statement of Affairs and list of creditors must be prepared to be presented at the Meeting of Creditors on the prescribed Form 4.4 (Scotland), a copy of which is enclosed.

2.   Further credit in respect of goods or services must not be taken.

3.   No payments or dispositions of assets should be supplied or returned to any supplier or customer, the value if which could be used as a set-off against an existing debt.

4.   No goods or other assets should be supplied or returned to any supplier or customer, the value of which could be used as a set-off against an existing debt.

5.   Any bank account which is overdrawn must not be used.

6.   All necessary steps should be taken to preserve and protect the assets of the Company for the benefit of the creditors.

7.   Adequate insurance cover must be maintained.

Failure to comply strictly with the advice hereinbefore described may result in penalties or personal liability being incurred under provisions of the Insolvency Act 1986.

Yours faithfully

MacRoberts

B3. Notice of Extraordinary General Meeting

<u>ROCOCO COCOA CO LIMITED</u>

NOTICE is hereby given that an EXTRAORDINARY GENERAL MEETING of the Company will be held at Trades Hall, Glasgow on the [*date*] at 12 noon for the purpose of considering, and if thought fit, passing the following Resolutions which will be proposed Number (1) as an EXTRAORDINARY RESOLUTION and Number (2) as an ORDINARY RESOLUTION of the Company:

RESOLUTIONS

1. THAT it has been proved to the satisfaction of the meeting that the Company cannot, by reason of its liabilities, continue its business and that the Company be wound-up voluntarily.

2. THAT David Flint, Solicitor, of MacRoberts, Solicitors, 152 Bath Street, Glasgow G2 4TB be appointed liquidator for the purposes of such winding-up.

Dated the [*date*].

BY ORDER OF THE BOARD

(sgd) U R Broke

<u>Company Secretary</u>

A Member entitled to attend and vote at the above Meeting is entitled to appoint a proxy to attend and, on a poll, to vote instead of him. A proxy need not be a Member of the Company.

<u>Registered Office</u>
1 Main Street
Glasgow

B4.   Agenda for Extraordinary General Meeting

<u>AGENDA FOR EXTRAORDINARY GENERAL MEETING</u>

<u>OF THE MEMBERS OF ROCOCO COCOA CO LIMITED</u>

<u>held at Trades Hall, Glasgow</u>

<u>on [*date*] at 12 noon</u>

[Quorum:	As provided by Articles of Association, otherwise two members in person [CA s.370(4)]	
	Note: A member may be represented by proxy who is considered to be present in person if that member is another Company. A total attendance of one member, who may or may not also be a proxy for another member, does not constitute a quorum unless so directed by the Court. A total attendance of one member and the proxy, who is not a member, of another member, constitutes a quorum. [CA 375(2)]]	
	Chairman: A nominated Director or an elected member.	[CA Table A, Reg 42 CA s.370(5); Table A, Reg 43]

1.   Introduction

Explanation of purpose of meeting:

Establish validity of proceedings
Consider voluntary winding-up of the Company
Appoint a Liquidator

2.   Validity of proceedings

Documents Laid on Table:

By Statute: Nil

By Habit: Notice of meeting
Related certificate of posting

Period of Notice:

(a) Minimum of fourteen days	[CA s.369(2)(b)(ii)]
(b) Waiver of (a) by 95 per cent of nominal value of voting shares	[CA s.369(3)(b); CA s.369(4)(a)]
Receipt of Forms of Proxy	[CA s.372]

3. Consider, pass and sign Extraordinary Resolution No. 1 and Ordinary Resolution No. 2.	[CA s.378(1) IA s.84(1)(c)]
4. Receive written consent from Insolvency Practitioner to act as Liquidator.	[Rule 4.19(2)]

5.   Close of meeting.

B5. Minute of Extraordinary General Meeting

> MINUTE of EXTRAORDINARY GENERAL MEETING of the MEMBERS of ROCOCO COCOA CO LIMITED held at Trades Hall, Glasgow on [*date*] at 12 noon

Present: I B Broke (1) (Shareholdings in parenthesis)
                 U R Broke (2)

1. The meeting was held to be properly constituted [, notwithstanding that shorter notice than that specified in section 369(2) of the Companies Act 1985, or in the Company's Articles of Association, may have been given].

2. The following Resolutions, respectively extraordinary and ordinary, were passed:

    2.1 That it has been proved to the satisfaction of the meeting that the Company cannot, by reason of its liabilities, continue its business and that the Company be wound-up voluntarily.

    2.2 That David Flint, Solicitor, of MacRoberts, Solicitors, 152 Bath Street, Glasgow G2 4TB be appointed as liquidator for the purposes of such winding-up.

3. It was noted that the aforesaid David Flint is an insolvency practitioner qualified under section 230 of the Insolvency Act 1986 to be the liquidator and that, in terms of rule 4.19(2) of the Insolvency (Scotland) Rules 1986, he consents so to act, a written statement to that effect being provided.

U R Broke

<u>Chairman</u>

B6.   Print of Extraordinary Resolution

THE COMPANIES ACT 1985

COMPANY LIMITED BY SHARES

EXTRAORDINARY RESOLUTION

(Pursuant to section 378 of the Companies Act 1985)

of

ROCOCO COCOA CO LIMITED

Passed [*date*]

At an EXTRAORDINARY GENERAL MEETING of ROCOCO COCOA CO LIMITED duly convened and held at Trades Hall, Glasgow on [*date*] the following Resolution was passed as an Extraordinary Resolution of the Company

"THAT it has been proved to the satisfaction of the meeting that the Company cannot, by reason of its liabilities, continue its business and that the Company be wound-up voluntarily."

"U R Broke"

Director

Registered Office
1 Main Street
Glasgow

B7. Notice of Meeting of Creditors

ROCOCO COCOA CO LIMITED (IN LIQUIDATION)

Registered Office: 1 Main Street, Glasgow

Trading Address: Paradise Way, Ibrox, Glasgow

Notice is hereby given that, in terms of section 98 of the Insolvency Act 1986, a meeting of the Creditors of Rococo Cocoa Co Limited will be held at the Trades Hall, Glasgow at 12 noon on [*date*] for the purposes of choosing a person to be Liquidator of the Company, and of determining whether to establish a Liquidation Committee in terms of sections 99, 100 and 101 of the Insolvency Act 1986. The attention of Creditors is drawn to the following:

1. All creditors whose claims are unsecured, in whole or in part, are entitled to attend in person or by proxy.

2. A Creditor is entitled to vote only if he has submitted his claim (Form 4.7 (Scotland)) to the address mentioned below and his claim has been accepted in whole or in part.

3. A Resolution at the meeting is passed if a majority in value of those voting vote in favour of it.

4. Proxies may be lodged at or before the meeting at the offices of MacRoberts, Solicitors, 152 Bath Street, Glasgow G2 4TB marked for the attention of Mr David Flint.

5. Claims may be lodged by those who have not already done so at or before the meeting at the said offices.

6. The provisions of rules 4.15–4.17 (as amended by Schedule 1) and of rule 7 of the Insolvency (Scotland) Rules 1986.

7. A list of names and addresses of the Company's Creditors will be available for inspection, free of charge, at the offices of MacRoberts, Solicitors, 152 Bath Street, Glasgow G2 4TB during the two business days prior to the said meeting.

If you are in any doubt as to any of these matters, you should consult your Solicitor immediately.

Ian B Broke
Director

Dated the [*date*]

B8.   Agenda for First Statutory Meeting of Creditors (Section 98)

AGENDA FOR FIRST STATUTORY MEETING OF CREDITORS OF

ROCOCO COCOA CO LIMITED – IN LIQUIDATION

held at Trades Hall, Glasgow

on [*date*] at 12 noon

in terms of section 98 of the Insolvency Act 1986

[Quorum:	One creditor in person or by proxy	
	entitled to vote	Rules 7.7; 7.16
Chairman:	A Company Director]	Section 99(1)(c)

1.   Introduction

Explanation of purpose of meeting:
To adjourn the meeting if no quorum is present and
for the chairman to give notice of the date and time
of the adjourned meeting   Rule 7.8(5)

To inform the meeting of any payments made in
connection with:

(a) the preparation of the Statement of Affairs   Rule 4.9(2)
(b) the summoning, advertisement and holding
     of the meeting   Rule 4.14A(2)

To lay before the meeting a Statement as to the
Affairs of the Company   Section 99(1)
                                                        Rule 4.7

To choose a Liquidator   Section 100(1) and (2)
                                                        Rule 4.19

To establish a Liquidation Committee   Section 101(1) and (4)
                                                        Rule 4.41

Documents Laid on Table:

By Statute:	Directors' Statement of Affairs	Section 99(1)(b)
		Rule 4.7(5)
By Habit:	Notice of Meeting	Section 98(1)(b)
		Rule 7.3(1)
	Related Certificate of Posting	Rule 7.23(1)
	Edinburgh Gazette	Section 98(1)(c)
	Two Newspapers	Section 98(1)(c)
		Rule 7.3(3)

2.   Insolvency Practitioner

No involvement with Company or directors prior to ....

Payments made in connection with:

(a) preparation of Statement of Affairs   Rule 4.9(2)
(b) summoning, advertisement and holding of the
     meeting   Rule 4.14A(2)

3. Report by Insolvency Practitioner

    (i)   Company History
    (ii)   Statement Deficiency
    (iii) Directors' Statement of Affairs
    (iv)   Estimated Statement of Affairs   Section 99(1)(b)
    (v)   where the Directors' Statement of
           Affairs differs from the Estimated
           Statement of Affairs, an explanation
           of that difference   Rule 4.7(6)

    Questions

4. Appointment of Liquidator

    (a) Report Resolutions of Meeting of Members   Section 100(1)

    (b) Members' nominee or assisting Insolvency
         Practitioner as sole nominee:

         Exhibit Consent to Act and certify
         appointment   Rule 4.19(2)

    (c) Two or more nominees:

         Exhibit Consent to Act and certify
         appointment   Rule 4.19(2)

    One vote is required if one nominee has a clear
    majority in value of claim over all the other
    nominees   Rule 7.12(3)(a) and (b)

    Several votes are required if no one nominee has a
    clear majority, the nominee with the least support
    withdrawing at each subsequent vote   Rule 7.12(3)(c)

    (d) No nominee:

         Notify Registrar of Companies of Resolution
         of members and invite dissolution of Company

         Advise directors and members at their liability
         continues for twenty years

5. Establishment of Liquidation Committee

    Explanation of Composition and powers:

    Composition: At least three and not more   Rule 4.41(1)
    than five creditors or their   Section 101(1)
    representatives, plus up to   Section 101(2)
    five contributories or their
    representatives (who shall   Rule 4.54(1)
    have no voting rights) if so
    agreed by the creditors (plus   Section 101(3)
    Deposit Protection Board
    if the Company in liquidation
    is Bank and Board exercises its
    Right to join the Committee)   Rule 4.41(6)
    Powers: To assist the Liquidator in the
    winding-up to audit the
    intromissions of the Liquidator   Rule 4.32(1)
    to determine the outlays and
    remuneration of the Liquidator   Rule 4.32(2)

to review the adequacy of caution
obtained by Liquidator   Rule 7.28(2)(b)

[NOTE: Except with the prior leave of the Court or of
the Liquidation Committee, a member or any
person who has been a member within the
last twelve months, shall not enter into any
transaction whereby he receives any payment
for services given or goods supplied, or
obtains profit, or acquires any part of the
liquidated assets.   Rule 4.58

A member shall be reimbursed for any
reasonable travelling expenses incurred
in attending meetings of the Liquidation   Rule 4.57(1)
Committee excepting those in respect of
a meeting held within three months of a
previous meeting]   Rule 4.57(2)

Obtain written Consents to Act, with full   Rule 4.42
names, addresses and telephone numbers.

If formed, then hold first meeting after close
of this meeting.

6.   If no Liquidation Committee is established the liquidator   Rule 4.32
shall:

(a) advise creditors that until or unless a   Rule 4.12(3)
liquidation committee is later established
applications shall be made, at the appropriate times,
to the Court for approval of the liquidator's
remuneration and expenses bases on the time records
of his firm.

(b) put resolutions to the meeting for approval:

■ to dispense in whole with the settlement of a list of contributories.

■ to fix [*date*] as the date on or before which all creditors are to prove
their debts or claims or be excluded from the benefit of distribution made before those debts are proved.

■ to appoint Solicitors in the Liquidation to assist the Liquidator in
the performance of his duties.

7.   Close meeting.

B9. Minute of Statutory Meeting of Creditors

MINUTES OF STATUTORY MEETING OF CREDITORS of ROCOCO COCOA CO LIMITED – IN LIQUIDATION – held at Trades Hall, Glasgow on [*date*] at 12 noon

PRESENT:
ATTENDING:

1. The meeting was deemed to be properly constituted.

2.** The meeting was informed that payment of the sum of £[ ] had been made to [*name*] as an expense of the Liquidation in respect of the preparation of the Statement of Affairs.

2.** The meeting was informed that no payment had been made in respect of the preparation of the Statement of Affairs and that such payment would be authorised by the Liquidation Committee, if appointed, or the Court.

3.** The meeting was informed that payment of the sum of £[ ] had been made to [*date*] as an expense of the Liquidation in respect of the summoning, advertisement and holding of the meeting.

3.** The meeting was informed that no payment had been made in respect of the summoning, advertisement and holding of the meeting, and that such payment would be authorised by the Liquidation Committee, if appointed, or the Court.

4. The Insolvency Practitioner, on behalf of the Directors, reported on the History and the Statement of Affairs of the Company, and answered the questions of the creditors.

5.** It was resolved to appoint as Liquidator David Flint, Solicitor, of MacRoberts, Solicitors, 152 Bath Street, Glasgow G2 4TB and a Certificate of Appointment was duly issued after the Chairman had been provided with a written statement to the effect that the said David Flint was a duly qualified insolvency practitioner and that he consented so to act.

5.** No nominations were received for the appointment of Liquidator, and the meeting was advised that [*name*], previously appointed by the members, would consequently remain as liquidator.

5.** No nominations were received for the appointment of Liquidator, and the meeting was advised that the Accountant in Bankruptcy would be appropriately advised.

6.** A Liquidation Committee to act with the Liquidator was elected comprising:

....

....

....

....

Its members agreed to act and the Liquidator issued a Certificate of Constitution.

6.** A Liquidation Committee to act with the Liquidator was not elected, and the Meeting was informed that the outlays and remuneration of the Liquidator would be determined by the Court and resolved:

6.1 that the liquidator be empowered in terms of rules 4.14A(4) and 4.9(4), where applicable, to make payment to his firm of the costs of summoning, advertising and holding of the creditors' meeting under section 98, and the expenses of preparation of the Statement of Affairs under section 99, where the funds of the liquidation permit, at his discretion.

6.2   to dispense in whole with the settlement of a list of contributories

6.3   to fix as the date on or before which all creditors are to prove their debts or claims or to be excluded from the benefit of any distribution made before those debts are proved

6.4   to appoint MacRoberts, Solicitors, 152 Bath Street, Glasgow G2 4TB, as Solicitors in the Liquidation to assist the Liquidator in the performance of his duties

OR

1.   The meeting was adjourned until [*date*] at [*time*]

....
Chairman

** Delete as appropriate

B10. Advertisement of Appointment of Liquidator

<u>ROCOCO COCOA CO LIMITED (IN LIQUIDATION)</u>

Notice is hereby given, pursuant to section 109 of the Insolvency Act 1986, that by resolution of the creditors dated [*date*], David Flint, Solicitor, 152 Bath Street, Glasgow G2 4TB was appointed liquidator of Rococo Cocoa Co Limited, having its Registered Office at 1 Main Street, Glasgow, of all of which intimation is hereby given.

IN RESPECT WHEREOF

(sgd) A Wiseman

Solicitor,
152 Bath Street,
Glasgow G2 4TB

<u>Agent for the Liquidator</u>

B11.   Minute of First Meeting of Liquidation Committee

MINUTE of the FIRST MEETING of the
LIQUIDATION COMMITTEE Appointed to
Assist the LIQUIDATOR of ROCOCO
COCOA CO LIMITED held at Trades Hall,
Glasgow on [*date*] at 12.30pm

PRESENT:
IN ATTENDANCE:

It was reported that:

1.   MacRoberts, Solicitors, 152 Bath Street, Glasgow G2 4TB have been
     appointed as solicitors in the liquidation, to assist the liquidator in the per-
     formance of his duties, in terms of paragraph 12 of Part III of Schedule 4 to
     the Insolvency Act 1986.

It was resolved:

1.   To dispense in whole with the settlement of a list of contributories in terms of
     section 165(4) of the Insolvency Act 1986

2.   To fix [*date*] as the date on or before which all creditors are to prove their
     debts or claims or to be excluded from the benefit of any distribution made
     before those debts are proved.

3.   To meet as required within the terms of rule 4.45(1) of the Insolvency
     (Scotland) Rules 1986 and to waive written notice thereof under rule 4.45(3).

4.   That the Liquidator sends to every member of the Liquidation Committee a
     written report setting out the position generally as regards the progress of the
     winding-up and matters arising in connection with it, all in terms of rule
     4.56(2) of the Insolvency (Scotland) Rules 1986, as and when the liquidator
     considers it appropriate.

5.   That the Liquidator be empowered in terms of rules 4.14A(4) and 4.9(4),
     where applicable, to make payment of the costs of summoning, advertising
     and holding of the creditors' meeting under section 98, and the expenses of
     preparation of the Settlement of Affairs under section 99, where the funds of
     the liquidation permit, at his discretion.

6.   That the Liquidator will give notice to the Committee of any intention to dis-
     pose of any property of the Company to a person who is connected with the
     Company under section 167(2) of the Insolvency Act 1986.

7.   That the Liquidator investigates the following:

     ....

     ....
                       Chairman

B12. Letter to Creditors from Liquidator re Date for Lodging of Claims/Settlement of Debts

<u>ROCOCO COCOA CO LIMITED</u>

(In Liquidation)

I, David Flint, Solicitor, of MacRoberts, 152 Bath Street, Glasgow G2 4TB have been appointed Liquidator of Rococo Cocoa Co Limited by a Resolution of a meeting of creditors duly convened and held on [*date*].

Persons claiming to be creditors of the Company who have not already lodged statements of their claims with me are requested to do so on or before [*date*] and all parties indebted to the Company are requested to make payment forthwith.

<u>David Flint</u>
Liquidator

MacRoberts
Solicitors
152 Bath Street
Glasgow
G2 4TB

[*date*]

B13.   Notice of Annual Meeting of Creditors

INSOLVENCY ACT 1986

<u>ROCOCO COCOA CO LIMITED – IN LIQUIDATION</u>

NOTICE IS HEREBY GIVEN that, in terms of section 105(1) of the Insolvency Act 1986, a meeting of the creditors of the above Company will be held within the offices of MacRoberts, Solicitors, 152 Bath Street, Glasgow G2 4TB at [*date*] on [*date*], for the purpose of receiving an account of the Liquidator's acts and dealings and of the conduct of the winding-up for the year ended [*date*].

All creditors are entitled to attend in person or by proxy, and a resolution will be passed when the majority in value of those voting have voted in favour of it. Creditors may vote whose claims and proxies have been submitted and accepted at the meeting or lodged beforehand at the undernoted offices.

....
Liquidator

MacRoberts
Solicitors
152 Bath Street
Glasgow G2 4TB

[*date*]

B14. Minutes of Annual Meeting of Creditors

MINUTES OF STATUTORY MEETING OF CREDITORS OF ROCOCO COCOA CO LIMITED – IN LIQUIDATION held at [*address*] on [*date*] at [*time*] in terms of section 105 of the Insolvency Act 1986

Present:

In Attendance:

1. The meeting was deemed to be properly constituted.

2. The Chairman gave an account of the Liquidator's acts and dealings and of the conduct of the winding-up for the year ended [*date*] which was accepted by the Meeting.

OR

1. The meeting was deemed to be properly convened.

2. It was noted that there was no quorum.

3. An account of the Liquidator's acts and dealings and of the conduct of the winding-up for the year ended [*date*] was deemed to have been tabled.

....
Chairman

B15.   Notice of Meeting of Creditors to Remove Liquidator

INSOLVENCY ACT 1986

ROCOCO COCOA CO LIMITED – IN LIQUIDATION

NOTICE IS HEREBY GIVEN that, in terms of section 171(2) of the Insolvency Act 1986 a meeting of the creditors of the above Company will be held at 152 Bath Street, Glasgow G2 4TB on [*date*] at 12 noon to consider a proposal for the removal of [*name*] as liquidator.

In the event that the removal of [*name*] is approved, the meeting will require to determine under sections 173(2)(a) or (b) of the said Act whether or not he is granted his release and may also resolve to appoint another liquidator to fill the vacancy.

The attention of creditors is drawn to the following:

1.   A Creditor is entitled to vote only if he has submitted his claim (Form 4.7(Scotland)) to the address mentioned below and his claim has been accepted in whole or in part.

2.   A Resolution at the meeting is passed if a majority in value of those voting vote in favour of it.

3.   Proxies may be lodged at or before the meeting at the undernoted offices marked for the attention of Mr D Flint.

4.   Claims may be lodged by those who have not already done so at or before the meeting at the said offices.

5.   The provisions of rules 4.15–4.17 (as amended by Schedule 1) and of r.7 of the Insolvency (Scotland) Rules 1986.

If you are in any doubt as to any of these matters, you should consult your Solicitor immediately.

....
Liquidator

MacRoberts
Solicitors
152 Bath Street
Glasgow
G2 4TB

...............................(Date)

B16. Notice of Meeting of Creditors for Release of Liquidator – following resignation

INSOLVENCY ACT 1986

<u>ROCOCO COCOA CO LIMITED – IN LIQUIDATION</u>

NOTICE IS HEREBY GIVEN that, pursuant to rule 4.28(1) of the Insolvency (Scotland) Rules 1986, a meeting of the creditors of the above company will be held at 152 Bath Street, Glasgow G2 4TB on [*date*] at 12 noon for the purpose of considering proposals for the resignation of the liquidator under section 173(2)(c) of the Insolvency Act 1986 and rule 4.29(4) of the said Rules.

In the event that the resignation of [*name*] is approved, the meeting will require to determine under sections 173(2)(c) of the said Act whether, and, if so, from what date the liquidator should receive his release, and may also resolve to appoint [*name*] or another liquidator to fill the vacancy.

The attention of creditors is drawn to the following:

1. A Creditor is entitled to vote only if he has submitted his claim (Form 4.7 (Scotland)) to the address mentioned below and his claim has been accepted in whole or in part.

2. A Resolution at the meeting is passed if a majority in value of those voting vote in favour of it.

3. Proxies may be lodged at or before the meeting at the undernoted offices marked for the attention of Mr D Flint.

4. Claims may be lodged by those who have not already done so at or before the meeting at the said offices.

5. The provisions of rules 4.15–4.17 (as amended by Schedule 1) and of rule 7 of the Insolvency (Scotland) Rules 1986.

If you are in any doubt as to any of these matters, you should consult your Solicitor immediately.

....
Liquidator

MacRoberts
Solicitors
152 Bath Street
Glasgow
G2 4TB

..............................(Date)

B17.   Agenda for Meeting of Creditors to Accept Resignation of Liquidator

<u>AGENDA FOR MEETING OF CREDITORS OF</u>

<u>ROCOCO COCOA CO LIMITED – IN LIQUIDATION</u>

<u>held at 152 Bath Street, Glasgow, G2 4TB</u>

<u>on [*date*] at [*time*]</u>

<u>in terms of rule 4.28 of the Insolvency (Scotland) Rules 1986</u>

[Quorum:	One creditor in person or by proxy entitled to vote	Rule 7.7, 7.16
Chairman	The Liquidator	Rule 7.5(4)
Note:	If no quorum is present, the meeting is deemed to have been held, the resignation of the liquidator being immediately effective]	Rule 4.29(6) and (7)

1.   Introduction

Explanation of purpose of meeting:

To accept the resignation of the Liquidator due to: Rule 4.28(3)

(a) ill health; or
(b) intention to cease practice as an insolvency practitioner; or
(c) conflict between interest having arisen; or
(d) such a change of personal circumstances as to make continuation in office impracticable

To choose a succeeding Liquidator   Rule 4.29(5)

To specify the terms on which the former liquidator be remunerated

Documents Laid on Table:

By Statute:	None	
By Habit:	Notice of Meeting	Rule 7.6(3)
	Related Certificate of Posting	Rule 7.23(1)
	Edinburgh Gazette	
	Two Newspapers	Rule 7.3(3)
	Letter of resignation	

2.   Elect another Chairman, who will:

(a) determine the release of the Liquidator, who will lodge with the Court and the Accountant in. Bankruptcy   Section 172(6)

Form 4.15(Scotland) and 4.16(Scotland)

(b) invite nominations for a succeeding Liquidator under procedures given in Rules 4.19, 4.20, 4.27 and 7.12 of the Insolvency (Scotland) Rules 1986.   Rule 4.29(5)

3. The succeeding Liquidator will take the chair and:

    (a) invite proposals for the determination of the fee and outlays of the former Liquidator.
    (b) discuss any other relevant business.
    (c) close meeting.

B18. Agenda for Meeting of Creditors to Remove Liquidator (Creditors' Appointment)

<u>AGENDA FOR MEETING OF CREDITORS OF</u>

<u>ROCOCO COCOA CO LIMITED – IN LIQUIDATION</u>

<u>held at [*address*]</u>

<u>on [*date*] at [*time*]</u>

<u>in terms of section 171 of the Insolvency Act 1986</u>

[Quorum:	One creditor in person or by proxy entitled to vote	Rule 7.7; 7.16
Chairman:	The Liquidator or his nominee	Rule 7.5(1)]

1. Introduction

   Explanation of purpose of meeting:

To remove the Liquidator at the request of more than 25 per cent in value of the creditors	Section 171(2)(b) Rule 4.23(1)
To release or not to release the Liquidator	Section 173(2) Rule 4.25
To choose a succeeding Liquidator	Rule 4.27

   To specify the terms on which the former Liquidator be remunerated
   Documents Laid on Table:

By Statute:	None	
By Habit:	Notice of Meeting	Rule 7.6(3)
	Related Certificate of Posting	Rule 7.23(1)
	Edinburgh Gazette	
	Two newspapers	Rule 7.3(3)

2. Elect another Chairman, who will:

   (a) propose resolution to remove the Liquidator and, if adopted, determine his release and issue
   Certificate of Removal   Section 171(2)(b)
   (Form 4.10(Scotland), copies of which will be lodged with the Accountant in Bankruptcy by the former Liquidator.)

   (b) invite nominations for a succeeding   Rule 4.27
   Liquidator under procedures given in Rules 4.19, 4.20, 4.27 and 7.12 of the Insolvency (Scotland) Rules 1986.

3. The succeeding Liquidator will take the chair and:

   (a) invite proposals for the determination of the fee and outlays of the former Liquidator.
   (b) discuss any other relevant business.
   (c) close of meeting.

B19. Agenda for Meeting of Creditors – Removal of Liquidator (Court Appointment)

AGENDA FOR MEETING OF CREDITORS OF

ROCOCO COCOA CO LIMITED – IN LIQUIDATION

held at [*address*]

on [*date*] at [*time*]

in terms of section 171 of the Insolvency Act 1986

[Quorum:	One creditor in person or by proxy entitled to vote	Rule 7.7, 7.16
Chairman:	the former Liquidator or his nominee	Rule 7.5(1)]

1. Introduction

   Description of Appointment:

By the Court	Section 108(1)

   Meeting can only be convened:

(a) if the liquidator thinks fit; or	Section 171(3)
(b) if the Court so directs; or	Section 108(2), 173(3)
(c) if not less than 50 per cent, in value, of the creditors have requested it	Section 171(3)(b) Rule 4.26

   Explanation of Purpose of Meeting:

   To replace the Liquidator .

To release or not to release the Liquidator	Section 173(2) Rule 4.25

   To choose a succeeding Liquidator
   To specify the terms on which the former
   Liquidator be remunerated.

   Documents Laid on Table:

By Statute:	None	
By Habit:	Notice of Meeting	Rule 7.6(3)
	Related Certificate of Posting *Edinburgh Gazette*	Rule 7.23(1)
	Two newspapers	Rule 7.3(3)
	Court Interlocutor of removal	Section 108(2)

2. Elect another Chairman, who will:

(a) propose resolution to remove the Liquidator and, if adopted, determine his release and issue Certificate of Removal (Form 4.10 (Scotland), copies of which will be lodged with the Accountant in Bankruptcy by the former Liquidator.)	Section 171(2)(b)
(b) invite nominations for a succeeding Liquidator under procedures given in Rules 4.19, 4.20, 4.27 and 7.12 of the Insolvency (Scotland) Rules 1986.	Rule 4.27

3. The succeeding Liquidator will take the chair and:
    (a) invite proposals for the determination of the
         fee and outlays of the former Liquidator
    (b) discuss any other relevant business
    (c) close meeting.

B20.   Minutes of Meeting of Liquidation Committee

MINUTES OF A MEETING OF THE LIQUIDATION
COMMITTEE APPOINTED TO ASSIST THE
LIQUIDATOR OF ROCOCO COCOA CO LIMITED
held at [*address*] on [*date*] at [*time*]

Present:
In Attendance:

1.   The meeting was held to be properly constituted.

2.   The Liquidator gave an account of the winding-up to date which was
      accepted by the meeting.

3.   The amount of caution obtained by the Liquidator was reviewed and was
      deemed adequate.

4.   It was agreed that the following dividends should be paid to the various rank-
      ing creditors:

          [   ].

5.   It was agreed that the Liquidator should receive an interim fee of £ plus VAT.

6.   It was agreed that the Liquidator could be released from his office subject to
      the concurrence of the final meeting of creditors held pursuant to section 106
      of the Insolvency Act 1986.

....
Chairman

B21. Sederunt Book – Creditors' Voluntary Winding-up

SEDERUNT BOOK

in terms of rule 7.33(1) of the Insolvency (Scotland) Rules 1986

CREDITOR'S VOLUNTARY LIQUIDATION

ROCOCO COCOA CO LIMITED

Certificate of appointment	
External notices of appointment	
Copies of relevant *Edinburgh Gazettes*	
Copies of relevant newspapers	
Certificates of posting and related circulars	
Certificate of specific penalty (pre 1 April 1993)	Insolvency Practitioner Regulations 13(1)
Copy of Borderaux (post 1 April 1993)	Insolvency Practitioner Regulations 13(1)
Certificate of Constitution of Liquidation Committee	
Claims endorsed with date of receipt	
Notice of change of Registered Office	
Statements of Affairs received from directors	Rule 4.8(2)
Reports on administration	
Minutes of meeting of creditors	Rule 7.13(3)
Proxies used for voting at meetings	Rule 7.17(3)
Minutes of meetings of Liquidation Committee	Rule 4.55(5)
Professional valuations of assets	Rule 4.22(1)(b)
Reports on conduct of directors	
Periodic accounts	
Dividends paid	
Approval of fee	Rule 4.32
Release	

Any other document necessary to give a correct view of the administration of the Liquidation.

Note 1 When any document is of a confidential nature (such as opinion of counsel on any matter affecting the interests of the creditors), the Liquidator shall not be bound to insert it, or exhibit it to any person other than a court official or a member of the Liquidation Committee.   Rule 7.27(1)

Note 2 The Sederunt Book shall be retained by the Liquidator for a period of 10 years from the date of dissolution of the company.   Rule 7.33(5)

B22. Letter to Creditors

Our Ref

Your Ref

[*Date*]

Dear Sirs

ROCOCO COCOA CO LIMITED – IN LIQUIDATION

I was appointed Liquidator of the above named company on [*date*]. All goods and services supplied by the company during the liquidation will only be supplied on condition that they will be paid for in full, by the due date, without deduction or set off against any monies you may be owed by the company. Your acceptance of goods or services will constitute acceptance of these terms and conditions of sale. You should note that I am not in a position to give any guarantees or warranties in a personal capacity for goods or services supplied.

Please remit to me any amounts which are owed to the above company.

I look forward to hearing from you as soon as possible.

Yours faithfully

Liquidator

[Notes:

i   *To be sent to all customers.*
ii   *Where set off is known to be a potential problem, this letter is to be specifically addressed and sent by recorded delivery and an acknowledgement obtained.*
iii   *Where the company's terms and conditions are inadequate, consideration should be given to attaching new terms and conditions drafted by liquidator's solicitors.]*

B23.   Section 204 Early Dissolution Checklist

Statutory Reference

1   Although not a statutory requirement, it is good
practice to send to all known creditors as an
estimated statement of affairs and a brief
circular indicating that the company assets are
insufficient to cover the expenses of the winding
up and that it is the Liquidator's intention to
apply to the court for early dissolution in terms
of section 204 of the Insolvency Act.

2   Send letter to law agent requesting application   s.204
to the relevant court under section 204. (The
relevant court being the court where the
company was wound-up). Law agent will
require:
-   Copy interlocutor of appointment
-   Estimated statement of affairs
-   Minute of the section 138 meeting

3   Send court order to Companies House for   s.204(4)
registration accompanied by Form   s.172(7)
4.28(Scotland) within 14 days from date
of order. The company will be dissolved three
months from the date of registration of order.

4   Submit Form 4.12(Scotland) to the Accountant   s.174(4)
of Court requesting release of the Liquidator,   IR4.25
enclosing sederunt book of liquidator's
documents.

5   Accountant of Court will issue Forms 4.13 &   IR4.25
4.14(Scotland), the certificate and notice of
release.

6   Copies of Forms 4.13 & 4.14 (Scotland) should
then be submitted to Companies House
forthwith.

C – MEMBERS' VOLUNTARY LIQUIDATION

C1. Letter to Directors

Our Ref

Your Ref

[Date]

Dear Sirs

PROPOSED MEMBERS VOLUNTARY LIQUIDATION
Further to our meeting today I am writing to outline the issues to be considered, a proposed course of action, and the likely costs involved in placing the above company into members' voluntary liquidation.

I understand that your outline plans comprise [*i.e.* the disposal of the company's freehold shop, the realisation of trading stocks and debtors, the settlement of trading liabilities and the realisation of most of the company's investments. Once these steps have been completed, the company's assets will comprise cash, unlisted investments and the investment property. There are also likely to be tax liabilities arising from the sale of the freehold shop and the realisation of investments.]

It is on this basis that I have compiled this letter.

BASIC PRINCIPLES

The principal objective of a proposed members' voluntary liquidation is to maximise the return of monies (or other assets) into shareholders' hands.

Two issues impact significantly on this objective, namely taxation and professional costs. Effective planning, and agreement between directors and professional advisers regarding their respective responsibilities is essential to minimise these costs.

The impact of taxation is two fold. First, the company is likely to generate taxable profits as assets are either realised for cash or distributed to shareholders. This latter option is known as a 'distribution in specie'. The realisation of assets can occur either before liquidation or after liquidation.

Secondly, the shareholders may suffer capital gains tax on any gain arising on the return of funds (as cash or assets) as capital distributions on their shares following liquidation, or income tax if dividends are paid prior to liquidation.

Professional costs usually arise in four categories:
i   Agents' fees in producing valuations and assisting in asset realisations.

ii   Legal fees in dealing with the sale of assets to third parties or the transfer of assets to shareholders.

iii   Accountancy, tax and liquidator's fees incurred in concluding the affairs and life of the company (these are estimated at the end of this letter).

iv   Tax fees incurred in establishing the shareholder's personal tax positions following liquidation of the company. Depending on circumstances this could involve research into the history of individual shareholders acquisitions of shares and of the value of the shares at dates of acquisition and at March 31, 1982. If we are to act as tax advisers to shareholders personally, we will require appropriate letters of engagement. We would be pleased to discuss this further.

It should be noted that the powers of the directors cease upon the appointment of a liquidator. As a further general principle, therefore, the directors should aim to deal with as many of the company's affairs as possible prior to liquidation.

The duration of the liquidation is usually dependent on the time required to conclude the company's taxation affairs with the Inland Revenue. This is likely to fall within the range of six months to two years following completion of asset realisations.

Issues to be Considered Prior to Commencement of Liquidation

In this particular case, there are several matters which I believe require consideration prior to liquidation:

i   Pre liquidation tax planning, particularly relating to the disposal or cessation of the business and freehold premises (including VAT consequences) the timing of the date of liquidation and whether dividends should be paid prior to liquidation. Issues which are likely to emerge, and have a tax effect are, for example, employment termination costs and one-off contributions to pension funds.

ii   The tenancy arrangements of the company's investment property.

iii   Obtaining a valuation of the company's unlisted investments.

iv   Obtaining a valuation of the company's investment property.

v   Disposing of the company's motor vehicles.

vi   Investigating the effects of liquidation on the company's pension fund(s) and taking appropriate action.

vii   Determining which shareholder(s) is/are to receive the unlisted investments and investment property as distribution in specie.

viii   Individual shareholders' tax positions.

ix   The likely timing of distributions where this might have an impact on tax liabilities.

Matters to be Completed Prior to Liquidation

I have set out in Appendix I a comprehensive list of matters to be completed prior to commencement of the liquidation.

It is particularly important for the directors to settle as many liabilities of the company as possible before liquidation. This is because the liquidator is obliged to pay statutory interest on any liabilities settled after his appointment. Such interest is not payable on taxation liabilities as long as these are paid by the due dates.

Commencement of Liquidation

I have set out in Appendix II the detailed procedure leading to commencement of the liquidation. There are two principal components, a directors' meeting and an extraordinary general meeting.

The principal purpose of the directors' meeting is to summon the extraordinary general meeting of shareholders, which is required to pass the special resolution that is required to place the company into liquidation. The extraordinary general meeting will be summoned on not less than 21 days' notice.

The extraordinary general meeting of shareholders will also need to give sanction to the liquidator to distribute assets in specie to the shareholders (*i.e.* the unlisted investments and the investment property) during the ensuing liquidation.

Liquidation

Once appointed, I, as liquidator, will deal with the matters listed in Appendix III. I will be assisted by [*date*], members of my staff who is/are experienced in dealing with this type of liquidation. I am authorised by [*name*] to act as an insolvency practitioner.

I would expect most of the tax aspects of the liquidation to be dealt with by [*date*].

Fees

The proposed liquidation gives rise to three costs:

i   Liquidator's disbursements eg statutory advertising and liquidator's bond. Approximate cost £.

ii   Solicitors' fees for acting for the liquidator to effect the distributions in specie of the unlisted investments and the investment property to shareholders. I propose to utilise the services of MacRoberts, Solicitors who have given an indication of their fees to be in the region of £.

iii   Liquidator's fees. At this stage, I anticipate the fees for my involvement in the planning of this liquidation, and the execution of the work set out in Appendix III to be in the range £.

Once you have had an opportunity of considering the contents of this letter, I would recommend a further meeting to discuss any matters arising and the issues to be considered prior to liquidation, so that the plan of realising the shareholders' interests in the company, culminating in liquidation, can be concluded. At that point I should be able to estimate my own fees as outlined above with greater precision and also estimate the other fees required to deal with taxation planning before the liquidation and dealing with ongoing matters thereafter.

Yours faithfully

APPENDIX I

MATTERS TO BE COMPLETED PRIOR TO LIQUIDATION

1   Annual returns filed up to date.

2   Ensure memoranda of satisfaction filed in respect of any outstanding mortgages on the Companies Register.

3   Complete all necessary accounts to 31 March.

4   Agree corporation tax liability to 31 March.

5   Accounting events post 1 April:
- Accounts to date of extraordinary general meeting.
- Ensure, prior to drafting that as many liabilities as possible have been paid.
- Agree corporation tax liability on these (unaudited) accounts (carried out during the liquidation).

6   Prepare statement of assets and liabilities for declaration of solvency.

7   VAT – consider deregistration.

8   PAYE/NIC – effect all final outstanding returns for [ ] and [ ] (P35 etc).

9   Company pension fund:
- Independent trustee requirements?
- Any effect if company wound-up?
- Any further contributions to be made?

APPENDIX II

**Detailed Procedure Leading
to a Members' Voluntary Winding-up**

Sections 89 and 90 of the Insolvency Act 1986 define the circumstances in which a company may be wound-up voluntarily under the control of the shareholders.

Section 89 provides that, where it is proposed to wind up a company voluntarily the directors, or, if more than two, the majority of them, may at a board meeting make a statutory declaration that they have inquired into the company's affairs and have formed the opinion that it will be able to pay its debts in full within a specified period not exceeding twelve months from the commencement of winding-up.

This declaration is ineffective unless:

i   it is made within the five weeks preceding the date of the passing of the resolution for winding-up, or on that date but before the passing of the resolution and

ii   it contains a statement of assets and liabilities as at the latest practicable date.

This declaration must be delivered to the Registrar of Companies within fifteen days after the passing of the resolution.

A director who makes this declaration without reasonable grounds for his opinion is liable to imprisonment or a fine or both. Further, if the company is wound-up but its debts are not paid in full within the specified period, it is presumed (unless the contrary is shown) that the director did not have reasonable grounds for his opinion. This provision puts the burden of proof on the director concerned.

The declaration of solvency is normally completed at a directors' meeting which subsequently summons an extraordinary general meeting of the shareholders. Twenty-one days' notice of the extraordinary general meeting is normally required.

The short notice provisions of sections 369 and 378 of the Companies Act 1985 may be invoked to enable the extraordinary general meeting to be held immediately after the directors' meeting. Procedure at the meeting is governed by the company's Articles of Association.

A special resolution is required to place the company in liquidation, and it is normal for the liquidator's appointment to be included in the special resolution.

Winding-up commences at the time of the passing of the resolution and the liquidator's appointment is effective immediately. The directors' powers cease at this point.

The chairman of the meeting certifies the appointment of the liquidator when the liquidator provides him with a statement of his qualification and consent to act.

APPENDIX III

Work to be carried out by liquidator

Prior to Appointment

1   Draft minutes of directors' meeting and extraordinary general meeting.

2   Arrange for despatch of notice of extraordinary general meeting to shareholders.

3 Liaise with directors to ensure that pre-liquidation planning concluded and put into effect.

4 Arrange for representation at extraordinary general meeting.

Following Appointment

1 Arrange for the liquidator's bond to be obtained and deal with statutory advertising and filings.

2 Set up liquidation bank account.

3 Take control of the company's bank balances and unrealised assets, and realise the latter as appropriate.

4 Agree and pay the claims of any outstanding creditors.

5 Estimate the corporation tax payable by the liquidator on the distributions in specie of the unlisted investments and the investment property.

6 Make a substantial interim cash distribution to shareholders.

7 Arrange for the conveyance of the unlisted investments and the investment property to the relevant shareholder(s).

8 Agree with the Inland Revenue the corporation tax liabilities on income and chargeable gains arising in the liquidation and for any earlier period including the period up to the date of liquidation.

9 Prepare statements of receipts and payments, as required by statute (every 12 months and on completion), for distribution to shareholders and filing with the Registrar of Companies.

10 Make a final cash distribution to shareholders.

11 Deal with statutory meetings (every 12 months and on completion) and filings throughout as necessary.

C2.   Final Checklist for Members' Meeting

Date   Prepared by

1   Prepare minutes for directors' meeting

2   Arrange for Declaration of Solvency
     to be sworn

3   Prepare resolutions for members' meeting

4   Prepare attendance list

5   Complete proxy summary

6   Photocopy history (if any) and
     declaration of solvency – adequate
     for numbers attending

7   Prepare liquidator's consent to act

8   Prepare certificate of appointment
     of liquidator

9   Prepare minutes for members' meeting

C3.   Minutes of Meeting of Directors

MINUTE OF MEETING of the DIRECTORS of
ROCOCO COCOA CO LIMITED held at 152 Bath Street,
Glasgow G2 4TB on [*date*] at 12 noon

PRESENT: I B Broke

U R Broke

ATTENDING:

I B Broke occupied the Chair.

The financial position of the company was discussed and it was resolvd that an
Extraordinary general Meeting be convened at which the resolutions aftermentioned would be put.

[The Chairman submitted a draft Declaration of Solvency embodying a Statement
of Assets and Liabilities as at [*date*] and bringing out an estimated surplus, after
paying all debts in full, of £100,000 conform to the copy of the Statement of
Assets and Liabilities attached to this Minute.

The financial position of the Company as evidenced by the said Statement was
examined in detail pursuant to section 89 of the Insolvency Act 1986, and the
Statement was formally approved.

The Directors present, who comprised [all/a majority of] the Directors of the
Company, made and signed the solemn declaration required by the Declaration of
Solvency in the presence of Alan Neil Other, Notary Public, this solemn declara-
tion being in the following terms:

> "We, Ian Barry Broke residing at "Duntradin", Kilmacolm and Uriah
> Rodney Broke residing at "Tumbledown Cottage", Bridge of Weir being all
> the Directors of Rococo Cocoa Co Limited do solemnly and sincerely declare
> that we have made a full inquiry into the affairs of this company, and that,
> having so done, we have formed the opinion that the company will be able to
> pay its debts in full within a period of twelve months, from the commence-
> ment of the winding-up, and we append a statement of the company's assets
> and liabilities as at [*date*] being the latest practicable date before the making
> of this declaration. And we make the solemn declaration, conscientiously
> believing the same to be true, and by virtue of the provisions of the Statutory
> Declarations Act, 1835."

U R Broke as Company Secretary, undertook to file the Declaration of Solvency
with the Registrar of Companies within 15 days of the commencement of the
winding-up.]

[Note: if the Declaration of Solvency is not available or complete this will be
omitted]

It was resolved that an extraordinary general meeting be convened at [*time*] on
[*date*] at which the following resolutions would be put:

1   A Special Resolution "that the company be wound-up voluntarily and that
     David Flint, Solicitor, 152 Bath Street, Glasgow G2 4TB be appointed liq-
     uidator of the company for the purposes of the voluntary winding-up"

2   A Special Resolution "that the Liquidator be and is hereby authorised to
     value the company's assets for the purpose of a distribution *in specie* and to
     distribute the assets amongst the Members accordingly".

3   An Ordinary Resolution "that the liquidator's remuneration be based upon MacRoberts' time costs and that the liquidator be authorised to draw remuneration on account".

[*Amend as appropriate*].[1]

It was noted that the aforesaid David Flint is an insolvency practitioner qualified under the Insolvency Act 1986 and that in terms of the Insolvency (Scotland) Rules 1986 he, on the passing of the resolution for his appointment, will consent so to act.

[It was understood that all the members would agree to the Meeting being convened on shorter notice than that set out in section 369 of the Companies Act 1985 and to the Resolutions to be submitted to the Meeting being passed as Special Resolutions of the Company notwithstanding that less than twenty-one days' notice had been given therefore.]

MacRoberts, Solicitors, on behalf of the Secretary, be instructed to send to the shareholders of the company notice of the meeting.

MacRoberts were instructed:

- [to assist the directors in the preparation of the Declaration of Solvency and other information to be laid before the meeting of shareholders.]

- to advise the directors in the financial control and supervision of the business between the date of this meeting and the date of the passing of a resolution for winding-up.

The proper charges and disbursements in connection with the above be paid out of the assets of the company **and that there be deposited with MacRoberts the sum of £[ ] plus disbursements plus VAT in respect of services to be rendered by them**, it being clearly understood that these services are required and given for the benefit of the company.

Mr U R Broke or failing him Mr I B Broke, being directors of the company be appointed to take the chair at the meeting of shareholders.

This concluded the business of the Meeting.

"I B Broke"
Director

---

[1] It is important that the wording of the Minutes of the Meeting of the Directors concerning the resolutions is the same as the actual resolutions to be passed by the members.

C4. Notice of Extraordinary General Meeting

<u>ROCOCO COCOA CO LIMITED</u>

NOTICE IS HEREBY GIVEN that an EXTRAORDINARY GENERAL MEETING of ROCOCO COCOA CO LIMITED will be held at 152 Bath Street, Glasgow G2 4TB on [*date*] at 12 noon for the purpose of considering and, if thought fit, passing the following Resolutions :

RESOLUTIONS

1   A Special Resolution "that the company be wound-up voluntarily and that David Flint, Solicitor, 152 Bath Street, Glasgow G2 4TB be appointed liquidator of the company for the purposes of the voluntary winding-up".

2   A Special Resolution "that the Liquidator be and is hereby authorised to value the company's assets for the purpose of a distribution *in specie* and to distribute the assets amongst the Members accordingly".

3   An Ordinary Resolution "that the liquidator's remuneration be based upon MacRoberts' time costs and that the liquidator be authorised to draw remuneration on account".

Dated the [*date*]

BY ORDER OF THE BOARD
"U R Broke"
Secretary

<u>Registered Office:</u>
1 Main Street
Glasgow

A Member entitled to attend and vote at the above Meeting is entitled to appoint a proxy to attend and, on a poll, to vote instead of him. A proxy need not be a Member of the Company.

C5. Minute of Extraordinary General Meeting

MINUTE of EXTRAORDINARY GENERAL MEETING of ROCOCO COCOA CO LIMITED held at 152 Bath Street, Glasgow G2 4TB on [*date*] at 12 noon

PRESENT: I B Broke
ATTENDING: U R Broke

I B Broke occupied the Chair.

The Chairman, having ascertained that the necessary quorum required by the Articles of Association was present, declared the Meeting duly constituted.

[The Chairman submitted a letter signed by all the Members of the Company agreeing to the Meeting being held on shorter notice than that specified in section 369 of the Companies Act 1985 and to the resolutions being submitted to the Meeting being passed as Special Resolution notwithstanding that less than the requisite notice had been given thereof.]

On the motion of the Chairman, the Notice convening the Meeting was taken as read. The Chairman moved that the following Resolution be passed as a Special Resolution of the Company:

"that the company be wound-up voluntarily and that David Flint, Solicitor, 152 Bath Street, Glasgow G2 4TB be appointed liquidator of the company for the purposes of the voluntary winding-up"

U R Broke seconded this motion.

Before putting the Resolution to the Meeting the Chairman invited questions regarding it but none was asked. He then put the Resolution to the Meeting and, after taking a vote by a show of hands, declared that it had been carried unanimously as a Special Resolution of the Company.

The Chairman then moved that the following Resolution be passed as a Special Resolution of the Company:

"that the Liquidator be and is hereby authorised to value the company's assets for the purpose of a distribution *in specie* and to distribute the assets amongst the Members accordingly".

The Chairman invited questions regarding it but none was asked. He then put the Resolution to the Meeting and, after taking a vote by a show of hands, declared that it had been carried unanimously as a Special Resolution of the Company.

The Chairman then moved that the following Resolution be passed as an Ordinary Resolution of the Company:

"that the liquidator's remuneration be based upon MacRoberts' time costs and that the liquidator be authorised to draw remuneration on account".

The Chairman invited questions regarding it but none was asked. He then put the Resolution to the Meeting and, after taking a vote by a show of hands, declared that it had been carried unanimously as an Ordinary Resolution of the Company.

The Solicitors of the Company were instructed to arrange for a signed print of the Resolutions to be filed with the Registrar of Companies and with the Accountant in Bankuptcy and Notice of the Resolution for voluntary winding-up to be advertised in the *Edinburgh Gazette*.

This concluded the business of the Meeting.

"I B Broke"
Chairman

C6. Print of Resolutions

THE COMPANIES ACT 1985

COMPANY LIMITED BY SHARES

RESOLUTIONS

of

ROCOCO COCOA CO LIMITED

Passed [*date*]

At an EXTRAORDINARY GENERAL MEETING of ROCOCO COCOA CO LIMITED duly convened and held at 152 Bath Street, Glasgow G2 4TB on [*date*] the following Resolutions were passed as Resolutions of the Company.

RESOLUTIONS

1 As a Special Resolution "that the company be wound-up voluntarily and that David Flint, Solicitor, 152 Bath Street, Glasgow G2 4TB be appointed liquidator of the company for the purposes of the voluntary winding-up".

2 As a Special Resolution "that the Liquidator be and is hereby authorised to value the company's assets for the purpose of a distribution *in specie* and to distribute the assets amongst the Members accordingly".

3 As an Ordinary Resolution "that the liquidator's remuneration be based upon MacRoberts' time costs and that the liquidator be authorised to draw remuneration on account".

"U R Broke"
Secretary

Registered Office:
1 Main Street
Glasgow

C7.   Advertisement of Appointment of Liquidator

<u>ROCOCO COCOA CO LIMITED (IN MEMBERS' VOLUNTARY
LIQUIDATION</u>

Notice is hereby given, pursuant to section 109 of the Insolvency Act 1986, that by resolution of the members dated [*date*], David Flint, Solicitor, 152 Bath Street, Glasgow G2 4TB was appointed liquidator of Rococo Cocoa Co Limited, having its Registered Office at 1 Main Street, Glasgow, of all of which intimation is hereby given.

MacRoberts
Solicitors
152 Bath Street
Glasgow

<u>Agents for Liquidator</u>

C8. Letter to Creditors

Our Ref

Your Ref

TO THE CREDITORS

STRICTLY PRIVATE & CONFIDENTIAL

NOT FOR PUBLICATION

[*date*]

Dear Sirs

ROCOCO COCOA CO LIMITED (IN MEMBERS' VOLUNTARY LIQUIDATION)

At an extraordinary general meeting of the above named company held on [*date*], a special resolution was passed placing the company into members' voluntary liquidation and appointing me as Liquidator.

The directors have made a declaration of solvency under S89 of the Insolvency Act 1986, to the effect that the company will be able to pay its debts in full, together with statutory interest, within 12 months from the commencement of the winding-up [or amend to] [lesser period] as per Declaration of Solvency.

Please would you send details of your claim to me at the address below within the next 21 days.

Yours faithfully

Liquidator

C9.   Notice of Annual Meeting of Members

<u>ROCOCO COCOA CO LIMITED (IN LIQUIDATION)</u>

Notice is hereby given that a meeting of the members of Rococo Cocoa Co Limited having their Registered Office at 1 Main Street, Glasgow, will be held at 152 Bath Street, Glasgow G2 4TB at 12 noon on [*date*] for the purpose of receiving a report on the Liquidator's intromissions during the preceding year. The attention of members is drawn to the following:

(1)   Members are entitled to vote at said meeting according to the rights attaching to their shares.

(2)   A resolution at the meeting is passed if a majority in value of those voting vote in favour of it.

(3)   Proxies may be lodged at or before the meeting at the offices of the Liquidator, Messrs MacRoberts, Solicitors, 152 Bath Street, Glasgow G2 4TB marked for his attention.

(4)   The provisions of rule 7 of the Insolvency (Scotland) Rules 1986.

If you are in any doubt as to any of these matters, you should consult your solicitor immediately.

> MacRoberts
> Solicitors
> 152 Bath Street
> Glasgow
>
> <u>Agents for the Liquidator</u>

C10. Minutes of Annual Meeting of Members

MINUTES OF STATUTORY MEETING OF MEMBERS OF ROCOCO COCOA CO LIMITED – IN LIQUIDATION held at 152 Bath Street, Glasgow G2 4TB on [*date*] at 12 noon in terms of section 93 of the Insolvency Act 1986

Present:

In Attendance:

1.* The meeting was deemed to be properly constituted.

2. The Chairman gave an account of the Liquidator's acts and dealings and of the conduct of the winding-up for the year ended July 31,1990 which was accepted by the Meeting.

OR

1.* There were no members present in person or by proxy and, accordingly, there was no quorum.

....
Chairman

C11. Letter from Liquidator regarding Annual Meeting

Our Ref

Your Ref

TO THE MEMBERS

[*Date*]

Dear Sir / Madam

ROCOCO COCOA CO LIMITED – IN MEMBERS' VOLUNTARY LIQUIDATION

I am now in a position to report on the liquidation to date and enclose an account of my receipts and payments for the year ended.

[Outline of principal events during the past year]

There remain certain matters to be resolved in relation to:

[Detail as necessary]

Notice is hereby given pursuant to section 93 of the Insolvency Act 1986 that a meeting of members of the above named company will be held at [*address*] on [*date*] at [*time*] for the purpose of receiving an account of the liquidator's acts and dealings and of the conduct of the winding-up to.

[The following resolutions will be put to the meeting:

                                                                            ]

The attention of members is drawn to the following:

(1) Members are entitled to vote at said meeting according to the rights attaching to their shares.

(2) A resolution at the meeting is passed if a majority in value of those voting vote in favour of it.

(3) Proxies may be lodged at or before the meeting at the offices of the Liquidator, Messrs MacRoberts, Solicitors, 152 Bath Street, Glasgow G2 4TB marked for his attention.

(4) The provisions of rule 7 of the Insolvency (Scotland) Rules 1986.

If you are in any doubt as to any of these matters, you should consult your solicitor immediately

At this meeting a report similar to this will be given and as the meeting is purely formal, there is no necessity to attend unless you so wish.

Yours faithfully

David Flint
Liquidator

C12. Notice for Extraordinary General Meeting for Removal of Liquidator

<u>ROCOCO COCOA CO LIMITED (IN LIQUIDATION)</u>

Notice is hereby given that a meeting of the members of Rococo Cocoa Co Limited having their Registered Office at 1 Main Street, Glasgow, will be held at 152 Bath Street, Glasgow G2 4TB at 12 noon on [*date*] for the purpose of removing David Flint, Solicitor, 152 Bath Street, Glasgow G2 4TB as Liquidator of the Company.

The meeting may also resolve to appoint [*name*] or another liquidator to fill the vacancy.

The attention of members is drawn to the following:

(1) Members are entitled to vote at said meeting according to the rights attaching to their shares.

(2) A resolution at the meeting is passed if a majority of those voting vote in favour of it.

(3) Proxies may be lodged at or before the meeting at the offices of the Liquidator, Messrs MacRoberts, Solicitors, 152 Bath Street, Glasgow G2 4TB marked for his attention.

(4) The provisions of rule 7 of the Insolvency (Scotland) Rules 1986.

(5) The provisions of section 173(2)(a) of the Insolvency Act 1986.

If you are in any doubt as to any of these matters, you should consult your solicitor immediately.

MacRoberts
Solicitors
152 Bath Street
Glasgow G2 4TB

<u>Agents for the Liquidator</u>

C13.   Notice of Meeting to Receive Resignation of Liquidator

<u>ROCOCO COCOA CO LIMITED (IN LIQUIDATION)</u>

Notice is hereby given that a meeting of the members of Rococo Cocoa Co Limited having their Registered Office at 1 Main Street, Glasgow, will be held at 152 Bath Street, Glasgow G2 4TB at 12 noon on [*date*] for the purpose of receiving the resignation of David Flint, Solicitor, 152 Bath Street, Glasgow G2 4TB as liquidator of the Company.

The meeting may also resolve to appoint [*name*] or another liquidator to fill the vacancy.

The attention of members is drawn to the following:

(1)   Members are entitled to vote at said meeting according to the rights attaching to their shares.

(2)   A resolution at the meeting is passed if a majority of those voting vote in favour of it.

(3)   Proxies may be lodged at or before the meeting at the offices of the Liquidator, MacRoberts, Solicitors, 152 Bath Street, Glasgow G2 4TB marked for his attention.

(4)   The provisions of rules 4.28A and 7 of the Insolvency (Scotland) Rules 1986.

If you are in any doubt as to any of these matters, you should consult your solicitor immediately.

> MacRoberts
> Solicitors
> 152 Bath Street
> Glasgow G2 4TB
>
> <u>Agents for the Liquidator</u>

C14.   Notice of Final Meeting

ROCOCO COCOA CO LIMITED (IN LIQUIDATION)

NOTICE IS HEREBY GIVEN that a final meeting of the members of the Company will be held at the offices of MacRoberts, Solicitors, 152 Bath Street, Glasgow G2 4TB on [*date*] for the purpose of having an account laid before them by the liquidator (pursuant to section 94 of the Insolvency Act 1986) showing the manner in which the winding-up of the company has been conducted and the property of the company disposed of, and of hearing any explanation that may be given by the liquidator.

A member entitled to attend and vote at the above meeting may appoint a proxy to attend and vote in his place. A proxy need not be a member of the Company.

....
David Flint
Liquidator

Date [*date*]

D – INSOLVENT MEMBERS' VOLUNTARY LIQUIDATION

D1. Minute of Meeting of Creditors

MINUTES of MEETING of CREDITORS of ROCOCO COCOA CO LIMITED held at 152 Bath Street, Glasgow G2 4TB on [date] at 12 noon

David Flint, Solicitor, Liquidator of the Company, presided.

The Certificates of Posting of the Notices convening the Meeting were tabled together with copies of the *Edinburgh Gazette* and *The Herald* newspaper giving notice of the Meeting.

The Chairman having ascertained that the necessary quorum was presented declared the meeting duly constituted.

On the motion of the Chairman it was agreed that the Notice convening the Meeting be taken as read.

The Chairman explained to the Meeting that by Special Resolution of the Company dated [date] it was resolved to wind up the Company voluntarily and that he was appointed Liquidator for the purposes of such winding-up. He further explained that prior to that Meeting all the Directors of the Company had signed a Declaration of Solvency to the effect that they had formed the opinion that the Company would be able to pay its debts in full within twelve months from the commencement of the winding-up.

The Chairman tabled a Statement of Affairs of the Company in the prescribed form and confirmed that, in his view, based on the Statement of Affairs, the Company would be unable to pay its debts in full within the twelve month period referred to in the Statutory Declaration.

The Chairman pointed out that in terms of section 95 of the Insolvency Act 1986 the winding-up would accordingly require to be converted from a Members' Voluntary Winding-up to a Creditors' Voluntary Winding-up.

The Chairman moved that a Resolution be passed that he be appointed liquidator for the purposes of the winding-up and that a Liquidation Committee be appointed to assist the liquidator.

The Chairman put the Resolution to the Meeting and after taking a vote declared that it has been passed.

The liquidator's law agents were instructed to publish in the Gazette and deliver to the Accountant in bankruptcy a notice of his appointment using Form 4.9(Scotland), and to publish notice in The Herald newspaper.

This was all the business.

"David Flint"
Chairman

E – MISCELLANEOUS

E1. Deed of Appointment of Independent Trustee

DEED OF APPOINTMENT

By

the Liquidator of

[ ] LIMITED

appointing

MACROBERTS TRUSTEES LIMITED[1]
as Independent Trustee
of the
[ ] LIMITED PENSION SCHEME

---

[1] MacRoberts Trustees Limited is a Scottish company offering independent trustee services to insolvency practitioners and others.

DEED OF APPOINTMENT

between

(1) [ ] LIMITED, incorporated in Scotland under the Companies Acts (no. [ ]) and having its registered office at [ ] (the "Company") acting by [*name and address of liquidator*] (the "Liquidator"); and

(2) MACROBERTS TRUSTEES LIMITED, incorporated in Scotland under the Companies Acts (No. 241503) and having its registered office at 152 Bath Street, Glasgow, G2 4TB (the "New Trustee")

WHEREAS:

A. The Liquidator is acting as an insolvency practitioner in relation to the Company in accordance with the Insolvency Act 1986 having been appointed as such pursuant to [*instrument*] dated [ ] and granted by [*court*].

B. The Company is the principal employer of the [ ] Limited Pension Scheme (the "Scheme"), an occupational pension scheme established under a trust and presently governed by a Definitive Trust Deed and Rules dated [ ] as amended to date (the "Governing Documentation"). This deed is supplemental to the Governing Documentation.

C. Pursuant to section 23(1) Pensions Act 1995 (the "Act") the Liquidator is obliged to satisfy himself that at least one of the trustees of the Scheme is an independent person within the meaning of section 23(3) of the Act ("Independent") and, if not so satisfied, appoint, or secure the appointment of, an independent person as trustee of the Scheme.

D. The current trustees of the Scheme are [*specify names and addresses of trustees*] (the "Continuing Trustees").

E. Having investigated the position the Liquidator is not satisfied that any of the Continuing Trustees are Independent but is satisfied that the New Trustee is Independent and, accordingly, wishes to appoint the New Trustee as independent trustee of the Scheme pursuant to section 23(1)(b) of the Act.

NOW THIS DEED WITNESSES AND IT IS HEREBY DECLARED as follows:

1. APPOINTMENT OF INDEPENDENT TRUSTEE

In exercise of the power conferred upon him by section 23(1)(b) of the Act the Liquidator hereby appoints the New Trustee to be the independent trustee of the Scheme in terms of the Act. The appointment shall take effect from the last date of execution of this Deed.

2. ACCEPTANCE OF OFFICE BY NEW TRUSTEE AND CONFIRMATION OF INDEPENDENCE

The New Trustee hereby accepts office as trustee of the Scheme and confirms to the Liquidator that it is Independent.

3. UNDERTAKING BY NEW TRUSTEE RELATING TO INDEPENDENCE

The New Trustee undertakes to the Liquidator that if it ceases to be Independent, in fulfilment of the obligation imposed upon it section 25(4) of the Act, it shall immediately give written notice of this fact to the Liquidator.

4. LIQUIDATOR NOT LIABLE FOR ACTINGS OF INDEPENDENT TRUSTEE

The Liquidator signs this Deed in fulfilment of the statutory requirements imposed on him by section 23(1) of the Act and neither he nor his partners, firm, employees, agents, executors or personal representatives shall incur any personal liability in respect of any matter relating to the Scheme which is or may be attributable to any act or omission of the New Trustee or its directors, employees or agents whilst acting or purporting to act as independent trustee of the Scheme.

5. GOVERNING LAW

This Deed shall be governed by the Law of Scotland.

6. STAMP DUTY

The parties hereby certify that this Deed falls within category A in the Schedule to the Stamp Duty (Exempt Instruments) Regulations 1987.

IN WITNESS WHEREOF this Deed is executed as follows:

SIGNED on behalf of the Company by
[*specify name*] acting as Liquidator at on the day ....
of 200[ ] before this witness [*Liquidator's name*]

....
Witness's signature

....
Full name (in capitals)

....
Address

....
Occupation

SIGNED for and on behalf of MACROBERTS ....
TRUSTEES LIMITED by one of its Directors at *Director*
on the day of 200[ ] before this witness

....
Witness's signature

....
Full name (in capitals)

....
....
Address

....
Occupation

E2.   Form of Proxy

Rule 7.15 The Insolvency Act 1986   **Form 4.29[Scot]**
PROXY

Pursuant to rules 7.14 and 7.15 of the Insolvency (Scotland) Rules 1986a

a Insert name of
the company

a **ROCOCO COCOA CO LIMITED**
_____

b Insert nature
of Insolvency
proceedings

b [ ] LIQUIDATION
_____

Name of Creditor/Manager_____

Address _____

_____

_____

_____

(hereinafter called "the
_____principal").

c Insert the
name and
address of the
proxy-holder
and of any
alternatives.
A proxy-holder
must be an
individual
aged over 18

Name of proxy-holder (c) 1 _____

Address _____

_____

whom failing 2

_____

_____

whom failing 3

_____

_____

_____

I appoint the above person to be the principal's proxy-holder
at

* Delete as
appropriate

• [all meetings in the above Insolvency proceedings relating
to the above company]

• [the meeting of *creditors/members of the company to be
held on or at any adjournment of that meeting].

Voting Instructions

The proxy-holder is authorised to vote or abstain from voting
in the name, and on behalf of the principal in respect of any
matter*/s, including resolution*/s, arising for determination
at said meeting*/s and any adjournment*/s thereof and to
propose any resolution*/s in the name of the principal,
either

i   in accordance with instructions given below or,

ii   if no instructions are given, in accordance with his/her
own discretion.

Rule 7.15 The Insolvency Act 1986   **Form 4.29[Scot]**
PROXY

d Complete only if you wish to instruct the proxy-holder to vote for a specific person as liquidator.	d 1 To *propose/support a resolution for the appointment of _____ of _____ whom failing _____ _____ as liquidator of the company.
e Delete if the proxy-holder is only to vote as directed in 1.	e [in the event of a person named in paragraph 1 withdrawing or being eliminated from any vote the proxy-holder may vote or abstain in any further ballot at *his/her discretion.]
f Set forth any voting instructions for the proxy-holder. If more room is required attach a separate sheet.	f 2 _____ _____ _____ _____ Signed _____ Date

Name in **BLOCK LETTERS**

_____

Position of signatory in relation to the *creditor/or member or other authority for signing.

_____

Notes for the Principal and Proxy-holder

1   The chairman of the meeting who may be nominated as proxy-holder, will be the insolvency practitioner who is presently *liquidator/receiver/administrator/nominee under the voluntary arrangement or a director of the company.

2   All proxies must be in this form or a form substantially to the same effect with such variations as circumstances may require. [Rules 7.15(3) and 7.30].

3   To be valid the proxy must be lodged at or before the meeting at which it is to be used. [Rule 7.16(2)].

4   Where the chairman is nominated as proxy-holder he cannot decline the nomination. [Rule 7.14(4)].

5   The proxy-holder may vote for or against a resolution for the appointment of a named person to be liquidator jointly with another person, unless the proxy states otherwise. [Rule 7.16(4)].

6   The proxy-holder may propose any resolution in favour of which he could vote by virtue of this proxy. [Rule 7.16(5)].

7   The proxy-holder may vote at his discretion on any resolutions not dealt with in the proxy, unless the proxy states otherwise. [Rule 7.16(6)].

8   The proxy-holder may not vote in favour of any resolution which places him, or any associate of his, in a position to receive remuneration out of the insolvent estate unless the proxy specifically directs him so to vote. [Rule 7.19(1)].

9   Unless the proxy contains a statement to the contrary the proxy-holder has a mandate to act as representative of the principal on the creditors' or liquidation committee. [Rule 4.48].

INDEX